BRING IT ON HOME

BRING IT ON HOME

PETER GRANT, LED ZEPPELIN, AND BEYOND—THE STORY OF ROCK'S GREATEST MANAGER

MARK BLAKE

DA CAPO PRESS

Da Capo Press
Hachette Book Group
1290 Avenue of the Americas, New York, NY 10104
dacapopress.com

@DaCapoPress, @DaCapoPR

Printed in the United States of America
First Edition: December 2018

Published by Da Capo Press, an imprint of Perseus Books, LLC, a subsidiary of Hachette Book Group, Inc. The Da Capo Press name and logo is a trademark of the Hachette Book Group.

The Hachette Speakers Bureau provides a wide range of authors for speaking events. To find out more, go to www.hachettespeakersbureau.com or call (866) 376-6591.

The publisher is not responsible for websites (or their content) that are not owned by the publisher.

Editorial production by Lori Hobkirk at the Book Factory
Print book interior design by Cynthia Young at Sagecraft

Library of Congress Cataloging-in-Publication Data has been applied for.

ISBNs: 978-0-306-90283-3 (hardcover); 978-0-306-90285-7 (ebook)

LCCN: 2018959321

LSC-C

10   9   8   7   6   5   4   3   2   1

To Matt B.

(Not to be read until you're at least eighteen)

"*The truth is rarely pure and never simple.*"

—OSCAR WILDE

"*Always look in their eyes, not the face,
the eyes . . .*"

—PETER GRANT

CONTENTS

PROLOGUE

*I*t's a Saturday evening in summer 1982. I am seventeen years old, sitting in a porn cinema in London's Soho. I'm with five teenage friends, male and female, and we're passing out cans of cheap lager from supermarket bags stashed between our feet.

The tiny theater smells of last week's cigarettes, disinfectant, and bodies. We are not alone. In the shadows we can see a homeless man slumped across two seats, fast asleep and snoring. Behind us, someone is coughing loudly, as a cloud of dope smoke wafts down the aisle.

One weekend a month, this cinema abandons its timetable of adult movies to show Led Zeppelin's *The Song Remains the Same*. The film isn't available on video yet, and very few people we know own a VCR anyway.

Listening to Led Zeppelin in 1982 is a peculiar, often isolating pastime. The band broke up two years earlier following the death of drummer John Bonham, and their lead singer, Robert Plant, has just released his first solo record.

The compact disc is about to arrive, and we're in a brand new decade with brand new groups. Nobody's supposed to care about Led Zeppelin anymore. And yet here we are.

We've already watched forty minutes of the movie. "Rock and Roll," "Celebration Day," and the rest have been delivered with fast-moving close-ups of Robert Plant and guitarist Jimmy Page, swaggering and peacocking across the stage of New York's Madison Square Garden. Then, suddenly, the film cuts to a dressing room somewhere in America.

It doesn't take long to notice this backstage anteroom, with its strip lights and drab paintwork, is about as glamorous as the dressing rooms in most British provincial civic halls. But all that matters is it's backstage at a Led Zeppelin concert.

On screen, there's an argument taking place between an American, whose clothes and haircut suggest he's some kind of authority figure, and an enormous, bearded Englishman, whom we recognize as Zeppelin's manager Peter Grant. He looks like a gypsy pirate and sounds like he should be throwing drunks out of pubs in Soho. Which isn't far off what he once did for a living.

We've already seen Grant briefly at the beginning of the film: playing a Mafia-style capo in one of the movie's awkward fictional sequences, but that was a silent role.

In the backstage scene, the rolling cadence of Grant's South London accent and his scattergun profanities ("Don't fucking talk to him! It's my bloody act!") stay with us long after the film has ended. Led Zeppelin is the star of *The Song Remains the Same*. Their manager is its unsung hero.

Peter Grant always looked like he'd wandered in off the set of a movie and chosen to remain in character. Unbeknown to us then, he'd been an actor in a past life. The wild hair and beard, the antique rings, and the silk scarves were part of his costume.

Grant came from the pre–Second World War era, a world of variety theater and gramophone records, long before television and rock 'n' roll. He was a generation older than Led Zeppelin.

London's West End had been Peter Grant's domain in the late fifties and early sixties. It hadn't changed much by 1982. Twenty-first-century Soho, with its al fresco dining and cosmopolitan bar culture, wasn't even a developer's dream then.

After the film, we left the cinema and headed for the nearest pub. Turn down any Soho alley in the early eighties and you entered a rabbit's warren of peepshows, clip joints, and what tabloid newspapers called "dirty book shops." It wasn't so different in Grant's day.

Less than five minutes' walk from the cinema is Old Compton Street. Here, the twenty-one-year-old Peter Grant took the tickets at the 2i's coffee bar, while British rock 'n' roll wannabes played on a stage made from milk crates in the cellar. Nearer still, on Wardour Street, had been the Flamingo— the all-night jazz and blues club where Grant policed the door in the era of Georgie Fame and the Blue Flames.

From the Flamingo, you could be at what was once Murray's Cabaret Club on Beak Street in less than ten minutes. In the late fifties, members of the royal family and East End gangsters sipped champagne side by side at Murray's, while Grant stood in the doorway in his concierge's cap and uniform, ordering cabs for crooks and their showgirl mistresses.

In the early sixties, when he'd worked for Sharon Osbourne's father—the promoter Don Arden—Grant had been a familiar presence in the music publishers' offices on nearby Denmark Street and at venues such as the original Marquee and the 100 Club.

When the original American rock 'n' rollers Gene Vincent and Chuck Berry first came to Britain, Grant was there, driving them between gigs and collecting their fee. Later, after homegrown pop acts such as the Animals and the Yardbirds came of age, Grant was there again, shaking down rogue club owners who tried to cheat them out of their money.

Like a giant, moustachioed Zelig, Peter Grant was always somewhere in the picture as this ramshackle, fly-by-night operation evolved into the modern-day music business.

Ten years after first seeing *The Song Remains the Same* in a West End porn cinema, I was at the Marquee when word spread that Led Zeppelin's fabled ex-manager was in the building. All heads turned away from the stage toward the tall, bearded gentleman standing near the bar. Grant's costume had changed: the scarves and rings replaced by a somber business suit, and there was much less of him than there had been in the movie.

By now, I'd convinced a couple of bottom-rung-of-the-ladder music magazines to let me write for them. They were generous with concert tickets and free records, less so with paychecks. But after the show I was allowed entry to the Marquee's green room, where I was introduced to Grant. Out of nowhere, he asked my opinion of the group we'd just seen.

Was there a right answer, I wondered? I told him I wasn't sure. He told me he wasn't either, but that the guitarist was good. I wondered what it must be like trying to judge any new guitarist when the yardstick was Jimmy Page. He sounded just like he did in *The Song Remains the Same* but without the expletives.

Grant was now a long way from Led Zeppelin and Madison Square Garden, but certain things hadn't changed. He had a minder with him, rhythmically chewing gum, his eyes scanning the room left to right and back again, as if he were watching a particularly slow game of tennis. Nobody was going to bother Grant, but I soon became aware that everyone nearby was craning their necks to get a glimpse of him.

For the next hour, Grant entertained a small gathering of us with several choice tales. This was a man who'd spent most of his working life on tour buses and planes. He was a well-schooled storyteller and divulged how a drunk Gene Vincent once tried to run him over in his own car, and how the first time he'd met Robert Plant he'd pleaded for advice about his tortuous love life. "He told me he was in love with two sisters," revealed Grant, with a conspiratorial grin.

Some months later, I ran into Grant again at an awards ceremony. Old business acquaintances, musicians, and acolytes hovered expectantly around him. You could overhear snatches of the conversation: "I dunno if you remember me, Peter; I toured with Bad Company in '76." And so it went on.

Everybody in the room knew about Grant's reputation. We'd heard tales of violent altercations and verbal intimidation. Some older music critics' faces still darkened whenever his name was mentioned. In 1992, though, we were told he'd changed; that he'd softened in his old age. But had he, really?

Years later, Peter's son, Warren, told me of the time they were leaving a charity dinner, when somebody dashed over to say hello to his father. Peter responded with a tirade of abuse.

His victim listened in stunned silence. Only later, while Peter and Warren were outside waiting for a taxi, did Grant realize he'd mistaken the poor man for somebody else.

It's a story that sums up Peter Grant's reputation. Nothing about Grant was quite how it seemed. He was a master at allowing the mythology, the gossip, and the rumors to spread—to keep the "real" Peter Grant under wraps.

Grant, the pioneering manager, revolutionized the business and helped shape the modern music industry. At the time of his death in 1995, a proposed film about his life had been in development for more than five years. It was never going to get made. And if it had, nobody would ever have believed it anyway.

Peter Grant's story began for me in a Soho cinema in 1982. More than thirty years later it turned out to be a celebration, a cautionary tale, and a compelling human drama—far stranger than any fiction.

1

The Battle of
Streatham Common

"Nobody knew Peter Grant. All these people
who crow on about him know nothing about
his subtleties and his magnificence."

—ROBERT PLANT

*P*eter Grant was an ordinary man who led the most extraordinary life. He was also a man with secrets. He took many with him. An envelope of papers relating to his mysterious family background even went with him in the coffin.

It made sense. During his lifetime, Led Zeppelin's manager rarely discussed his family background, even with his ex-wife and children. He was brought up by a single mother and always claimed he'd never known his father. But the missing pieces in the familial puzzle continue to fascinate and perplex his daughter, Helen, and son, Warren.

With Led Zeppelin's fame and success, some of the spotlight fell on their fearsome giant of a manager. In the absence of hard facts about Grant's early life, an alternative history took shape, assisted by books, magazine articles, and television documentaries. Some of the information was true, some was wild speculation, and some was completely false.

Grant himself contributed to this confused backstory. As his reputation grew, it was to his advantage to let people believe what they wanted. The truth might have been too mundane or revealed too much about the person he really was. "He was a complex man," says Helen. "You could never really know him."

This much we *do* know: Peter Grant came into the world on April 5, 1935. Contrary to other reports, he never had a middle name. The building in which he was born, Thurston House, 11 Birdhurst Road, in South Croydon, Surrey, still stands at the junction of two suburban south London streets.

Thurston House is a listed Victorian building, which is now divided into flats. A steep turret juts into the skyline above its three floors. In 1935, though, it was the Birdhurst Nursing Home—a small cottage hospital.

Peter's mother, Dorothy Louise Grant, was unmarried and forty-two years old when she gave birth to her only child. Dorothy's father, Harry James Grant, was a civil service clerk, originally from Chesterton, near Cambridge. Her mother, Catherine Anne Bradley, came from Petersfield, Hampshire—an area where her grandson would spend time during the Second World War.

By the time Harry and Catherine met, they were both living just south of London in Thornton Heath, Croydon, one of the metropolitan suburbs taking root since the arrival of the railways.

The couple were married at the local Church of the Holy Saviour in 1892. Dorothy was born the following year in a house on Buxton Road, Thornton Heath. A brother, Ernest, arrived six years later in 1898.

Dorothy never married, and by the time she was expecting Peter she was employed as a private secretary by the Church of England Pension Board in Westminster.

In 1934, she'd moved into a small, terraced house at 33 Norhyrst Avenue, in Norwood, four miles north of Thornton Heath. She remained there on and off for most of the next forty years, most likely as a sitting tenant and with the assistance of the church pensions board, which helped provide housing for retired clergymen. Peter eventually bought the house outright for her.

An unmarried woman giving birth in her forties in prewar Britain would have faced great prejudice. "Dorothy was a Christian, a churchgoer," says Helen. "So you can imagine what it was like, having a baby at that age out of wedlock."

The Birdhurst Nursing Home was especially popular with single mothers. It was close to the Mission of Hope at Birdhurst Lodge, a Christian organization and adoption agency, whose members were regular visitors at the hospital. Their brochures promised to take care of unmarried mothers "of otherwise good character" before encouraging them to give up their babies "to Jesus."

Dorothy didn't succumb. She was twice the age of most new mothers and presumably thought she'd never get another chance to have a child. She left the hospital with Peter, registered his birth, but never listed a father's name on the certificate.

"The surname "Underwood" is the only clue we have, and we're not entirely certain of that," says Helen. Peter's ex-wife Gloria also suggested his father could have been a Canadian serviceman: "My mum told me she thought he might have been a soldier."

Despite inheriting some of Dorothy's diaries, Helen never found any information about her grandfather's identity. However, on one of Peter's school admission forms, Dorothy listed his father's profession as "senior clerk." It was the same job as her own father, but it's the only surviving clue.

"If Dad knew anything, he never said," insists Helen. "I asked him once, 'Aren't you curious to know who your dad was?' He said no. I told him I was and kept asking, and he told me to stop: 'Helen, I don't want to talk about it.'"

"I think he felt rejected, and that's why he couldn't handle rejection, as it reminded him of this part of his childhood. Maybe that's where the blowouts came from. There was something within him that made him take it out on people."

The late music manager Malcolm McLaren spent several years in the eighties and early nineties working with Grant on a film about his life. Try as he might, Grant would never tell him anything about his childhood. "I think he never wanted anybody to be able to get to him," said McLaren, "and I think that's the Golden Rule of any godfather."

However, McLaren's researcher/writer Mark Long gleaned some information from Grant during hours of interviews. In Peter's account, Dorothy intimated to her son that she knew where his father was, but he was unable to be with them. "It was quite a while before he realized she didn't know," says Long, "and he was, to all intents and purposes, nonexistent."

Grant inherited his height from Dorothy, who was six feet tall. Nobody's certain where the dark hair and piercing eyes came from. Grant's old friend, the late record producer Mickie Most, was certain Peter told him he was half Jewish.

"A lot of people thought he was Jewish," says Helen, "but nobody knew. We thought it might have been in his background. In his seventies heyday, he always looked like a Romany."

"I remember Jimmy Page asking Peter if he was Jewish," remembers Led Zeppelin's former tour manager, Richard Cole. "Peter asked why, but didn't actually reply." In a business with so many Jewish managers, attorneys, and agents, perhaps Grant thought it was a point in his favor to pretend he was. Or he just liked to keep people guessing.

With the outbreak of the Second World War in September 1939, the government commissioned a census of every man, woman, and child in Britain. Approximately 40 million people were accounted for in sixty-five thousand record books. The four-year-old Peter Grant wasn't one of them.

According to this official record, Dorothy was still working as a secretary, but now living away from her son with a retired solicitor, his wife, and his domestic staff in a cottage in Haslemere, Surrey.

Nevertheless, Grant told Mickie Most he'd spent time in a children's home because his mother was too poor to look after him. Helen Grant heard a similar tale: "There was talk of an orphanage."

Grant began his education in May 1940 and spent the next three years at a school in Grayshott, a village in Hampshire. In summer 1943, he was back in South London and enrolled at St. Walter John School in Battersea, where he remained for the next five years.

The school's admission forms show four handwritten addresses for Dorothy, each one crossed out, as she spent the war years moving between flats and houses in Grayshott and Hindhead in Surrey. "What was she doing, and where was my dad?" Helen wondered.

In a 1974 interview with *Melody Maker*—the British weekly music magazine—Grant spoke briefly about this time. He revealed that his school in Battersea had been evacuated to Charterhouse, a public school in Godalming, Surrey. At the time, thousands of city-dwelling children were billeted in rural towns and villages to avoid the German Luftwaffe's bombing raids.

Grant joined them and spent just under two of the war years boarding at Northbrook House—the Charterhouse headmaster's private home—which had been turned into a residence for the Battersea boys.

Grant painted a vivid picture of deprived urban kids coming up against their rich, privileged counterparts. "World War Two was on, and there was another war going on down there, which nobody knew about," Grant told *Melody Maker*. "There used to be great battles, and we'd beat them up."

Grant owned a photograph of Northbrook, on the back of which Dorothy had written the dates of his attendance and that "Peter was very happy here." She was either ignoring the "great battles" or didn't know they were happening.

In interviews, Grant often referred to being illegitimate and always mentioned his mother and her struggle. Sherry Coulson, the widow of Bad Company's handler Clive Coulson, remembers long conversations with Peter.

"He told me he'd had this really impoverished background," she says. "He talked about this grinding poverty. How little food they had and how they'd cook and prepare it.

"He told me his mother was very hardworking and kept their heads above water. He loved his mother and told me *her* mother was involved in his life as well. He suggested the two of them brought him up." Catherine Grant's family background in Hampshire might explain her daughter living in the same county during some of the war years.

By the end of the war in September 1945, Peter and his mother had returned to the house on Norhyrst Avenue. He remained at St. Walter John School until February 1948.

Like most of London, Norwood and its surrounding areas bore the scars of the German bombing campaign but not all were visible. A generation would grow up without fathers, uncles, or brothers, and some of those who returned from the conflict were damaged by the experience. The physical and emotional cost to the survivors was immense.

In interviews, Grant described having a "bad, bad education" and how it had been severely disrupted by the war. The impression given was of a twelve-year-old boy who'd fallen between the cracks of the school system and been forgotten.

After Battersea, he continued his education at Rockmount School on Chevening Road, Upper Norwood. He lasted six months, until he was presumably asked to leave. "When I was older, we used to sit up and talk," says Warren Grant, "and one of the things he told me was he'd never done anything at school."

"Peter told me that once a week he was taken out of school and sent to a place for special counseling," remembers Mark Long.

These child psychology sessions came about from Grant being deemed "out of parental control" by his teachers, and, presumably, his mother: "His mum and the school sent him to this class for problem kids."

On one visit Grant wondered if his behavioral difficulties might run in the family. His cousin, Uncle Ernest's son Geoffrey, who was a couple of years' Peter's junior, was attending the same counseling session.

Grant sometimes told journalists he'd quit education at thirteen to work as a stagehand. However, in August 1948, after Rockmount, the thirteen-year-old Peter enrolled at Ingram County Secondary School for Boys in Thornton Heath.

"Ingram Road," as it was commonly called, was a secondary modern school for children who hadn't passed the "Eleven Plus" examination. This test, introduced under Britain's 1944 Education Act, determined whether a child was suitable, or not, for a coveted grammar school place.

In class-conscious, postwar Britain, passing or failing the Eleven Plus could have a major impact on a child's prospects. The same Act promised to create more technical schools, called Secondary Moderns, for those with practical rather than academic abilities, but it didn't happen.

Secondary Moderns, such as Ingram Road, were soon filled with young people of wildly different abilities and one thing in common: they had failed the government's exam or not even taken it. Peter Grant was among them.

When Grant arrived at his new school, its recently appointed headmaster, a former Royal Air Force officer Frederick T. B. Wheeler faced an insurmountable challenge. World War II had wreaked havoc, and the school was still recovering from the aftershocks in peacetime. Ingram Road lacked teachers and basic facilities. It was easy for a child to disappear or be ignored.

According to former Atlantic Records senior vice president Phil Carson, the school had an intimidating reputation in the 1950s. Carson, who'd passed his Eleven Plus, was a pupil at St. Joseph's College—a grammar school in Beulah Hill, Upper Norwood. The two schools were fierce rivals, with the enmity fueled by jealousy and social division.

Carson remembers an incident just before he enrolled. "Some of our St. Joseph's boys had been attacked by some lads from Ingram Road," he says, "and it was decided the two schools would have it out in an organized fight."

The designated battleground was Streatham Common, a stretch of parkland near both schools. "St. Joseph's had a sixth-form for older teenagers, so we sent down our football first eleven, some of whom were as old as eighteen," he recalls. "Apparently, Ingram Road sent just eight or nine kids, most of them only fifteen, and they absolutely battered our football eleven—beat the living shit out of them."

Years later, when the two men discussed their childhoods, Carson mentioned the fight on Streatham Common. Peter told him he'd been one of Ingram Road's foot soldiers.

"I like to think of it as being like that time in the Boer War where Gandhi, Winston Churchill, and the future prime minister of South Africa [Louis Botha] were on the same battlefield," he joked, referring to the Battle of Spion Kop, where the lives of three future world leaders briefly intersected. "Though, of course, not of quite such devastating importance."

Carson remembers the fight happening shortly before he joined St. Joseph's in the summer of 1955, but Grant had left Ingram Road five years earlier. "I remember Peter telling me he was there," says Carson. "And I still like to think he was, *somehow* . . . because, of course, it's such a great story."

It's a story that brilliantly illustrates his ability to let music business gossip further his reputation. The idea of the young Grant battling rival school pupils three years his senior dovetailed with the later Peter Grant bawling out a building manager in Led Zeppelin's film *The Song Remains the Same*. The reality was more complicated.

Grant's approach to academia didn't improve and led to a damning report from Frederick Wheeler. "His headmaster said, 'This man will never make anything of his life. Useless, hopeless,'" says Helen. "It made him think, 'Sod you, I am going to do something.'"

Decades later, Grant still sounded like a man trying to prove his detractors wrong. "I know some of these big shots at record companies cringe when they're with me," he said in 1974. "They have to do it because of what you represent, which is great."

"I don't think money was Peter's driving force," said Malcolm McLaren. "His driving force was respect."

*P*eter Grant left Ingram Road on April 4, 1950, the day before his fifteenth birthday. The school records give his reason for leaving as "employment" rather than expulsion. He left without a single qualification and spent the next eight years in the army and low-paying jobs, slowly finding his way toward the entertainment industry.

Later, the more successful Led Zeppelin became, the less inclined Grant was to discuss his life before the music business. However, he was surprisingly candid in a 1970 interview with the women's magazine, *She*. "When I was thirteen I became a stagehand at the Croydon Empire," Grant said. "I also tried to work in a sheet metal factory, but after five weeks I knew it wasn't for me."

"Peter wanted to build bicycles," says Mark Long. "Dorothy took him to [British bike manufacture] Claud Butler's factory in Clapham Junction." Then he found out how poor the money was for an apprentice and walked out.

Instead, he ended up working at Visco's Engineering in Waddon, Croydon. Grant was employed as "dolly boy," climbing inside huge steel drums and holding the rivets while his co-worker drilled them from above. He lasted five weeks.

Britain was rebuilding itself after the war, and jobs were plentiful. After Visco's, Grant waited tables at the chic Italian restaurant Frascati's, an hour's bus ride from South Norwood on London's Oxford Street. Then came a brief stint as a messenger boy at Reuter's news agency. As long as there was money to be made, it didn't matter how he made it.

Arguably, the most important of all these jobs, though, was the one Grant always claimed was his first: working as a stagehand at the Croydon Empire after school and earning what he remembered as "fifteen bob a week," less than a sterling pound or a dollar in modern currency.

The Empire Theatre of Varieties first opened its doors in North End, Croydon, in 1906. For most of the next fifty years, this regal hall, with its velvet furnishings and stained-glass roof light, hosted the cream of Britain's music and variety acts.

"I was fascinated by the theater," Grant told McLaren. "There were plate spinners and another act where a guy drove a motorcycle around a huge steel cage. It seemed pretty glamorous and better than the steel factory."

Variety was Britain's version of American vaudeville: fast, cheap entertainment performed in provincial theaters by singers, comedians, and dancers—anyone who could raise a smile, coax a tear, or hold an audience's attention during their stint in the spotlight.

By the time Peter Grant was sweeping the floor and working the stage curtain, the Empire's velvet furnishings had faded, and variety was dying a slow death because of the arrival of the "talking pictures." By 1950, the world's biggest stars were movie actors such as all-American hero John Wayne or wisecracking song-and-dance men Bob Hope and Bing Crosby.

That year, the Croydon Empire's fifteen-year-old stagehand would have seen the Piccadilly Nudes, playing twice a day for six days a week. The act had been rushed in from London's Soho to bring some risqué glamour to Croydon and bump up the takings.

They were an ensemble of naked women, carefully arranged in static poses. Britain's Victorian censorship laws didn't permit a nude woman to

move on stage. This *tableau vivant*, as it was called, might have titillated audiences in the 1900s but would have seemed sad and dated by 1950.

Peter Grant would spend the best years of his working life standing in the
wings on stages all over the world, watching others bring sex and glamour to
an expectant audience—and it started at a South London theater.

In 1975 Led Zeppelin's run of dates at London's Earls Court was billed as
"An Evening With Led Zeppelin" and sold with a retro poster that wouldn't
have looked out of place at the Croydon Empire.

"Peter learned how a show would work," said Mickie Most. "How you get
an audience, how you hold back and then a deliver a decent encore."

By April 1953, the eighteen-year-old Grant had briefly quit show business and was working as a trainee hotel chef. Then he received his "call-up"
papers. All healthy British males between seventeen and twenty-one were
called up to undertake two years' compulsory national service in the armed
forces.

The Beatles' Ringo Starr once said the abolition of national service in 1960
was a blessing for British pop music: "We were the first generation that didn't
go into the army and were allowed to turn into musicians."

Until then, young conscripts were taken away from their civilian jobs and
loved ones and billeted in military garrisons up and down the country. They
were taught to march and point a gun and told when to eat, sleep, and shit.

Grant was assigned to the Royal Army Ordnance Corp—the division for
military supplies and repairs—and put in charge of the mess hall at its barracks in Kettering, Northamptonshire. He also resumed his theatrical career:
"We used to have shows at the army base every two months, and when they
found out I'd worked as a stagehand, I helped run them."

Grant assisted the Navy, Army, and Air Force Institutes (NAAFI) with
stage shows by making sure they had the same quality lights and drapes used
at the Croydon Empire. Grant was thrilled when the celebrated postwar comedian and drummer Max Bacon was booked for a show and made sure he
had the best possible stage production.

Grant was promoted from private to lance corporal in summer 1955 and
completed his national service the following April. He'd done his duty, but
the twenty-year-old was now back home and looking for work.

Grant returned to the hotel business. After taking a vacation on the island
of Jersey he started working as an entertainment manager in the same hotel
in which he'd stayed. Grant was soon booking some of the same song-and-
dance acts that had played the Empire a decade earlier. But the entertainment
business was slowly evolving.

At the time, dance bands and homegrown romantic balladeers such as Dickie Valentine or their suave American counterparts, Al Martino and Dean Martin, dominated popular music in Britain.

Then in August 1955 America's Bill Haley and His Comets upset this gentle status quo with the rock 'n' roll hit "Rock Around the Clock." Haley and his men were moonlighting jazz and swing players, who'd cannily repurposed black rhythm and blues for a young white audience. It worked. Dance band leaders and romantic balladeers were appalled and hoped this new music was just a passing fad.

Then came Elvis Presley: twenty years old, swiveling hips, lacquered hair, and excess testosterone. "This man is dangerous," proclaimed the British film magazine *Picturegoer*. "His powerful voice rises above the din like a mating call in the jungle."

In Europe, Presley's music found an immediate home on Radio Luxembourg, the commercial rival to Britain's state-sanctioned BBC. Grant, like every other adolescent or early twentysomething, listened to the station.

Elvis's effect on a generation of British teenagers was immediate and profound. His UK hits in 1956, including "Heartbreak Hotel" and "Blue Suede Shoes," turned him into a parent-baiting sex symbol and a poster boy for a glamorous new world without bombsites and ration books.

Other rock 'n' roll stars Jerry Lee Lewis, Chuck Berry, Gene Vincent, and Little Richard, soon followed. "Rock 'n' roll was about sex, hound-dogging, getting plenty of it, playing with your poodle," Malcolm McLaren explained. "Even the words 'rock' and 'roll' signified the sexual act."

In a bedroom in suburban Surrey, Led Zeppelin's future leader, a twelve-year-old Jimmy Page, was similarly smitten. "It was all so primeval," he said. "Young people were drawn to it. I was no exception."

Grant was also seduced. Barrie Keeffe, the first scriptwriter hired by McLaren to work on the film about Grant's life, interviewed Peter in the 1980s. Grant showed him a signed photograph of Elvis Presley and said, "I did it all for this."

Elvis would affect Grant's life in ways that would have seemed unimaginable in 1956. Later, he would meet the singer, befriend his manager Colonel Tom Parker, and try to bring Presley to Britain for what would have been an inaugural UK tour.

"One of the greatest highs I ever experienced was when we went to see Elvis performing in Los Angeles," he said. "His band members were all out of time, and he stopped, announcing to the audience: 'We've got Led Zeppelin here, and we're going to start again, so we look like we know what we're doing.'"

In 1957, Grant's next job would bring him slightly closer to Elvis's world. The 2i's Coffee Bar at 59 Old Compton Street took its name from its founders, brothers Freddie and Sammy Irani. Inspired by the introduction of the Gaggia espresso coffee machine, bars like the 2i's tried to bring cosmopolitan color and panache to the capital. "Soho has become espresso land," declared the *Sunday People*, one of Britain's oldest Sunday newspapers. "Bright with colored neon lights."

In spring of 1956, the 2i's was taken over by a pair of aspiring entrepreneurs, Ray Hunter and Paul Lincoln. Both had recently arrived from their native Australia where they'd worked as champion wrestlers. Lincoln would be instrumental in Grant's next career move.

It was Lincoln's idea to feature singers and groups in the 2i's' tiny basement, with its stage made from milk crates and planks of wood. Soon after, Tommy Hicks, a twenty-year-old merchant seaman from Bermondsey, South London, was spotted performing in the cellar.

Hicks signed a record deal and changed his name to Tommy Steele. His first single, "Rock With the Caveman," tried hard to imitate American rock 'n' roll and came up short, but it didn't matter. The song became a hit in summer 1956. More would follow.

Teenagers were inspired. Many daydreamed of becoming the next Elvis but gravitated toward something more achievable. For a short time, the skiffle craze ran parallel to the rock 'n' roll boom in 1950s Britain.

Skiffle music was rooted in American blues and country and was played on cheap acoustic instruments. An old-fashioned washboard and a length of string tied between a tea chest and the top of a broom handle often supplied the rhythm. It was raw and primitive, and anybody could do it.

In 1955, skiffle topped the British charts, thanks to its newly anointed king, jazz musician turned singer Lonnie Donegan. His debut hit, "Rock Island Line," inspired the future members of the Beatles, the Who, and Led Zeppelin. In 1957, a teenaged Jimmy Page made his BBC TV debut, singing and strumming an acoustic guitar with his own JG Skiffle Group.

Now, night after night, teenagers flocked to the 2i's to listen to the big Wurlitzer jukebox on the club's ground floor or the skiffle groups and rock 'n' rollers thrashing away in the cellar. There was money to be made in this newfangled strand of show business.

Paul Lincoln charged one shilling at the door. And although the club's official capacity was 60, more than 150 would squeeze in on a busy Saturday night. Record company scouts now made trips to the 2i's in their quest to find the next Lonnie Donegan or, better still, the English Elvis.

Lincoln was soon managing two homegrown rock 'n' roll singers. Neither Terry Dene nor Wee Willie Harris would challenge Elvis Presley for star quality but for a time both had hits.

Dene was arguably the first rock 'n' roll casualty, suffering a nervous breakdown while doing his national service and dropping out of the music business altogether. Meanwhile, Harris, who stood just five feet two inches, made up for what he lacked in height with a frenetic stage act and brightly colored dyed hair.

There wasn't an instruction manual on how to make a career out of this new music. Everybody knew it could all end tomorrow, and they'd be back on the factory floor. "Nobody was actually managing anyone," says former 2i's regular Derek Berman, who met Grant in 1960. "Paul Lincoln was a businessman who thought, 'There's a guy who can sing; I will manage him.' Then his friends decided to do the same."

Now, though, wherever teenagers gathered, there was an even greater need for security. The 2i's and other coffee bars recruited doormen to keep their patrons in line and see off Soho's less desirable elements. Paul Lincoln would employ various imposing looking characters in the months ahead.

There was twenty-two-stone "Big" Roy Heath, who intervened when an East End mob armed with axes and a shotgun came looking for one of the 2i's' skiffle players. Later came men known by the nicknames, "2i's Norman," "Lofty," and Henry Henroid, who was a sometime wrestler who later worked for the Beatles and Peter Grant's early employer Don Arden.

"You had a lot of hard people who used to strut around down at the 2i's," said singer-songwriter Tony Sheridan. "All these characters in Italian suits and pointed shoes."

In 1958 Lincoln appointed a colleague from the wrestling world, Tom Littlewood, to manage the 2i's while he was on tour with his acts. Lincoln's first job in England had been as a bodyguard, and Littlewood was a professional judo instructor. Their mutual background was a bonus in London's wild West End.

Where there was cash money to be made, there was always someone trying to cut themselves in on the deal. Protection racketeering and intimidation were rife. When Lincoln opened another coffee bar, The New i's, a gang tried to extort money from him, and one of his doormen ended up scarred for life after a hatchet blow.

Rock 'n' roll's popularity had also seen the rise of the Teddy Boy youth cult. "Teddy Boys" were named after their taste for Edwardian-era drape jackets. The look was completed by drainpipe trousers, crepe-soled "brothel creepers," and long hair fashioned into an exaggerated quiff, *à la* Elvis.

When the first rock 'n' roll movie, *The Blackboard Jungle*, opened in 1956, some Teddy Boys were so enthralled by Bill Haley and His Comets' soundtrack they slashed the seats of their local cinema and were arrested for public disorder. Having saved Great Britain from Nazi Germany, parents and grandparents worried that Elvis and his disciples would finish what Hitler had started.

Peter Grant began policing the door at the 2i's in 1957. Food and a wage were of paramount importance for him. "You got a meal and a quid a night," he said. To many who remember him from back then, Grant was just the latest in a long line of 2i's bruisers. "By the time Grant worked there, the job description was more realistic: he was a bouncer," said sixties historian Barry Miles.

The late agent Peter Harrison booked Grant's clients the Yardbirds to play London's Last Chance Saloon club in 1967. "Their road manager was a big hulk of a man with shrewd eyes," he said. "He was puffing and panting, as he heaved the equipment down to the semi-basement club." After a couple of minutes Harrison recognized him as the ex-bouncer from the 2i's.

As a teenager, Harrison had worked for a Soho jukebox company supplying discs for the coffee bar's Wurlitzer: "I often bumped into the menacing figure of Peter Grant. We got on fine, but neither of us could have forecast the future."

It was at the 2i's that Grant forged the friendship that would lead to one his earliest business partnerships. During the 1960s, the late Mickie Most produced hits for Herman's Hermits, Donovan, and the Animals. In the 1970s, Most also became a household name as a judge on the TV talent show, *New Faces*, where his waspish comments cast him as a reality TV villain long before *The X-Factor*'s Simon Cowell.

In the mid-1950s, though, Mickie Most was still known as Michael Hayes—a West London teenager, who dressed like his hero, the surly adolescent played by James Dean in *Rebel Without a Cause*. Like Peter Grant, Hayes left his secondary modern school at fifteen and, like Grant, drifted into a job as a dolly boy at his local steelworks. Then came the accident.

Hayes was helping move a large metal vat when it dropped on his foot, severing one of his toes. "From that day on, I was sort of 10 percent disabled," he said, "which got me out of doing national service, which I was quite pleased about."

Even before the injury, Hayes had been ducking out of work to hang around Soho's music shops, trying out guitars he couldn't afford to buy, and making a cup of coffee last for hours at the 2i's. Before long, he was working at the club, serving Coca Cola and operating the espresso machine.

"Mickie poured the coffee, and I sold the tickets at the top of the stairs," recalled Grant.

Hayes was friends with Terry Dene and watched enviously as he became a pop star. Though hired to make drinks, Mickie would often dash out from behind the counter to sing in the basement—until Paul Lincoln told him to shut up and get back to work.

Hayes's fascination with the hip new lingo overheard in American movies or songs led to him describing any record, film—or girl—he liked as "the most." The catchphrase stuck and by 1957, Michael Hayes had become Mickie Most. Soon after, Hayes and another 2i's regular, Alex Wharton (who would go on to produce and manage the Moody Blues), had formed a singing duo—the Most Brothers—and hassled Lincoln into becoming their manager.

What the 2i's waiter and doorman shared was a willingness to seize any opportunity to make money. "The music business wasn't particularly wanting either Peter Grant or myself," said Most. "We had to occupy our time doing other stuff."

Paul Lincoln hadn't abandoned his earlier career. He began wrestling soon after he arrived in England. When he began wearing an executioner-style black mask and billing himself as "Doctor Death," his popularity soared, and he was soon topping the bill around the country.

Nobody knew whether rock 'n' roll and coffee bars would turn out to be passing fads. So Lincoln set up a wrestling promotions company and began shaking up the sport's staid image. Lincoln understood the power of a good gimmick and showbiz glamour. He'd copied the idea of dyeing Wee Willie Harris's hair pink from an American fighter called Gorgeous George. Paul Lincoln Promotions were soon pulling in crowds, thanks to such exotic characters as the Mighty Chang, Jungle Boy, and the Wild Man of Borneo.

According to Mickie Most, his and Grant's move into wrestling came when they were paid to put up the ring at Wembley Town Hall. However, Grant told McLaren and his filmmaking partner Mike Figgis that he began wrestling after being appointed by Paul Lincoln to drive his acts to their engagements around London. At first, Grant was employed as a timekeeper during the bouts. Then he became a "plant" in the audience.

Among Lincoln's performers was a Hungarian dwarf, whose act involved bending metals bars with his neck and claiming he could lift the heaviest person in the audience. Grant said he made his wrestling debut at the Streatham Regal in south London, where he pretended to be a member of the public and volunteered to be lifted.

Grant wasn't as heavy then as he would become, but his weight still presented a challenge. He lay on a plank of wood with a rope joining each end and supported by two stools, while the Hungarian stood on a third stool in between and lifted the rope with his mouth. "I used to get two quid for doing that," said Peter.

When one of the wrestlers failed to turn up one day, Grant took his place. Led Zeppelin's future manager climbed onto the canvas, while Mickie Most, Britain's future record producer, presumably excused from fighting on the grounds of his missing toe, shouted encouragement from the ropes.

Mentions of Grant's wrestling career appeared after the *Daily Mirror* interviewed him in October 1970. Until then he'd managed to keep it from the press. "I was a wrestler for about eighteen months when I needed to make some money," he revealed.

From here on, though, the "ex-wrestler" tag usually accompanied any mention of Grant in the music papers. "It's a fact of history he's anxious to consign to oblivion," suggested *Melody Maker* in 1974.

Like the fabled Battle of Streatham Common, Grant's wrestling career has acquired a life of its own. Atlantic Records' music mogul Ahmet Ertegun added to the myth, claiming, "Peter wrestled at carnivals, where he would take on anyone in the audience."

Malcolm McLaren also talked about Grant frequenting "fairgrounds in the 1950s, which is what all the gypsies and outlaws did . . . where things were loose and free."

The image of Led Zeppelin's manager taking on all comers, like some Victorian bare-knuckle brawler, is irresistible. The reality was far less glamorous.

*P*aul Lincoln staged many of his events at Granada cinemas and bingo halls in the provinces. Less than ten years earlier, these drab venues, with their cream and bottle green decor had hosted variety acts. Very little had changed.

Grant told his friend—Dire Straits' manager—Ed Bicknell he'd fought under the name His Royal Highness Count Bruno Alessio of Milan. He told the *Observer*'s Tony Palmer he'd wrestled as Mario Alassio. Others remember the name Count Massimo. There are many variations.

As a wrestler, Grant perfected many of the tricks he used later on those who crossed him, including his signature move: the four-fingered jab under the ribcage. In reality, it was all about putting on a show. It wasn't a good night at the wrestling until at least one elderly woman in the audience had left her seat, shouting abuse and banging a rolled-up umbrella on the canvas.

When it was over, His Royal Highness Count Bruno would change in a cold, grubby dressing room and get paid extra to take the ring down later.

Drummer Mick Underwood, who worked with Grant in the 1960s, remembers Peter's wrestling days. "My father-in-law loved wrestling and thought he'd seen Peter fighting under one of his names," he says now. "He rated him, said he was great."

"I once asked him, 'What moves did you have, Peter?'" remembers Ed Bicknell. "He replied, 'I used to push 'em over and fall on them. Fucking hell, I never lost a bout.'"

Bad Company's crew boss Phil Carlo remembers an incident on tour in America. "We were backstage, and there was a tannoy piping horrible music into the dressing room," he says. Without warning, Peter swung his arm back, walloping the speaker with the flat of his hand: "The whole thing disintegrated like confetti over the floor. I said, 'What the hell was that?' He said, 'It's a wrestler's slap, Phil.'"

Between 1957 and the early 1960s, Grant earned his living with wrestling, door work, and anything else that helped him to get by. "I first met Peter when he was at the door of the Flamingo," says retired music critic and PR Keith Altham. "All I knew about him was that he'd wrestled for Paul Lincoln and was one of his bouncers. I don't think any of us expected him to become what he did."

The Flamingo on Wardour Street was a mecca for blues and jazz artists and attracted the sharply dressed modern jazz crowd, later known as mods. By the early 1960s, its weekend all-nighters were run by former boxer Rik Gunnell. He paid off the police to ensure the club could stay open until 6 a.m. and was on good terms with East London's infamous criminal siblings, the Kray twins.

Gunnell's weekly drama of booking acts, sweet-talking managers, bribery, and schmoozing gave Grant a vital education. He was paid to stand in the Flamingo doorway, taking tickets and dispensing the odd wrestler's slap, but he was also watching and learning.

The Flamingo would make headlines in 1962 for its part in Britain's great political scandal. Jack Profumo, the government's secretary of state for war, was revealed to have been sharing a lover, Christine Keeler, with a Soviet naval officer and a Jamaican singer and hustler known as "Lucky" Gordon. Gordon had his face slashed by a jealous rival one night at the Flamingo.

Ten minutes' walk away was another of Grant's haunts: Murray's Cabaret Club on Beak Street, where Peter was employed as a doorman and Christine Keeler later worked as a showgirl.

An advertisement for Murray's promised the most "lavishly staged floor show in town, with the loveliest showgirls." The club was run by a well-traveled old roué named Percival Murray, who instructed his employees to call him "Pops."

"There was a pervasive atmosphere of sex, with beautiful young girls all over the place," wrote the late Keeler in her 2012 memoir, *Secrets and Lies*. "We star showgirls walked bare-breasted onto the stage, and the hostesses moved among the wealthy and aristocratic male diners and drinkers."

One night, Christine recalled smuggling her politician lover into Murray's, even though he wasn't a member: "I whispered to Peter at the front door who Jack was. And Peter made an exception and allowed him in." It's likely, though, that Grant had left by the time Keeler worked at Murray's, and she was referring to the club's long-standing manager Peter Batchelor.

"I learned a lot at Murray's cabaret club," Grant said. "When you're getting cabs for those punters in your uniform or stood on the reception desk, you get to talk to big people—'Good evening sir, how are you?' It was a great training ground."

When "Pops" Murray found out Grant had previously worked in theater, he also asked him to operate the stage curtain and help with the running of the show. "I wasn't married then," he said. "And what with me being the only man around and about forty girls backstage . . . it was alright."

It was through Murray's that Grant met another occasional employer. After Peter's death, Mickie Most divulged that his friend had worked as a minder to the infamous slum landlord Peter Rachman, another Murray's Cabaret Club member and one of Christine Keeler's lovers.

By the late 1950s, Polish refugee Rachman had acquired more than a hundred properties in Notting Hill and its surrounding area. Many of these were let to West Indians denied accommodation by other agents. Rachman considered himself the savior of the immigrant community. The authorities felt differently, and he was vilified as a slum landlord, who ran prostitutes and used intimidation to collect rents and evict tenants.

Rachman's collectors included many wrestlers, boxers, and nightclub doormen. Grant was one of them. By the early 1960s, there was a thread connecting the landlord with many people hustling on the fringes of the entertainment business.

The radio DJ Nicky Horne met Grant in the 1970s but became aware of the connection when he started in the business as a teenager in the late 1960s.

"I was working for the DJ Emperor Rosko," he says. Rosko's manager was former 2i's doorman, Henry Henroid. "Henry seemed to be very well connected with the West London boys, and I used to drink with them all in the Moscow Arms pub in Bayswater. There I was, this little eighteen-year-old schnook, with all these gangsters."

The Moscow Arms' clientele included Peter Grant's future bodyguard, the actor and criminal John Bindon, and Jimmy Houlihan, "a wonderful character whose claim to fame was that he'd once collected rents for Peter Rachman," says Horne.

However, not all of Grant's jobs at this time required strong-arm tactics. "I wanted to be an actor," he admitted in 1989, "but I was never really good enough."

Nevertheless, Grant made several credited and uncredited appearances in British films and TV shows in the late fifties and early sixties. He turned up in the police drama *Dixon of Dock Green*, played a cowboy in an episode of the *Benny Hill Show*, a barman opposite future James Bond star Roger Moore in *The Saint*, and appeared as "an Arab with a large saw" in a sketch for the children's variety show *Crackerjack*.

He even made a brief appearance on stage playing a waiter in a mime act with the American vaudeville star Eddie Vitch. "We did a Connie Francis TV special together," Grant later told Malcolm McLaren.

In 1958, Peter made his movie debut, playing a sailor in *A Night to Remember*, a black-and-white drama about the sinking of RMS *Titanic* in 1912. Grant was required for a winter night shoot at West London's Ruislip Lido, an open-air swimming pool, which contained a replica of the ocean liner and several lifeboats.

Leading man Kenneth More played the ship's second officer Charles Lightoller. When the extras refused to jump into the icy water, More offered to go first. "Never have I experienced such cold," he said. "It was like jumping into a deep freeze. The shock forced the breath out of my body. My heart seemed to stop beating. I felt crushed, unable to think."

Gasping for air, More tried to warn the extras not to follow, but it was too late. Somewhere in the scene, among the sailors crowded on the deck of the capsized ship or floating in the water, struggling to catch their breath, is a twenty-two-year-old Peter Grant.

In winter 1960, Grant was among the extras on set for the romantic epic *Cleopatra*, starring Elizabeth Taylor. "It was originally being filmed at Pinewood Studios," he said, "and I always remember her turning up every day on set in a white Phantom 5 car, wearing a fur coat. She'd get out of the car, decide it was too chilly, and go straight back to the Hilton Hotel."

This routine continued for two weeks, with the weather becoming worse and the temperature plummeting. "I didn't mind," Grant said. "I was getting paid £15 a day, which back then was a lot of money."

The three hundred extras wiled away their time in a marquee, drinking tea and playing endless games of cards. Many, including Grant, were dressed as slaves or soldiers and daubed with brown body paint to make them look Middle Eastern. "I was a Macedonian guard, wearing rubber armor," he said.

Elizabeth Taylor eventually arrived to shoot the scene in which Cleopatra makes her grand entrance into Rome. 2i's regular Mim Scala, later to become a film and theater agent, was with Grant when director Rouben Mamoulian summoned them to the set.

"Peter Grant was a huge fellow I knew from Soho," remembered Scala, "and I stood next to him in the front line." The director swooped toward Scala and his giant friend seated on a crane-operated boom. He leaned forward and quietly told Scala he was too small and should stand at the back, before summoning Grant to the front.

Neither Peter nor Mim would make the final cut. "In the end, we managed to get about seven minutes of film in the can, before they scrapped everything," said Grant. Mamoulian resigned, and *Cleopatra* was shot in Italy with a new director.

Grant fared better in other movies, even if he was still difficult to spot on screen. He was actor Anthony Quinn's stand-in and stunt double on the hit 1961 war drama *The Guns of Navarone*. The film's setting of the Greek mountains and the Aegean Sea was re-created at Pinewood Studios.

A violent storm scene was staged using eight hundred thousand gallons of water, several wind machines, and an aeroplane motor. Quinn was knocked off his feet, injuring his back and reopening an old war wound. Which is, presumably, where Grant came in.

For a time, Grant doubled for the portly British actor Robert Morley in several films, including 1962's knockabout comedy caper, *Go to Blazes*. Morley played a fire chief in the movie but was nervous about traveling at high speed in an open-cab fire engine. Grant took his place: "They had to pad me out quite a bit. And I would also put on a bald wig. I had hair then."

In the same year, Grant also appeared in Stanley Kubrick's comedy-drama, *Lolita*. "All I had to do was walk across the set, playing a bell hop," he explained, but he walked too fast for the fastidious director, and Kubrick "gave me a good dressing-down."

Ten years later, Grant wrote to Kubrick asking if he'd consider directing what became *The Song Remains the Same*: "And I added in a little message at the end, reminding him of the incident. He wrote back declining the offer and said he did recall my performance . . . and hoped that I'd improved since then."

Grant's appearance in *Lolita* lasts for just a few seconds, and he's only glimpsed in profile. However, he's visible, wearing a white jacket and sauntering through a hotel lobby, as actor Peter Sellers and actress Sue Lyons lean across the check-in desk.

By then, though, Grant had acquired the item that would transform his working life. Part-time actor, doorman, wrestler, and rent collector, Peter Grant had bought himself a minibus.

2

Soup for Christmas

"Peter Grant had been on the road with
Wee Willie Harris and Gene Vincent
in the bad old days. He had his own
way of getting things done."

—ROBERT PLANT

In spring 1958, the London Planetarium was the capital's latest tourist attraction. Inside the domed building on Marylebone Road, visitors stared at the tableau of galaxies and stars overhead. Outside, back on planet Earth, the men tasked with driving America's rock 'n' roll stars met in the drivers' canteen on Allsop Place.

Peter Grant was a regular at the café. Here, he'd drink tea and swap stories with his fellow drivers before rounding up his acts and putting them on the bus. There were the American headliners, shivering in the cold and straining to understand the English accents. There were the warm-up acts: teenagers with teetering quiffs and oversized guitars. And then there were the variety-style entertainers—the comedians who shared the same agent as these musicians and hoped some of their rock 'n' roll gloss would rub off on them.

For the next few years, Grant drove them all: from Gene Vincent and Little Richard, to Cliff Richard and the Shadows, to sibling comedians, Mike and Bernie Winters, to yodeling crooner Frank Ifield. His job was to get them there, get them onstage, and get them paid.

Grant's passport listed his profession as "Theatrical Manager." There was some wishful thinking involved. In spring 1960, he spent four months in Italy with Wee Willie Harris. The UK pop TV show, *6.5 Special*, had beamed Willie's theatrical stage act into the nation's living rooms. Harris didn't have the studied coolness of Elvis or Gene Vincent. With his dyed orange hair and caveman-style, leopard-skin tunic, he was a comic strip brought to life.

Harris's backing musicians in Italy included guitarist Derek Berman (who used the stage name Dave Burns). "We traveled in an Alfa Romeo Superlight Sprint, and Peter Grant followed in the van with all our gear," he recalls. "We played every night, and I don't think anyone slept. It was sixteen weeks of hell."

The band, dressed as English city gents in pinstriped suits and bowler hats, pretended to look shocked when Harris bounded on stage, skinny white legs shaking beneath his animal-print loincloth. It worked every time. Willie was hugely popular in Italy where he had appeared in two movies that year: the travelogue *Mondo di Notte* and a knockabout comedy, *Tototruffa '62*.

In Britain, a government committee protested to the BBC that he was promoting "teenage decadence." Grant later told the press the Pope had banned Harris from appearing on Italian TV. Whether it was true didn't matter. It added to the myth.

Derek Berman remembers Grant as reliable and unfailingly funny. "I don't know where that other Peter Grant came from. I heard all the stories later, and I can only assume it was the drugs and the people he was hanging around with. I also remember Peter as struggling. He had *nothing*. Nobody was making a penny."

Three specific events characterize the hand-to-mouth nature of Grant's working life during this time. In the late fifties, the teenage Phil Carson briefly played bass guitar for Cal Danger, a singer cheekily billing himself as "Britain's Gene Vincent." Danger convinced one promoter he was the real thing, upsetting Don Arden, who represented the real Gene Vincent. Arden arranged to have this imposter stopped at his next gig.

Carson remembers sitting in the back of an Austin Somerset van on the way to the show when the vehicle came to a sudden halt: "The driver's door opened, and Cal was dragged out. The drummer and me were in the back, and we could hear all this banging and thumping. We were teenagers, scared shitless. Then the passenger door jerked open, and this big head appeared—'Who the fuck are you?' 'We're in Cal Danger's band,' we whispered. 'Not any fucking more you're not. Get out!' And that was my first encounter with Peter Grant."

Had Phil Carson been watching television on December 6, 1960, he'd have seen the same man in the BBC comedy series *Citizen James*. In an episode titled "The Money," actor Sid James, playing a Soho con man, hosts a lottery to win £250. Grant appeared in a nonspeaking role as one of the ticket holders. It was good casting. Off-screen, Grant was a man in urgent need of £250, and he was always searching for ways to find it.

That same year, the American singer Chubby Checker launched a dance craze with his hits "The Twist" and "Let's Twist Again." Fifteen-year-old Jeff Dexter, who'd later become a club DJ and festival compère, was banned from London's Lyceum for performing the dance. "It was considered obscene," he says now. However, the publicity secured him a job with the Cyril Stapleton Orchestra and a visit from Peter Grant.

"I knew Peter as a 2i's character," Dexter explains. "I'd seen him around Soho. After I did one of my stints with Cyril, he came backstage at the Lyceum." That day, Grant was accompanied by the future DJ and TV presenter Jimmy Savile. After his death in 2011, Savile was exposed as a serial sex offender: "Back then, nobody knew he was such a pervert."

At the time, Savile was a dancehall manager and part-time wrestler—another would-be entrepreneur on the make. The two men had a proposal for Dexter: "Peter, bless his heart, suggested I'd make a lot of cash if I became 'The Twisting Wrestler,' fighting and dancing in a swimsuit." Dexter declined, and another moneymaking scheme was abandoned.

*B*y late 1961, though Grant was also employed as an occasional driver and stage manager for the Noel Gay Agency in London's West End. Rock 'n' roll had arrived but hadn't conquered everywhere. Gay's clients included song and dance acts, trampolinists, and magicians, which were hired to play holiday camps, working men's clubs, and a circuit of faded Embassy ballrooms in English seaside towns.

Among the acts were the Jeanettes—three young singing sisters, Jean, Sue, and Gloria Cutting, from Hull in Yorkshire. Peter met the trio during rehearsals in Denmark Street for an upcoming tour of North and South Wales, sponsored by Gallaher Cigarettes. "My mum first noticed my dad's eyes," says daughter Helen.

Soon after, Peter and Gloria became a couple. The show business trade journal, *The Stage*, reported on the tour: "The company includes compère Larry Burns, the Jeanettes, Kovari, a young Hungarian magician, Jimmy Rodgers, pianist from Preston, and as stage manager/driver, Peter Grant, who has appeared in many films and TV plays and is well-known for his tough guy parts, as he is six-feet three-inches tall and weighs over eighteen stone."

The tour notched up 162 performances in fourteen weeks up to Easter 1962. Grant drove the acts from town to town, stayed in the same boarding houses, and even joined them onstage to sing out of tune during the grand finale. Grant told the singing sisters he should become their manager. They laughed, as he hadn't managed anyone. By the end of the run, Peter and Gloria were engaged.

Grant's last movie, *The Guns of Navarone*, was a box office hit, but none of the profits filtered down to lowly stunt doubles. He later told a journalist that he and Gloria were so poor their first year together, they'd shared a can of soup for Christmas dinner.

In June, Grant joined the Jeanettes for shows at the British army base in Tripoli. The couple married in Hull that summer and moved into Norhyrst Avenue with Dorothy. It wasn't easy for the newlyweds. Despite having an illegitimate son, Dorothy was quite Victorian in her outlook.

"My grandmother was very straitlaced," says Helen. "She wasn't that keen on my mum, not really. They didn't always get on." Gloria, however, was just twenty-four years old and had been working in the theater since she was a teenager. "Mum was tiny but very feisty, and didn't stand for any shit."

Soon after, Gloria discovered she was pregnant. The couple moved into a tiny flat in Dorrington Court at the top of South Norwood Hill. Later, Grant would make enough for them to move to Cromwell Road near Shepherds Bush.

"For the time being, Dad had to work two or three jobs," says Helen. "He was still driving the groups, and he was also driving a cab. They had nothing. He was putting pieces of cardboard inside his shoes when they wore out and nicking pints of milk off people's doorsteps."

When money became too scarce, Grant went to work full time for Don Arden. Asked about Grant later, Arden (who died in 2007) was scathing. In his autobiography, *Mr. Big*, Arden accused Grant of being a thief, disputed the story he'd ever worked as a wrestler, and described him as "a three-hundred-pound bag of shit."

Part of the problem for Arden was the apprentice became the master. Despite their later enmity, Grant always admitted he'd learned a lot from Arden. Don was an old vaudeville star who relished his reputation as the so-called "godfather of rock 'n' roll." By the end of his life, though, Arden was just as easily known as "Sharon Osbourne's dad."

Arden had been born Harry Levy into a Jewish family who'd fled Russia after the revolution and arrived in Manchester. He later spoke of a childhood blighted by anti-Semitism and violence but claimed to have won over his tormentors by killing the rats in his local scrapyard and displaying their corpses: "It put a question mark in the minds about what I was capable of."

By the time he was in his teens, Levy was calling himself "Don Arden" and mimicking popular singers and impersonating Hollywood tough guys Edward G. Robinson and James Cagney on the variety circuit. Then, at the Blackpool Palace in 1956, a heckler encouraged him "to sing in his own voice." Soon after, Arden heard Elvis Presley and sensed his time was up. "There was no point hanging around, trying to prove I could sing louder than these kids," he reasoned.

Instead, Arden reinvented himself as a promoter and agent. He'd performed at US army bases around the UK and Germany and realized they rarely booked acts the troops wanted to see: "The soldiers would ask for Elvis and end up with Fritz the local yodeler and his dancing bear."

At first Arden found it difficult to crack the monopoly of Britain's showbiz agencies, but his break came when one of his veteran contacts asked if he'd heard of a new American singer named Gene Vincent. "You'll love *her*," they told him. "*She's* marvelous." Arden convinced New York's William Morris Agency to let him promote Vincent in the UK.

Although native rock 'n' rollers such as Cliff Richard and Marty Wilde were producing hits, British audiences craved the real thing. Arden's sales pitch was to offer Vincent a theater tour but also include some lucrative dates at the American military bases.

To shore up his transatlantic connections, Arden formed Anglo-American Artists at 35 Curzon Street in London's Mayfair. The address was soon being used by a growing network of agents, promoters, and willing chancers; many of whose businesses would intersect in the years ahead.

Number 35 also housed showbiz agent Colin Berlin and future Van Morrison manager, Phil Solomon, both of whom would make use of Grant's services; and dance band leader-turned-agent Vic Lewis, who'd sell his management agency to the Beatles' manager Brian Epstein. Epstein's company, N.E.M.S., would later poach Arden's management clients, the Midlands rock group Black Sabbath.

Arden also became a partner in the Star Club, the red-light district venue in Hamburg, Germany, in which the Beatles learned their craft. Don saw a gap in the market and began filling it, just as Grant did later with Led Zeppe-lin. He wrested Gene Vincent away from other promoters and was soon compèring tours for other American acts including Johnny Preston and Brenda Lee. They weren't all rock 'n' roll singers, but it didn't matter: the most important thing was they were American.

Don and his wife, a former dancer nicknamed "Paddles," lived in Brixton, South London, with his son David and daughter Sharon. Their house on An-gell Road also accommodated Arden's office and whichever of his gofers needed a bed for the night. Among his associates were wrestlers-turned-pop managers Les Bristow and Paul Lincoln, while 2i's regular Henry Henroid was soon on the payroll as Gene Vincent's driver and minder.

It was a cash business, and as the cash flow increased, so did Don's retinue of film extras, stunt doubles, and men hired simply because they looked like they could handle themselves. "They were all on the fringes of show business and hired because they knew someone who knew someone," says Sharon Osbourne.

Among them was Stan Simmonds, also an extra in *Cleopatra* and *Citizen James*, and Black Sabbath's future co-managers, film heavy Patrick Meehan Sr. and Wilf Pine, whose associates later included the Kray twins and New York crime boss Joe Pagano.

Arden first met Peter Grant while compèring a show at one of the US military bases. Grant was driving the trad jazz act Dick Charlesworth and His City Gents at the time. "Peter was just a kid in his twenties," remembered Arden, "but he had a Volkswagen bus."

Before long Grant had joined the gang—on £50 a week, from which he had to pay his own petrol. "Peter was one of my dad's heavies," Sharon Os-bourne said. "I remember him because he used to take us to school, and he'd often be at the gates later to pick us up."

However, Arden was soon making use of Peter's size and demeanor. In October 1962, Don brought Gene Vincent, soul star Sam Cooke, and "Tutti Frutti" singer Little Richard to Britain. Henry Henroid was now running the Star Club in Germany, so Arden appointed Grant as Vincent's driver and stage manager.

However, Peter soon acquired other duties besides chauffeuring the star. He was there to do whatever Don Arden wanted. Don had hired the *New Musical Express* writer Chris Hutchins as his press officer. Arden welcomed him into the fold but was furious when Hutchins changed his mind and re-turned to his old job.

Little Richard's backup band was the British group Sounds Incorporated, whom Arden was managing. After a show in London, Hutchins joined them for a drink at their Kensington hotel. At 2 a.m., the porter told Hutchins he had an urgent telephone call. He went to reception where, instead, he was bundled into a car by Peter Grant.

Grant drove the journalist to Brixton, where Arden screamed, cursed, and cross-examined him for hours, convinced Hutchins was trying to lure Sounds Incorporated away and manage them himself. "I don't remember exactly what he threatened," wrote Hutchins in his 2005 memoir, *Mr. Confidential*, "but I can still recall the air of menace and wondered whether I would ever leave in one piece."

Finally, with dawn breaking over South London, Arden accepted Hutchins's innocence and told Grant to take him home. The two men shared the awkward journey back to Hutchins's flat in Chelsea. Besides being held prisoner, what also unsettled Hutchins was how it happened in the same room in which he'd socialized with the Arden family weeks earlier. He'd gone from a friend to an enemy overnight for nothing.

The late-night interrogation was a familiar scenario in the Arden household. "There was always some drama going on," admitted Sharon Osbourne. "Someone had done something against my father, and he'd be threatening to kill the bastards. From as early as I can remember, people were frightened of him."

Grant and Stan Simmonds were also present the night Don attacked a journalist for insulting him in front of his son, David. In hindsight, there were parallels with Grant's later treatment of a security guard who pushed over his son Warren backstage in America. "I walloped him hard and watched his feet lift off the ground," bragged Arden. "He actually landed on top of my car."

"I never stopped performing," admitted Don. "But instead of performing on stage I was performing in real life." Tales of Arden's threats and violent behavior, whether real or imaginary, were repeated in the offices of *Melody Maker*, at the music publishers on Denmark Street, and in De Hems, the Ship, or any of the West End pubs in which writers, musicians, and their handlers gathered. These stories would become enhanced with each retelling.

"The music industry is made up of two separate groups—drama queens and wannabe gangsters," explained Arden, "and they're always gossiping among themselves."

In his mind, Arden was still marching through the streets of Manchester, swinging dead rats by their tails. Except now he was doing it through the

music business in London. It was all about "the power of fear," a trick Grant
would later use to his advantage.

In 1962, the job titles "roadie" and "tour manager" didn't exist. "How it
worked was Don or Colin Berlin would give me an itinerary," said Grant. "I'd
pick up the act from the airport, book the hotel, get them set up, take them
round the gigs, and get them paid."

However, Grant also had to deal with the problems: the crooked club
manager fixing "the count" of tickets at the door, the singer too drunk to
perform, or the besotted fan who'd slept with the headline act and couldn't
understand why he wouldn't marry her.

Then there were the rogue promoters who booked groups on several con-
secutive dates—they paid on time and lulled their agents into a false sense of
security. Finally, they'd book the act into a huge theater, sell more tickets than
ever, and promise a check as payment. The check would fail to appear, by
which time the promoter had disappeared. Those who brazened it out with
those they'd ripped off found a tough adversary in Arden. Don, like Peter
Rachman, gained a reputation for using debt collectors who always collected.

Sometimes arguments over money and rivalry between promoters spilled
over into violence. Grant and Mickie Most arrived one night at a club in
Hitchin to see a gang waving machetes at the bouncers outside. It was revenge
for some misdemeanor by the club's promoter.

On other occasions, the altercations were more comical than terrifying.
When Arden and Rik Gunnell fell out over money, the two promoters sent
separate gangs of heavies to each other's offices. Grant recalled the two
teams meeting at 35 Curzon Street: Arden's men were coming down the
stairs, as Gunnell's were going up. Realizing they'd all been paid up front,
they piled into the nearest pub and spent the rest of the afternoon getting
drunk together.

For the artists themselves, the dying world of variety and the new world
of pop music weren't so different. Everybody still craved money, sex, and attention—and they were all looking for ways to ease the tedium of traveling
between shows. "It was the same sort of lunacy, the same silly things," said
Grant, who remembered watching as a bored Tubby Hayes, the feted jazz
saxophonist, set light to his farts in a dressing room. Later, when America's
newest pop heartthrob Brian Hyland toured Britain, Grant had to smuggle
him out of the Guildford Odeon after teenage girls smashed their way into his
dressing room, showering him with glass.

Each passing week, Grant witnessed some stunt or scam. One of his final
jobs in 1962 was driving B. Bumble and the Stingers on a month-long jaunt

around the provinces. The American group had just had a hit with "Nut Rocker," a souped-up version of Tchaikovsky's "March of the Toy Soldiers." When Grant went to collect them from the airport, he found a group of unglamorous session musicians instead of pop stars.

"Nut Rocker" was the work of a producer and his hired hands. When the record became a hit, the label put together a fake group to promote it. Four years later, Grant was involved in a similar sleight of hand with the New Vaudeville Band and its hit, "Winchester Cathedral."

B. Bumble and the Stingers may not have been the real thing, but Gene Vincent was—and neither Tubby Hayes's farts nor Brian Hyland's wild female fan base could prepare Grant for life with Vincent.

*I*n 1955, the singer born Eugene Vincent Craddock in Norfolk, Virginia, had just reenlisted in the US Navy. Then came the motorcycle accident that left him with a damaged left leg and ended his military career. One year later, Craddock had changed his name to Gene Vincent and bagged a record deal. Gene Vincent and His Blue Caps' first single, "Be-Bop-A-Lula," with its stuttering, drawled vocal, was one of their first great rock 'n' roll records and would sell 2 million copies in one year.

There would be other hits. However, Vincent's appearance on the UK TV music show *Boy Meets Girl* and his subsequent tour in December of 1959 boosted his career in Britain, just as it was tailing off in America. Usually clad in black and hunched over his microphone stand, Vincent was the prototype for every sullen, leather-clad rock star to come, but he was prone to even darker behavior offstage.

Gene had refused his doctors' recommendation to have his ruined leg amputated and was in chronic pain. He'd also contracted osteomyelitis, which caused the limb to rot. His response was a perilous combination of painkillers and alcohol. Few of those watching Gene Vincent onstage at the Tooting Granada knew he used the microphone stand for support, and when the adrenaline and pills wore off, he needed crutches to walk.

By 1963, Vincent was living in the UK and was being managed by Don Arden. He became a frequent visitor to Angell Road and later taught Sharon Osbourne to swim, "with his strange, withered leg dangling in the water," she recalls.

Coming to England put the singer beyond the reach of his two ex-wives and the Internal Revenue Service, and it was where he met his next wife, an English dancer and ex-Murray's showgirl named Margie Russell. Before long,

Arden and Peter Grant had become responsible for every aspect of the singer's life and career.

When Peter took over, Don gave him a simple instruction: "Make sure
that fucker gets to the shows in one piece and stays off the whisky." Grant had
witnessed Vincent's volatile behavior before. In May 1962, Gene had toured
on a double bill with the West Indian singer Emile Ford and had daubed Ku
Klux Klan signs on his dressing-room door.

Most days began with a fortifying shot of scotch or vodka and continued
until he ran dry or Grant confiscated his booze. Roused from his flat or hotel
room, Gene would slide awkwardly into the passenger seat next to Peter, a
bottle of something alcoholic concealed about his person. If Grant wasn't
driving fast enough for his liking, he'd jam one of his crutches onto the
accelerator.

"One day, Peter told me he'd gotten rid of everything, but Gene was still
getting drunk," Barrie Keefe recalls. "He couldn't understand where the
booze was coming from. Then he picked up Gene's crutches and found one
was heavy and the other was light. The heavy one was full of miniature bottles
of sweet martini."

Music journalist Keith Altham added to the trove of great Peter Grant stories, when he joined Vincent for two performances at a theater in Aylesbury.
While Grant was collecting the cash after the first show, Gene and Margie had
a violent row on the coach. "Gene had hold of his wife by her hair and was
hitting her head against the window," remembers Altham. "Peter jumped on
the bus and separated them. He was furious—'I'm trying to pick up the fucking readies here.'" When he went back outside, the marital dispute resumed:
"Except this time it was the wife banging Gene's head on the window."

Grant dragged them apart again. However, in the hour before the next
performance, Vincent consumed most of a bottle of vodka, fell over, and
trapped his good leg between the seat and a vertical pole. Grant then had to
intervene and bend the bar to free the now swollen limb.

Arden, mindful of Gene's behavior, included a clause in his contract stating he only had to appear on stage to get paid. Grant hoisted the star to his
feet and despite him having two damaged legs, maneuvred him into place as
the curtain rose. Grant had found a novel way to keep him upright.

"He'd shoved a microphone stand up through the back of Gene's jacket,"
says Keeffe. "It was just enough to keep him steady." The story goes that Vincent croaked a few lines of the opening number before passing out. Grant
then picked him up and carried him offstage "like a pig on a spit" before going to collect the cash.

During one of Vincent's early British tours, it was rumored an impersonator in Scotland was replacing him. Furious Teddy Boys stormed the dressing room of the Hawick Drill Hall, where the real Gene Vincent confronted them with a loaded gun.

Gene had a macabre fascination with weapons. He often carried a revolver, a knife, and, later, a bullwhip, which he'd flex with scant regard for anyone within striking distance. He was certainly trigger-happy during his first Christmas in London. In Don Arden's version of events, Gene's new wife, Margie, telephoned him in a panic, claiming her husband was threatening her with a gun. Gene was back from a tour and accusing her of cheating on him.

Arden and Grant raced over to the couple's flat. By then, Gene had convinced himself his wife was having an affair with their neighbor and had gone to confront him. "Gene stuck the barrel of the gun through the letterbox and started firing," said Arden. "He got three or four rounds off before Peter wrestled him away from the door."

Grant supposedly smashed his way into the flat to see if Vincent had shot anybody. Mercifully, the tenant was away for Christmas. When he returned, Arden paid him off.

Peter apparently had to disarm Gene Vincent on other occasions. One story retold in the Swan Song Records office had him confiscating a starting pistol, after Vincent began firing at guests in a Brighton hotel. The police tried to persuade him to surrender. "Peter pushed past the coppers, shouting 'Gene, you silly cunt!' and took the gun off him," remembers one who heard the tale.

There were also times when Vincent turned on his handler, and Grant turned on him. One night, Gene commandeered Peter's car in a cinema car park and tried to run him over. In Italy, Don Arden claimed Grant and Vincent had an altercation, and Peter accidentally fell on him, causing even more injury to his cursed leg. "It nearly finished Gene off for good," Arden claimed. "He had to be put into plaster up to his waist and flown back to London."

For Grant, it was part of a vital learning curve. "If I hadn't been on the road with Gene Vincent and the rest, there's no way I could've coped with the events of the past five or six years," he told *Melody Maker*, when Led Zeppelin were in their pomp.

Grant was also with Vincent when he witnessed his first vandalized hotel room. It was at the Cumberland in London's Marble Arch, and it wasn't Vincent's room; it was his co-star Eddie Cochran's. After a call from the concerned manager, Grant arrived to find Cochran's door lying on its side in the passageway.

Apparently when Eddie refused to let Gene Vincent in, he broke the door down. "I thought they were fucking lunatics," Grant marveled. "So I went down and negotiated a settlement with the manager. I said to them later, 'We don't do things like this in England.' It was over a chick—a bird was involved somewhere along the line."

Working with Vincent also introduced him to Arden's beloved "power of fear." "Peter pretended to carry a gun," says Ed Bicknell. "What Gene Vincent and all those acts suffered with was guys in the audience resenting the effect they had on their girlfriends. Peter said they were sometimes bothered by the lads, so he'd warn them off by patting his jacket pocket, pretending to have something inside—and it always worked."

Grant, however, claimed to others that he did occasionally carry a weapon because Vincent insisted on it. Outside a gig at Rotherham Baths, Grant found his '57 Chevy surrounded by "a local team of tearaways" looking to attack the pop star. "I said to them, 'I don't give a shit about you people,' opened my jacket, and showed them the holster. They fucking ran."

Like Derek Berman, though, some who remember Grant from this time struggle to equate the man they knew with Led Zeppelin's fearsome manager. This later "Peter Grant" was still a work in progress.

In the summer of 1963, the British instrumental group the Outlaws toured as a backup band to Gene Vincent and Great Balls of Fire singer Jerry Lee Lewis in the UK and Germany. Grant was their tour manager. The Outlaws included bass guitarist Chas Hodges (later of pub-rock duo Chas 'n' Dave), Deep Purple's future guitarist Ritchie Blackmore and drummer Mick Underwood, who'd later play with Deep Purple's singer Ian Gillan. Grant assumed the role of surrogate boss, older brother, and co-conspirator.

"Peter was a hoot," says Mick Underwood now. "You knew not to mess with him, but sometimes he enjoyed the lunacy as much as we did." The band quickly discovered Grant had nicknames for most people ("Peter called Gene Vincent 'the Finger,' but I have no idea why"), and an extensive lexicon of cockney rhyming slang. When one of the party went to chat to a girl in their Hamburg hotel, Grant gave him a quizzical look. "Not the bird with the hairy scotches?" he whispered.*

---

* "Scotches"—"scotch eggs": cockney rhyming slang for "legs."

"I saw Peter misbehave," admits Underwood, "but it was only verbal. He liked Gene Vincent but treated him as he needed to be treated. You couldn't let Gene be silly—that was a danger. But Peter was wary of Don Arden. One of his sayings was, 'Don'll go up the fucking wall.' We heard it many times when things weren't going to plan."

However, there were times when Grant indulged in mischief himself. At one date in a grim civic theater, the Outlaws discovered Mrs. Mills—the roly-poly pub pianist—was playing later.

En route to collect the money, Grant passed her empty dressing room and spotted an outfit on a hanger. Minutes later, he reappeared in the Outlaws' dressing room wearing Mills's dress, the garment straining over his big back and arms. The group burst out laughing while Grant regarded them with a poker-straight face: "What d'ya think, lads?"

In July 1963, Gloria gave birth to their daughter, Helen. "I don't know whether I was planned or not," she says now. "Mum wanted to be a singer and wanted to be in the music business, and I stopped everything in its tracks. Mum had so much ambition, and I think she was quite cross about having to give it up."

Peter's passport from 1963 records his countless trips to Europe. "My mum was still young and wanted to see friends and family back up north in Hull, so I spent a lot of time with my grandmother at Norhyrst Avenue. I re-member reading one of Dorothy's diaries, and it said, 'Poor little Helen's been left with me. . . . Gloria's gone off again.' That was their life."

Grant told Malcolm McLaren that he believed Gloria was envious of his success. Later, Grant landed his wife a job as Duane Eddy's backup singer for some UK dates. However, when Arden sent him to Glasgow Airport at a mo-ment's notice to meet the American singing group the Shirelles ("cos they didn't have work permits"), he and Gloria had a row.

"She really hooted about me going away," he told McLaren. "She couldn't deal with it. The Shirelles being three great-looking chicks probably didn't help."

"Mum didn't put up with any bullshit and was quite a jealous person," adds Helen. "Rightfully so in that business. I'd probably be the same."

Mick Underwood remembers Peter excusing himself from the Vincent tour not long after his daughter's birth. Grant asked him to "look after Gene" in his absence. The Outlaws were rock 'n' roll fans, but being Vincent's backup group tested their admiration. "Gene was a handful, and I got a hand-ful of it," says Underwood. "When Peter asked me to help, I remember thinking, 'Why don't you get someone else to do this?' I was the youngest, so Granty thought he could get away without paying me extra."

Vincent and the band had weekend shows booked in Belfast. Grant entrusted Underwood with the star's travel ticket and gave him strict instructions not to let him have it. When they arrived in Northern Ireland, Gene was in a foul mood. He'd just come back from a hospital appointment, and it had not gone well.

"None of us knew what was wrong with his leg," admits Underwood. "He'd had a cast put on it with a leather block underneath, like a built-up shoe." The block was too large and exaggerated Gene's limp. "He kept saying, 'It's too damn high, man.' And then, 'Can you cut the bottom off this thing, man?'

"We got a saw off the caretaker, put Gene's leg up on a chair, and started cutting," says Underwood. "It was hard work." After several minutes, Underwood still wasn't even halfway through the block. Then another act on the bill—singer and comedian Kenny Lynch—strolled into the dressing room: "I said, 'Here, Ken, can you give us a hand?' And, bless him, Kenny took over."

After the show, Vincent limped over to Underwood and made the demand he'd been dreading: "He said, 'Mick, I want my ticket, man.'" They still had a gig to play the following night, but Gene had decided he was going home. Underwood tried to reason with him, but he couldn't refuse. "He was a hero of mine. What could I do? So in the end, I gave him his ticket."

Underwood was in bed at his parents' house on Sunday morning when the telephone rang. It was Grant. "He exploded at me—'What have you fucking done?' He was ranting and raving, swearing, calling me every name under the sun. I told him, 'Peter, there was no way I could have stopped him. . . . He wanted his ticket; there was nothing I could do.'"

At which point, Grant's anger subsided, and he started laughing. "This was Peter. He'd get mad at you, but after a while he'd start laughing. He said, 'Mick, You'll never guess what happened when he got home? The Finger only got himself banged up.'"

Back in London, Vincent had accused Margie of cheating on him again and pointed a loaded German Luger at her head. This time, she called the police instead of Don Arden. "The Finger" was arrested, later fined £20 for possession of unlicensed firearms, and conditionally discharged for a year.

Don Arden stuck by Vincent and continued promoting his tours to ever diminishing returns. Vincent would launch several comebacks but never reached the heights he had before. With each new year came a new backup group and new stories: Vincent later told musicians his damaged leg was the result of a covert military operation during the Korean War. He passed away in October 1971; the cause of death was a ruptured stomach ulcer. By then his former minder and driver was managing the biggest rock 'n' roll group on the planet.

The Outlaws survived until 1965. In the late 1970s, Mick Underwood joined Ian Gillan's band and drummed on several hit singles and albums. Before then, he and Peter Grant crossed paths on the touring circuit. In 1968, the pair ran into each other in a London club, where Mick was playing. "Peter said, 'This sounds a bit odd, but I'm doing some stuff with Jimmy Page. He's re-forming the Yardbirds, and we've got shows in Scandinavia. We're not fixed for a drummer yet. Are you interested?'"

Underwood said yes, but was asked to join a new group the next day. He called Grant back and told him he'd changed his mind. "Peter was fine about it. I didn't turn down Led Zeppelin," he says carefully. "They didn't exist. And it would never have worked, because John Bonham was their perfect drummer."

Mickie Most, the 2i's' singing waiter, came back into Peter Grant's life in 1963. Mickie had left England at Christmas 1958. He'd met his future wife, Christina, when she was on holiday in London that summer. After a whirlwind romance, he joined her at her family home in South Africa, where they lived for most of the next four years.

The Most Brothers had signed to Polydor and, in Mickie's words, "toured for a year and a half and made a few ghastly records." However, South Africa was a country starved of rock 'n' roll. Mickie formed Mickie Most and His Playboys and enjoyed eleven number one hits, usually with covers of American artists' songs. Discovering South African engineers had never made rock 'n' roll records, he also learned how to produce them himself.

Mickie and his band opened for Gene Vincent when he toured South Africa in 1961, which is where they met Don Arden. "Don was a likeable crook," says Mickie's widow, Chris Hayes. Two years later, with Most weary of playing the same dancehalls, they moved back to England.

"Mickie looked me up, as he had no work," Grant said. "So I got him on the tours as an opening act and occasional compère while I was working for Don." Pop stardom eluded Most back home in London. He managed a couple of modest hits but ran aground when his cover of Frankie Ford's "Sea Cruise" was banned by the BBC after the Greek cruiseliner, the *Lakonia*, went down off the coast of Madeira and 128 passengers and crew drowned.

However disparaging Don Arden was about Peter Grant later, by spring 1963 he'd employed him as an agent at Curzon Street. Grant and co-agent Mark Wildey had a deal with Arden to be paid 10 percent commission on every act they found, which they'd then split between them: "Though Don rarely paid us." Around this time, Grant also started managing the Flintstones, an instrumental group whose guitarist Terry Slater would later manage the 1980s pop group A-ha.

Chris Hayes, meanwhile, began working as a promoter. "Don had lots of bands and told me to speak to Peter," she says. "I'd listen to the radio, pick songs I thought would become hits, and book the groups for very little money. You had to move fast because when they got in the charts, the price went up."

Grant had learned well from Arden. "He tried it on a few times," Chris laughs. "He'd say a band was already in the chart and he had to put the price up, but I wasn't having it."

There were changes afoot. The Beatles—a British group raised on Elvis and Gene Vincent—had conjured a new sound and image and were now poised to conquer America. Don Arden hadn't taken the Beatles seriously, and it cost him dearly. "They killed everything," he said later. "People who had been stars all their life suddenly became milkmen."

Arden had already tried to bring Elvis to the UK and had one trump card left to play. Chuck Berry was the original rock 'n' roll guitar hero and had given Britain's ration-book kids a tantalizing glimpse of American culture. "He was singing about 'hamburgers sizzling night and day,'" said Jimmy Page. "We didn't have hamburgers in England. We didn't even know what they were."

Arden set out to bring Chuck Berry to Britain. There was just one catch: Berry was in jail for transporting an underage Native American girl across state lines. However, Arden's offer of a UK tour was waiting by the time Berry was released. According to Grant, it was he who flew to Chuck's hometown of St. Louis, Missouri, and then to Chicago to close the deal.

"Don said, 'I want you to make a deal,' and he gave me an envelope of money," he revealed, before recounting a story illustrating America's racial divisions and the era's uneasy manager/artist hierarchy.

Grant was shocked when Berry himself collected him at the airport to take him to his hotel. When Peter invited him in for a drink, Chuck refused. "It was my first time in America. I didn't realize it was because he was black."

The following day they traveled to Berry's label Chess Records to meet company boss Leonard Chess. "The place was like a double-fronted shop,"

Grant said. "Like a speakeasy, and there was Leonard in braces, smoking a cigar—'Oh, you're the limey guy.'"

Grant completed the deal with Chess, and Berry's lawyer and handed over Arden's envelope of cash. Berry's involvement was minimal. "Chuck said, 'The only thing you have to do for me is get me a real good piano player.'" Afterward, and again to Grant's astonishment, Leonard Chess told Berry to drive Peter to the airport.

"We went out the back of Chess Records, and it was like a used car lot full of Cadillacs," said Grant. "Chuck chose one, and we set off." En route, Berry told him the Cadillac used too much gas, and he couldn't drive him all the way. Instead, he dropped him off at the downtown bus terminal. Grant had plenty to think about on the ride to the airport. Earlier, he'd asked Berry how many records he'd sold. Chuck didn't know; his manager never told him: "And I thought that was terrible."

The Chuck Berry tour was booked, though not until the following year. In the meantime, Arden brought singing siblings, the Everly Brothers, and Mississippi R&B guitarist Bo Diddley to Britain in a last-ditch attempt to head off the Beatles.

Diddley couldn't afford to bring over a full band and showed up with just his lamé-jumpsuited female co-guitarist, nicknamed the Duchess, and a maraca player Jerome Green, whom Peter immediately befriended.

"Jerome always carried a radio with him that didn't appear to work," said Grant. "One day I asked him why. He took the back off, and there was nothing inside, just half a bottle of scotch. He whispered, 'Don't tell Bo.'"

Decades later, the Everly Brothers paid a glowing tribute to Peter Grant, describing him as the "the best road manager we ever had." In 1963, though, the Everlys sold so few tickets for their first dates, Arden had to beg Little Richard to co-headline.

Lower down the pecking order and highlighting the old and new guard were Mickie Most in one corner and the Beatles' rivals, the Rolling Stones, in another. Grant loved the Stones' grimy, British take on American R&B. When the BBC invited Bo Diddley to record a session for its Saturday Club radio show, Grant suggested he borrow the Stones' bassist Bill Wyman and drummer Charlie Watts. Diddley agreed but the BBC didn't.

"They'd auditioned the Stones earlier and turned them down because they weren't considered good enough," Grant recalled. "I got a call from the producer telling me it wasn't such a hot suggestion. I replied, 'No Stones, no Diddley'—and they got the job."

Grant had helped broker the Rolling Stones' first broadcast on the BBC. Within a year the group had recorded four BBC sessions of their own. "I have no musical knowledge," Grant admitted. "It's purely a feel thing." His gut instinct was right.

Following a show at the Newcastle Odeon in October, Grant, Mickie Most, and Jerome Green visited the Club A'Gogo, where they caught the Alan Price Rhythm & Blues Combo. "I was so impressed, I signed them up," Grant said. "I became their booking agent and co-manager, and they changed their name to the Animals."

Grant said the Animals signed to Arden's agency after Don promised them a slot on the Chuck Berry tour. It was the Holy Grail for any aspiring British blues band: "That was the inducement, and Mark Wildey and I were supposed to get 10 percent of what Don made."

However, Derek Berman remembers Grant embellishing the facts. Berman was now playing with an East London group, the Echoes, who were headlining over the future Animals that night.

"Peter introduced himself to the Animals as *our* manager," he says. "He was never the Echoes' manager, but he told the Animals he was, and I think it helped convince them he was for real."

Back in London, Grant told Arden about his new discovery. He brought the Animals to London to play the Scene Club in Piccadilly. Afterward, Grant, Arden, and Mickie Most crowded into the dressing room. The group already had a manager, Mike Jeffery, a Newcastle club owner, who'd later co-manage Jimi Hendrix and die in a plane crash over France. "He was a bad manager," said Grant. "We did more managing than he did."

When Don Arden announced Peter Grant would take day-to-day care of the Animals, and Mickie Most would produce their records, there was no argument from the band or Jeffery.

When the Animals arrived at Arden's office to sign a contract, their lead singer, Eric Burdon, sidled over to Peter. "He said, 'We've met before, but you don't remember,'" Grant recalled. "Eric said, 'You once threw me down a corridor.'" A year earlier, Burdon, the excited fan, had gatecrashed Gene Vincent's dressing room, and Grant introduced him to the door.

The day the Animals signed to Don Arden was the day Don lost control of Peter Grant. He'd empowered his apprentice to look after what would become a hit group. David Arden, who'd soon move into the family business, remembered Grant and Mickie Most suggesting to his father they start a record company and split the money three ways. It never happened. One year later, after the Animals had a hit, "The old man said, 'Where's the record company?' And Mickie said, 'Oh, goodbye!' That was it."

It would be months before Grant and Most struck out on their own, though. In the meantime, Chuck Berry arrived in the UK in May of 1964. The tour's special guest was another of the Beatles' heroes, Tennessee guitarist Carl Perkins, who'd had a hit before Elvis with "Blue Suede Shoes." Berry's backup band was Brit hopeful King Size Taylor & the Dominoes, and his support acts included the Animals and Grant and Mickie Most's next protégés the Nashville Teens, whose pianist John Hawken became the "real good piano player" Berry had requested.

On tour, the Animals quickly fell into line. When Burdon arrived late for a show, Grant picked him up and threw him across the room. "I was never late again," Burdon admitted. "Peter was what I needed. He was what *we* needed."

Grant's uncompromising stance with acts lower down the bill meant he could concentrate on the headliner. By 1964, Chuck Berry was well versed in the exploitative nature of the music industry and had seen the inside of several jail cells. Show business and prison time had made him embittered and suspicious. Chuck wouldn't play a note until he'd received every last shilling or cent of his fee.

Grant and Arden were once seen on their knees outside Berry's dressing room, feeding pound notes under the door. When the fee was three shillings short one night, Grant promised Chuck he'd get the rest later, but Berry refused to pick up his guitar until he had it all. When Peter couldn't scavenge enough loose change, he found the nearest cigarette machine, delivered a wrestler's slap, and scooped out the coins. Chuck was playing, whatever it took.

These were career lessons learned the hard way, and which Grant would later apply to Led Zeppelin. Once Chuck Berry had his money, it was like someone pressed a switch and the lights came on. Watching from the wings in May '64, Grant studied the way he worked the crowd; cocking the guitar, jutting his chin out and performing his trademark "duck walk" to a chorus of cheers. Grant also spotted a way to make his stage entrance more dramatic.

"I talked the MC into doing a long lead-in," he said. "You could hear John Hawken the piano player, and you could *hear* Chuck playing." But, crucially, the people couldn't see him. "Then he'd appear, doing the duck walk, and the audience just exploded." According to Grant, a young Jimmy Page watched spellbound, as Berry strutted onstage for the tour's opening night at London's Finsbury Park Astoria.

Berry wasn't the only one using showbiz tricks to win over an audience. Each night, most of the groups finished their sets with a fast number, but nobody could out rock 'n' roll Chuck Berry. Instead, the Animals finished with their brooding version of an old folk song, "House of the Rising Sun." It was slow and dramatic, and it made a lasting impression.

The Animals recorded the track with Mickie Most producing at London's Kingsway Studios. "They came in at seven in the morning and did it in one take," Grant recalled. In June, "House of the Rising Sun" reached number one in the UK and would do the same in America two months later. It was Grant's first hit single.

*I*n April 1970, Led Zeppelin played the Miami Beach Convention Hall in Florida. After the show, Grant took them to see Little Richard performing at a nearby resort. Peter had phoned ahead and booked a table, but they arrived late and in the middle of a song. "Richard did a double take," Grant said, "and stopped the number he was playing."

The elderly audience, a sea of blue and pink rinses, turned to squint at the bearded giant and his long-haired companions picking their way through the throng. "See that man there," trilled Richard, pointing at Grant. "That's Mr. Peter. . . . He saved my life in Paris."

In June 1964, "Mr. Peter" spent two weeks in Europe with Little Richard. In the late 1950s, Richard had suddenly found God and denounced rock 'n' roll for gospel. When Don Arden dangled a large paycheck under his nose, he embraced the devil's music again and thrilled audiences on a subsequent UK tour.

Little Richard was playing rock 'n' roll, but getting him onstage was often a problem. In the Swan Song Records office and hotel suites around the world, Grant regaled his audience with Little Richard stories. In one, Richard announced he wouldn't be playing that night's show at the Lewisham Odeon and refused to leave his hotel bed. Grant told how he'd wrapped the singer in a sheet and carried him over his shoulder to a waiting car.

Richard had another episode during his European tour. Despite having flown from the United States to the continent, he claimed to have a phobia of air travel. Richard needed to catch a connecting flight from Dusseldorf to Paris, but he refused to board another plane.

This time, there wasn't a hotel bed sheet to roll him up in. "I had to get a cab driver to take us all the way from Dusseldorf to Paris," Grant said, "but that's the game. You've got to get your artist there, whatever it takes."

After arriving late in the French capital, the promoter refused to pay Richard his full fee. There was an argument and the gendarme arrived. Punches were thrown and Grant intervened: "The policemen got a bit rough, and I slung two of them on the floor."

In Miami, Little Richard told his audience the whole story, conjuring an enduring image of the camp showman and his burly minder making their getaway through the Parisian streets, with unconscious gendarmes laid out in their wake.

In 1992, Richard played London's Wembley Arena and met Grant again for the first time since Miami. "Mr. Peter! Mr. Peter!" he declared loudly. "Feel my ankle! Feel my ankle!"

Richard hiked up his trouser leg, and Grant cautiously touched the singer's sock. Inside were a credit card and a roll of cash. Grant had once warned Richard never to leave his valuables in the dressing room. And he was still heeding the warning three decades later.

Like Don Arden before him, tales of Grant's bullish dedication to the cause spread around the business. In a 2012 interview, David Arden insisted that despite his father's bad reputation, Don was a great believer in talent: "He always thought, if you've got talent, you can do whatever you like and get away with it. If you haven't got talent, he'd go, 'Fuck off, or I'll knock you down the stairs.'" He could have been describing Peter Grant.

Besides embracing Arden's power of fear, Grant had also discovered the power of suggestion. Whether it was pretending to carry a gun or telling the Animals he was managing a band when he wasn't, people believed what he said. As Don Arden admitted, "Peter Grant learned from me that you can overcome anything if you've got enough front."

Grant would put this thinking into practice again with the Nashville Teens. Peter had discovered the Surrey pop group, signed them to the agency, and put them on the Chuck Berry tour. Meanwhile, Mickie Most signed them to Decca and became their producer.

The Teens' first single, "Tobacco Road"—a song written by country songwriter John D. Loudermilk about growing up in North Carolina—survived the trip across the Atlantic and would become their biggest hit.

Grant looked after the group on tour while they promoted the single. "Peter was a big, lovable bear," remembers lead singer Ramon Phillips. "His catchphrase was an exasperated 'Come on *fellas.*' He changed drastically when he got into power with Led Zeppelin; he'd had a good teacher in Don Arden."

One thing troubled Grant about the Nashville Teens: they weren't teenagers. "Peter came up to me before a gig once and said, 'Get rid of those whiskers,'" says ex-vocalist Arthur Sharp. "I'd shaved but missed a bit. Peter wasn't having it—'You ain't gonna look like a fucking eighteen-year-old with them, Arthur.' I was twenty-four, which was a problem."

With "Tobacco Road" inching slowly up the charts, Grant employed the power of suggestion. Ramon Phillips had met a smitten fan at a show in Hastings. Susan Penry-Davey was the seventeen-year-old daughter of a prominent local solicitor and followed the group to their next date in Welwyn Garden City. It gave Grant an idea.

"We were back at my flat after the show, when Peter rang up—'Come and meet me now and bring that girl with you,'" says Phillips. The following day the *Daily Mirror* ran a story, 'Police Stop a Beat Romance,' claiming Penry-Davey's father had called the police after she ran away from home with the Nashville Teens' lead singer.

"Peter saw pound notes and the opportunity to sell some records. Susan was happy to go along with it, and we were photographed arriving in a police car," says Phillips. Except the vehicle in the newspaper's photo wasn't a police car, and the so-called plainclothes policeman guarding the young lovers was Peter Grant. Nobody challenged the story, and "Tobacco Road" went top ten in Britain and top twenty in America.

*O*ne story followed Don Arden to his grave and would do the same for Peter Grant. In 1965, Arden began managing the Small Faces, a group of pint-sized, East London teenagers whose lead singer was former child star Steve Marriott. Arden paid the bills for the band's shared house and settled the accounts they ran up at London's fashionable boutiques. He also kept everything they earned from their hit records. The Small Faces were penniless.

When challenged by the boys' parents, Arden told them their sons had spent all their money on drugs. The ensuing legal battle and bitter war of words between Arden and the Small Faces continued for decades, long after the group had disbanded.

Arden's treatment of the Small Faces would see him forever typecast as a showbiz supervillain. Whatever the similarities between the two men, "Don was the manager Peter told me he didn't want to be like," says Barrie Keeffe. "Peter detested the way Don treated his artists."

However, Grant also told Keeffe and Ed Bicknell that he was party to Don's most notorious act. Manager Robert Stigwood later oversaw the careers of Eric Clapton and the Bee Gees, before moving into film production with the hit movies *Saturday Night Fever* and *Grease*.

In the early 1960s Stigwood had tried to lure the Small Faces away from Don Arden. Don's retribution was sudden and shocking. Like most Arden and Peter Grant stories, it changes with each retelling. However, Stigwood, who died in 2016, never denied the incident.

Enraged at the prospect of losing his group to a rival, Arden supposedly rounded up several of his heavies. The number varied from twenty to as few as five, depending on who was telling the story. Arden briefed the men on what they had to do, almost rehearsing them as actors in a play.

Arden and his gang arrived unannounced at Stigwood's fourth-floor office in London's Cavendish Square. Once inside, Don ignored Stigwood's greeting, picked up a heavy glass ashtray, and smashed it down on his desk with such force the wood below splintered.

Arden then dragged the terrified manager from his chair toward the balcony. Don always insisted he meant only to show Stigwood the street below and warn him he'd "end up down there" if he tried to steal one of his acts again. But the hired help had arranged to play a prank on their boss.

Arden's men apparently rushed forward and shouted that Stigwood was "going over, right now." They picked him up, forced him over the edge of the balcony, and held him upside down. Arden later claimed Stigwood was wearing fashionable Chelsea boots, and his attackers had to keep a tight grip on his ankles to stop him from sliding to his death.

Depending on who's telling the tale, Stigwood either fainted or defecated in his trousers—or both—before his attackers heaved him back inside and dumped him on the office rug.

Grant told Barrie Keeffe he'd been one of those dangling Stigwood upside down that day. "He had disgusting skinny ankles, Barrie," he confided. Asked about the incident by Ed Bicknell, Peter was more circumspect. "'Ed . . . I merely introduced him to the view.'"

But did he? Stigwood was certainly threatened and probably held over a balcony by Don Arden's minders. However, nobody else has ever confirmed Peter Grant was involved. The power of fear and suggestion was sufficient. The tale of Robert Stigwood and the balcony became an evergreen rock 'n' roll anecdote told and retold for decades to come.

By 1965, though, Don Arden's empire was crumbling. Robert Stigwood had promoted Chuck Berry's second UK tour that year and had nearly gone bankrupt after tickets failed to sell. The Beatles, the Rolling Stones, and other British groups had taken Berry and Little Richard's music, twisted it into bold new shapes, and sold it to a younger generation.

Don Arden would find new artists and battles to fight in the years ahead. So too would his apprentice.

3

The Diving Horse

"Peter knew the business.
He was a master at it."

—JIMMY PAGE

O ne afternoon in 1965, Sharon Osbourne came home, and Peter Grant was gone. "It was like one day he was waiting for us outside school, and the next it was taboo to mention his name," she said. When Grant and Don Arden met later in the street, Sharon remembers them coming to blows, and her father's minders dragging them apart. Unfortunately for Don, Grant had committed the cardinal sin of luring one of his acts away.

For all his ambition, Don Arden had missed an opportunity. Arden's tours helped Gene Vincent and the rest sell records, but he didn't see any royalties himself. When those acts stopped selling tickets, Arden stopped making money. Arden would get rich managing Black Sabbath and Electric Light Orchestra in the seventies but would spend the rest of the sixties struggling to play catch-up.

The record label Grant and Mickie Most talked about launching with Arden never happened. Instead, Most struck out on his own. In the summer of 1964, he launched RAK Music Management, RAK Publishing, and RAK Records and took over a sixth-floor office at 155–157 Oxford Street. It was a sparse affair: a couple of desks, a couch, a dartboard, and a receptionist named Irene. Peter Grant came with him.

The building's landlords were the camping store Millets, whose shop occupied the ground floor, and who took a casual attitude to maintaining the facilities. Number 155's rickety metal elevator was notoriously unreliable. If Grant arrived for work and found it wasn't working, he often went home again.

"Sometimes I try to foot it up," he told a journalist, before claiming he'd befriended somebody on the third floor, enabling him to stop for a cup of coffee "and a quick recuperation" on the way.

While Most launched his companies, Grant continued to look after the Animals. However, his relationship with Don Arden was tested during their first US tour. That summer, "The House of the Rising Sun" echoed out of every car radio in the States. The Animals' tour began with headlining dates at the Paramount Theatre in New York's Times Square. It was a celebration for the visiting Brits—less of one for Little Richard and Chuck Berry lower down the bill.

During the tour, Grant made the shocking discovery that Arden had two different contracts for the Animals with the William Morris Agency. The band had signed a contract for $1,200 per night, but Arden had a separate deal with the agency and was being paid three to four times as much: "There were two sets of contracts, both on William Morris–headed paper, and I never questioned it. So the shit hit the fan."

Backstage at the Paramount, Grant, Mike Jeffery, and the Animals were supposedly introduced to Allen Klein, an accountant from New Jersey who'd recently become business manager to soul singer Sam Cooke. Klein was a great opportunist and keenly aware of what the American press were calling "the British invasion." Over the next few years, he would woo all the great British groups, including the Beatles, the Stones, the Kinks, and the Who, but it began with the Animals.

While auditing record companies and music publishers as an accountant, Klein discovered how little money was reaching the artists. He proved his mettle when investigating Roulette Records' mob-connected boss Morris Levy. Impressed by his persistence and nerve, Levy befriended his investigator. The relationship would hold Klein in good stead later.

Allen Klein knew what pop stars and their handlers didn't—or else chose to ignore: that their record companies were ripping them off. His pitch was simple. He offered to renegotiate the Animals' contracts and make everybody, including Peter Grant, a lot of money. Klein told them he wouldn't charge a fee, only a commission, and if he failed, they'd lost nothing.

As a sign of his good intentions, he promised Grant and Mike Jeffery he could get the Animals $10,000 for an appearance in the new Nancy Sinatra movie, *Get Yourself a College Girl*. Klein was as good as his word. Soon after, he flew to London to meet Mickie Most.

By now, Most had produced records for the Animals, the Nashville Teens, and Herman's Hermits—a Mancunian group who'd had a hit with "I'm Into Something Good" and were poised to do the same in America. But he wasn't making money. Most almost had to beg American labels to take his singles, and he was earning a paltry 50 percent royalty on US sales. He was easily seduced by Klein's promise of a big payday.

Allen Klein's meeting with Most's paymasters at EMI in London was a prime display of bullishness and bullshit. Really, Klein could barely afford his airfare or his suite at London's Grosvenor Hotel. Appearance was everything, though, and he played up to his image as the moneyed American with whispered Mafia connections.

To begin with, he curtly refused his hosts' offer of a cup of tea before explaining that Mickie Most would ignore any existing contract and stop making records unless he received more money. Klein's terribly English hosts were stunned, and even more so when he ignored their threat of legal action. Nobody had ever challenged the managing director of Britain's biggest record company like this. The power between the artist and the label suddenly shifted.

EMI was appalled by Klein's manner and attitude, but they gave in to his demands. Mickie Most appointed Klein his business manager and secured a better deal, larger royalties, and the chance to produce artists for other companies in America. Klein delivered on his promise and secured a huge commission for himself on all Mickie's future productions, with ramifications for the producer further down the line.

Klein's later financial dealings with the Beatles, especially, would see him cast as the unscrupulous bean counter who helped destroy the world's greatest pop group. Yet his coup on Mickie Most's behalf was a precursor of what Peter Grant would achieve for Led Zeppelin. Klein showed Grant that the artists held the power.

This willingness to call anyone's bluff was something Grant later excelled in. "It was the essence of Peter's genius," believes Abe Hoch, a former vice president of Swan Song Records. "When you have a client that is willing to say, 'Fuck you' and walk away, then you have power beyond belief."

Grant learned from Klein, just as he'd learned from Arden, except Don's days were numbered. "It was Peter Grant who broke the news to me," Arden said. "Part of his job with the Animals was to collect the money and bring it back to me. When he got back to London he claimed he didn't have any. He told me the band had been poached by Allen Klein, and I would need to talk to him."

The double dealing over the Animals' contract was one thing, but Arden had also failed to pay Grant and Mark Wildey their commission. Don now owed Peter £1,800. Years later when Arden was living in Los Angeles and spotted Grant on Sunset Strip he'd shout across the street, "Don't worry, Peter, the check's in the post." It became a running joke.

Grant raged at the injustice until his friend, the agent Harold Davison, took him aside and told him to consider it part of the cost of learning how the music business worked. Grant had outgrown Don Arden but would spend the next twenty years of his working life chasing someone for money.

*L*aurence Myers first met Grant in 1965. Myers was the Rolling Stones' accountant and remembers discussing pensions with Mick Jagger: "He said, 'Laurence, it's not as if I'll be singing rock 'n' roll when I'm *fifty*.'" Mickie Most hired Myers to take care of his finances and gave him 10 percent of his companies in lieu of payment.

Myers had been present at Allen Klein's meeting with EMI and was there again when Most and Grant tried to collect overdue money from Don Arden: "Mike Jeffery told Mickie there was a discrepancy in the Animals' accounts, and Don owed them. So he asked Mickie and Peter to collect." It gave him an insight into Grant's working methods.

The three men arrived at Arden's office and waited in reception while he finished a phone call. "I could hear Don screaming down the phone—'I'll break your facking legs!' I thought, 'I'm an accountant. What have I got myself into here?' Beforehand, Peter said to me, 'Look, there will be aggravation with Don, but don't worry.' Like he was warning me he would be putting on an act."

Inside the office, Arden regarded his visitors with a mix of disinterest and outright disdain. Myers started talking: "I said, 'I am the authorized representative of the Animals, and the accounting shows you owe them six thousand pounds' in my best accountant's voice. In the meantime, Peter starts thumping on the desk, then picking it up and banging it up and down on the floor, shouting 'Give us the money, Don! Come on, you bastard!'"

Myers tried to talk over the noise. Arden finally acknowledged him. "He said, 'What do you want, you little pisher?'—a Yiddish expression." Myers explained he would be issuing a writ for the money. Arden calmly opened a desk drawer containing a tray full of writs. "He said, 'Oh, you're going to give me a writ?' And he picked up the tray and the writs and threw the lot out the window, shouting, 'If you're not out of here in five minutes you're going to follow them.'" Arden had called their bluff. Nobody was getting a penny.

For all Grant's bravado that day, Myers often found him softly spoken and even unsure of himself. The idea of Grant managing a hit group struck him as unlikely.

"I never imagined Peter having the success he did," Myers admits. "He wasn't educated and didn't appear to be very bright. However, I was never with him when he was required to be very bright. If everyone else in the office was chatting about world affairs, Peter wouldn't join in. That wasn't what he was about. Did I underestimate him? Yes, I did."

"There were two Peters," adds Chris Hayes. "One was like a Rottweiler in business, and there was also the gentle Peter. Everybody thought he was this big villain, but he was incredibly sensitive. I saw it straight away."

With Mickie Most's career in the ascendant, Grant tried to cast his net wider than RAK. In May 1965, *The Stage* ran a notice announcing the formation of Peter Grant Associates, "An employment agency for persons in the entertainment industry" at 101 Dean Street, but the company never seemed to have materialized.

That same month, Grant visited Canada. The Toronto group—the She Trinity—was an all-female ensemble that played their own instruments and were considered a novelty in less enlightened times. The group moved to London, where Mickie Most produced several singles for them, including a cover of "Yellow Submarine," but they failed to achieve a hit. Grant later described the experience of managing the band as "a disaster."

He fared slightly better with the late Canadian comedian Ray Cameron, an acquaintance made during Grant's bus-driving days. Cameron was living in England and had compèred on many Don Arden promotions. Peter managed him for most of the 1960s, but he achieved greater success later as a scriptwriter for DJ and TV host Kenny Everett. Cameron's stand-up career would be eclipsed by that of his son, the comedian Michael McIntyre.

With his management career slow to take off, Grant returned to America with the Animals and Herman's Hermits. He made a lasting impression on Eric Burdon and the Hermits' manager. In his autobiography, *I Used to Be an Animal, But I'm All Right Now*, Burdon recounted two incidents he thought gave an insight into Grant's background.

On their way to the Memphis Coliseum, the Animals' tour bus was flagged down by the Ku Klux Klan, which was handing out leaflets. Apparently, Grant was furious. "He was yelling, red-faced, straight at the Klansmen—'Go wipe your asses on it, you shitheads!'" claimed the singer.

Later, Burdon described how Grant also challenged a Holiday Inn manager who refused entry to the Animals' black roadie. The singer presumed Grant was particularly sensitive to the prejudice because he was Jewish. Grant never told him otherwise.

Later on tour, the Animals were joined by Mickie Most's youngest clients, Herman's Hermits. Herman was lead singer Peter Noone, and he and the group were barely out of their teens. Their manager, Harvey Lisberg, considered Grant the best chaperone during their first trip to Los Angeles. He'd heard all the stories: about Gene Vincent and his gun, and Little Richard and the bed sheet: "It was folklore even then." He was also impressed by Peter's protective instincts and droll humor.

Grant had put on weight, which he partly blamed on bad eating habits in America. In LA with Herman's Hermits, he'd decided to go on a health kick, but it wasn't going to plan.

"I was in the Beverly Hilton when I saw a waiter walking past carrying more than a dozen glasses of orange juice," says Lisberg. "I had a hunch and followed the waiter all the way to Peter's room. I said, 'What's all this?' Peter said, 'I'm on a diet, Harvey.' There must have been a million calories in those drinks.

"Peter made me laugh," he adds. "And he kept on making me laugh, which is one of the reasons we became friends."

*A*fter the uncertainty of the previous few months, 1966 would be a better year. In February, Gloria gave birth to their son, Warren. The family would also move back to South London and into a house in Beulah Hill in Croydon. Soon after, Peter would discover his first hit act, but there would be further setbacks and drama along the way.

When the British folk singer Donovan ditched his original managers, Grant was keen to take over and approached Allen Klein. He played him Donovan's song "Catch the Wind," convinced it would be a hit. "Klein said, 'Listen, if you can get Mickie to put it all together with Donovan, I'll give you a piece of the action.'"

Unfortunately for Grant, Donovan was already committed to a new manager. Nevertheless, he helped close the deal. Mickie Most's first Donovan production, "Sunshine Superman" (recorded with session musicians Jimmy Page and John Paul Jones), would become a top-five hit in America and the UK. Months after its release, though Grant was still waiting for his money.

Just as he'd done with Don Arden, Grant visited Klein in his office. One apocryphal story claims Grant slammed Klein's hand in a desk drawer until he agreed to pay up. Another claims Klein's armed minder chose not to intervene, and even complimented Peter on his persuasive powers. Grant himself claimed, "I helped Allen out of his chair by his lapels." Either way, Klein sent his attorney to the bank to withdraw Grant's promised $12,000 in cash.

Having missed out on Donovan, Grant found an unlikely replacement through the singer's ex-manager. Geoff Stephens had composed Dave Berry's big hit "The Crying Game" and had just written "Winchester Cathedral," a gentle parody of the prewar dance band era. He'd recorded the song with session musicians and credited it to the fictitious New Vaudeville Band. Released in the summer of 1966, nobody imagined it would become a hit, but "Winchester Cathedral" started creeping up the British and American charts. The nonexistent band was invited to appear on *Top of the Pops* and audition for the Royal Command Performance. Stephens hastily assembled a group and appointed Peter Grant to take care of them.

Among the hired hands was ex-Bonzo Dog Doo Dah Band trumpeter Bob Kerr. "Geoff turned up at this theater in South London with this huge guy and said, 'This is Peter. He's your manager,'" remembers Kerr. "We all looked at him and said, 'OK, then.' Peter was not the sort of guy you'd argue with."

Richard Cole would go on to become Peter Grant's lieutenant and one of his closest friends. In 1967, the twenty-one-year-old heard Grant was looking for a tour manager and went for an interview. Growing up in Northwest London, Richard had hustled his way from a job welding milk crates in a factory and working as a scaffolder to a stint as the Who's and Unit 4+2's driver and road manager.

"Colesy was straight off the scaffolding," recalled Grant. "Rough and ready and likeable. He had a lot of front. He knew what he was doing."

"Peter told me the pay was twenty-five pounds a week," says Cole now. "I said I wanted thirty—take it or leave it—and he agreed. He told me later, he'd figured if I could talk to him like that, I'd be good at getting money out of promoters.'" Before he left, Grant issued Cole with a warning. "He said, 'If you ever repeat anything you hear in this office, I'll cut your fucking ears off.'"

Despite the threat, Cole quickly realized neither Peter nor Mickie took themselves entirely seriously. "Half the time I had no idea what their business consisted of," he says. "They had a desk each side of the room, and if Mickie was on the phone, Peter would be trying to distract him, pulling faces. Then vice versa when Peter was on the phone.

"It was a fun business then. I remember sitting with the Beatles in the Scotch of St. James club in 1965, and they couldn't believe their luck that they were getting paid to play music. It was the same with all of us."

Cole joined Grant for the New Vaudeville Band's US tour in spring 1967. It was an eventful trip. During an overnight bus journey from Philadelphia to New York, their hired driver fell asleep at the wheel, and Bob Kerr stepped in, despite never having driven a bus before. It was only when they'd reached the New Jersey Turnpike that Grant woke up and strolled to the front of the coach. "Peter went absolutely mad," Kerr admits. "He didn't speak to me for some time after that."

Incredibly, "Winchester Cathedral" reached number one in America, meaning they would get a coveted appearance on the *Ed Sullivan Show* and more incongruous live dates. "Places like Las Vegas and Reno, Nevada—the cabaret circuit," remembered Grant. "They weren't exactly a rock band."

The group were reminded of their novelty status in the New Jersey resort, Atlantic City. Here, among the casinos and Ferris wheels, they shared the bill with Frank Sinatra Jr. and a diving horse.

"This old stagehand told us not to go over our twenty minutes because everybody would leave to watch the horse," says Richard Cole. "We thought, 'Fuck that.' But they did—everybody left. This horse was hoisted in a harness with a girl on its back before plunging thirty feet into a tank of water." It was a flashback to the days of variety; the world from which Grant had escaped.

It was at a show in Washington that the band witnessed their manager's skill at talking his way out of trouble. "There was a Musicians Union ruling that if a British band played America, there had to be an exchange with an American band," Kerr explains. "The promoter wanted to know who we'd exchanged with. We said we didn't know, but he wasn't giving up."

Grant had clearly chosen to ignore the ruling. When the promoter asked him the same question, he didn't miss a beat. "Peter said, 'We're on exchange with the Count Basie Orchestra'"—dropping the name of America's revered bandleader. "It was rubbish—this little chap was terribly impressed. And that's when I thought, 'This guy is a good manager. He thinks on his feet.'"

Without Don Arden to answer to, the band and the tour were Grant's sole responsibility. From sleeping bus drivers and missing paperwork to a novelty animal act, he took it in his stride. The New Vaudeville Band lasted eighteen months. They made an album and won a Grammy Award for "Winchester Cathedral," a song later covered by Frank Sinatra and Dizzy Gillespie.

Before then, another opportunity had come Grant's way. "By the time we came to an end," says Bob Kerr. "Peter was planning what would become Led Zeppelin."

*P*op music had come a long way since the 2i's cellar. By 1967, even the traditional single had been challenged. "The House of the Rising Sun" was one of the first 45s to break the three-minute mark. A year later came Bob Dylan's "Like a Rolling Stone," six minutes of musical poetry hinting at some profound truth or whatever its listeners imagined it to be. Where once pop music had been the soundtrack to dancing, fighting, and having sex, it was now making the audience think.

Social commentary, politics, and drugs all fed into the mix. The phrase "psychedelic" was soon randomly applied to anything that suggested the influence of the hallucinogenic LSD. That summer, the Beatles released *Sgt. Pepper's Lonely Hearts Club Band*, an album of unparalleled scope and imagination.

Where the LP was once seen as a vehicle for twelve random songs, it now offered a musical journey in several movements, closer to a classical symphony. The Rolling Stones and the Who would follow the Beatles' lead, with *Their Satanic Majesties Request* and *The Who Sell Out* albums, though with variable results.

Grant and Most saw these changes happening. However, Mickie's forté was the pop single, and while Grant might have wanted to manage the hippie prince Donovan, he didn't buy into the rhetoric. Visitors to 155 remember Peter grinning beneath his mandarin's moustache and gently teasing any starry-eyed minstrels and poets wandering about the place.

"In the flower power era, when artists and their managers were preaching peace and love, Mickie and Peter were making fun of them," remembers Chris Hayes. "They didn't take any of it seriously."

Somehow, though, Peter Grant inherited England's premier psychedelic R&B group, the Yardbirds. It was his happiest accident yet. The Yardbirds had formed in the London suburbs five years earlier and became the house band at Richmond's Crawdaddy Club, the crucible of the booming R&B scene. The Rolling Stones's former handler, Giorgio Gomelsky, originally managed the band before passing them on to a young entrepreneur named Simon Napier-Bell.

The Yardbirds' first star turn was their mercurial lead guitarist Eric Clapton. In the spring of 1965, when the group moved away from pure blues toward pop, Clapton, a blues purist, quit in disgust. His replacement was another gifted player, Jeff Beck, who'd been recommended by his friend, fellow guitarist Jimmy Page.

Between 1965 and 1966, the Yardbirds released a run of singles, including "For Your Love," "Shapes of Things," and "Happenings Ten Years Time Ago," which subverted pop and American R&B with trancelike rhythms, Indian ragas, and guitar solos that sounded like air raid sirens.

The thrilling chaos of the music was sometimes matched by turmoil onstage and off. Page witnessed a tumultuous performance in Oxford, where drunken lead singer Keith Relf harangued the audience.

"Keith was rolling around on stage, blowing his harmonica in all the wrong places, and singing nonsense words," he said. Relf apparently ended the show with a broken hand after karate-chopping a chair: "Keith did a sort of punk act. It was so in advance of punk that even some band members weren't ready for it."

Bassist Paul Samwell-Smith was one of them and left immediately. Almost without thinking, Page offered to play bass. The arrangement lasted a short time, until Beck missed a show and Page had to go back to guitar. Eventually, rhythm guitarist Chris Dreja switched to playing bass full time.

"Sometimes it was fantastic with Jeff and Jimmy both playing guitar, and sometimes it wasn't," remembers drummer Jim McCarty. "Jeff was hyper, Jimmy was superconfident." The Yardbirds secured their place as England's hippest group with an appearance that summer in Michelangelo Antonioni's swinging London movie *Blow-Up*. And like Clapton before him, Beck was unhappy.

In May 1966, Beck had moonlighted from the group to record a session at London's IBC Studios with Page, bass guitarist John Baldwin (later known as John Paul Jones), pianist Nicky Hopkins and the Who's drummer Keith Moon. Their fiery, guitar-heavy reworking of Ravel's "Bolero" was christened "Beck's Bolero."

The track wouldn't appear until March 1967, when it turned up as the B-side of Beck's first solo single, "Hi Ho Silver Lining." It was indicative of the music he and Page wanted to make in the future, even if neither quite knew it yet.

In August, the Yardbirds joined the Dick Clark Caravan of Stars tour across America. They shared a rundown tour bus with Sam the Sham & the Pharaohs, of Wooly Bully fame, and played gigs in a shopping mall and on an ice rink. More than once, they were left waiting in a dressing room while a jobsworth tried to determine which American act they were on the Musicians Union exchange with; Grant's stock answer of the Count Basie Orchestra only worked once. It was all too much for Beck, who quit, pleading illness, after just a few shows, leaving Page as the Yardbirds' sole lead guitarist.

Beck's departure was also a turning point for the Yardbirds' manager, Simon Napier-Bell. He'd grown tired of difficult pop musicians and offered Mickie Most their management. Then Grant spoke up.

"My first impressions of Peter—ugly, coarse, and unattractive," admits Napier-Bell now. "I'm sorry, but I think that's what most people's first impressions were, and Peter used it to his advantage. I discovered later, he had quite a sensitive streak inside him and would never let it show."

Just before Christmas of 1966, *Melody Maker* announced Peter Grant was now managing the Yardbirds. Or was he? "The whole thing was odd," says Jim McCarty. "We thought Simon was sharing management with Peter, but Simon disappeared, and Peter said, 'I'm your manager now.'"

Having already been passed between Giorgio Gomelsky and Napier-Bell, nobody asked too many questions. McCarty, like most people, found Grant imposing. "I never had any problems with him," he insists. "My only worry was sharing that lift at Oxford Street. Peter was a big man, and we'd all be looking at each other, thinking, 'Are we going to make it to the sixth floor?'"

Before quitting, Napier-Bell had taken Grant aside: "He said, 'There's a troublemaker in the band, a real pain in the arse.' I said, 'Who's that?' He said, 'Jimmy Page.'"

Page told Grant they'd been touring nonstop, recording singles, and had just appeared in *Blow-Up*, but they weren't making any money: "Jimmy was the only one with the balls or the savvy to stand up and say, 'This is not good enough.'"

Unlike Mickie Most, Grant had never been a performer or a musician and "couldn't carry a tune in a bucket," according to his family. Instead, he committed himself to nurturing Jimmy Page's talent, which meant protecting him from the outside world and offering a curious, unstinting loyalty.

Many close to Grant believe Jimmy played a greater role in his life than anyone, except his children. "There was this wonderful, mutual respect," says Helen, "but it was also a case of 'Whatever Jimmy wants.'"

Born in West London in January 1944, James Patrick Page enjoyed a comfortable postwar upbringing in suburban Epsom, Surrey. Like Grant, Jimmy was brought up as an only child: "Until I was five, I was totally isolated from kids my own age," he said. "That early isolation probably had a lot to do with how I turned out."

In 1958, the thirteen-year-old Page appeared with his grammar school skiffle group on the TV show *All Your Own*. Jimmy strummed a Hofner President almost as big as him. Later he was interviewed by gently patronizing host Huw Weldon. When asked if he wanted to become a musician after leaving school, Page famously replied, "No, I want to do biological research."

Jimmy Page was a younger version of the teenagers Grant had seen at the 2i's. While Peter was dragging a drunken Gene Vincent to the stage at the Aylesbury Granada, Jimmy was in his bedroom obsessively playing his records to learn guitarist Cliff Gallup's solos.

News of Jimmy Page's talent spread quickly. Within two years of his TV debut, Page was playing with Neil Christian and the Crusaders, who had to promise Page's parents they'd return their underage son safely after each gig. Following a bout of ill health, Jimmy gave up playing live for a time and enrolled at Sutton Art College.

It was a temporary diversion. By 1963, Page was playing sessions for songwriters John Carter and Ken Lewis, who'd also formed their own group, Carter-Lewis and the Southerners. Grant later claimed he first came across Page playing with the Southerners.

John Carter offered an insightful description of their young guitarist at the time. "Jimmy was a guy you'd get a good performance from without trying," he said in 2001. "He was a very fast player, he knew his rock 'n' roll. . . . He was very quiet, a bit of an intellectual and interested in all sorts of odd cult things."

Most of Page's contemporaries were survivors from the original rock 'n' roll era. Jimmy was at least seven years their junior and became their equal, dashing around London from the studio to the Tube station and back again to play as many as three sessions a day, six days a week.

Among hundreds of hits and misses, Page could be heard on "Lulu's Shout," the Rolling Stones' "The Last Time," Tom Jones's "It's Not Unusual," and Donovan's "Hurdy Gurdy Man." He was a regular on Mickie Most's productions. "Mickie thought Jimmy was a genius," says Chris Hayes. "He knew Jimmy would always get it done."

Page was soon branching out, writing his own songs and working for Andrew Loog Oldham as an in-house producer for his label, Immediate Records in an office next door to RAK's.

Page joined the Yardbirds almost on a whim, and was immediately frustrated by their next single, the Mickie Most–produced "Ha! Ha! Said the Clown." It was a jaunty pop song at odds with the Yardbirds' experimental live show. On stage, the noise of the Staten Island ferry horn was sampled in one song, while Page played spectral-sounding guitar with a violin bow on another. The Yardbirds were already becoming the prototype Led Zeppelin.

This experimental approach was mostly curtailed on their next album, *Little Games*. "Mickie understood singles," said Page. "I knew how he'd set about making an album—you had three hours to get as many songs down as possible." Just as Grant would wrest control away from the labels in favor of the artist, Page wanted to take control of the music from the producer.

Peter Grant's arrival had a positive and immediate impact on the Yardbirds' bank account. America's politicized youth were now marching against the Vietnam War and its groups preached peace and goodwill. However, the message hadn't reached the promoters, and it was still a struggle to get paid.

"Simon Napier-Bell was a big deal as a manager," says the Yardbirds' bassist Chris Dreja, "but he wasn't hands-on. Peter was. He came on tour with us in the States and for the first time ever, we started making money."

The cash flow increased partly because of Grant's no-nonsense approach and honesty. "If Napier-Bell booked a Yardbirds' tour for, say, $100,000, he'd cop his commission and fuck off to the Bahamas," Grant told McLaren. "Then I discovered their promoter, Frank Barsalona, owned the limousine company they were using. So I trod on all those kickbacks."

Now thirty-two, Grant had ten years on his band and had been on the road for almost as long. "I warmed to him straight away," Dreja continues. "One of the first things Peter taught me was never to use room service in America, because it was too expensive. He knew all the tricks, all the short-cuts, and that's what we needed."

"Having the manager on the road was unusual for the time," adds the Yardbirds' American roadie Henry "The Horse" Smith. "I don't remember Robert Stigwood or people like that on the bus. Peter was an involved manager, and you can't do that sitting at a desk, you have to be in the trenches—and only Peter was."

It was at a state fair in Canada that Chris Dreja witnessed another incident for which Grant would always be remembered. The Yardbirds' fee for the gig was $2,000. They'd received half up front, but when bad weather delayed their arrival the organizers tried to withhold the balance.

"I think the two guys running the show were Mafia connected," says Dreja. "I know they were being very Italian about it. They came on the bus and told Peter we weren't getting the rest of the cash."

When Grant demanded they pay up, one of the promoters pulled a gun. Grant recalled the incident in a previously unpublished interview from 1994: "I said, 'What are you doing? He said, 'I'm going to shoot you, motherfucker.'

I said, 'I'm a British citizen; you don't want to do that. You'll cause an international incident.'"

"Peter turned up his Englishness," remembers Henry Smith. "He would do cockney or aristocratic—or a bit of both. He knew how to sound intimidating. And it worked."

A disbelieving Dreja watched as Grant walked into the muzzle of the gun, and carried on walking, bouncing his would-be assailant back down the aisle: "It was comical really. Peter stomach-butted this guy all the way to the front of the bus. By the time they'd got there, they'd become the best of friends—and we got the money."

"They're not going to shoot you for a thousand dollars," Grant reasoned, "but they count on frightening you with the gun. Once they see you're not frightened, they back down."

The Yardbirds were now making money, though not enough to stop the rot within the band. Their next single was a curious-sounding cover of Harry Nillson's "Ten Little Indians." Page wasn't impressed. While he was pushing the Yardbirds in bold new directions on stage, in the studio they were still half stuck in the beat-pop era of three years earlier.

Page had seen Eric Clapton's new group Cream conquer America, and Jimi Hendrix "crashing onto the scene like an express train" and challenging every other guitarist on the planet. While touring the United States, both Grant and Page had glimpsed an alternative world and one that was the polar opposite of Mickie Most's "hit factory."

America's new FM radio format allowed its DJs to play longer album tracks uninterrupted. It was radio for the post–*Sgt. Pepper* generation. "Instead of trying to get played on top-forty radio, I realized there was another emerging market," said Grant. "The scene was changing."

The tour had also given him an insight into Page's reputation in America. In New York, Grant and his guitarist were on Fifth Avenue when a car screeched to a halt alongside them. Inside was the songwriter Burt Bacharach ("in a white tuxedo, with a beautiful woman in the back," remembered Grant). He jumped out and greeted Page like an old friend. The two men had met when Page played guitar on his album, *Hit Maker! Burt Bacharach Plays His Hits!* "All the important guys in the US biz already knew Jimmy," Grant said.

In spring 1968, Page, with his ruffled shirts and Regency-dandy hairdo, already looked like a seventies rock-star-in-waiting. The rest of the Yardbirds were trailing behind. By the time they set off for another American tour, the group was falling apart.

Richard Cole had been tour managing the New Vaudeville Band but was drafted in by Grant to look after the Yardbirds. He was shocked by what he found. "Jimmy had assumed leadership of a band capsizing at sea," he said.

When the group arrived in Los Angeles, Cole and Page noticed a palmist at their hotel on Sunset Strip and went for a reading. The fortune teller scrutinized Jimmy's palm and told him, "In a very short time, you are going to make a decision that will change your life."

Two days later, Jim McCarty and Keith Relf announced the Yardbirds were over. Page was shocked. While they'd struggled to find a coherent sound in the studio, he was still convinced their live show signposted the way forward. Then the pair dropped another bombshell: they wanted to form a harmony pop group in the style of the Turtles, who'd had a hit the year before with "Happy Together." "My jaw dropped," Page said.

In the meantime, though, there were still shows to be played. Cole and Henry Smith quickly realized the band had split down the middle. McCarty and Relf were in one camp. Page and Chris Dreja, who wanted to keep the Yardbirds going, were in another. Both sides offered new jobs to their road crew.

"Jim and Keith came first and said, 'We're starting a band, we'd like you to join us,'" says Smith. "Then a day later, Jimmy Page said the same thing. Peter pointed me in Jimmy's direction. He knew the potential of Jimmy's playing and the excitement he generated. Peter already had a vision."

In tandem with FM radio was a growing circuit of college halls and clubs. The Yardbirds' final tour included hip underground venues such as Detroit's Grande Ballroom and San Franciscan promoter Bill Graham's Fillmore Auditorium. These were the people and places Grant and Page needed to woo next time Jimmy played America.

Not everyone in the group agreed. Miami's Thee Image club, a repurposed ballroom with its own designated meditation space, was a perfect example of these new venues. The owner Marshall Brevetz offered the Yardbirds $5,000 to play a gig on their day off. "Jimmy and Chris wanted to do it," said Grant. "The others didn't—and there was a big row in the Holiday Inn." It was the end of the Yardbirds.

Two photographs from the time encapsulate Peter Grant's role. The Yardbirds' 1967 Christmas card showed the band members perched awkwardly on motorcycles while their manager stood between them dressed as Santa Claus.

On the last day of their final American tour, Chris Dreja took a portrait of Grant with the spoils of war. Peter grinned for the camera with hundred dollar bills stuffed in his mouth, ears, and nose and more piled around his feet.

The photographs showed him having fun and said much about how the Yard-birds perceived their manager and how he perceived himself.

Back in Britain in July, the band members went their separate ways. Years later, Peter Grant pinpointed the birth of Led Zeppelin to a car journey he took with Page soon after: "We were driving down Shaftesbury Avenue by the Savile Theatre one day. I said, 'What are you going to do? Go back to doing sessions?' And he said, 'No, form a new band.'"

Grant saw his opportunity and took it. "Once Jimmy was sure Peter was on his side, they made a perfect team," says Simon Napier-Bell. "Jimmy was inherently fragile and sensitive, and Peter provided him with some armor."

In the coming days, various singers were mentioned, including Steve Winwood and the Small Faces' Steve Marriott—names previously bandied around during the "Beck's Bolero" session. But Page had another vocalist in mind. Terry Reid was a Cambridgeshire teenager, whose gravel-throated roar later earned him the soubriquet "Superlungs." Page had seen him perform two years earlier on a package tour with the Yardbirds. His voice fuzzed the boundaries between soul, blues, and pop: "And he was exactly what I was looking for."

Grant was tasked with tracking down Reid only to discover he'd just signed to Mickie Most. Terry was summoned to RAK, where he later said Grant and Most reminded him of the American TV cartoon duo, Heckle and Jeckle, a pair of identical magpies; one blatantly confrontational, the other underhand. Reid then watched as they tossed a coin to decide who would manage him. Grant won.

Reid considered Jimmy Page's offer to join his new band: "He was just formulating what he might be doing. I was very flattered and said, 'Let's have a go when I come back off tour.'" Reid was opening for Cream on their fare-well US dates. "But Jimmy said, 'No, I want to put something together now.'"

It was then Reid suggested a vocalist he'd seen performing with a group in Derbyshire. "Terry said, 'I know a singer who'd be really great—a blues singer—go and see him,'" Grant recalled. His name was Robert Plant.

Asked for his thoughts on Peter Grant now, Plant replies, "He was like my older brother, and I still think of him that way." It was on July 20, 1968, Grant first met this surrogate younger sibling. Plant was singing with his group Obs-Tweedle at a teacher training college in Walsall.

Grant, Page, and Chris Dreja arrived at the venue where they were met by a tall, rangy youth wearing a University of Toronto sweatshirt and an explo-sive frizz of curly hair. Everybody presumed he was a roadie. "Then he came back, and it turned out to be Robert," Grant said.

Born in West Bromwich in August 1948, Plant was very much Peter Grant's and Jimmy Page's junior—something which would have consequences on his relationship with both men. Plant's father was a civil engineer and wanted his son, a promising grammar school pupil, to become a chartered accountant. However, Robert abandoned his accountancy course after just two weeks. "I was that kid who'd discovered Elvis Presley and had his head turned," he said.

The teenage Plant was fascinated by Elvis, Gene Vincent, and the blues. His favorite anecdote involved his irate father chopping the plug off his Dansette record player after he'd spun New Orleans singer Chris Kenner's "I Like It Like That" "seventeen times in a row."

Having abandoned a good job in an office, Plant became a fixture on the Midlands blues scene. The money was poor, and he worked for a time laying tarmac for a building firm: "I got the piss taken out of me because of my barnet and because I kept telling everyone—'Hey, this is an interim thing because I'm going to be incredibly successful.'"*

Plant recorded two solo singles for CBS, which failed to sell. British bluesman Alexis Korner took Robert under his wing and record company A&R men showed a cautious interest in his latest group, the Band of Joy. But the big break never seemed to come.

When Grant and his entourage arrived in Walsall, Plant was just a few weeks shy of his twentieth birthday. He'd promised his pregnant girlfriend, Maureen, if he hadn't made it in music by then, he'd give it up. He was in luck. Neither Page or Grant cared for Obs-Tweedle, but they thought the singer was excellent.

Plant's voice wasn't so far removed from Terry Reid's. It was raw and unpredictable, but it had a disarming power and urgency. "He wasn't the frontman with his shirt open that you saw in 1972," said Page, "but I could see he was a serious, ballsy singer."

On Page's instruction, Grant sent a telegram to Plant: "Priority—Robert Plant. Tried phoning you several times. Please call if you are interested in joining the Yardbirds."

"He sent me a couple of telegrams—'You want to join the Yardbirds'—and I thought someone was taking the piss," Plant told me. He wavered for a day or so and then agreed to a further meeting. "I knew the Yardbirds had cut some great records—I'd seen them play with Eric. I didn't have anything to lose."

---

* "Barnet" or "Barnet fair": cockney rhyming slang for "hair."

Page invited Plant to his house at Pangbourne, Berkshire. It was an audition/vetting process. Page had recently acquired an elegant riverside property with its own boathouse from the proceeds of his session work. "I knocked on the door and Jimmy's girlfriend, Lynn—this spectacularly alternative-looking American woman—opened the door," Plant said. The house itself was just as impressive. "It was a beautiful place—all rings and birds and trinkets and beautiful things everywhere."

Plant spent several days at Pangbourne, listening to records and Page outlining his musical vision. The Yardbirds had been playing an electrified version of folk singer Jake Holmes' "Dazed and Confused," and Page wanted to bring a similar treatment to Joan Baez's "Babe I'm Gonna Leave You." He played Plant both songs. "I wanted the group to be a marriage of blues, hard rock, and acoustic music with heavy choruses," he said.

Plant passed the audition, but by the time he joined, Chris Dreja had excused himself from any new band. Dreja had studied photography at art school and wanted to take it up as a profession. "I was committed to becoming a photographer," he says now, "and you should always follow your love. I never had any regrets."

The day before his trip to the Midlands, Page had taken a phone call from fellow session musician, John Paul Jones. "It was my wife, Mo, who noticed an item in *Disc*, saying Jimmy was forming a new band out of the old Yardbirds," said Jones. "She prompted me to phone him up. It was the chance to do something different at last."

Jones and Peter Grant's paths had crossed many times. As a teenager, John had toured with ex-Shadow Jet Harris's group the Jet Blacks when he opened for Gene Vincent. "I was 17 and earning £30 a week," Jones said. "And that's when I first met Peter."

John Paul Jones was a stage name. John Baldwin was born into a show business family in suburban Kent in January 1946. His parents had worked as a comedy act in the variety era, and his father had been an arranger for dance orchestras. Their son studied music at London's Christ's College and was an organist and choirmaster when still in his teens.

As a multi-instrumentalist and arranger, Jones was soon in demand. By 1964 he was playing regular sessions and performing on several Mickie Most productions, including the Yardbirds' *Little Games*. He'd also played bass on "Beck's Bolero."

"I could compete with most bass players," says Chris Dreja, "but I couldn't compete with John Paul Jones. Jimmy now had one of the top session musicians in the country." Jones's quiet demeanor and disregard for any notion of celebrity would prove a blessing in the years ahead. Not least for his manager. "He was an incredible musician and the vital link," offered Grant.

By the end of July 1968, three-quarters of what would become Led Zeppelin was in place. Jimmy Page still needed to find a drummer. At which point, Peter Grant flew to America. He had another group to manage.

4

The Kicking Trick

"Peter didn't see it as the manager and the act.
He saw it as 'us' versus 'them.'"

—ATLANTIC RECORDS' PRESIDENT,

AHMET ERTEGUN

Nobody liked Rod Stewart. Or that was how it seemed in summer 1968. The singer had been working the Soho clubs since 1962, which is where Peter Grant first encountered him. Known as "Rod the Mod" after his dapper dress sense and rooster's haircut, Stewart had sung with several groups before Jeff Beck hired him for his. It wasn't an auspicious start. Apparently, Stewart loped onstage for his first show at the Finsbury Park Astoria with his fly undone shortly before the stage curtain collapsed.

The previous spring, Beck's debut single, "Hi Ho Silver Lining," a boozy pub-rock sing-along with a reluctant Beck on lead vocals, had been a British hit. Beck had tried to persuade producer Mickie Most to let Stewart sing, but he refused. "Mickie didn't want to know," Beck claimed. "He said, 'You're the star.'"

Beck disliked the song and was soon telling the press he much preferred the B-side, "Beck's Bolero." Their identity crisis continued on their next two Mickie Most–produced singles. Listeners who turned over the A-sides—"Tallyman" and "Love Is Blue"—heard Rod Stewart rasping over some wonderful heavy blues.

The Jeff Beck Group in the summer of 1968 was Beck, Stewart, piano player Nicky Hopkins, drummer Mickey Waller, and bass guitarist and future Rolling Stone Ron Wood. After some disastrous British dates, the band was close to splitting.

One afternoon, Beck arrived at Oxford Street for crisis talks, where he ran into Peter Grant. "Jeff was ready to quit," said Grant. "I said '*Don't*—I'll get you an American tour.'" It was what Beck wanted to hear. During his last stint with the Yardbirds, Beck had noticed a booming underground club scene and the rise of FM radio. Like Jimmy Page, Beck wanted to make albums not singles.

"Peter Grant saw I had a shit-hot blues band with Rod," Beck said, "and realized America was where I should go." This meant Mickie Most would be passing the guitarist on to his partner. "Mickie's attitude was, 'Good luck, but it's not going to happen. Go and do your underground thing,' recalled Beck. "And we did, and we never came back."

The Jeff Beck Group had just completed its first album, *Truth*. While listed as its producer, Most's involvement had been minimal. Grant later claimed he'd made the record. "I produced the album, although I didn't get a credit," he insisted. "Mickie was contracted to produce, but he was recording Donovan at the time."

More than Led Zeppelin, it was the Jeff Beck Group that marked the beginning of the end of Grant and Most's partnership. There was no great falling out. Peter went to America, and Mickie stayed in England. It changed everything. In the space of less than one month, Grant found himself juggling the careers of not one but two world-class guitarists, who'd soon end up in competition with each other.

Grant left Jimmy Page looking for a drummer and joined Beck's group on its inaugural US tour in July. They opened for California's premier underground act, the Grateful Dead, at New York's Fillmore East, and in Beck's words "blew the town apart."

Epic Records was interested in Beck's group but wouldn't commit because there wasn't an obvious hit single on *Truth*. Grant contacted label head Len Levy. "I said, 'This album is wonderful.' He said, 'Don't tell *me* the record business. You're from England, for a start.'" Levy was on his way to a record company convention in Las Vegas and put the phone down.

Grant now had the bit between his teeth. The following day, the *New York Times* published a glowing review of the Fillmore show by its star critic

Robert Shelton. Grant photocopied the article, tracked down Levy in Las Vegas, and sent it by courier with a note reading, "Do you want this band or don't you?"

Epic wanted them and told Grant they still had one reservation: "They said, 'Get yourself a proper singer.'" Nobody, it seemed, liked Rod Stewart.

*W*hen Jeff Beck's touring party reached San Francisco, Peter Grant received the phone call that would change his life. It was from Jimmy Page in London: "He said, 'G, I saw a drummer last night; he's so good, so powerful, clubs won't book them if he's in the group.'" The drummer's name was John Bonham.

Drummers, including session aces Clem Cattini and Procol Harum's BJ Wilson, had been considered for Page's new group. Grant remembered ex–Jeff Beck Group drummer Aynsley Dunbar's name being put forward, while Mickey Waller claimed Peter also approached him about the job. But it would only ever belong to one man.

John "Bonzo" Bonham was Robert Plant's former band mate. Born in May 1948, he was the same age as Plant and a fellow Midlander from Redditch, Worcestershire. By the time Bonham was sixteen, he had followed his father into the construction trade but was also playing drums in various semi-pro groups.

His reputation quickly preceded him. Besides playing at a punishing volume, Bonham sometimes stood on his kit and stripped to the waist, to the chagrin of conservative club owners. Plant met Bonham in 1967, when they played together in the Midlands act Crawling King Snakes and later, Band of Joy.

A friendship developed based around familial bickering and a shared humor. "John and I were best mates," said Plant. "Page and Jones were never mates."

Like Plant, Bonham had commitments: he'd promised his new wife, Pat, he'd give up music after they married, but he was still playing after the birth of their son, Jason. On Robert Plant's recommendation, Page saw Bonham playing with folk singer Tim Rose in a North London club. Unlike on previous occasions, the venue's management didn't ban him for being too loud and outlandish, but Page was astonished by the power of his performance. "He was incredible. I didn't just hear him, I *felt* him."

Bonham didn't have a telephone, and Grant supposedly sent between thirty and forty telegrams, before he responded. Bonham had his doubts about joining the new group. He was earning £40 a week with Tim Rose and wasn't sure this new group could do better. Peter assured him they could and offered him £50: "And John later offered to drive the van as well for another fifty."

"Bonzo's missus, Pat, said, 'You're not going with Planty; you know what happens when you go with him,'" Plant said. "I had a lot of harebrained ideas that were a little left of center when it came to putting bread on the table. We were both precocious and antagonistic. You either got it or you crossed the road to avoid it."

Peter Grant and Jimmy Page were opposites but drawn to each by a mutual affinity. Grant and Bonham were more obviously alike. "He was the best mate I ever had," Peter said later. Even at Zeppelin's height, neither quite lost the fear that it might end tomorrow, and they'd be back driving a van. Both also had a bluff exterior that hid these insecurities.

It was barely more than one month since the previous Yardbirds group had returned from America. On August 12, the new version played together for the first time in a basement in Gerrard Street in London's Chinatown.

They spent two hours together, thrashing through the old Yardbirds favorite, "Train Kept A-Rollin'," among others. It sounded so good, Page would talk later about an "ESP-like connection" between the musicians and suggest "the gods were looking down" on them all.

Further rehearsals continued at Page's house in Pangbourne. Then after one session, Bonham sheepishly told Grant he had a problem. He'd accepted a one-off gig with blues singer Chris Farlowe on the Isle of Wight and had been paid up front.

The promoter was the Flamingo club's formidable ex-manager Rik Gunnell. Bonham was terrified of cancelling and couldn't afford to pay back the money. Grant knew Gunnell going back to his Soho days, made a call, and the matter was resolved.

"Both John and Robert were a bit naïve in those days," Grant explained.

"Me and Bonzo had just dropped off the conveyor belt," confirms Plant now. "We had no idea what the fuck was going on."

Grant booked the New Yardbirds—as they were now called—on a short Scandinavian tour. Without record company support, Grant, Page, and Jones funded the shows themselves. Peter had stayed away from rehearsals, and first saw the group at their inaugural date in September.

The Teen Club was a school gymnasium in Gladsaxe, Copenhagen. Grant watched from the side of the makeshift stage, as Page conducted the band through "Dazed and Confused," "How Many More Times," and "Communication Breakdown"—songs that would soon appear on the first Led Zeppelin album. "There was this incredible chemistry," Grant declared. "It was the best thing I ever heard."

During their car ride through London's West End, Grant had asked Page who he wanted to produce his new group. "Jimmy said, 'I'll produce it myself, and if I don't cut it, *then* I'll get a producer in.'"

Page wanted to pay for and produce the album himself, without any outside interference. Then, when it was done to his satisfaction, it would be licensed to the highest-bidding record company.

However, Page still needed an engineer. He and Glyn Johns had known each other since they were almost teenagers. Johns had gone on to engineer hits for the Who and the Rolling Stones, and he agreed to work with the New Yardbirds, believing he'd also receive a percentage of royalties on the finished album. Or so he thought.

What would later become Led Zeppelin's debut album was recorded at West London's Olympic Studios in September and October of 1968. It was completed in thirty hours and cost Page £1,782, including the cover artwork. The band worked at a furious pace and to Page's instructions. Plant listened; Bonham less so.

On his first meeting with the band, Bonzo had spotted Grant and asked who "the big fat bloke was." Page told him to be quiet; it was their manager. Laurence Myers remembers hearing about Grant's threats after Bonzo misbehaved in the studio: "Peter was supposed to have said, 'Could you play drums in a wheelchair?' The other one was, 'Do as I say Bonham, or you'll be leaving by different doors.'"

On another occasion, Grant took the drummer aside, pointed at Jimmy Page, and quietly said, "Do what this man says or fuck off." The threats were comical but also menacing.

In between sessions, the group dashed up and down the country playing college halls and clubs, but not everybody was interested in Jimmy Page's new group. Ed Bicknell was a student and entertainment secretary at Hull University, and was responsible for booking groups to play his college. In October, he traveled to London to see agents Chris Wright and Terry Ellis at the newly formed Chrysalis agency.

"Chrysalis was on the first floor at 155 Oxford Street, and Mickie and Peter were upstairs," says Bicknell. "This man I realized later was Peter Grant walked into the Chrysalis office. He cut quite a figure, with his big top half and skinny legs. The New Yardbirds were playing the Marquee, and he was trying to get these bookers to go and see them. They were all saying, 'Oh, fuck off, Peter, we don't want to see your band.' Nobody cared."

Bicknell went instead. "I walked down Wardour Street where the club was, and there was a line of people almost as far as Old Compton Street," he recalls. The show itself was a sensory overload. "They were still called the Yardbirds or the New Yardbirds. I was completely blown away, mainly by the energy level and the noise. There were loud bands at that time, but this was something else."

The *New Musical Express* (*NME*) critic Keith Altham also saw the show but lasted through only three songs. "They were painfully loud," he says. "They were good musicians, but they didn't have their sound together yet. Peter called me the next day, and I told him what I thought. Of course, he never *ever* let me forget it, even years later. Peter was wedded to that band."

Grant had also been trying to persuade a BBC producer to see his group. He'd even sent a limousine to their office, and nobody came. "I said to the band then—'Bollocks! You've got the kids in the street, these are your people, fuck television!'"

The decision to ignore the media was not Grant's to make. It was Page's. Soon after, Jimmy told the press Led Zeppelin wouldn't be releasing any singles. It was a bold move and a huge commercial risk, and Grant accepted it. "I don't think Peter was in awe of musicians," says Chris Dreja. "He was in love with musicians. And he had this unshakable belief in Jimmy's talent. He would do anything for him."

Before the UK tour was over, there was another important change: the group's name. Grant always insisted Page acquired the rights to the Yardbirds' name during their final American tour: "In my very ambitious way—and without a lawyer—I got them to sign a letter which gave Jimmy use of the name."

Chris Dreja denies this. "Not true," he says now. "Jimmy told me had a piece of paper proving he owned the name, which is why they started using it. I wrote to Peter Grant and told him I own the name. I still have a copy of the letter I sent, and I *still* own the name."

By the end of October, the Yardbirds/New Yardbirds had become "Led Zeppelin," a variation on a name conjured up by Keith Moon at the "Beck's Bolero" session. Moon and the others had been discussing a "super group" and speculated how badly it would go down with the respective bands.

"Keith said, 'This'll go over like a lead Zeppelin,' instead of a lead balloon," Grant recalled. "The only thing I didn't like was 'lead.'" Grant was worried it would be pronounced "leed." "So I wrote it down on a piece of paper and crossed out the A." He pitched the new spelling to Page, who agreed, and the grammatically challenged Led Zeppelin was born.

The new name would have repercussions a year later when Zeppelin played a show in Denmark and was introduced to the Danish aristocrat Countess Eva Von Zeppelin. Her grandfather had built the famous Zeppelin airship, and she was unhappy about them using her family name.

The countess agreed to meet the group and their manager backstage. Grant charmed her sufficiently, and then she spotted the sleeve of Zeppelin's first album, showing an airship in flames. The countess denounced the group as "shrieking monkeys" and threatened to sue if they continued to use the name. The band played that evening under the name "the Nobs," but no legal action ever ensued.

Having recovered from the sensory overload of their Marquee gig, Ed Bicknell booked what he thought were the New Yardbirds for a date at Hull University. "They never played," he says, "They had a better offer. But I have a contract where somebody has crossed out 'New Yardbirds' and written 'Lead Zeppelin' and signed it Jimmy Page."

Twenty years later, Bicknell showed the contract to Grant and pointed at the signature. "I said, 'Peter, this is not Jimmy Page's handwriting; this is yours.' He said, 'Yes, it is. . . . I never liked to take a risk.'"

With a new name in place, Grant began shopping for a record deal. He didn't have to look far. Turkish-born blues aficionados Ahmet and Nesuhi Ertegun had launched their Atlantic label in 1947 and pioneered black music in the postwar years. By 1968, they were hip to the prevailing trend for long-haired white boys with guitars. Atlantic had signed Cream, which had just broken up as Led Zeppelin came on the market.

In Zeppelin folklore, it was pop singer Dusty Springfield who tipped off Atlantic Records' executive vice president Jerry Wexler about the band. Grant backed up the story: "She was down at Wexler's house and told him about this new group that were in the offing. . . . She'd worked with John Paul Jones on arrangements." Page and Jones had played on Dusty's sessions, but Jimmy insists she played no part in Zeppelin joining Atlantic.

"I first met Jerry Wexler and Ahmet Ertegun when I was a studio musician in 1965," Page recalled. He had been in New York where Bert Berns—the composer of "Hang on Sloopy" and "Twist and Shout"—was trying to persuade him to move to America. Berns introduced Wexler and Ertegun to the English boy wonder.

The Yardbirds had barely split before Grant put the word out that Page was starting a new group. "Wexler jumped on the phone and said, 'I want this new band that Jimmy Page is doing,'" remembers former Atlantic Records president Jerry Greenberg. "And that was before knowing Robert Plant was the singer."

Grant and Page's first move had been to create Superhype Tapes, a company with Page as its main shareholder, through which all band business would be funneled. Superhype Music and Productions would follow soon after. "The title came from Jimmy being aware of the hype that surrounded us at the time," Grant said. This meant Led Zeppelin would never sign directly to a record company and would be able to retain their autonomy. Grant, meanwhile, would receive an executive producer's credit on their albums.

News of the group spread quickly and other record executives started circling, even before the album was finished. "Mickie Most got calls from Allen Klein and Clive Davis [Columbia Records president] at Epic," recalled Grant. Mickie said, "You better sort this one out, Peter."

Klein had a blanket deal with Most and Epic, which had been the Yardbirds' label in the States. Both Klein and Clive Davis automatically presumed they'd get Page's new band. Page, who'd joined the Yardbirds later, wasn't tied to the label, and Grant was free to take him wherever he wanted, rowing both Most and Klein out of the deal. "Zeppelin was too heavy for Mickie, anyway," he said later.

Interviewed in 1994, Grant admitted he was inexperienced when it came to negotiating Led Zeppelin's deal. "This was a big thing for me. I didn't have a lot of knowledge." But he had street sense and followed his gut instinct. Grant and Page flew to New York at the end of October with the master tapes of the album. By now, Mo Austin at Warners and Chris Blackwell at Island Records were also in the picture. Grant used this as leverage over Atlantic.

During negotiations, Wexler invited Grant and Page to Miami to spend time on Atlantic's luxury boat. The Jeff Beck Group was touring America, where Truth had become a top-twenty hit. Beck joined them in Florida. Grant might have been negotiating with one of the world's biggest record companies, but he switched from businessman to minder in a heartbeat. When a couple of passing sailors made fun of the fey English rock stars, Grant intervened, lifting the bigger of the two off his feet and growling, "OK, what's your trouble, Popeye?" The other one apparently fled.

Grant used similar tactics on Atlantic. He wouldn't budge until they did as he asked. Zeppelin signed an unprecedented deal, which allowed them to license their music to the label and also control the production and the artwork. Atlantic's job was to promote and sell the finished product. Later, when their in-house producer Tom Dowd suggested some tweaks to the LP mix, Page flatly refused. That wasn't part of the deal.

A photograph taken on the day Zeppelin signed with Atlantic shows Ahmet Ertegun sitting next to Jimmy Page with Grant towering over them like a smiling giant in a suit and tie. "Although the exact terms are secret, it can be disclosed that it is one of the most substantial deals Atlantic has ever made," declared Atlantic's press release. By keeping the figure secret, the power of suggestion took over, though the sum usually quoted, including by Grant, was $200,000.

Jerry Wexler later revealed Atlantic had given Zeppelin a five-year contract with a $75,000 advance for the first year and four one-year options. When Grant's lawyer offered world rights for an extra $35,000, Wexler asked Atlantic's British distributors Polydor to pay $20,000 toward the cost. Polydor refused, missing out on a piece of one of the biggest groups of the seventies.

Atlantic wanted an option for six albums. Grant insisted on five. In a prescient move, he included a "no motion picture soundtracks" clause in the contract, meaning Zeppelin later kept the rights to their 1976 soundtrack, *The Song Remains the Same*. Grant always believed it was his dogged refusal to budge that brought him closer to Atlantic's president, Ahmet Ertegun.

Although Jerry Wexler signed Zeppelin, he stepped back soon after. "Ahmet took over," he told Ertegun's biographer Robert Greenfield. "I don't think I could have tolerated them. I got along fine with Peter Grant, but I knew he was an animal. Ahmet plunged into it heart and soul. He became their friend."

While corporate giant Warners Brothers had just acquired Atlantic, the label retained a certain cachet. To music obsessives Page and Plant, Ahmet Ertegun was a fascinating character. Born in 1923, Ertegun was steeped in the history of popular music, and he retained a tireless appetite for the business and all its attendant glamor. "Ahmet was a man of stories and adventures," Page told me. "A real party animal, and he was passionate about music."

Ertegun quickly identified where the power was. He indulged the band and their manager and wasn't afraid to lock horns when necessary. Grant and Ertegun would argue frequently, but Grant always respected him. "Ahmet was the finest record man of all time, and every time we negotiated and he said, 'Peter, shake on it,' you knew it was done."

Like many of Grant's close friends and colleagues, Ertegun quickly acquired a nickname. "Dad always called him 'Omelette,'" says Helen. Soon after, Ertegun presented Grant with a gift: a necklace decorated with Peter's Aries star sign.

"Peter was very good at relationships," says Phil Carson. "The rough diamond approach worked really well with my boss Ahmet. He got Peter, and Peter got Ahmet, and they became very good friends."

News of Grant's boardroom maneuvres spread quickly. Clive Davis had been shocked when Zeppelin didn't sign with Epic. Island Records boss Chris Blackwell, whose office had been on the first floor at 155 Oxford Street, said he and Grant had even shaken on a deal. Later, Blackwell, who went on to sign Bob Marley and the Wailers and U2, insisted he was glad Grant broke his promise, saying Zeppelin's music and aura was "too dark" for Island.

However, Grant hadn't been alone in these negotiations. He'd used his American lawyer, Steve Weiss. Grant told Mark Long he'd first come up against Weiss in a legal skirmish involving the Animals and their double set of contracts. "Peter said Weiss threatened him and said he'd never work in the States again, so a settlement was arrived at." When Grant and Page put Zeppelin together, Grant realized he needed a good attorney and called Weiss, who by then listed Jimi Hendrix, Herman's Hermits, and Vanilla Fudge among his clients.

"Steve [Weiss] was an excellent attorney and a very important person in my life," says Harvey Lisberg, manager of Herman's Hermits. "Whether he was entirely straight or not depends on who you talk to."

Stevens H. Weiss died in 2008. Like Grant, he had an intriguing history. There were many stories: how he'd supposedly dated Marilyn Monroe, how he'd brokered a controversial grain deal between the United States and the Soviet Union, how he was chauffeured around in a purple Rolls-Royce, and how he'd reputedly worked for mob accountant Meyer Lansky. Many suggested Weiss was similarly connected.

"I don't think he was a mafia lawyer," says Lisberg, "but he certainly knew people in that realm."

"Our manager, Phil Basille [who died in 1996], was mob connected, and Steve was Phil's attorney," explains Vanilla Fudge's ex-drummer Carmine Appice.

Basille ran several East Coast venues, including a Long Island club called the Action House, which regularly hosted Vanilla Fudge and other rock groups. When one of New York's Mafia families tried to claim protection money from Basille, Weiss sat down with the family and negotiated a reduced percentage. "From 5 percent to 1," says Appice.

Henry Smith remembers checking into a New York hotel with the Yardbirds and waking the next morning to discover the truck with all their equipment had been stolen. "I called Steve's office, and by lunchtime the truck had
been returned," he says. "Steve Weiss knew everyone."

"Steve was Peter's *consigliere*—as the Italians say," offers music manager
and ex–Swan Song employee Mitchell Fox. "He was very well placed in terms
of Warners' corporate hierarchy. He had access to those people two tiers
above Ahmet Ertegun. He went to the *very* top."

In the years ahead, Weiss would often be seen in photographs taken at
record company parties, rarely standing more than 2 feet away from the talent and sometimes dressed as much like a rock star as they were. In *The Song
Remains the Same* movie, when Grant is seen arguing backstage, Weiss is
there, silently observing from behind dark glasses.

*P*eter Grant spent Christmas Day of 1968 with his family. Page, Plant, and
Bonham spent it in bungalows at the Chateau Marmont Hotel in Los
Angeles. Led Zeppelin had a gig to play in Denver on December 26—the first
of a twelve-date American tour. Grant had been dreading telling them about
this tour since October. "It was one of the few times I never went, and I re-
gretted it so much I thought, 'I'm never going to not go with them again.'"

Richard Cole went in his place. Cole had been touring America with Vanilla Fudge and more recently, Terry Reid. Cole collected Plant and Bonham
up from the airport on Christmas Eve, where they surveyed their new alien
surroundings. "It was the first time I saw a cop with a gun and the first time I
saw a 20-foot car," admitted Plant.

"They were both rather sweet," remembers Cole, who had Christmas dinner with a girlfriend in Laurel Canyon, leaving Bonham and Plant to fend for
themselves. By the end of the day, a delegation of LA's beautiful people, its
scenesters, and Sunset Strip party girls had found their way to the Chateau
Marmont to meet what Atlantic Records was calling "the hot new English
group."

John Paul Jones arrived in time for Zeppelin's first American gig—an un-
billed slot at the Denver Auditorium, opening for heavy psychedelic rockers
Vanilla Fudge. Promoter Barry Fey had to be persuaded to put them on the
bill. It it didn't hurt that Zeppelin and Vanilla Fudge shared the same
lawyer.

"I'd love to say it was a life-changing event, but it wasn't," says Carmine
Appice. "Robert Plant stood very still on stage. I remember saying to him

later, 'You should move a bit more.' But you could tell there was something there."

It would only get better, and quickly. "You could tell by the fourth night, in Portland," says Cole. "I'd never heard anything like the drummer, and I suddenly thought, 'OK, this is going to be enormous.'" Cole had spent the past year hopping between bands and tours. "And I'd had enough. As soon as Peter turned up, I asked for a full-time job with Zeppelin. And that was it from then onward."

Grant arrived in time for January's four-night stand at San Francisco's Fillmore West, the nexus of the West Coast's underground scene: "I said to the band, if you don't crack San Francisco, you can go home." Zeppelin opened for local heroes Country Joe and the Fish, but the headliners' ramshackle folk-rock couldn't withstand the assault.

The message was driven home when Zeppelin's self-titled debut arrived at the end of the Fillmore run. The cover, which so upset Countess Eva Von Zeppelin, showed an eerie monochrome image of the Hindenburg airship going down in flames. The picture matched the music.

Songs such as "Dazed and Confused," "Babe I'm Gonna Leave You," and "Communication Breakdown" were a masterclass in drama and dynamics. There were few restrictions, and Page encouraged every band member to show their true musical personality. For Bonham, whose drumming was considered too forceful by some, the freedom was unprecedented.

Atlantic had distributed a few hundred white-label copies to key DJs and writers, and by the end of the tour the album had cracked the Billboard top ten and sold five hundred thousand copies. It would go Gold by the summer.

Two weeks after San Francisco, Led Zeppelin played for four hours at the Boston Tea Party, bumping up their set with Beatles and Who covers, after the audience wouldn't let them leave. It was a pivotal moment when everybody, including Grant, realized they'd made a breakthrough.

"Peter was absolutely ecstatic," remembered John Paul Jones. "He was crying—if you can imagine that—and hugging us all. You know, with this huge grizzly bear hug. I suppose it was then we realized just what Led Zeppelin was going to become."

By the time they reached the East Coast at the end of January, Grant could start making demands. Peter and the Fillmore manager Bill Graham would fall out badly in the late seventies. In 1969, the relationship was cordial, if cautious. "Bill didn't like the Yardbirds," claimed Grant, "because Jeff Beck kept walking out." Graham agreed to put this latest version on at his new New York venue, the Fillmore East.

Zeppelin were booked to open for Iron Butterfly, an American group, which, like Vanilla Fudge, played what critics were calling "heavy rock." The same description was soon being used for Led Zeppelin.

Grant approached the Fillmore East dates like a wrestler preparing for a championship brawl: "I knew they could nail Iron Butterfly's arse well and truly into the ground. So, I said to Bill, 'We're not going to open.'"

It was a remarkable display of bravado. Graham did as he was asked and booked another act—country-blues duo Delaney & Bonnie—putting Zeppelin second on the bill. And still the headliners ran scared. "When Iron Butterfly's management found out, they wanted Zeppelin off the bill," Grant said. "They didn't want us near them."

"Peter was so committed to what we did," Plant told me. "His tough guy image came out of there being so many cowboys around and the way musicians were taken advantage of. Peter just bluffed everybody out."

Grant relished the competition, believing headline acts were there to be toppled. But while he'd never forget the victories, he could never forgive the slights. Weeks later, *Rolling Stone*, America's new taste-making music magazine, gave Zeppelin's debut a critical mauling, with writer John Mendelssohn suggesting it "offers little its twin, the Jeff Beck Group, didn't say as well or better three months ago."

That particular comment stung. Grant had played Jeff Beck an acetate of the Zeppelin album, unaware it contained a cover of the blues song "You Shook Me," a track also featured on *Truth*. "I thought, 'Oh, this is a great tribute to us. OK, now where's the album?'" Beck recalled. "And Peter said, 'This *is* the fucking album; you're listening to it.'"

Jimmy Page insisted he'd never heard *Truth* until after Zeppelin had recorded its album: "It was a total freak accident." However, it didn't help that John Paul Jones had played on Beck's version as a session musician, or that Grant would tell anyone who listened that he, rather than Mickie Most, had produced *Truth*.

"When *Truth* was finished, I sent Jimmy a white-label copy," said Grant. "Some time later Jimmy asked me why I hadn't told him that Jeff had done "You Shook Me." This was after Led Zeppelin's version had been recorded. I told him about the white label, and he hadn't even gotten around to hearing it." If it seemed like an oversight on Grant's part, there was another plausible excuse. He hadn't noticed. "*Truth* was the only album I produced," Grant admitted. "I'm not a musician, and I don't profess to know much about music."

The comparisons between the two albums were inevitable. Page and Beck shared the same influences, but as bands, Led Zeppelin and the Jeff Beck Group were very different beasts. Grant and Page had already generated an "us-versus-them" attitude toward the outside world. There was no such spirit in Beck's group.

Furthermore, while Peter Grant sold himself as the artists' champion, he still observed a pecking order. However much Grant defended Rod Stewart, the feeling wasn't mutual. "Jeff was well looked after, and the band was totally ignored," complained Stewart. "I remember [Ron Wood] Woody and I having to scrounge around Peter and Mickie Most's office to see an accountant, who would make us wait five or six hours to get paid."

Beck was a gifted musician, but by his own admission he wasn't a band leader like Jimmy Page. He was also envious of Led Zeppelin's rhythm section. In February, Beck asked Grant to fire Ron Wood and Mickey Waller.

Richard Cole, their then road manager, remembers the call. "They got in this Australian bass player who did the gig in bare feet," he recalls. "He was terrible, and they had to get Ronnie back. Of course, he said 'Fuck you. I want twice as much money.'"

"I loved hearing Peter Grant squirm," admitted Wood, who insists Grant also offered him a job with the New Yardbirds. "I said, 'I'm not joining this fucking bunch of farmers.' And they became Led Zeppelin. Not my scene at all."

*A*t home, Led Zeppelin's album had attracted positive reviews and gone top ten, but there was still suspicion in the industry that they couldn't live up to Atlantic's astronomical advance. Zeppelin polarized opinion. For a time, Grant hid the press cuttings from Robert Plant when critics made scathing comments about his voice ("Plant sings notes that only a dog can hear"). Ron Wood wasn't the only musician unimpressed. Glyn Johns played a test pressing of the album to George Harrison and Mick Jagger, and neither liked it.

The us-versus-them mentality prevailed, even with those who thought they were close to the group. Soon after Zeppelin landed the deal, Grant told Glyn Johns he wouldn't be getting a royalty as discussed (although Jimmy Page insists a royalty was never agreed to in the first place).

It set a pattern. Several engineers, including Eddie Kramer and Glyn's brother, Andy Johns, would work with Led Zeppelin later. However, Page never wanted a studio technician to become so close they could take any credit for their sound: "I had this idea of what things should sound like, and I didn't want things to be directed from the outside."

The pace at which Led Zeppelin worked throughout 1969 was unforgiving. Back from America in February, the group toured the UK and Europe in March before making a second US visit in April. Zeppelin was now being paid on average $5,000 a night, and Grant still bagged up the cash, just as he'd done in the Gene Vincent era.

The days of private planes were some way off. To save money, Richard Cole had taken advantage of Trans World Airlines' "Discover America" budget promotion, which enabled them to fly at low cost from city to city. "It meant I had to carry a huge book of tickets like a telephone directory," he says.

They traveled with a small crew led by Richard and the late soundman and technician Clive Coulson, a U-Haul truck, and a minibus and slept in Holiday Inns. Even hiring a rental car was difficult, as nobody owned a credit card.

"Peter knew America, and I learned what I knew about America from him," says Cole. "He asked me to do something once, and I said, 'I can't.' And he said, 'You *can't*? There's no such a word in my dictionary.' You found a way to do it. When I look at those tour itineraries now, I think 'How?'"

The band covered thousands of miles by road, experiencing America at its best and worst. They were spat at for having long hair in the Midwest and then feted like kings on the West Coast.

Zeppelin was now playing what Grant called "opinion-making places," such as Miami's Thee Image Club and the Boston Tea Party, on its own terms and for more money. Many venues staged two "houses" a night, but as Zeppelin took a cut of the gate money as part of their fee, Grant insisted the halls were cleared before the second performance, so nobody could watch the next show without paying.

One night, Grant spotted a bootleg ticket seller outside Chicago's Kinetic Playground. "This guy was taking five dollars from the guys in the queue," he recalled. "So, I joined the line, and as I came for my turn, I shouted, 'Gotcha!'" Grant took him back to the dressing room and made him empty his pockets. "We took every last nickel and dime off him."

If Led Zeppelin's music was untamed and unpredictable, so too was the atmosphere around them. In every city, they were met by a welcoming party of dealers, DJs, and wide-eyed, underdressed teenage girls, most of whom were fascinated by the dandyish guitar player and his woolly-headed lead singer. Grant had seen it before when female fans smashed into squeaky-clean heart-throb Brian Hyland's dressing room. But not like this. "There was always that groupie scene in those days," he said. "But things were a lot more innocent."

America's groupies were organized and resourceful. Zeppelin's 1969 US dates introduced them to several retinues of women who'd join them whenever they came to town. Among them were the GTOs (which later stood for Girls Together Outrageously) from LA's Sunset Strip. "I'd heard that Led Zeppelin was really dangerous guys and you'd better stay away from them," said former GTO, now writer, Pamela Des Barres.

Before the tour was over, "Miss Pamela" would become Jimmy Page's LA girlfriend. Ushered into Zeppelin's dressing room before a show, she would later talk of parking herself on "Peter Grant's ample lap," while Page and Plant teased their hair in the mirror before heading onstage.

"There was a certain amount of hedonism that was involved, and why not?" admitted Page. "We were young, and we were growing up."

America's *Life* magazine sent journalist Ellen Sander to cover the last three weeks of the second US tour. Sander never published her story until 1973 when it appeared in her book, *Trips: Rock Lives in the Sixties*.

She described the bleak reality of touring—"Exhaustion, anxiety, release, sex, drugs, traveling"—and in the final scene told of being mauled by two unidentified band/crew members (one of whom was John Bonham). "I fought them off until Peter Grant rescued me, but not before they managed to tear my dress down the back," Sander wrote.

It wouldn't be the last time Grant had to intervene when Bonham misbehaved, or when he worried about a damaging story finding its way into the press. In a bizarre counterpoint, Sander had spent time before the tour with Peter and Gloria. "They treated me with respect, support, and affection," she says now. "They even had me over for dinner, and Peter's wife made the best shepherd's pie I've ever had." It illustrated the schizophrenic nature of Grant's working life: family man and perfect host one day, brawling bodyguard the next.

Back home in June, Led Zeppelin toured the UK including a headline date at the Pop Proms at London's Royal Albert Hall. The Proms compère was Jeff Dexter, to whom Grant had offered the job of "The Twisting Wrestler" seven years earlier. Dexter had seen Zeppelin's earlier rehearsals and was struck by the transformation. "They staggered everybody," he says. "They communicated on stage so much more than many other groups."

With this onstage communication came one-upmanship. *NME* reported on the Pop Proms and noted the dynamic between Page and Plant: "In one way or another they seem to be fighting each other for dominance," they wrote. "Plant employs his voice as a fourth instrument. . . . Page evens the score by using his instrument as an extra voice." *NME*'s observation predicted the tug of war Grant would have to mediate in the decade ahead.

Elsewhere on the tour, Zeppelin's support groups, the Liverpool Scene and Jethro Tull, noticed how the manager preferred to keep his act hidden away. "All the groups met up before the first date in Birmingham," recalls ex–Liverpool Scene guitarist Andy Roberts. "Peter made Zeppelin stay in their dressing room away from the rest of us. His strategy broke down after a few days when Robert stuck his head round our dressing room door. You could tell Peter wanted to create an aura—especially with Jimmy."

The tour was a success, but not every date sold out, and there were gaps in the audience at Bristol Colston Hall: "Peter was extremely pissed off."

Right now, America wanted Led Zeppelin more than Britain did. Grant brought them back to the States for two more tours that year. Starting in July, they played more than forty shows, including festival dates, and notched up thousands of road miles. Faced with the long haul from Salt Lake City to Oregon, Richard Cole remembers giving John Bonham a handful of amphetamines and letting him get behind the wheel.

Grant turned down an offer, though, to play that year's biggest festival. Woodstock was being pitched as "Three Days of Peace and Music" on a stretch of farmland in upstate New York. The event was being filmed and the Who and Hendrix were among those appearing.

Atlantic was shocked by Grant's decision, but he had his reasons. At Woodstock, half a million people descended on a site equipped for a fraction of that number. By Sunday, military helicopters were flying in food and medical supplies. The drama and spectacle dwarfed the music. "I said no, because we'd have just been another band on the bill," Grant explained. Furthermore, most of the bands were performing for free—and that would never do.

On the festival circuit, groups including Vanilla Fudge, which had headlined over Zeppelin a few months earlier, were now playing below them. "I always wondered who would blow us offstage," admits Carmine Appice. Grant, meanwhile, had gone from thinking like a wrestler before a brawl to a boxing coach ordering his fighter to draw blood. "I used to tell them, 'Go in there and tear the place apart, take the roof or canvas off,'" he said. "'I don't want to see you afterward unless you succeed.'"

With so many acts on the festival bills, Grant still had to fight his corner. At the Atlanta International Pop Festival, the hotly touted blues and soul group Blood Sweat & Tears played past its curfew and delayed Zeppelin's set. Grant stood on the stage steps, arms folded, like a scowling English Buddha, and refused to let their crew pass until the band unplugged.

The day after Atlanta, George Wein, promoter of the Newport Jazz festival, cancelled Zeppelin's planned appearance, claiming one of them had taken ill. There'd been gate crashers and violence earlier in the festival, and he worried Zeppelin would incite a further disturbance.

"Nobody ever cancelled because they were ill," stresses Richard Cole. "You had to break a finger or something serious. Zeppelin didn't cancel." Grant and Steve Weiss threatened Wein with legal action, and Zeppelin was reinstated. They finished a late-night set with a version of Little Richard's "Long Tall Sally," while "Mr. Peter" watched dotingly from the wings.

After Newport, Zeppelin acquired a new roadie. Guitarist Joe "Jammer" Wright was traveling around the United States at the time "in a bus full of hippie girls with my 1964 Les Paul, trying to figure out my future." When Clive Coulson fired one of Zeppelin's helpers for being drunk and incapable, Joe took his place.

It gave him his first experience with Peter Grant. Before one gig, John Bonham, who'd been downing Southern Comfort all afternoon, fell asleep over his kit, leaving the band to start the show without him.

"Peter told me to wake him up," says Joe. "'What do you mean, wake him up? He's drunk.' 'I don't fucking care, wake him up now.' I'm shouting 'Bonzo!' and he's growling like Frankenstein. Then Peter says 'Hit him!' I said, 'What? I have your permission to hit him?' So I slapped him."

It had the desired effect, but Bonham then seized the gong hanging beside his kit and threw it at his assailant. "It knocked me off the stage and into Peter. The gong landed on both of us and cut my knuckles—blood everywhere. At which point Peter turns around and says, 'Is he awake *now*?'"

The Jeff Beck Group was also touring the States, off the heels of their second album, *Beck-Ola*. But theirs was not a happy camp. Beck's new drummer, Tony Newman, called a strike over band wages before a headline appearance at New York's Schaefer Beer Festival. Steve Weiss apparently wrote a check to each of the hired hands just to get them onstage. Their days were numbered.

Beck's road manager at the time was the late Don Murfet. After a short stretch in prison in London in the late fifties, Murfet went to work for band leader/agent Vic Lewis, which is when he first met Grant. Peter apparently challenged Murfet backstage at the Edmonton Regal: "He said, 'Who are you? And where do you think you're going?'" In 1966, Don launched a chauffeur service for musicians and actors, later followed by a security company Artistes Services. "And I found myself in the dubious role of becoming Peter's trouble shooter."

On tour in the States, Murfet had a ringside seat when Grant dispensed rough justice at a Beck show in New York. After a tearful fan complained about a man pestering her in the bathroom at the Schenectady Aerodrome, Grant cornered the offender and demonstrated what Murfet called "his celebrated kicking trick"—a volley of blows to the shins that left the "groper" in agony.

Not everyone was treated quite so harshly. Future rock star and Bruce Springsteen guitarist Nils Lofgren followed Beck's group around on the same tour. "I was always trying to get backstage," he admitted, "and Peter Grant was *always* trying to throw me out."

Grant's problem solving didn't always require violence. Beck was playing a show at the Singer Bowl in New York's Flushing Meadows, and Zeppelin had a day off and joined them for an onstage jam. Partway through, a drunken John Bonham decided to undress.

While a nude Bonzo flailed away behind the kit, the police made their way backstage. As soon as the song finished, the crew smuggled Bonham away and locked him in a changing room, where he passed out. It didn't take the police long to find him, and they were determined to make an arrest.

Peter Grant's sudden arrival in the changing room changed everything. "Like a giant mother hen hell-bent on protecting her chicks, he almost took the door off its hinges," Murfet later recalled in his memoir, *Leave It to Me*. After demanding to know who was in charge, Grant introduced himself to the police chief and requested they be left alone.

The chief sent everyone else out of the room. Ten minutes later, Grant and the policeman emerged, the best of friends. Grant had shown what Murfet called "his unique brand of diplomacy" and paid the cops off ("Only $300, Don"). Over the next few years, Murfet watched Grant throw ever-increasing amounts of money at problems to make them go away.

The past twelve months had been a life-changing experience for everyone, including Grant. Robert Plant and John Bonham felt it the most. "Up in the Black Country, we were big fishes in a small pond," admitted Plant. "Suddenly, we were sitting on planes, not knowing which cutlery to use." Bonzo, especially, would get bored, miss home, drink too much, and act up, sometimes with appalling consequences. And he saved his worst behavior for America.

It was when Zeppelin played the Seattle Pop Festival in late July that the most infamous episode in its history took place. Bored and stoned, Richard Cole and his accomplices, Vanilla Fudge's drummer Carmine Appice, and organist Mark Stein, had been joined at their hotel by a teenage groupie remembered only as Jackie.

The Edgewater Inn was on a pier overlooking the Pacific inlet, Puget Sound. Earlier, Cole and John Bonham had gone fishing from the balcony of Bonzo's suite and filled the bath with mud sharks and red snappers. Cole started fooling around with Jackie, while Stein filmed them on his 8mm movie camera. At some point, Cole introduced the head of a dead fish into the girl's vagina. In doing so, a deathless rock legend was born.

"We were in the room when it happened," Plant told me. "In fact, we were invited to bring our wives in to take a look, but after a while we left because it was all a bit unsavory." Not everybody in Led Zeppelin saw the incident, but everybody heard about it.

In 1985, the Led Zeppelin biography, *Hammer of the Gods*, brought the anecdote into the mainstream. "What amazed me is they didn't write about the *octopus*," joked Grant in a later interview. Scriptwriter Barrie Keeffe recalls Peter telling him the story of the groupie and the fish. "He was joking, 'Who needs a vibrator, Barrie, when you've got a shark?'" says Keeffe now. "I also remember thinking, 'How the fuck am I going to dramatize this?' It would have been too much for the filmmakers."

Led Zeppelin's misadventures stoked the mythology, but it wasn't the stories that were selling records. "It's the music that's lasted," insisted Page, years later. "It's not about one stupid incident that happened in Seattle on a day off."

Ellen Sander summarized Zeppelin's appeal at the time. It had been two years since the so-called Summer of Love, and America was still fighting the Vietnam War and seeing young men shipped home in body bags. "These kids sought out a music that represented their desperation, anger, fear, and, more than anything, hope," Sander wrote. On a simpler level, Zeppelin filled a void. It was still the sixties, but they sounded like the new decade had come early. The music was a thrilling combination of sex, noise, and some strange, dark power.

Led Zeppelin II, released in October 1969, had all that and more. It had been recorded on the move between London, New York, and LA, and it bottled the frantic energy of the road. Jerry Wexler was so impressed after hearing a sample, he sent Grant a telegram: "On the strength of these three tracks . . . I would have to say it is the best white blues I have ever heard."

It began with the libidinous "Whole Lotta Love," where Jimmy Page's guitar riff suggested a revving Harley Davidson, and Robert Plant wailed as if

in the throes of orgasm. Meanwhile the rest of *Led Zeppelin II* swung from
similarly carnal blues-rock to fragile love songs and all points in between.

"Peter left the music to Zeppelin, never interfered," says Richard Cole,
"but I remember him playing me the second album and being amazed. We
thought the first album was good, but they'd topped even that."

Grant also couldn't resist playing it to those who hadn't liked Zeppelin a
year earlier. "I thought, 'Fuck, have I got this wrong,'" admits Keith Altham.
"Now I was getting calls from Peter Grant—'What do you think of the band
now, Keith?'"

Agents and fellow managers, including Chris Wright of the Chrysalis
Agency also took Grant's calls. Among Chrysalis's acts were virtuoso
blues-rockers Ten Years After, which had just completed a new album,
Shhhh. . . .

"We believed we had a monster on our hands," said Wright. "My excitement was tempered when I got a call from Peter. He said, 'Colonel, have you
got a minute? I wanna play you something.'"

The Kentucky Fried Chicken franchise had just opened its first London
restaurant, and Grant had decided Wright bore a strong resemblance to its
founder, Colonel Sanders. Wright had a bigger problem, though, than the
"Colonel" nickname. As Grant played him "Whole Lotta Love," Wright's
heart sank. Ten Years After's *Shhhh* . . . didn't stand a chance.

Even *Rolling Stone*'s John Mendelssohn, who'd savaged Zeppelin's debut,
offered tongue-in-cheek praise: "This is one fucking heavyweight album! . . .
I very nearly had my mind blown!"

Led Zeppelin II included a likeness of Peter Grant on its cover. The sleeve
showed a doctored photograph of the German Luftwaffe's Jasta Division, with
the pilots' faces swapped for the band's. Bluesman Blind Willie Jefferson,
Richard Cole, and Grant's heads were also added to the bodies of the surrounding airmen. Mischievously, the face of English actress Glynis Johns of
Mary Poppins fame was also included, as a play on Johns's name. Jimi Hendrix's engineer, Eddie Kramer, had replaced Johns on the new record.

Led Zeppelin II would go on to reach number one in Britain and the
United States, where it deposed the Beatles' *Abbey Road* from the top spot.
Fired up with excitement, Atlantic prepared to release "Whole Lotta Love" as
a single in Britain but hadn't checked with Peter Grant first.

A tlantic Records' Phil Carson and Grant hadn't met face to face for almost
ten years—since Carson was in a Gene Vincent impersonator's backing
band, and Grant dragged the musicians out of their Austin Somerset van.

Since then, Carson had played bass guitar in the Springfields and worked in the music and the food industry.

"I'd been headhunted for a gig with Danish Bacon," he says now, "but I kept getting calls from Atlantic Records." The Ertegun brothers wanted him to head up the company in Europe, and so began his close and sometimes fraught relationship with Peter Grant.

Carson recalls being with Zeppelin and their handlers at a club in Newcastle. The band attracted some unwelcome attention, and a scuffle broke out. "I used to do a Japanese martial art called aikido," Carson says. "So I ended up having a go, and because of that, Peter and Richard went, 'Oh Carson's OK.' Typical Zeppelin. Nothing to do with the fact I was good at running a record company."

Phil's unique role would see him employed by Atlantic *and* becoming Grant and Led Zeppelin's confidante: "What's the saying? Running with the fox and hunting with the hounds?"

The plan almost didn't work. America's FM stations were playing "Whole Lotta Love" regularly, and there was now interest from AM top-forty radio. At five and a half minutes, though, it was deemed too long for mainstream stations. Jerry Greenberg, Atlantic's head of promotions, called Grant and asked if Jimmy Page would consider an edit for radio in America. "Peter said, 'We're not a singles band, we're not interested.' Click," says Greenberg. "But I kept getting the calls from pluggers and top-forty DJs, so I kept calling Peter."

In the end, Greenberg oversaw an edit—excising the instrumental mid-section—and sent it to radio stations for airplay. However, full-length versions were also pressed as singles and gave Led Zeppelin a hit in the United States and other territories around the world. When Atlantic in the UK tried to release the edited version as a single, Carson was summoned to a meeting with Zeppelin's manager.

"Peter said, 'We don't do singles,'" recalls Carson, who'd already had the singles pressed. "And I remember saying, 'I have a strong background in marketing. I know what I'm talking about.' Peter said, 'You don't fucking know enough.' It was very daggers drawn."

The two men argued back and forth, both convinced they were right, but there would be only one victor. "Eventually I got a telex from Ahmet saying, 'Back off, withdraw all the singles now,'" says Carson. "And I did as I was told."

Atlantic was astonished at the missed opportunity, but Grant's refusal to release singles in the UK added to Zeppelin's precious mystique. Furthermore, if British audiences wanted to hear "Whole Lotta Love," they had to buy the album.

The song still became a hit months later, when Mickie Most and Alexis Korner's studio project, CCS, released an instrumental version as a single. It was then licensed to BBCTV's *Top of the Pops* and became its theme tune throughout the 1970s and beyond. Led Zeppelin let someone else have the "hit" but pocketed the royalties.

Despite initially butting heads, Grant and Phil Carson became friends. "Peter had a house on Beulah Hill not far from my old school. He was with Gloria—and Helen and Warren were tiny kids—and we'd just hang out. Those first few years were great fun."

"I learned straight away how Zeppelin worked," he adds. "Peter and Jimmy were joined at the hip. Peter always agreed things with Jimmy, first, and then told the rest of them. Nobody gave them any argument because the success was so incredible."

Their strategy of doggedly touring America had succeeded. By the end of 1969, Led Zeppelin had earned more than $5 million from touring America alone.

"Jimmy had money, he'd been in the Yardbirds," points out Carson, "and Jonesy had made some as an arranger and session musician. But Robert and Bonzo had never seen cash flow like it."

When Bonham joined the New Yardbirds, he'd been living with Pat and Jason in a caravan in his parents' back garden. Within a year, they'd moved into a flat in Dudley, and Bonzo was tooling around the Midlands in a XK 150 Jaguar. For Peter Grant, too, the days of stealing milk bottles off doorsteps were long gone.

Wee Willie Harris's ex-guitarist Derek Berman was on Shaftesbury Avenue one day, when a Rolls Royce mounted the pavement and stopped right in front of him. "I'd been living overseas and hadn't seen Peter since the early sixties," Berman says. "He recognized me. He jumped out and gave me a big hug. I couldn't believe it was him, *and* he was driving a Rolls."

By 1970, the Rolls was joined by a Jaguar, a Mercedes, and a Ford Capri ("For the wife to do the shopping in," he said). That same year, the Grants moved into a large redbrick house at 15 Rose Walk on a private estate in Purley, Surrey. They lived opposite TV comedian Ronnie Corbett and his family. Peter hung a stuffed black tuna he'd caught in Miami on one wall and built an outdoor swimming pool to go with the house's beautiful Japanese garden.

"Our agent friend Harold Davison was fascinated," remembers Richard Cole. "He'd phone up, and Peter would think it was about some urgent business, but Harold just wanted to ask him a question about his fucking pool."

Davison had known Grant when he was still driving the Everly Brothers and scrabbling around for petrol money. Peter had proved everybody who doubted him wrong. In an interview the following year, Grant revealed he was now "a half-millionaire."

Helen Grant remembers living at Rose Walk as one of the family's happiest times. "It was lovely," she says now. "Unfortunately we wouldn't live there for very long." There was more money to be made, a bigger swimming pool to be built, and an even bigger house to move into.

5

On the Bus or Under the Bus

"My greatest strength as a manager?
Being able to say 'no.'"

—PETER GRANT

*M*ark London's earliest memory of Peter Grant is seeing him throw a bag filled with thousands of English pounds under a pub table. Others have similar memories to those of singer Maggie Bell's old co-manager. The size and style of the bags change, but they're always stuffed with cash and being thrown somewhere: under a table, into the back of a car, or once left—forgotten—in the restroom at London's Dorchester hotel.

The discarded bags could be a metaphor for Grant's early scattershot style of management. After struggling to find a hit act, he'd taken on the New Vaudeville Band, the Yardbirds, Terry Reid, *and* the Jeff Beck Group—unaware Led Zeppelin would overtake them all.

However, by 1970, Reid had found new management, and the Jeff Beck Group had disintegrated. Rod Stewart signed a solo deal and formed the Faces, and Beck tried to put a new outfit together with Carmine Appice and Vanilla Fudge's bass player Tim Bogert.

"We went to London and met Peter Grant, our manager," says Appice. "We hung out in the Speakeasy and were all set to go. Then Jeff had a car crash, and that was it."

The accident put Beck out of action for months. When he went to see Led Zeppelin at the Royal Albert Hall, he was still recuperating and couldn't bear the noise. Beck was also envious of what he saw and heard on stage. "Peter did the right thing and shut me down and went off with Zeppelin," he admitted later.

Grant's remaining clients could only watch Led Zeppelin's rise and hope their manager still had time for them.

Mark London, a songwriter/producer, who'd just co-written Scottish pop star Lulu's big hit, "To Sir With Love," brought Cartoone to Grant in 1967. London had grown up in Canada and the States and was now married to Lulu's manager, Marion Massey.

"Peter was back from the States with the New Vaudeville Band, and we went for lunch in a pub near the RAK office," London says. He noticed Peter was carrying a brown bag, which he casually tossed under a table when they went to the bar. "A couple of hours later, Peter opened the bag, and there were bundles of cash inside. Thousands of pounds—the New Vaudeville Band's tour money—and he'd been walking around with it like it was nothing."

Grant and London launched a company to look after Cartoone, called Color Me Gone. "Nobody worked as hard for an act as Peter did," London recalls. "He was incredibly honorable, and he made me laugh."

Cartoone's debut LP came and went unnoticed, but their guest guitarist Leslie Harvey had his own band, Power, with girlfriend and singer Maggie Bell. Maggie had been working the Scottish ballroom circuit, before teaming up with Leslie, the younger brother of singer Alex Harvey. Power spent a year playing the same military bases in Germany that Grant had toured with Gene Vincent.

Power now performed several nights a week for club owner, John Waterson, in their native Glasgow. Leslie Harvey persuaded Grant and Mark London to make the trip to see them. "They arrived in a big limo with Richard Cole," says Maggie Bell now. "The whole place was buzzing about how these guys were coming from London."

Grant's appearance didn't go unnoticed, and neither did Cole's. "I'll always remember Ricardo was wearing a striped T-shirt, leather trousers, and a leather hat. He looked like a French onion seller," laughs Maggie. The Glaswegians wondered if this was how all London music-biz types dressed.

Grant and London both loved Maggie's soulful voice and offered to manage the band and bring them to London. However, John Waterson believed they were under contract to him and not going anywhere.

"It was a wonderful moment," says Maggie. "Peter sent Richard to get a couple of gin and tonics, and then he walked over to Mr. Waterson, this little Scotsman in a tweed suit and glasses, with the whole club watching. Waterson said, 'You're not going to take my band away, are you?' Peter replied, 'We've already done that; they'll not be back tomorrow. Alright? Have a good life.' And we all went off in the limo and never came back."

Power moved into a house in Hampstead, North London, which the group shared with the cast from the hippie musical *Hair*. They changed their name to Stone the Crows and, in 1970, released two Mark London–produced albums. Sales were sluggish, but it was the beginning of Maggie's enduring friendship with Grant. And, like many women, she quickly saw the other side to the bluff public persona.

"Peter and I would have these conversations about him being illegitimate, because something similar had happened in my family," she says. "Nobody cares now, but it was seen as a terrible sin in those days. Peter had all this going on as a child, but I met his mum who clearly adored him."

Early on, though, Maggie saw how Stone the Crows and Grant's other acts took second place to Jimmy Page. "I watched the beginnings of Led Zeppelin. Jimmy was the shyest man in the world, and he and Peter almost had a father/ son relationship. Peter's thing was, 'Just concentrate on the music, and I will look after everything else.' But looking after everything else was always going to take over his life."

Stone the Crows weren't the only new arrivals at 155 Oxford Street that year. Teenage guitarist and roadie Joe "Jammer" Wright moved to London in late 1969. "I was Peter's little Chicago mascot," Wright says. "Him and Mickie were trying to sell me as this new American guitarist in London."

Joe Jammer put a group together, played sessions, and later joined Maggie Bell's touring band in the seventies. He spent days in the office, watching Grant and his foot soldiers on maneuvres.

"What I got from Peter was a sense of family," he says. "You were either on the bus or *under* the bus. There was also a chain of command there, like you'd see in the military or the mafia. Richard Cole watched how Peter operated and became the nexus of the multijunction mayhem. He saw and heard everything. That Zeppelin organization reminded me of guys I'd seen in Chicago, the kind that would blow your brains out and then offer to pay for the funeral," he adds, laughing.

This mix of crushing intimidation and impeccable manners amused Joe. "They observed the old gangster habits of respecting the 'old dolls,' as they called them in those Frank Sinatra movies. My mum would come to London, and Peter would roll out a red carpet —'How are ya, Mrs. Jammer?' Later, he had a box at the Albert Hall, and when she was in town he'd let her use it *and* send a limo to pick her up. They treated her better than they did me."

At the end of June, the Joe Jammer Band joined headliners Led Zeppelin way down the bill at the Bath Festival of Blues and Progressive Music in Somerset. Grant and Zeppelin had not been idle in the months before. They'd written songs for a third album, toured the UK and Europe, played in Iceland, and returned to America for a blitz of the Midwest and the South.

The three-day Bath festival had Woodstock-style aspirations and a lineup that included Pink Floyd, Jefferson Airplane, and the Byrds. Grant had first met its organizer, Freddy Bannister, when he'd been one of Gene Vincent's promoters.

"Peter always appeared most considerate and charming," said Banister, who was surprised to receive a call one day from Vincent complaining Grant had beaten him up. Peter had apparently intervened when the singer started hitting his long-suffering wife, Margie.

Banister realized Gene's old road manager had come up in the world when he had to pay £20,000 up front for Led Zeppelin's bill-topping Sunday night appearance. In fact, Grant had turned down $200,000 for two dates in New York the same weekend, believing a big UK show was more important. However, he'd leave nothing to chance. After discovering where the stage at Bath was going to be built, he contacted the Met office to find out what time the sun went down. He discovered it was eight o'clock and informed Banister that Led Zeppelin would go on stage only then.

Freddy agreed, but foul weather and huge traffic jams threw the festival's schedule into disarray. When John Paul Jones was delayed getting to the site, Grant had him flown in by helicopter and collected from a nearby field by a cortege of Hell's Angels. "I'd made a contact with the Angels in Cleveland," he claimed. "So we had no bother with them."

With all four of the group in place, Grant waited for the American jazz-rock ensemble the Flock to finish its set. At 7:50 p.m., the Flock was still playing, and Grant later claimed he went onstage to persuade them otherwise.

Zeppelin started late, but Grant's plan still worked. The sun went down slowly behind the stage, at which point he ordered the stage lights to be brought up. It was a simple but dazzlingly effective trick.

Until now, Led Zeppelin had felt like prophets without honor at home. Some 150,000 people watched a thrilling performance, partly lit by Mother Nature. "The pitch of excitement they achieved was frightening," gushed the reviewer from *Disc* magazine. "They did four encores, and they could have played all week."

Three months later, the readers of the music weekly *Melody Maker* voted Zeppelin the "top group" in their annual poll. It was the first time in eight years the Beatles hadn't made number one. "Bath was a turning point," said Grant, who joined the band at the *Melody Maker* awards ceremony in London's Savoy Hotel.

There was no ignoring Grant, as he strode into the Savoy's banqueting suite. Peter had recently told a journalist he could buy clothes only in America. "No style in this country for big men," he huffed. Nevertheless, he'd put his own spin on rock 'n' roll fashion. A drooping moustache trailed over his chin, and while his hairline had beaten a retreat, he'd let the remains grow down to his shoulders. Draped around his neck was an incongruously elegant silk scarf.

"I still think my dad was acting, even when he was managing the band," says Helen Grant. "The clothes, the rings, and the scarves were his regalia." It was the regalia that Peter Grant the man wore when he became Peter Grant the music manager. For a time, the two would become indistinguishable.

While Led Zeppelin was thundering through "Whole Lotta Love" at the Bath Festival, Grant had been underneath the stage. He had spotted bootleggers recording the show and had grabbed the nearest thing at hand. "I threw a bucket of water over the equipment," he recalled, "and then waded in with a fire axe, chopping everything up."

The market for unauthorized live recordings had boomed in the late 1960s, and the more popular Led Zeppelin became, the more demand there was. It was an illegal trade, but many record shops sold bootlegs openly. The maximum fine in the rare event of being charged was £25. For Grant, the bootleggers and their vendors became another enemy to be quashed, especially when Zeppelin returned to America in the summer.

Having gone from clubs to theaters, the band had graduated to 10,000-seat arenas and convention centers, with the fees to match. Zeppelin's next tour culminated in September with a $200,000 payday for a matinee and evening performance at New York's Madison Square Garden. The visit inspired another of Grant's great sayings: any visit to the New York venue was now described as "going in for a quick garden."

Not everyone was welcome at the show, though. Phil Carson was with Grant at the LA Forum, where bootleggers recorded the performance and issued it as the *Live at Blueberry Hill* album.

Grant and Carson tried to stem the tide of bootlegs with legal action. "In Germany the situation is terrible," Grant told *Melody Maker*. "There were attempts to record us at every venue, cables on broomsticks hanging over hall balconies."

Grant took a hands-on approach when he spotted a bootlegger with a machine crouched right in front of the stage. He ripped the spool of tape from the recorder and bundled the culprit out of the venue. Besides the loss of revenue, Grant considered the bootlegs' poor sound quality an affront to Zeppelin's high standards. Tapes were later impounded in Hamburg, and arrests were made. Like Metallica's battle with Napster in the twenty-first century, it was an unwinnable war.

Still, Grant resumed his quest to stop the trade at every turn. He'd become so worried he'd started taking tapes home from the studio at the end of recording sessions, to the annoyance of the band's engineers. He'd also begun personally confiscating bootlegs from record shops. One of his targets was a store in London's Chancery Lane whose manager, Jeffrey Collins, was nicknamed "the Bootleg King."

Grant and Collins were later interviewed for the BBC TV news show *24 Hours*. Collins played down the confrontation, while Grant claimed he walked into his shop and simply demanded the discs. When the BBC's interviewer asked if he wasn't worried about Collins employing "heavies" to deter him, Grant snorted, "Well they don't get much heavier than me, do they?"

In truth, Grant had brought Richard Cole and Mickie Most with him. There was a lot of swearing and finger pointing, until Collins handed over the merchandise. "I threw the records all over the place and made a bit of a mess," said Grant, before smashing a broomstick on the shop's counter and marching out.

There was an absurd punchline to the story, when Collins phoned Grant at RAK just hours later to tell him three men had come into his shop and confiscated Zeppelin's records, and could he find out who they were? Peter and Mickie could hardly contain their laughter. "He obviously didn't know who I was," said Grant. "He called two or three more times, and then someone must have told him."

The BBC had interviewed Grant at home in Rose Walk. Pictured behind him were three original lithographs by the Art Nouveau painter Alphonse Mucha. Those who only knew Grant in his day job were often surprised to discover his passion for art and antiques. It was a hobby he shared with Jimmy Page and one of Page's closest friends, Paul Reeves.

In 1967, Reeves was in what he calls "a psychedelic freakout group" with David Bowie's schoolfriend and bandmate George Underwood, who'd signed to RAK. "Mickie Most didn't think psychedelia would last and wasn't interested in us," says Reeves now. Paul swapped making music for creating clothes for rock stars—including for Led Zeppelin—antique collecting, and interior design.

Reeves was soon joining Page and his manager on antique-buying trips. "The three of us used to drive around in my minivan looking for bargains." Grant had begun by collecting Victoriana and had now moved on to Art Nouveau. The late American dealer Lillian Nassau was the first to spot the trend for Art Deco and Art Nouveau in the early 1970s, and Grant and Page became regulars at her shop on New York's East 57th Street.

"Peter had deeper pockets than I did and ended up with a big collection of original Mucha posters," remembers Reeves. "He also had some fantastic Tiffany chairs." Later his tastes extended to early-English and pre-Raphaelite furniture, including a Louis Majorelle desk and an exquisite Burne-Jones bed. "I'm thinking of starting a bed shop with Jimmy Page," Grant joked in 1970.

Atlantic's Jerry Greenberg also saw a different Peter Grant away from the boys-club atmosphere of the band. Besides the tours, Peter often came to New York on business. "One day he was complaining he never went anywhere," Greenberg says, "only the same restaurants. So I invited him up to my house for dinner."

Grant was delighted to be invited, but Greenberg lived eighty miles away in New Haven, Connecticut. "I said to Ahmet, 'How do I get him there?' He suggested I hire a limo. So I did, and we turned up to meet my now ex-wife and my two girls, who were nine and eleven."

Grant spent a pleasant evening with the Greenbergs, whose daughters thought he looked like a fairy-tale giant. "After he'd left, the girls said, 'Who *was* that?' They were taken aback. Peter was so charming to my family." Greenberg saw a man driven by loyalty and looking for the same trait in others. "Family was important to him. He met mine, and there was an immediate warmth."

*I*n October 1970, a month after the American tour, Grant oversaw the release of *Led Zeppelin III*. It was a collection of music as eclectic as the butterflies and flora depicted in its kaleidoscopic cover art.

Led Zeppelin III was the product of a long bonding exercise. Page and Plant had written much of it in a remote cottage in the Welsh countryside, without electricity or inside plumbing. The deprivation suited them. "It was the first time Jimmy and I really sat down together and got to know each other," said Plant.

One track, "The Immigrant Song," about Vikings pillaging their way around Europe, had a brutal riff, but Grant named the album's ballad "Tangerine" as one of his favorite Zeppelin songs ever. The presence of several acoustic numbers confused those who'd pigeonholed Zeppelin as an ear-bleeding rock band. "When we did the third album, all these people said, 'Well, there's no 'Whole Lotta Love,'" Page told me. "Our approach was to be radically different every time."

"I remember John Bonham coming offstage in New York and asking, 'What's the single gonna be?'" says Jerry Greenberg. "I said, 'John, there's nothing.'"

In fact, Atlantic released "The Immigrant Song" in America, and *Led Zeppelin III* became another number-one hit. But Jerry insists, "It didn't do as well as the first two." Reviews were also mixed. "This album lacks sparkle," claimed *Disc & Music Echo*. "Doesn't Zeppelin care anymore?"

If it was a blow to their confidence, Grant didn't let it show. "I leave the music to the boys. I look after the business," he told the *Daily Mirror's* Don Short. Zeppelin was one of the biggest bands in the world, but they didn't release singles or appear on television, making them an unknown quantity to many newspaper readers. Grant's interview was a PR exercise on their behalf.

Short interviewed Peter just before the album's release and offered a breathless précis of his home life: "Grant runs a Rolls-Royce, lives in a Surrey country mansion, has a pixie-sized wife called Gloria and two tots." It was a rare opportunity for self-publicity, but Grant preferred to talk about "the boys," offering brief descriptions of each one. "John Paul is like a recluse," he explained, "and Jimmy is known as Led Wallet because he's always got a heavy wallet and it stays in his pocket."

Like every interview with Grant, it also mentioned his size ("He weighs 23 stone and his friends joke that when he lies down he looks like a Zeppelin!"). Peter brushed it aside and told the *Mirror* he no longer wore suits and owned just three pairs of trousers: "You don't have to be flash anymore." However, his big appetite and sweet tooth was impacting his health. His mother suffered from diabetes and had now lost a leg to the illness.

Peter's weight could also make everyday life uncomfortable and embarrassing. Clive Coulson's wife, Sherry, first met Grant when Zeppelin played

Hawaii in 1970. She spent the night at the band's resort in Honolulu's Black Point and woke to an extraordinary sight.

"We were in this luxury estate, and there was a VW dune buggy in the driveway," she recalls. "It had tipped over, and I could see a man trapped inside—and it was G." Roadies struggled with the vehicle while Grant swore furiously. "They couldn't get it righted, and G couldn't get out."

That year, Grant checked into Enton Hall—a health farm in Sussex—and shed nearly 30 pounds in two weeks, "with lemon and water, and all that," he divulged. It wouldn't be his last visit or his last battle with the scales.

*I*n spring 1971, Peter still shared an office and a dartboard with Mickie Most, and they still listened to each other's phone calls. One afternoon, Mickie had been astounded to hear Peter turn down $1 million for a Zeppelin show on New Year's Eve. The offer came from an American company that wanted the band to play a concert in West Germany to be broadcast around the United States by satellite. "They said, 'We'll give you half a million dollars,'" Grant recalled. "I said, 'Oh, I dunno'"

Grant contacted the Met office, and someone apparently told him satellite sound could be adversely affected by snowstorms. "Maybe not snowstorms like we think of them, but miles high," Grant explained. Peter said no to the Americans, and then they bumped up their offer to $1 million. Grant still refused. When Peter finally put the phone down, Mickie couldn't believe what he'd just heard.

In his recent BBC interview, Peter had suggested *Live at Blueberry Hill* was created by bootleggers using radio transmitters relaying signals to a recording truck outside the venue. It was nonsense, but with wireless technology in its infancy, few would have challenged him. It was the same with snowstorms in outer space. It was a telling moment in his relationship with Led Zeppelin: even a million dollars couldn't persuade Grant to do anything that might compromise his band. "I'm not really up on that technical stuff," he confessed, "but it's their arses on the line."

Grant had another reason to feel cautious. After *Led Zeppelin III*, critics had found a chink in their armor. "*Melody Maker* and all that lot were saying Zep was getting too big for their boots with their US tours," he admitted. The reality was Grant had helped make Led Zeppelin huge, but the speed at which it happened had caught them all off guard.

Grant's solution was to book a tour of small UK venues and keep ticket prices low. The Marquee club's manager, Jack Barrie, who'd known Grant forever, thought it was a hoax when he took the call. Barrie couldn't believe

Zeppelin wanted to play the Marquee again. "He had to call me back to be convinced," said Peter.

Zeppelin's "Back to the Clubs" tour ran through spring 1971. "We are playing those clubs for exactly the same money as we did in the old days," explained Jimmy Page. "These shows are a thank you to promoters and audiences alike." Among the promoters was Geoff Docherty, who ran venues in Wearside in the north of England. Docherty championed the late-sixties underground scene and had brought Pink Floyd and Jethro Tull to Sunderland's unprepossessing Bay Hotel. In 1969, he'd booked Led Zeppelin for a date, which Grant cancelled when they went to America instead.

Docherty didn't take it lightly and had threatened to sue Grant for breach of contract. "I'll always remember Peter's reply. 'That's your prerogative, but they won't be there,'" he recalls. "After that, he put the phone down." Peter had a new secretary, Carole Brown, whom he'd poached from Don Arden. Carole became used to regular calls from "Geoff in Sunderland," wanting to rebook Led Zeppelin. Grant never returned his calls.

Whenever Docherty visited London on business, he'd stop by the RAK office. Grant was always on tour. Instead, Carole and the other secretaries made Docherty tea and listened sympathetically. While he sat there drinking, he noticed a map of America on the office wall. It was covered with colored pins for the cities on Zeppelin's latest US tour. With each visit, there seemed to be more pins.

Grant finally got in touch, offering Docherty Led Zeppelin on the "Back to the Clubs" tour. Docherty was shocked to hear from him, and traveled down to London on an early morning mail train to finalize the deal. He asked for a signed contract, but Peter said his handshake was enough.

Docherty booked Zeppelin into the Newcastle Mayfair, placed a single ad, and sold all three thousand tickets within two hours. "My fee was 10 percent of a gig that didn't need any promoting," he explains. Docherty sensed his refusal to back down had been a point in his favor with Grant. "In some strange, reciprocal way, I'd gained his respect."

Demand outstripped supply throughout the rest of the tour. Zeppelin was too big for these venues, and, unavoidably, thousands of fans were left disappointed. The music had also grown bigger. It was at Belfast's Ulster Hall in March when Led Zeppelin played "Stairway to Heaven" for the first time. This new song was a long way from "Communication Breakdown" and almost classical in its construction. It condensed every facet of Zeppelin's sound into a little more than eight minutes. It was subtle and loud, intimate and widescreen. "It crystalized the essence of the band," offered Page. "It had everything."

Grant remembered Robert Plant writing "two-thirds of the song's lyrics in the studio while we were recording." Those lyrics would be subject to wild conspiracy theories and rumors into the next century. "Stairway to Heaven" would become Led Zeppelin's biggest song and sounded like it meant *something*. What that was would always be open to speculation.

Grant pleaded musical ignorance, but the old showbiz carny in him recognized the song's importance. Phil Carson remembers Peter approaching the group after a few dates. "He said, 'You've really got to shut up after this song, Jimmy. Don't check your guitar tuning. . . . Bonzo, don't hit the snare drum.'" Grant thought if the band treated "Stairway to Heaven" with hymn-like reverence, the audience would as well. It worked.

Northern Ireland was riven with civil unrest at the time, but Belfast wasn't the only city marred by violence. The disturbance Zeppelin encountered in Italy that summer set the tone for the next few months. It was Grant's first visit to the country since touring with Wee Willie Harris. "I knew what a dodgy place it could be," he said, "so I got all the money up front and made sure we got the air tickets back in advance."

Zeppelin was headlining a government-sponsored festival in Milan. As soon as they drove into the Vigorelli Stadium, they knew something was amiss. "We noticed the whole militia was out," said Page. It had been a long, punishingly hot day for the fifteen thousand inside the arena, while a crowd of ticketless fans were creating a disturbance outside. By the time Zeppelin came on stage, the police were fractious and on edge. Plant pleaded with everybody to "Cool it," but when people stood up and danced, the cops threw canisters of tear gas.

The atmosphere grew worse when the police were pelted with bottles. Clouds of smoke soon enveloped the stage, and the band, their eyes streaming, staggered into the wings. "We had to flee, and I'm not that good at running," said Grant. "We barricaded ourselves in the medical room and stayed there till it all cooled down." Meanwhile, the crew tried to save the equipment from stampeding fans and a volley of missiles. Bonham's roadie, Mick Hinton, was struck on the head and carried away, bleeding, on a stretcher.

By the time Grant and the band re-emerged, the stadium was strewn with debris. It was the last time Led Zeppelin played Italy. In the 1990s, Grant walked into a bathroom at London's Café Royal and spotted the show's promoter at one of the urinals. "This guy saw me and pissed all down himself because he thought I was going to have him, but you can't account for the actions of the Italian police."

Milan was a turning point. What Mickie Most had dismissively called "the underground thing" had become a vast, money-spinning enterprise. Zeppelin's artistic credibility discounted singles and appearing on *Top of the Pops*, but the fiscal rewards discounted the notion that they were still an underground group.

The riot also brought home the harsh new reality of touring life. If the "Back to the Clubs" tour had proved anything, it was that Led Zeppelin couldn't go back. They were too big. Meanwhile, the margin for trouble increased exponentially with the size of their audience. Factor in overzealous policemen, unscrupulous promoters overselling tickets, and a smorgasbord of drugs, and it increased even further. Grant and his men were policing audiences five or six times the size of those in 1969.

One month after Italy they flew to Canada to start another North American tour, and Grant walked straight into trouble. Vancouver's Pacific Coliseum ice rink was filled to capacity with nearly eighteen thousand people. Among them was noise pollution officer Mac Nelson, there in an official capacity to monitor decibel levels. Unfortunately, Grant saw him crouched by the stage, holding a microphone, and presumed he was a bootlegger.

Nelson later claimed his noise-measuring equipment was smashed before "four men dragged me upstairs and started to beat me." "I went down and challenged the guy," said Grant. "He wouldn't answer me, so I took him backstage. I threw the piece of equipment down the stairs, and he was about to follow. Then the hall manager intervened, and it turned out he was the environmental health man taking a decibel reading."

Grant later told *Melody Maker* his victim wanted him arrested, but he was able to "smooth it out with the Mounties." This invites the question: How much did Grant pay them? Still, the police were preoccupied with thousands of people outside trying to get into the show. These fans didn't have tickets, but in the end, the promoter gave up and let them in. The gig had become unpoliceable.

There was now a dangerous edge to touring North America. Zeppelin had received a written death threat via a promoter in Chicago, and arena show audiences had a habit of setting off "cherry bomb" firecrackers during gigs, which meant every show was punctuated by what sounded like gunshots. Zeppelin's set now included two acoustic numbers, before which Plant had to ask the audience to "cool it" so they could hear what they were playing.

The drugs, too, had changed. There'd always been dope and acid, and now there were Quaaludes—heavy sedatives that plunged users into a waking torpor. At times it looked like the audience was scattered with zombies, clapping hands as if they were underwater or simply gazing into the middle distance.

In September, the tour reached Madison Square Garden in New York. Grant, refusing to leave anything to chance, hired empty trucks to follow their regular vehicles on the twelve-hundred-mile journey from Miami, in case of a breakdown. There was, but it was one of the emergency trucks that broke down. In the end, there was something fitting about Led Zeppelin following P. T. Barnum's circus into the Garden; some elephants were still in the building when Zeppelin's crew arrived.

In Berkeley, which had been a hotbed of student revolt and the hippie revolution, Plant introduced a new song—"Going to California"—with a toast. "Here's to the days when things were really nice and simple and everything was far out, all the time." There was a bittersweet note to the comment.

Richard Cole admits it was sometimes "too much hassle" to leave the hotel and find a club. It was much easier to bring the party to the band. And everything was available: women, drugs, booze, even British food. In Montreal, having sampled every dish on the hotel menu and drunk their bodyweight in Brandy Alexanders, Grant, Cole and Bonham ordered up plates of egg, chips, and brown sauce. They craved simpler home comforts.

The tour grossed $1 million, but nobody was allowed to stay home for long. A week after the final American show, Zeppelin played its first concert in Japan at Tokyo's Budokan Hall. Something had to give. The pressure-cooker environment of the road had generated tension between band and crew members. The night before the show, Cole and Plant had an argument, and insults and punches were thrown. A hotel concierge witnessed it and called the police. Peter stepped in, telling the cops they were his sons—and, in some ways, they were.

Meanwhile, the tension between Plant and Bonham finally reached breaking point at the venue. According to one insider, Robert could never resist goading the drummer: "Robert was good with words, whereas Bonzo wasn't an especially educated man."

Backstage at the Budokan, Bonham punched Plant in the mouth. The two men were arguing over a debt from the Band of Joy days in 1967. "Robert still owed Bonzo petrol money—but that's just how it was," Grant said.

"It was in between encores at the Budokan," Plant admitted. "We ended up scrapping in this ante area of the gig. Bonzo said, 'Fuck it! You're no good anyway. Just go out there and *look* good.'"

"We had a lot of fun, and we got up to a lot of mischief," Cole explains. "When we fell out, it was soon forgotten." A drunken fracas involving John Bonham on the Japanese bullet train culminated with Richard falling on top of their sleeping manager. "Peter hit me and then fired me."

The Japanese promoter was so disturbed by the incident, he called Ahmet in New York. "Omelette" reassured him Led Zeppelin and its manager hitting each other was nothing to worry about; it happened all the time. The following morning, with sake hangovers kicking in, mumbled apologies were made, and Cole resumed work. However, Grant gave Bonham and Plant an ultimatum: settle their differences or one of them was going home for good.

There was an added pressure to the tour. Led Zeppelin's fourth album should have been in the shops months ago. There were eighty-five thousand advance orders in Britain alone, but there'd been problems with the sound mix and the cover. After Milan, Grant had pitched headlong into an argument with Atlantic over the proposed packaging. The band refused to give the record a title and didn't want their name anywhere on the sleeve. "Names, titles, and things like that do not mean a thing," announced Page loftily.

There was talk of withholding the master tapes unless Atlantic agreed—a smart move, as Zeppelin was now responsible for around 25 percent of the company's total sales. "We had trouble initially, but Ahmet believed in us," Grant explained. "It was a case of following our instincts and knowing the cover would not harm sales." Led Zeppelin's untitled fourth album finally made the stores in November.

As Grant predicted, the absence of the band's name or a title made it only more appealing. The LP's front cover showed a nineteenth-century painting of an old man carrying a bundle of sticks, stuck to the side of a derelict building. The back cover showed an urban street scene. The images depicted the conflict between rural and modern life. And there was more. The inside gatefold was given over to an eerie impression of the Tarot's hermit ("Do you know the Tarot cards?" Page asked a journalist. "Then you know what the hermit means"). Meanwhile the LP's inner sleeve showed four runic symbols, one for each band member.

Zeppelin's latest was soon being referred to as *Led Zeppelin IV* or *Four Symbols*, and it created a problem in some record shops. Store managers would peer at the symbols, especially Page's "Zoso" rune and call the office. "The rack jobbers used to ask, 'How do you pronounce this? Or what language is this? Is this old Arabic or something?' We never let anyone know which symbol represented which member of the group until they came on tour and the symbols were on stage with us."

To Grant's amusement, trade magazines reprinted the runes when the LP sped up the charts to number one in the UK and number two in the United States. "For fifteen dollars a block we had the symbols actually printed in the Billboard and Cashbox charts," he boasted.

The whole package was designed to provoke the listeners' imagination. It was shrewd marketing. However, it wasn't the artwork that sold it. Musically, *Led Zeppelin IV* was the band's most complete work yet. "Black Dog" and "Rock and Roll" had enough brute force for those who just wanted their senses blasted, but there was also a subtle drama in "Going to California" and "The Battle of Evermore."

And then there was "Stairway to Heaven." As if already aware of its status, Page had the song's lyrics transcribed on the inner sleeve. "It was a cynical thing about a woman getting everything she wanted all the time without giving anything back," said Plant at the time, unaware he'd spend the next forty-five years and more being asked what it *really* meant.

"Radio went crazy for the song," remembers Jerry Greenberg. "It was the same situation as with "Whole Lotta Love"—no single. Peter said if people wanted to hear the song, they had to buy the album, and we ended up selling a lot of albums."

"It belonged on the album," stated Grant in 1976. "That was its home. As long as I have any control, it will always be on there, exclusively."

Like its predecessor, *Led Zeppelin IV* had been created partly in rural isolation. The band had rented Headley Grange, a repurposed sixteenth-century poor house in Headley, Hampshire. They discovered the dining hall had a fabulous drum sound, but the house was cold, damp, and haunted. "I was walking up the stairs, and I did see something on the top landing," Page told me. "I remember thinking, 'That's definitely an apparition.' It was like a shrouded, gray lady—a phantasm."

There were also ghosts at Headley Grange for Grant. "It was magic," he said. "I knew the area well because I'd been evacuated there." The old poorhouse was fifteen miles from Charterhouse School and fewer still from where Dorothy had lived during the war. It was the place Peter had spent some of his formative years.

*T*he specter of the Croydon Empire and the Noel Gay Agency loomed over Led Zeppelin's next UK dates in November and December. Among them were two at the Wembley Empire Pool, a venue usually reserved for pantomimes and ice shows. Grant asked Isle of Wight promoter Rikki Farr to stage the gigs. Farr remembered Grant requesting "something magical."

"Electric Magic Featuring Led Zeppelin" co-starred Stone the Crows and several circus acts, including trampolinists, trapeze artists, a plate-spinner (like the ones Grant had seen at the Croydon Empire), and performing pigs. Its promotional poster depicted Zeppelin as medieval minstrels in the style of Marvel comic artist Jack Kirby.

"Electric Magic" was a night of firsts: the first time a rock concert had been staged at the Empire Pool and the first time Zeppelin shared a bill with farm animals. Champion spinner Ollie Gray dropped his plates, and the pigs, dressed in Elizabethan ruffs and policeman's helmets, failed to do much more than leave a horrifying mess backstage. "I turned to Robert and said, 'Don't worry, he's just nervous—it's the first time he's played a big gig,'" remarked Grant.

The contrast between Led Zeppelin with the mysterious runic symbols and these old-time vaudevillian acts grabbed everyone's attention. Twenty thousand tickets sold out for the shows in less than one hour. "Peter was brilliant in how to present the band," said John Paul Jones. "'Don't do this or don't do that. We go here, but we won't go *there*.' That's always how he operated with us."

There were more flashbacks to Grant's past life, as they traveled around the country. "One night we took the Bentley to the army barracks in Kettering, where Peter had done his national service," says Richard Cole. "We drove in, and the guards saw the car and stood to attention. We drove round the whole place, including the hut Peter used to sleep in." It must have seemed like another lifetime to former Lance Corporal Grant.

Like Don Arden before him, Peter's reputation now preceded him wherever Led Zeppelin went. The early part of the tour included dates at Sunderland's Fillmore North and Newcastle City Hall, promoted by Geoff Docherty. After one show, a security guard brought an Alsatian dog into the building to intimidate a few fans loitering on the dance floor.

"Peter shouted, 'Get that fucking dog out of here!'" recalled Docherty. He then asked the security guard to step outside, and they'd settle the matter man to man. Instead, Geoff remembered the guard locking himself in an office and refusing to come out until Grant had left the building.

"Peter learned so much from Don Arden about how to intimidate people," says Laurence Myers. "He used his physicality in the same way." But where Arden believed his artists worked for him, Grant treated his artists with almost touching deference. Peter would trample over anyone and anything to defend his act and, like Arden, would also take great umbrage at any injustice.

Myers watched the rise of Led Zeppelin and Peter Grant's transformation with great interest. "Because of my deal with the RAK companies, there was a brief moment where I had 10 percent of Led Zeppelin," Myers says. "I remember Peter asking me about song publishing when he was putting together the publishing company. That was as far as it went."

Myers was in New York on business when Peter asked him to collect some money for him and bring it back to London. "Peter was always a great believer in the cash economy," he says. "I picked up this big thick envelope from someone—I don't know how much was in it—and took it back to my hotel."

Myers was staying at the Americana in Manhattan. He locked the envelope in one of the deposit boxes behind the hotel reception and went to bed. He woke the next morning to discover he'd lost the key. After an hour searching for it, Myers accepted defeat. "I had to speak to the hotel manager and arranged for an engineer to come in and drill open the box. It cost me a fortune, and I very nearly missed my flight. There was no way I could have gone back, faced Peter Grant and said, 'Sorry I don't have your money.'"

Future Bad Company and Led Zeppelin tour manager Phil Carlo first met Grant when he joined Zeppelin's crew for their winter UK tour. Carlo had shared a flat in Cambridge with Bonzo's aide Mick Hinton, and both men had roadied for a local band. Hinton moved to London and started working for Zeppelin. When they needed another pair of hands, Hinton called his former flatmate. "Mick said, 'We want someone reliable, hardworking, who we can have a laugh with and who can chat up birds.'" recalls Carlo.

Days later, Phil was on his way to Oxford Street, where he was introduced to Zeppelin's manager. "I said, 'Nice to meet you, Mr. Grant.' He said, 'Call me Peter, and this is my assistant Richard Cole.' I said, 'Hello, Richard.'" Cole paused and replied, "You can call *me* Mr. Cole."

Carlo made his Led Zeppelin debut at the St. Matthew's Baths Hall in Ipswich. The novice roadie arrived hours early with two of his friends, a couple of local builders, in tow, "Just in case it got rowdy like we'd heard these pop concerts could."

Once inside, Carlo's first task was to build a stage over the same pool in which he'd won medals in a school swimming competition.

Zeppelin still used a small crew, and each band member had a driver. Carlo quickly identified the chain of command. Grant deferred to Jimmy Page, but when Peter spoke, everybody, including "Mr. Cole," jumped. The whole operation had one purpose: getting Led Zeppelin to the stage.

"Peter had the knack of forming an inner circle. And even in those days it was organized to the point where Peter wanted Zeppelin to do as little as possible," says Carlo. "We sorted out everything. All they had to do was play."

"Peter kept everything else away," concurred John Paul Jones, "so we could just do what we wanted."

In truth, Led Zeppelin was now living in a bubble. Or as Mickie Most said, "They were living in a world where nobody says no to you." Bonham, Jones, and Plant were husbands and fathers, and Page and his girlfriend, French fashion model Charlotte Martin, now had a baby daughter, Scarlet.

They all had home lives, but the band came first. Helen and Warren saw their father's absences as part of that life. "Mum had been in the business and was used to traveling," says Helen. "And that's how it was. We became used to not seeing our dad for weeks."

Even when Grant was home, there were distractions: phone calls from Jimmy Page, promoters, and agents, and then, when America woke up, there were calls from Ahmet Ertegun and Steve Weiss. The Grants would often have holidays with Mickie Most and his family, but Grant was rarely off duty. Days by the pool could easily be disrupted by a phone call, and Peter would have to disappear.

"There were times when he could switch off," remembers Warren Grant. "We had some amazing holidays. I remember going to Cap Estel and getting an Arriva speedboat to the Monaco Grand Prix. Later on, we went shark fishing in Florida. I've still got a certificate for the shark we caught."

"We used to socialize with them a lot in the early days," says Chris Hayes. "Gloria was a good mother and good for Peter. I remember one of Led Zeppelin saying to him, 'You know, Gloria is the best out of all the wives because she doesn't put any pressure on you.'"

There was enough pressure from elsewhere, as the press began printing "Zeppelin to split" rumors. Grant's relationship with the music papers was cautious, but as Zeppelin never appeared on TV and was rarely played on daytime radio, the printed word was king.

While Grant didn't want Zeppelin to become too accessible, he understood the power of the press. Favored journalists would often be summoned to the Golden Egg café on Oxford Street, where Grant would turn up, chaperoning Plant or Bonham like a parent taking their kids to school. Here, the rock stars would hold court to a backdrop of scraping plates and rattling cutlery.

Zeppelin had a publicist named Bill Harry, whom Grant hired when he took on the New Vaudeville Band. Harry was an ex-journalist who'd been to school with John Lennon. Conveniently, he also had an office at 155 Oxford Street. "With Led Zeppelin, I was often there to keep the press away," Harry said in 2009. "The band was fine, but it was everything around them that could be a problem."

Those problems now included their drummer's wrecking sprees and punch-ups in Tokyo. When *Melody Maker* heard about the fight, Grant agreed to an interview. Both he and Harry regarded *Melody Maker*'s Chris Welch as a safe pair of hands. He'd championed Zeppelin from the beginning.

"Chris was considered *all right*," says Richard Cole. Welch was dispatched to interview Bonham, who stuck to an agreed-upon party line. "The American tour was great. . . . We kept seeing stories, 'Led Zeppelin is breaking up,' but really we have never been closer together," he insisted.

Grant's sense of family and loyalty also extended to the music press. If journalists wrote good things about his band, they were usually treated well. Nick Kent, the *New Musical Express*'s star writer, interviewed Zeppelin several times in the seventies and was considered an ally, "but Peter made it abundantly clear he wouldn't be at all happy if anything negative appeared in my write-ups."

No sooner had Grant quashed the "Zeppelin to split" rumor than another appeared about him taking over management of the progressive rock trio Emerson, Lake & Palmer. *Melody Maker* acknowledged the rumor by running a cartoon that depicted Grant as a corpulent whale with the members of Zeppelin and E.L.P. swilling around in its stomach and a plume of bank notes exploding from its blowhole.

When Grant saw the cartoon, he called the paper's editor, Ray Coleman, and threatened to sue. "If anybody did any small thing against him, Peter would get very hurt," says Chris Hayes. "He could never forget a slight." The culprit, Les Gibbard, moved on soon after and enjoyed a twenty-five-year career as *The Guardian*'s political cartoonist.

When it came to Led Zeppelin, Peter obsessed over every detail, every criticism, and every error. In January 1972, he received a letter from Bernard Chevry, head of the international music trade fair Marché International du Disque et de l'Édition Musicale (MIDEM). Chevry invited "Led Zeppelin and his musicians" to attend MIDEM's annual festival in Cannes.

It said much about Zeppelin's public profile that they could sell millions but still be mistaken for a solo act. Grant ignored the letter and then booked a full-page ad in several trade journals, reproducing it in full under the banner: "Mr. Zeppelin Regrets. . . . " To twist the knife further, the ads ran during the week of the MIDEM festival. "Led Zeppelin and his musicians" did not attend.

Grant dealt with Chevry's *faux pas* by embarrassing him in the press. However, *Melody Maker*'s cartoon had gotten under his skin. It wasn't just the grotesque illustration; he was terrified Jimmy Page would think he was deserting Zeppelin for another group.

"The fundamental thing that drives all managers is fear," says Ed Bicknell. "And it's a fear of being sacked. I had this conversation with Peter many times. Because in the end, every manager gets sacked, and it's not always for anything they've done wrong."

This fear, coupled with Led Zeppelin's box-office power only fueled Grant's imposing public image, but there was another factor. America was the land of opportunity, and Zeppelin had more opportunity than most. They rarely played a show in the United States where an admirer didn't slip them a gift of something to smoke or snort.

Marijuana was illegal, but a generation of musicians would have crashed and burned if it ever became unavailable. Similarly, the chore of getting a band thousands of miles across America became more tolerable with some sort of pick-me-up. In 1969, Richard Cole handed John Bonham a fistful of amphetamines and let him drive the hundred miles from Salt Lake City to the next gig.

By the end of the sixties, cocaine was becoming the drug *du jour* of rock stars and record executives. It wasn't a hippie drug; the high was harder and faster. Coke was darkly glamorous, prohibitively expensive, and soon oiling the wheels of an increasingly monied industry.

"It was a coffee-table drug," Grant said. "If you went to a high-powered movie executive's in Hollywood for dinner, they wouldn't offer you After Eight mints with the coffee. They'd pass around a small bowl of white powder with a straw."

Grant was in America and suffering from a toothache when someone suggested he "try this," and the buzz quickly outweighed the analgesic qualities. Cocaine banished fatigue, boosted confidence, and inflated its user's sense of well being and self-belief. Before long, the drug became a staple of Grant's working day.

Led Zeppelin played Australia and New Zealand for the first time in February 1972. "Warners had a deal with Air India, and we got a round-the-world trip for 500 quid," remembered Grant. Thirty-six hours after leaving

London, they arrived in Perth, where more than eighty thousand people filled the city's Subiaco Oval for Zeppelin's opening night. Hundreds more outside the stadium clashed with the police while trying to scale the perimeter fence.

There were similar scenes a few days later at the Sydney Showground, where thousands of extra people swarmed over the fence, bumping up the official twenty-eight thousand attendance figures. In footage from the show, Grant is seen patrolling the stage, wandering from behind Bonham's drum kit to the wings and back again.

Besides the invasion of ticketless fans, there was another cause for concern. The band had become a target for the police. Just hours after the first date in Perth, the police raided the band's hotel rooms, turning over mattresses and rifling through suitcases and wardrobes. Grant was too jet-lagged to realize. "Don't ask me about the drug bust," he told a journalist in 1994. "I slept through it."

The police left empty-handed, but Zeppelin escaped by luck rather than judgment. Nobody had had a chance to score drugs yet. However, even a fumbled raid brought home how vulnerable the band now was. Grant couldn't afford anyone getting busted. Led Zeppelin had another US tour coming up, and Peter was about to close his most audacious deal yet. Then tragedy struck.

*I*n May, Leslie Harvey, Stone the Crows' lead guitarist and Maggie Bell's partner, died on stage in a freak accident. The band was about to start its set at Swansea's Top Rank Suite. They hadn't played a note, when Harvey touched his guitar and an ungrounded microphone and was electrocuted. "It was as quick as that, as fast as that," says Maggie.

In spite of their loss, Stone the Crows refused to stop. Grant persuaded Fleetwood Mac's reclusive ex-guitarist Peter Green to join temporarily, but he never showed up. Harvey's place was eventually taken by fellow Scot Jimmy McCulloch. Grant wanted to support Stone the Crows and never wanted to let Maggie Bell down. "But Peter didn't have the time to commit to us," she says. "Looking after Led Zeppelin was now a full-time job."

One month after Harvey's death, Led Zeppelin played the first night of their next US tour in Detroit, but there was a major difference. The band was now receiving 90 percent of the door money. In a business where the artist usually took 60 percent at best and the promoter 40, this was a coup and a major blow to the agencies.

At the root of Grant's decision was his bad experience in the early sixties and his bullish sense of fair play. "I would see the money just fall into the hands of the promoter," he said in 1976. "On a tour with, say, Little Richard, the promoters were making more money than the acts were. That always went against my grain. I used to think, 'Why do they put the promoter's name up there? Who the hell is coming to see them?'"

Grant had a hunch Led Zeppelin no longer needed the agencies to advertise their shows. Ahmet Ertegun suggested they call a local radio station to announce the first date of Zeppelin's next tour. They did so, and within two hours, the show had sold out. Two days later, the station announced a second date, and the same happened again.

From now on, only those who accepted the 90/10 split could promote Led Zeppelin. Grant reasoned that 10 percent of Zeppelin was still a huge payday. It was, but there was also professional pride and principles at stake. At the time, New York promoter Frank Barsalona was at the top of the pyramid. Barsalona (who died in 2012) had launched the Premier Talent Agency in 1964 and had nurtured the American careers of The Who, the Yardbirds, and Herman's Hermits. By the early 1970s *Rolling Stone* magazine described him as "the most powerful person in the industry."

However, Barsalona wouldn't budge on the percentage and lost Led Zeppelin. From here on, the band would be represented by the Concerts West agency, headed up by Jerry Weintraub, the manager-turned-agent who'd recently promoted Elvis's first tour, and his partner Tom Hulett. Select promoters including Barry Fey and Bill Graham would still take care of certain cities.

Grant claimed everything was easier, and his profit margins increased with Weintraub involved. "Jerry could get the best deals on the buildings we played," Grant said. "He had the right connections in Washington for visas; he was a politically important, powerful man."

Led Zeppelin's deal with Atlantic and now with America's promoters made them the most powerful act in the industry. While Grant deserved the credit for the 90/10 split, he hadn't done it on his own. In his 2012 memoir, *Backstage Past*, the late Barry Fey recalled the day Grant rang Frank Barsalona to break the bad news. "He was the greatest agent. . . . And they just fired him," he wrote. "Frank was broken-hearted. It was the first time I'd ever seen him cry."

Fey remembered Stevens H. Weiss being on the other end of the line with Grant. By helping row out Barsalona, Weiss had immediately increased his stake in Led Zeppelin. "It's my understanding 90/10 was Steve Weiss's idea, but Peter made it happen," says Phil Carson.

"I think a lot of ideas were created by Steve, but he stood in the shadow of Peter," adds former Swan Song employee Sam Aizer. "I asked Peter about this. G said, 'Fuck those promoters. I'm not giving them 40 percent when we're the ones selling tickets. . . . ' Ninety/ten was a mix of him and Weiss. Steve was the guy who pulled the trigger."

"Peter had the clout of the band, so he could call the shots," explained Jimmy Page. "He didn't like the promoters, he felt they ripped everybody off. He could have done whatever he wanted because Zeppelin had exploded by that point."

By the summer 1972 US tour Led Zeppelin was a musical law unto themselves. At the LA Forum, the concert began with an eerie drone, like a muezzin call to prayer, pumped through the PA. Just as the baffled audience wondered where it was coming from, the band exploded into "The Immigrant Song." They played for two-and-a-half hours, cherry-picking songs from their first four albums and testing material from their unreleased fifth. The musical telepathy was tangible, and Jimmy Page would later describe some of the shows as Led Zeppelin's "artistic peak."

Throughout it all, though, there was one constant: Led Zeppelin's manager and his bag of money. It didn't matter where it was, at some point there'd be Peter Grant carrying his precious holdall. "Peter had a red flight bag in which he used to carry all the concert money," Barry Fey recalled. "Hundreds of thousands in cash." And there was now more than ever.

6

Crackpots in Jamaica

*"I used to be a wrestler, and I was still wrestling
long after I joined the music business."*

—PETER GRANT

*A*t the end of 1972, Peter Grant tried to stage a Led Zeppelin show on the concourse at London's Waterloo Station. "It would have been great—a completely covered hall and very good acoustics," he told *Melody Maker*. Inevitably, British Rail quashed the idea, and Zeppelin played Alexandra Palace instead. Their manager's fascination with the London landmark station endured.

Not long after, Grant spoke to his estate agent, Perry Press, about purchasing the disused Art Deco cinema next to the station's entrance. "Peter thought it was a pretty building," remembers Press. Nothing came of it, but by now Perry was used to finding unusual properties for his client.

Perry Press had launched London's first estate agency for buyers in 1967. His mission was simple: to find properties for busy people in the entertainment industry. "In the early seventies, it was strange how rock 'n' roll musicians moved to the suburbs, thinking they were in the countryside," he says. "My thing became moving people from suburbia to the proper countryside but near enough so they could still get to London."

Press took a proactive approach. He banged on the doors of rural mansions to ask if the owners would consider selling and often reversed his car quickly down the driveway when they objected. However, his approach often worked.

Press would find Plumpton Place and later the Tower House in London's Holland Park for Jimmy Page, as well as a neo-Gothic nunnery in Henley-on-Thames for George Harrison and rural retreats for Eric Clapton, Paul McCartney, and other members of Led Zeppelin. John Paul Jones was now living on the outskirts of Hertfordshire, and Robert Plant and John Bonham acquired farms in the Midlands.

"My first impressions of Peter Grant were unexpected," admits Press. "I have enough snobbishness in me to confess I didn't expect him to have quite such good taste. He was still living at Rose Walk, but he wanted a proper country house with history and charm."

Perry discovered Horselunges Manor, a fifteenth-century property set on 86 acres of farmland in the Sussex village of Hellingly. Its owner, Barbara Doxat, had lived there for many years with her late husband, Edmund. "When I heard it was on the market, I was down there like a shot," Press says. "I loved moated houses, and this one even had a drawbridge."

Among its other features were a secret passageway that had once led from the manor to the parish church opposite, and a 35-foot-long master chamber with a vaulted ceiling and oak beams. "Peter's four-poster bed looked small in there," remembers Press. "You could have lived in that room alone."

Warren remembers their father taking him to see the house and meeting the widow Doxat. Helen is certain he bought the house without telling their mother about it first.

The deal went through, and Grant sold Rose Walk. On the day its new owners arrived, he was running late to catch a plane. Dashing out the door, Peter later claimed he'd told the new occupants he'd mislaid an envelope containing £20,000 cash somewhere in the house, and he hoped they'd have better luck finding it. It was most likely a cruel if brilliant hoax.

Peter had taken his mother to see the manor before they moved in. Grant had bought Dorothy her house in South Norwood, but she hadn't realized how wealthy he was until now. But while Peter was on Zeppelin's 1972 US tour, Dorothy was rushed to the hospital.

"The band told me to go home, but my mother said, 'Don't you dare. You can't desert your duties. The boys need you,'" Grant recalled. Dorothy died the day after Peter returned from the tour. She was just a couple of months shy of her eightieth birthday.

Perry Press says Grant bought Horselunges Manor for £80,000, and paid a further £10,000 for fittings and fixtures, livestock, and farm equipment. Some beautiful furniture was included in the deal, but not everything was so desirable.

"Mrs. Doxat had these stuffed animals and boars' heads," remembers Helen. "Her husband had been a hunter, and a lot of bloody horrible stuff came with the house." Among the artifacts was a huge lion skin rug, complete with head and mane.

Horselunges Manor had a dark history. Thomas Fiennes, a sixteenth-century baron, had shot and killed a servant in the neighboring field and became the first nobleman executed for murdering a commoner. "Two young children had died there, years and years ago," believes Helen. "One of them fell down a well. There was always a vibe at Horselunges. It was a beautiful house, but an angry, melancholy house."

Nevertheless, Helen and Warren enrolled at the local primary school. Peter had a large swimming pool built and, in time, would install closed-circuit TV cameras around the grounds. "After we moved to Horselunges, I realized something important was going on," says Warren. "I'd lived in a big house before, but now we were down in the country in this huge place with a moat round it and all this land."

There would be no going back. By the end of the year, Led Zeppelin's fifth album was close to completion, and Atlantic expected another hit. It was around this time Aubrey Powell came into Grant's life. Known by everyone as "Po," Powell and fellow designer Storm Thorgerson had formed their design agency Hipgnosis in 1968. Operating from a studio on Denmark Street, they created unique artwork for many heavy and progressive rock bands, notably for their childhood friends in Pink Floyd.

Hipgnosis infuriated record companies with their uncompromising stance. Their cover for Floyd's *Atom Heart Mother* LP failed to include a title or the band's name, just a picture of a cow. Still, Po was surprised one day to take a phone call from Jimmy Page, who was asking if Hipgnosis would present ideas for Led Zeppelin's next cover. "He wouldn't give us a title, a lyric, or a clue," Po recalls. "Only that we should meet in the Oxford Street office in two weeks."

Storm and Po arrived at Number 155 to meet Peter for the first time. "Behind the desk was this enormous man with lank hair and a beard, wearing a sports jacket torn at the elbows," says Po, who was struck by the contrast between the exquisite Art Deco sculpture on Peter's desk and its owner.

The band members were also scattered around the room. "Jimmy was by the window, puffing on a cigarette, Robert was welcoming and gracious, John Paul barely said a word, and Bonzo looked as if he'd had a very rough night."

Grant told the visitors Zeppelin's new album was called *Houses of the Holy*. Storm and Po had drawn up several ideas ("on the back of napkins and cigarette packets," admits Po), but two caught the group's attention. The first was inspired by science fiction novelist Arthur C. Clarke's *Childhood's End*: "An image of a naked family, a mother, a father, and two children, crawling up rocks and disappearing into the sky in a ball of flame," explains Po. "The band loved it."

"The second idea involved going to the Plain of Nazca in Peru and carving Jimmy Page's runic symbol into the sand with a bulldozer and photographing it from a helicopter. They loved that idea, too." To Po's astonishment, Grant told them to create whichever image they preferred.

"We weren't used to this laissez-fare attitude. I said, 'Should we talk about budgets?' Peter said, 'Nah, whatever it fucking costs, see the girl outside, she'll give you some money.'" There was just one caveat: Zeppelin was about to tour Japan and needed the artwork when they returned. "'Just get on with it,' Peter said, 'and don't be late.'"

Storm and Po quickly agreed that bulldozing the Plain of Nazca would be problematic, if not impossible. Instead, they traveled to Northern Ireland and created their homage to *Childhood's End* at the Giant's Causeway, a coastal inlet famed for its patterned stepping stones. When bad weather and technical issues delayed the shoot, they missed Grant's deadline.

"Peter phoned us several times being rather threatening," says Po, "and I kept putting him off. In the end, he demanded to see the artwork, and we had no choice." Grant and Page were traveling back to London by train after playing in Birmingham. Po arranged to meet them at St. Pancras station, then drive them to Victoria Station, and show them the artwork before they continued their train journeys home.

Po was already nervous and became even more so when Grant maneuvered himself into the passenger seat of Po's tiny Mini Cooper. "He was so big, I couldn't move the gearstick properly and had to drive the whole way to Victoria in second gear." It was Peter's way of being subtly intimidating.

Once they arrived, Po opened the back of the car, took a deep breath, and presented the proposed artwork. Instead of a naked family as discussed, it showed multiple images of the same boy and girl clambering over the Giants Causeway. It was a striking, otherworldly image. There was a long pause. When Jimmy Page finally smiled, so did Grant.

"Peter said, 'Great, well done.'" At which point, a crowd of onlookers who'd gathered around the car gave Po a round of applause. Jimmy and Peter strode off to catch their trains, Page loping along in last night's stage clothes, and Grant towering over him in his tatty-elbowed jacket. "The crowd parted to let them through," Po recalls. "They were so intimidated by the sight of Peter."

Hipgnosis received several crash courses in Grant's management's style in the months ahead. When Atlantic's printers failed to reproduce the album's hand-tinted artwork to Hipgnosis's standards, Grant sent Po to New York to oversee the process. "I was told to see Ahmet Ertegun, show him the artwork, and tell him what we wanted," he says. When the printing company still couldn't reproduce the colors required, Po stormed out of their office, intending to fly home.

"I called Steve Weiss from the airport and told him I was done. Then Peter phoned and told me to go back. He'd called Ahmet and informed him he wouldn't be getting the new Zeppelin album until the artwork was done properly."

Po suspected the printers hadn't been trying their best, and he was right. When the LP's release was threatened, Ertegun placed a call, and the artwork was printed perfectly. "I realized then if Peter trusted you, he'd give you his unequivocal support," says Po.

Houses of the Holy was the beginning of a long, fruitful relationship between Hipgnosis and Led Zeppelin. However, being admitted to the inner sanctum meant Po's role sometimes went beyond designing album sleeves. In January 1973, Page and Grant sent him to Egypt on a mystical quest.

Led Zeppelin III's run-off grooves had been inscribed with the words, "Do What Thou Wilt, So Mote It Be." It was Jimmy Page's idea to include this abbreviated quote from Aleister Crowley's *The Book of the Law*. Before his death in 1947, Crowley had been a writer, painter, and occultist with a rock star–style ego. Calling himself "The Great Beast, 666," he'd founded a religion, Thelema—essentially a hotchpotch of Indian mysticism, Egyptian myth, and Satanism.

Crowley didn't consider the "devil" an evil force but an agent of freedom and self-expression. At the core of his philosophy was libertarianism: "Do what thou wilt . . . " including plenty of sex, drugs, and alcohol.

It was an attractive credo to a hedonistic rock star. "I do not worship the devil," Jimmy Page told *Rolling Stone*, "but I feel Aleister Crowley is a misunderstood genius." Besides Crowley's libertarianism, Page had also adopted his steely-eyed ambition; Zeppelin's world domination was testament to that.

On Zeppelin's records, Robert Plant's lyrics pinwheeled between sex, love, and hobbits (*The Lord of the Rings* was required reading in hippie circles). Plant had little interest in what he called "that devil stuff." But Page's fascination with Crowley fed Zeppelin's dark aura and the whispered rumor they'd sold their souls in exchange for fame and fortune.

Peter, who was irreligious when he wasn't letting people think he was Jewish, realized it had its drawbacks but was good for business. "Jimmy has an interest in black magic," he said. "But these stories just grew up around us, and we saw no reason to deny them. It helped build a certain mystique."

Grant was greatly amused to hear of the panic at Atlantic's New York office when Jerry Wexler received three esoteric-looking, Tarot-style cards in the post one day. "The staff thought they were having a hex put on them by Jimmy Page," he laughed. The cards turned out to be promotional artwork for a new Ginger Baker album.

However, in 1970 Page had bought Crowley's old home, Boleskine House, at Loch Ness, and was amassing a serious collection of Crowley ephemera, including books, wands, and priestly robes. In 1974, he opened Equinox, a shop specializing in esoteric books, on London's Holland Street. Grant was a shareholder in its parent company.

Also in Page's sights was the Stele of Revealing (sometimes known as the Stele of Ankh-ef-en-Khonsu), a painted, engraved tablet of great significance to Crowley's disciples. The stele was kept in the museum of Cairo. When Page heard Po was going to Egypt, he asked him to try and buy it.

"I called Peter in a panic and said, 'What shall I do? I'm completely out of my depth,'" remembers Po. "Peter said, 'Just try.'" Po was traveling to Egypt to photograph pyramids for Pink Floyd's next album, *The Dark Side of the Moon*. Page was delighted to learn Floyd was paying his airfare so Led Zeppelin didn't have to.

Egypt was preparing for another Arab-Israeli war, and the museum in Cairo was deserted and surrounded by sandbags in case of an air strike. Its director had never heard of Led Zeppelin, but he agreed to give Po a private viewing of the stele.

"He escorted me through a series of underground catacombs, walking by torchlight for what seemed like miles," says Po, "glimpsing dust-covered mummies and gold chariots and other relics. It was very spooky, and like something out of *Raiders of the Lost Ark*. We finally came to a box and opened it up and inside was the Stele of Revealing. I got chills just looking at it."

Po tried to bid for the artifact. "I said, 'How much do you want? Five thousand dollars, ten thousand.' I went up to twenty-five thousand dollars, but the director insisted it wasn't for sale." Eventually, he offered to make Po a plaster cast for $2,000, if Jimmy Page wrote a letter confirming he'd buy it. "I called Peter and told him about the offer. He said, 'Two grand? I'll have to ask Jim.'"

In 1980, Crowley acolyte Kenneth Anger released his film, *Lucifer Rising*, for which Page had composed the soundtrack. The guitarist appeared briefly in the movie, holding, presumably, a replica of the stele. Po's failed bid to buy the original was a rare instance of someone saying no to Led Zeppelin.

*P*eter's relationship with money was complicated. He'd spent most of his first thirty years without any, and now he had more than he'd ever imagined. While he delighted in screwing promoters out of their percentage and paid Zeppelin's road crew poorly, he could still be remarkably generous. Ignoring a budget and letting Hipgnosis pursue their wild ideas was typical.

A few months after Cairo, Po approached Grant with an idea. The longest-ever total eclipse (six minutes and 32 seconds) was due to take place at the end of June. The best place to observe this would be Chinguetti, a Berber town in Northern Mauritania.

"I wanted to photograph the eclipse and thought it would make a good Led Zeppelin album cover," explains Po. "Peter thought it was a great idea and agreed to pay for it, as long as the band owned the pictures."

Po and his team traveled to Mauritania in a military Land Rover, accompanied at various points by Tuareg tribesmen and BBC TV astronomer Patrick Moore. They set up cameras in Chinguetti and finally captured the eclipse.

"I must have taken hundreds of infrared pictures. It looked interesting, but it didn't quite work as an image," he admits. Then Po showed the photographs to Grant and Page. "They loved them, but they were never used for a cover. That was Peter—always open to creative ideas. I think he just liked the crack of it all, the adventure."

The trip cost Grant and Zeppelin £5,000, and the photos were discarded and never seen again. They could afford such indulgences. Peter now had the money to indulge his passions: Po's African expedition and buying vintage cars, antiques, and more property.

"Even after Horselunges, we were still looking at properties," says Perry Press. These included the House of the Northern Gate, a Victorian building in Caithness, boasting some of the finest views in Scotland, and, strangest of all, Hellingly's disused railway station. "Peter went after that, but it was sold off to the local council instead."

In the end, Grant settled on 41 Gloucester Place Mews in London's Marylebone. Peter and Jimmy Page had backed Paul Reeves's fashion boutique, the Universal Witness, since the late sixties. "With the arrogance of youth, I decided I'd had enough of the clothes business by 1973," says Reeves. "Peter said he wanted a place for 'Glo'—as he called Helen and Warren's mum—and would I refurbish it. He said he was too busy on tour and trusted my taste."

Reeves and his design partner, Jon Wealleans, took the commission with one proviso: "That Peter didn't come anywhere near the place while we were doing it." It would take them two years to complete, but Grant stuck to the deal.

Perry Press remembers browsing antique shops with Grant around this time, "And he'd sometimes stop at one of his favorite ones and buy me something." Others who were considered "on the bus" also benefitted from his largesse. "I was in London, and Phil Carson told me I had to call Peter," remembers Jerry Greenberg. "He'd met my family and wanted to return the favor and invited me to dinner at Horselunges."

Greenberg made the journey down to Hellingly, marveling as the regal manor came into view, complete with its moat and drawbridge. "We had a wonderful meal, and then Peter took me outside and showed me a car he'd had refurbished," he recalls. "It was a 1957 Rolls-Royce Silver Cloud, and it had just come back from the shop. I opened the door, and I'll never forget this wonderful smell. I said to him, matter-of-factly, 'Hey, maybe one day I'll own a car like this.' And Peter laughed."

Months later, Greenberg was back in the States when Steve Weiss telephoned him unexpectedly. "He said, 'Go to the dock; there's a shipping container for you.'" Greenberg did as he was asked. And found Grant's Rolls-Royce Silver Cloud, almost ready to drive straight out the crate and onto the street.

"I couldn't believe it," he says. "Peter had given me the car. I was amazed by his generosity. And then my ex-wife took it in our divorce."

Houses of the Holy was released in March 1973. The nudity on the cover upset Bible-Belt America, so Grant arranged for a paper band to be wrapped around the sleeve, obscuring the bare bottoms, "Just to shut Atlantic up." The music inside was a dazzling mix of hard rock and symphonic ballads, as well as funk and reggae. It confused some. "Limp blimp!" declared *Rolling Stone*.

However, neither lukewarm reviews nor naked children harmed sales. Zeppelin's fifth album reached number one in four countries, including Britain and the United States. That same month, the band played Scandinavia and Europe in advance of another US tour. His group might have been the biggest in the world, but at times Grant could have still been on the road with Little Richard.

In Lyon, France, the promoter refused to pay their fee before the show and left Grant standing with an empty hold-all. "Peter didn't trust this guy and told the band to stay at the hotel until we called them," remembers Richard Cole. The promoter was with a girlfriend, but when they walked out of the room, she left a handbag behind. On a hunch, Cole picked it up and found their fee in wads of hundred-franc notes inside. "We pocketed the lot and told the band to come down. The promoter and this woman came back, all smiles, thinking they'd had us over, and then she picked up her bag."

The gig at Lyon's Palais de Sport was a disaster. Hundreds of kids had broken into the venue, bottles were thrown, police and security seemed to be non-existent, and it fell to the crew to try and maintain order. Cole and some of the roadies were arrested later for being drunk and disorderly. "The police locked us all up but got so fed up with us singing songs they threw us *out* the jail."

As the band was catching a train to the next town, Grant had forgotten to give the crew any money before leaving. Cole remembers Mick Hinton frantically dashing down the platform, as the train pulled away. "Peter hung out the window throwing hundred-franc notes at him. Looking back, it was absolute insanity, but somehow it all worked out in the end."

Nothing would be left to chance in America, though. Zeppelin's next US tour began in May and would last three months and gross more than $4 million. Zeppelin was at the peak of their musical careers, but Peter couldn't risk another drug raid, like in Perth, or a repeat of the Milan tear-gassing. His solution was to build an even bigger wall around his group.

With a well-connected lawyer in Steve Weiss and the Concerts West agency on board, everything shifted up a notch. Former cop Bill Dautrich was brought in to manage security and used his contacts to provide a police escort for the band's limousines to and from every show.

Under his direction, Zeppelin was soon so well drilled they could exit the stage and be in the limos and on their way out of the venue within a minute. It was considered a very good getaway if the band was on the *Starship*, enjoying a drink while *still* listening to the sound of the crowd cheering through the security guards' two-way radios.

There would be Grant, Page, and Plant in limo number one; Cole, Bonham, and John Paul Jones in number two; Phil Carson, Steve Weiss, and other record-company minions in the third car. An additional security guard traveled in the front passenger seat of each vehicle. As Robert Plant admitted, "We were now prisoners of our own success."

The show itself was also grander than any Led Zeppelin had staged so far. Grant had been working with the sound company Showco since 1970. Showco provided state-of-the-art PA and had now expanded into lighting and special effects. The tour featured lasers, dry ice, mirrored backdrops, a kaleidoscope of lights, and a gong that burst into flames when Bonham struck it during "Whole Lotta Love."

Not every idea made the final cut. "I once came up with an idea I'd seen from my old stagehand days of using a real fountain behind the set to project the light," Grant said. "We were seriously considering this until we realized it would mean using fifty tons of water."

Very little in Zeppelin's world happened by accident, though. Having spent years keeping the press at arm's length, the band wanted more recognition. "We toured here in summer '72," Plant said. "That was the summer the Stones toured, and we knew we were doing more business than them. So we thought it time people heard something about us other than that we were eating women and throwing the bones out the window." Plant also thought more press would convince his skeptical father his musical career wasn't a waste of time.

The trouble was, the Rolling Stones' tour had attracted high-profile hangers-on such as Andy Warhol and author Truman Capote. "Jagger loved hanging round with princesses," recalls Richard Cole. "Before Springsteen, Zeppelin was the ultimate working man's band in America—and that didn't get written about."

Grant admitted the publicity the Stones generated had shocked him into hiring a publicist for the next US tour. Bill Harry had quit after John Bonham ripped off his trousers in a Soho pub, and been replaced for their recent UK dates by Bernard "B. P." Fallon, a DJ and occasional journalist who'd worked for the Beatles' Apple label.

"The Beep," who described himself as a "vibemaster," looked almost as much like a pop star as his other client, glam-rock elf Marc Bolan. This led to problems when Zeppelin played in Edinburgh. "Beep had the make-up and the glitter on and managed to get himself a good kicking outside the gig," Grant chuckled.

"The Beep" was still on the payroll and spreading his vibes. For America, though, Steve Weiss recommended Solters, Sabinson & Roskin, a PR company whose clients included Frank Sinatra and Barnum & Bailey's Circus. Its founder, Lee Solters, had hired twenty-two-year-old music critic Danny Goldberg to handle their rock 'n' roll clients. The pair flew to Paris to meet Grant during the European tour.

"Peter was not the kind of person I'd expect to see in Paris's Hotel George V," admits Goldberg now. "He was big and intimidating but also charming and gracious. He was nice to us. I'd told Lee beforehand how Zeppelin had a bad rep—that they'd supposedly assaulted a *Life* magazine writer, that people were scared of them.

"Lee, being this blunt, no-bullshit PR guy, said, 'Come on, tell Peter what you told me about how people view the band—like they're barbarians.' I always remember Peter grinning with those big teeth of his and saying, 'Yeah, but we're just *mild* barbarians.' The way he said it showed his humor and put me at ease."

The company landed the contract, and Danny Goldberg joined the US tour. "Where I had a crash course in all things Zeppelin," he says now.

There were nicknames to learn: "Jonesy," "Pagey," "Bonzo," and "Percy," while Grant was known as "G" and cocaine as "Charlie." There was also the private language: a mishmash of dialog from the surreal TV comedy show *Monty Python's Flying Circus*, cockney rhyming, Yiddish slang, and the usual violent expletives.

Then there was the subtle and not so subtle intimidation. Grant and Bonzo had a disconcerting habit of grabbing newcomers by their crotches and asking, "How's yer knob?" Sitting next to Peter in a limo could also be terrifying. "If you were sitting on the right and the car turned right, you had three hundred pounds crushing you," remembers Goldberg. "He knew exactly what he was doing."

The gods smiled on their new PR when Zeppelin played to more than forty-nine thousand people on their opening night in Atlanta, Georgia. Grant described Zeppelin as the biggest thing to happen to the city since *Gone With the Wind*. But he wished someone else had said it. Goldberg called his friend, music critic Lisa Robinson and pleaded with her to publish the quote. She did but credited it to Atlanta's mayor, Sam Massell. The story was picked up everywhere, and Massell never asked for a retraction.

It was a brazen publicity stunt, like the time Grant pretended the Nashville Teens' singer had run off with a local dignitary's daughter. It was also at odds with Zeppelin's rarefied image, but it worked. A day later, Goldberg scored another PR victory after Zeppelin smashed the Beatles' record at Shea Stadium in 1965 by drawing 56,800 to a gig in Tampa and grossing $312,400. Then Steve Weiss called and warned Goldberg never to reveal their gross earnings again: "Weiss implied that it invited the scrutiny of the IRS."

"The thing with Tampa is I didn't tell [the band] how big it was going to be," said Grant later. "When we drew up, Robert was going, 'Fucking hell G, where did these people all come from?' I just said, 'Don't worry, son, I know you're still on probation, but you'll be all right.' I was confident they could handle it. In fact, I knew they would rise to the occasion."

The probationary Robert Plant of 1968 was a distant memory. Plant now strutted across stages wearing a puff-sleeved woman's blouse slashed open to the waist. In fact, the entire band had overhauled its image. Page wore a black suit decorated with shiny moons and stars that made him look like a fey young wizard. Jones was modeling what he described as "a silly jacket with pom poms on," while Bonzo even had a scattering of glitter on his T-shirt.

However, it was Led Zeppelin's plane that truly demonstrated how big they'd become. Their first private aircraft was a nine-seater Falcon jet in 1972. "It was tremendous," said Grant, "but the band had to sit opposite each other all the time. And, of course, there were rows."

"It was supposed to have 'Led Zeppelin' painted on the side," adds Richard Cole. "But the lettering was stuck on with a transfer, and it blew off after we took off."

The Falcon was still being used one year later. Then, after a turbulent flight to LA, Grant, always a nervous flyer, insisted on a bigger plane. During a break in the tour, Cole arranged the hire of a forty-seat Boeing 720B jet, nicknamed the *Starship*, at $30,000 for three weeks. "It was a proper, grown-up plane," Page told me. "We didn't have to bend our heads to go in."

The interior boasted revolving armchairs, a thirty-foot couch, a bar, a fireplace, and an electric organ. There was also a double bedroom. "Yes, I did have first use," admitted Page. "In those days I rather liked the idea of a horizontal takeoff." As a final flourish, the jet's fuselage was spray-painted with the Led Zeppelin logo.

An NBC-TV news crew was allowed on the plane at New York's JFK airport. John Paul Jones was filmed playing "I Do Want to Be Beside the Seaside," while John Bonham sung along lustily, and Robert Plant, sprawled on the thirty-foot couch, and declared it "the best way to travel."

There was great practical value to the *Starship*. "Zeppelin could base themselves pretty much anywhere and just fly out to the gigs," says frequent passenger Phil Carson. However, there was no escaping the fact it also looked impressive.

Grant was delighted when they saw the *Starship* at Chicago's O'Hare Airport parked next to Playboy boss Hugh Hefner's personal jet. "All the press were there, and somebody said, 'Well, how do you think yours compares to Mr. Hefner's plane?'" recalled Grant. "I said, 'It makes his look like a Dinky toy.' Boomph! Headlines everywhere."

All major airports had a designated area for private flyers. The *Starship* would land, taxi to its spot, and be met by the band's limousines. Zeppelin then moved, in convoy, from the plane to the limo to the gig like a self-contained army, and nobody was searched for drugs.

Not everybody on the tour indulged, but Grant did. Peter was a man with big appetites, and this included what he called "the Peruvian marching powder." Sherry Coulson remembers seeing him blithely snorting cocaine from the bag rather than chopping out a line first. "I said, 'G, that's not good, you can't tell how much you're having.' But he wouldn't stop. He seemed to have the constitution of an ox."

"By 1973 cocaine had really started to come into the picture," admits Phil Carson. "By the time Peter moved to Horselunges, it was beginning to take a pretty serious hold of him. I could see the changes."

Grant wasn't alone in all this. "Led Zeppelin was a musician's dream," Page told me, years later. "It was euphoric, and you can't just switch off the adrenalin. For us, the way to wind it down was to go off and party. And before you know where you are, you've missed a night's sleep. Then two weeks later, you've missed a few nights' sleep, because you've been having such a good time."

Page's job was those two-to-three hours on stage. Grant's job was getting him there and keeping anything that might affect him at bay. "I think the thing that pushed Peter into drugs was not just their availability," offers Ed Bicknell, "but this high-wire act all managers are doing where at any minute you think you might fall off."

Danny Goldberg was a ponytailed hippie who preferred spiritual enlightenment to cocaine. He didn't partake in what he calls the "mountain of charlie" and saw how it affected rational thinking. "The threat of violence always seemed to be one bad mood away," he recalls. "I never saw Peter physically hurt anyone, but there was always the terror he might."

On many occasions, it was their surroundings that bore the brunt of the violence instead. John Bonham was homesick and self-medicating with Herculean amounts of coke and booze. "He would go wild if he couldn't get Pat on the phone," Grant told Mark Long. "That would always trigger him off."

Hotel suites would be decimated and TV sets thrown from balconies. It was around this time, Grant had his fabled conversation with a hotel manager. Everybody around him heard a version of the story.

"I heard about it at the time," insists Maggie Bell. "Peter was taking a hotel manager around the rooms to assess the cost of the damages after Zeppelin had stayed there. It was a mess. The manager said, 'This is nothing—the worst people we had in here were the Young Methodists.'"

Grant claimed it happened at Seattle's Edgewater Inn. "Apparently the Methodists didn't just throw out the TV sets and fridges—even the carpets went," he recalled. "I got talking to him more because he admitted he envied us because we could get rid of our frustrations by causing such damage, something that he'd always wanted to do."

Grant led him to his own suite and told him to do his worst. "I said, 'Here you are, have this room on Led Zeppelin.' And he went 'Oh yes!' and enjoyed himself, and it cost me $670."

Like the tale of Grant daring a promoter to shoot him for a thousand dollars, the one about the hotel manager destroying a room on Led Zeppelin's tab became another immortal rock myth.

"Some [stories] were very near the truth, some exaggerated, some underplayed," claimed Grant. "Musicians get up at midday, and the whole day is built up to eight o'clock, when the houselights go off and it's 'Led Zeppelin.' The whole day is a build from the beginning. You're not going to go off at the end of the night and get the Agatha Christies out."

Robert Plant, however, would play down the band's antics in later interviews. "There were just as many nights when nothing happened, and we all went to bed early with a good book," he joked. The trouble was, those weren't the nights anybody wanted to hear about.

Even if the reality was more mundane, Zeppelin's 1973 American tour was filled with episodes that, back to back, suggested one long riotous party. John Bonham celebrated his twenty-fifth birthday with a particularly lively soirée in the Hollywood hills.

Champagne and other substances flowed, George Harrison upended the cake on Bonzo's head, and everybody ended up in the pool. Except for Grant; nobody could or would throw him in. Instead, Peter tried to drive a car into the water. "But it got wedged between two palm trees," he complained.

It was during another party at the Hyatt that the band decided to dress up in drag. "Some girl suggested it would be a trip," said Page. Zeppelin raided their female friends' wardrobes and make-up bags. Bonham made the worst woman, Robert Plant the best in a Chanel dress, mink stole, and a pair of white high heels.

The "some girl" Jimmy Page referred to was fifteen-year-old Lori Mattix, the newest member of the cortege of groupies inhabiting LA's Rainbow Bar and Grill and DJ Rodney Binghenheimer's English Disco. Writer Lisa Robinson remembered Lori and her peers. "Teenage girls dressed in what appeared to be no more than two handkerchiefs, with platform shoes and frizzed-out hair," she wrote.

It was on the 1973 tour when Mattix, who claimed she'd lost her virginity to David Bowie, replaced "Miss Pamela" in twenty-eight-year-old Jimmy Page's affections. "That night we all wound up at the Rainbow, where I got approached by Led Zeppelin's manager, Peter Grant," she said in 2015. "He was scary as hell. He said, 'You're coming with me, young lady.' I wound up in a limo and didn't know where I was going. I felt like I was being kidnapped. I got taken into a room, and there was Jimmy Page. He wore a wide-brimmed hat and held a cane. It was perfect. He mesmerized me. I fell in love instantly."

News of this relationship would have broken the Internet today. But in the insular world of 1970s rock, where the moral compass pointed in all possible directions, nobody said a word.

"I think G accepted the girls as part and parcel of the industry," suggests Phil Carlo. "We all did. He liked them, and they liked him. G used to say, 'They're more honest than half the fucking suits I have to deal with. You can leave them in a hotel room, and they won't nick anything. So make sure they're looked after, make sure they get a drink, and make sure no one takes the piss.'"

Grant told Malcolm McLaren about an incident at the Chateau Marmont Hotel in LA, which summed up the casual attitude of the time. Peter walked into what he believed was an empty hotel room one afternoon to find a naked woman tied to the bed by her wrists and ankles.

"I said, 'Hello, what are you doing in here?' She said, 'I don't know, but guys keep coming in and fucking me.' I said, 'Oh, OK, well, have a nice day.' She seemed entirely happy."

"I found it deeply unsavory," admits Mike Figgis. "With the Me Too campaign and the current climate [of 2018], I'm stunned that rock 'n' roll has thus far escaped unscathed."

Mickie Most joined Grant for some dates on the 1973 tour. During a night of Caligulan excess at the Hyatt, Mickie saw the duality of Grant's life up close. During the party, Peter walked into a bathroom and saw a baby carrier with an infant inside abandoned on the floor.

"Peter took the baby to a quiet room, then went around the party until he'd found the mother and told her, 'Take your baby and yourself and go home,'" said Most. "He thought bringing a child to a party like that was terrible."

While it was Grant's job to keep Zeppelin's misadventures out of the press, it was made more difficult when a film crew joined them for the last week of the tour. Jimmy and Peter had always been wary of Zeppelin appearing on TV. It might damage the mystique. Zeppelin's Royal Albert Hall performance in 1970 had been filmed, but they weren't happy with the results, and it was canned for years.

What would become *The Song Remains the Same* movie began with a conversation in a hotel room. "Someone—I can't remember who—suggested it would be interesting to do a Led Zeppelin film," said Grant. "In order to give ourselves as much control as possible, the four members of the band and I all put in money."

Grant hired American director Joe Massot, a friend of Jimmy's and Charlotte Martin's. Massot had previously directed the psychedelic movie, *Wonderwall*, with its George Harrison soundtrack. "The idea for our film was that people who couldn't see Zeppelin play live could go to the cinema and watch us there," explained Page. "There was this massive demand to see us, and we couldn't always meet it."

It would take three years and two directors before the movie was released. However, Massot and his crew had their cameras running when Grant's men found a bootlegger selling pirate photos inside the Baltimore Civic Center. Grant was filmed questioning an unnamed man, presumed to be the building's manager, and Larry Vaughan, a stage manager from promoters Concerts East.

The encounter, filmed backstage, while Steve Weiss and Mickie Most looked on, defined "Peter Grant" in the minds of Zeppelin's audience for years to come.

"Don't fucking talk to him, it's my bloody act," Grant declares, rising from a chair and moving toward his opponent with surprising speed. "I bet it wouldn't happen in Europe."

"I don't know how the guy got in the building," the building manager replies. "This isn't Europe or England."

"No, I can see that because you're so inefficient."

When the building manager starts addressing Steve Weiss, Grant interrupts, "Talk to me, I'm the manager of the group. You had people inside this building selling posters, and you didn't know anything about it?"

"I didn't know about it. As soon as we found out about it we stopped it."

"As soon as *we* found out about it and told *you*. . . . How much kickback are you getting?"

"None. I knew nothing about it."

"Oh come on. . . . As long as we can screw an extra few bob out of the group."

When Larry Vaughan starts defending his position, Grant finally raises his voice and calls him "a silly cunt."

After more harsh words, Peter folds his arms and declares, "It doesn't matter, as long as there's an extra nickel to be drained by exploiting Led Zeppelin it's great. . . . With the fucking stars and stripes behind it."

Days later, Massot filmed Zeppelin performing at Madison Square Garden. There would be some sleight of hand before the footage made it to the final movie. For decades, though, these scenes of the band performing "Rock and Roll," "Stairway to Heaven," and the rest would be the only readily available moving images of Led Zeppelin.

As musically triumphant as it was, the tour's last week was blighted when Grant's cash economy came under attack. After the penultimate concert, Richard Cole had stashed an amount of cash, quoted as being between $180,000 and $220,000, in a safety deposit box at New York's Drake Hotel.

"Jimmy called me at three in the morning for some money because he wanted to buy a guitar," he recalls now. In Zeppelin's world, neither the time of the call nor the reason were unusual. "I went to the box and got some money out, and the cash was definitely there then."

However, when Cole returned to the box the following evening, the remaining money had disappeared. Richard was the prime suspect, as he'd had the only known key. He pleaded innocent, and to prove it, he agreed to take a lie detector test.

Grant told Zeppelin of the robbery after the show. Back at the Drake, they were besieged by press reporters, and Peter lost his temper with a photographer. "He took a flash and hit the back of my head with his camera. I said, 'Give us your bleedin' film,' so he did, and I threw it in the gutter. And the next day I got arrested."

Joe Massot's crew filmed Grant being driven away in a police car, but, unusually, he wasn't handcuffed. Grant later revealed one of the arresting officers had been in a group who'd once supported the Yardbirds on a college tour. Peter was taken to a communal cell and advised not to speak—so his fellow inmates couldn't hear he was English—and to remove his jewelry.

Steve Weiss made some calls, and Grant was released thirty-five minutes later without charge. However, the entire group was confined to their hotel suites until they'd been questioned in turn by the FBI.

The following day, Danny Goldberg arranged a news conference, in which Grant played the erudite Englishman to perfection. However, the news coverage highlighted how much cash money was sloshing around on a Led Zeppelin tour, something neither Grant nor Weiss wanted to draw attention to.

The money was never recovered, and nobody was ever charged with its theft. "To this day I do not know what happened," insists Cole. However, it didn't go unnoticed that Grant wasn't as perturbed by the loss as some expected him to be. Which suggests, had Zeppelin now become so blasé that $200,000 was considered small change? Or did someone else within the organization take the money? According to Grant at the news conference, Steve Weiss had been with Cole when the cash was deposited.

"Some people in Los Angeles genuinely thought it was something we staged for a bit of drama," Page told me in 2007. "I was led to believe it was one of the night porters, as he had a duplicate key for the safe. Of course, by the time they realized this, he was gone—off to Puerto Rico or somewhere."

Due to the robbery, Led Zeppelin flew home from America a day later than planned. When they collected their luggage at Heathrow, they found it had been searched since checking in. Looking for the missing money, the cops had rifled through suitcases filled with stage clothes and had even taken a pair of John Bonham's platform boots.

Years later, Page was having breakfast in New York with one of Grant's former security guards, Danny Francis, and a mutual friend—an NYPD detective. The conversation turned to the robbery.

"We wanted to know if the police files for the case were still around," says Francis now. "Our detective friend checked and found out they had been moved to a police warehouse. After weeks of searching the warehouse, the folder was eventually found, but it was empty." Somebody had made sure the case was closed for good.

Reunited with their families, everybody now had the task of reacclimatizing to the real world. It wasn't easy. Robert Plant told *NME* he was upset about missing his infant son Karac's first steps. "The kid just stands up and starts strolling around, and here I am in Tuscaloosa or wherever."

Jimmy Page said he'd developed several phobias while he'd been away. "I've become afraid of small places and of heights," he said. "I've also become a little bit paranoid of the motives of other people, but I'm still the same person."

Grant also found it hard to readjust—even more so when he picked up a letter waiting for him at home. "It was from some crackpots in Jamaica," he said, "stating what was in store for us when we toured again."

The message was scrawled in a mix of upper- and lowercase letters on headed notepaper from Kingston's Sheraton Hotel. It read, "Fat PIG, your money means nothing to us—we showed how easy it is to hit you when you are big. Next time you plan a tour in the USA, you better have 1 million dollars available. Since you can't get to us that could be a problem for you. Don't forget you are nothing without your boys. Now you wont [sic] want Robert to loose [sic] his voice or Jimmys [sic] Guitar to blow up. DON'T forget you are dealling [sic] with."

7

The Worst Job I Ever Had

"Peter Grant took us by the hand
and threw us into the stars."

—BAD COMPANY'S PAUL RODGERS

*H*elen Grant always knew when her father needed to be left alone. It was when Peter locked the great chamber. "When you saw this piece of leather string go through the door, it meant it was locked from inside, and the message was 'fuck off,'" she says. "Dad would come back off tour, sleep for two days and then be up and ready to go again."

After they moved to Horselunges, Peter and Gloria socialized with others from the village. "He'd go away and be surrounded by all the craziness and then come back to normality. Their friends weren't all in the music business. Some of them were my friends' parents," remembers Helen.

Peter would spend evenings in the Golden Martlet pub opposite the manor or the White Hart, in neighboring Horsebridge. It was a long way from LA's "Riot House" or the Rainbow Bar & Grill. After last orders, they'd sometimes invite their fellow drinkers back to Horselunges.

"Mum would say, 'Back to ours for sausage and mash,' and most of the pub would arrive," remembers Helen. "My bedroom was above the kitchen.

It would be two in the morning, and I'd hear all these voices and the smells of cooking wafting up."

The Grants regularly threw parties, including a medieval-themed bash, complete with a hog roast and jousters on the lawn. The pub's regulars, the local doctor, and the vicar mixed with Peter's music business friends.

However, when her husband was on tour, Gloria had no intention of simply waiting for him to return. Peter had a space at the side of the house converted into a dance studio. For the next three years, Gloria taught more than 150 pupils.

"She was very successful," says Helen, who was also a talented dancer. "Her pupils would compete in festivals all over the country. Mum needed something to do. No disrespect to the other Zeppelin wives, but she used to say, 'I'm not like them, spending days shopping on Bond Street . . . ' She needed to be busy."

Similarly, Grant's son and daughter became used to seeing his workmates roaming around the manor. "It was normal for Led Zeppelin and the roadies to be at the house," explains Warren Grant. "They were like uncles. We never knew any different. I always had the impression Jimmy and John Bonham were the *ones*. You could tell if they were all in a room together, those two would pair off more with Dad."

After the 1973 US tour, Led Zeppelin wouldn't release an album or tour again for two years. But neither the band nor their manager would remain idle. In the spring of 1974, work resumed on *The Song Remains the Same*.

The band's children would all appear somewhere in the finished film. However, after the death threat, Grant didn't want Helen and Warren involved. "Years later, I asked him, 'How come we're not in it?'" says Warren. "He told me there was stuff going on and didn't want the risk of a kidnapping."

Since shooting Zeppelin at Madison Square Garden, Joe Massot had also filmed "fantasy sequences" for each band member. "A manifestation of our personalities," explained Jimmy Page. It wasn't easy. Massot captured an otherwise reluctant John Bonham drag racing at Santa Pod Raceway in Northamptonshire and with wife, Pat, and son, Jason, on their farm.

John Paul Jones's sequence was an allegory on the conflict between touring and home life. He appeared as a masked marauder terrorizing local villagers before removing his mask and resuming his role as an ordinary husband and father.

Robert Plant and Jimmy Page were more engaged with the project. The singer dressed up as an Arthurian knight and was shown horse riding across a Welsh beach and rescuing a maiden in a tower at Raglan Castle. "It was a bit narcissistic, really," he admitted later.

Jimmy Page's sequence saw him climbing an escarpment outside Bole-skine House under a full moon. At the top of the cliff he was met by himself dressed as a hermit. "It was meant to portray the search for enlightenment," he told me. "And that's all I'm going to say about that."

Early in 1974, Massot assembled a rough cut of the footage and showed it to the band. He claimed Bonham burst out laughing when he saw Page in his hermit guise, while another band member complained Robert Plant's penis was too prominent in his jeans during the concert sequence. Much of the live footage was also unusable. "There were these huge gaps," Page complained. "Sometimes whole vocal verses missing from songs."

It was Grant's job to pull the trigger. He told Massot his services were no longer required and demanded all his film before appointing a replacement. Grant and Page already knew the Australian director Peter Clifton. He'd pre-viously filmed the Rolling Stones and Jimi Hendrix and had tried to use foot-age of Zeppelin at the Royal Albert Hall in his underground music movie, *Sound of the City.*

However, Page disliked the sequence in which Clifton created a montage of his guitars. Clifton was never told this until years later. "Instead, I waited months and months and couldn't get them to sign the contract," said Clifton (who sadly died shortly after being interviewed for this book). "So Led Zep-pelin was dropped from the film."

Clifton had been living in London with his family but was about to return to Sydney for a year. Their suitcases were in the hallway, and Clifton almost didn't pick up when the phone rang. "It was Peter Grant's secretary, Carol Browne," he said. "Then Peter came on the line and said, 'I need to see you today.'" Reluctantly, he agreed to visit Grant that afternoon.

When Clifton arrived at the RAK office, he found Grant and all four of Led Zeppelin waiting. He presumed they wanted to talk about *Sound of the City* and was shocked when they said they wanted him to make a film.

"Peter left me alone with the band in this room with a fridge full of Fos-ter's beer, and we talked for five hours," he said. "John Bonham wasn't inter-ested, but the others were."

Clifton proposed turning *The Song Remains the Same* into the ultimate Led Zeppelin concert movie, with the fantasy sequences in place of traditional interviews or narration. Page agreed, and Grant asked Clifton to produce a script. While his family set up home in Sydney, he checked into London's Churchill Hotel and worked frantically for the next three weeks.

In March 1974, Clifton drove down to Horselunges for the first time. "I gave Peter five copies of the script, and he disappeared inside the house. Gloria, a lovely woman, made me drinks and sandwiches and showed me round the manor, pointing out these amazing antiques."

After an hour, Grant reappeared and walked Clifton out to the garage where he kept his vintage cars: "I had a Bentley S3, which looked rather ignominious next to Peter's magnificent machines." Grant talked him through the finer points of his own car collection before finally telling him they had a deal.

"What I didn't realize until later was Jimmy Page had been hiding in the house all along," he said. "The two of them had read the script together." The secrecy and lack of communication would come to define the project.

Grant signed every page of the screenplay in lieu of a formal contract; a decision Clifton would later regret. Just as with Hipgnosis, Grant wouldn't discuss budgets. Instead, he told Peter to contact Joan Hudson at Zeppelin's accountants. "He said, 'Joan'll give you whatever money you need.'"

Before Clifton left Horselunges, he received an insight into Peter Grant's relationship with Jimmy Page. "Peter told me, 'You're an equal member of the team now. You will get an equal part of this film, but you must remember one thing—Jimmy Page is always the first man in the lifeboat.' Peter loved Gloria and his children, and he loved Jimmy Page. Jimmy always came first."

Months later, Clifton was there when Grant heard Page had injured his finger in a train door, jeopardizing Zeppelin's next American tour. "It was potentially a big problem for the band," he admitted. "But after the call, I don't think I ever saw anyone move so fast, especially a big man like Peter."

Grant understood that Jimmy Page's talent was the foundation on which he'd built his managerial career. However integral the others were, Zeppelin was Page's band, and Peter never wavered in supporting him, but it wasn't always a healthy relationship.

"When Peter wasn't with Jimmy, he was incredibly good company— funny, sarcastic, amusing," said Clifton. "When he was with Jimmy, there was an electricity there. You could almost put your hand out and feel the zap."

Clifton was thrilled to be directing the film but would encounter more hurdles than he'd have considered possible between now and the film's release. To begin with, most of Joe Massot's footage had to be scrapped. "It was all 16mm. We used what he'd shot as a template and reshot the rest at 35mm."

This meant later restaging the Madison Square Garden concert with a secret shoot at Shepperton Film Studios. Clifton was leaving nothing to chance and had hired the esteemed cinematographer Ernie Day, whose credits included *Lawrence of Arabia*, to operate the camera-crane at Shepperton. To ensure continuity, Zeppelin wore the same stage clothes, and Jones, who'd had his hair cut, was persuaded to wear a wig. Massot's and Clifton's footage was woven together. The idea of Zeppelin "faking" a concert went against the grain. "So we didn't shout about the fact," Grant admitted later.

Clifton's storyline now had Led Zeppelin being summoned individually to play in New York, with their fantasy sequences soundtracked by specific songs from the concert.

Peter and Gloria had already been filmed driving around the Sussex countryside in Grant's bright green Bentley Tourer. After reinstating Massot's discarded footage of Peter's backstage argument in Baltimore, Clifton wanted Grant's power reflected elsewhere in the movie.

Clifton knew about Grant's acting past and envisaged an opening sequence with Peter as a Mafia-style don overseeing a "hit" on a group of businessmen. "The promoters, bankers, ticket sellers—the people getting rich off Led Zeppelin."

Peter reluctantly agreed and was later filmed emerging from Horselunges, wearing a zoot suit and fedora. He was flanked by a machine gun–wielding Richard Cole and two henchmen played by a local car mechanic and a hairdresser friend of Richard's.

The hit squad was filmed driving in one of Peter's vintage cars to another country pile, Hammerwood Park. There, Grant watched as Cole and his accomplices ambushed and machine-gunned the scheming "suits."

The scene was loaded with imagery: Nazi swastikas, piles of "readies," a businessman dressed as a werewolf, and another rendered "faceless" by a bank robber's stocking mask. "Nobody got it, of course," said Clifton, "but anyone who saw the film was there for the music, not my wonderful filmmaking."

"The whole point of the bit where Peter plays a gangster was to show how it was just a joke," insisted Jimmy Page. However, the execution scene and Grant's backstage altercation only confirmed what people wanted to believe: that Led Zeppelin's manager was a tyrant and a gangster.

"The thing is, Peter loved having that image," insists Barrie Keeffe. "He told me about how he played up to it in business meetings. Someone would say, 'I don't want you to leave this meeting until you're happy, Peter.' And he'd get up slowly, walk to the boardroom door, fold his arms, and say very quietly, 'Nobody's leaving this meeting, till I'm happy.' He wasn't necessarily serious, but he'd look down at all these 'suits,' as he called them, and they were terrified."

His tactics could also be subtle and even comical. One former Warners executive watched Grant negotiating while lying flat on his back on the boardroom floor. "His huge mountain of a tummy rising up towards the ceiling and his tummy button like a volcanic crater in the middle of it," he recalled. Nobody was threatened or shouted at, but everybody felt slightly uneasy.

"That's why Dad went to a lot of big-shot meetings with a carrier bag," says Helen. "He liked to shock." And there was something shocking about producing great wads of cash from a budget supermarket carrier bag. "Dad used to say, 'When you're using a Marks & Spencer's bag, you know you've cracked it.'"

Grant had put his negotiating skills to good use of late. In October 1973, Led Zeppelin's five-album contract with Atlantic was due to expire. As a condition of staying with Atlantic, Grant requested they be given their own label, and so Swan Song Records was born.

Swan Song would be financed and distributed by Atlantic but with the cachet of being an independent label controlled by Led Zeppelin and its manager. Several bands before Zeppelin had launched their own imprints, most notably the Beatles with Apple.

Grant claimed Zeppelin had been considering its own label since Atlantic messed up some early pressings of *Led Zeppelin II*, "Because they didn't follow Jimmy's precise instructions on the master tape."

Being on Swan Song would allow Led Zeppelin even greater control. "Unlike the Beatles, Led Zeppelin wanted to actually break artists," says Danny Goldberg. The received wisdom was that musicians could spot new talent quicker than record company A&R men, and a rock star's endorsement would sell records.

"It took a long time to get Swan Song together," Grant admitted in 1976. "We couldn't think of a name. Whenever Zeppelin would get together to record a new album, Jimmy had this piece of music he'd wheel out at first rehearsals. Finally somebody said, 'Oh Christ, come on Pagey, that sounds like your swan song.' And that's where the name came from."

Goldberg also remembers Page telling him a swan's dying cry was "one of the most beautiful sounds in the world."

Swan Song's arrival spelled the end of Peter and Mickie's double act at 155 Oxford Street. Their careers had gone in opposite directions: Grant's band was the biggest albums act on the planet, and Most's RAK artists—Suzi Quatro, Hot Chocolate, and Mud—owned the British pop charts. When

Mickie moved to new premises in Mayfair, Grant took over a three-floor townhouse at 484 Kings Road in Chelsea and appointed Carol Browne his office manager.

Kings Road was the hub of London's fashion industry and was dotted with boutiques. The Swan Song headquarters was at the less salubrious end, close to the World End's council estate and a number of pubs often frequented by local villains.

Next to Swan Song was the original hippie clothes shop, Granny Takes a Trip, where drugs could be scored in a back room. Further along was Too Fast to Live Too Young to Die (soon to be renamed SEX), where Svengali Malcolm McLaren and designer Vivienne Westwood sold 1960s leather jackets to tomorrow's punk rockers.

The Swan Song building was owned by the British Legion. Mark London had rented an office there since the late 1960s: "And it was in our contract to let the Legion use our offices once a year to collect the poppies for Remembrance Sunday and count up the money afterward."

Every November, a group of elderly women would arrive loaded with bags of coins and begin their count. Most record company moguls would have resented the intrusion, but Grant liked hard cash and old ladies. "Peter used to make a real fuss of those old girls," remembers Maggie Bell. "He'd have food and drinks brought over for them, whatever they wanted. 'Everything alright, ladies?'"

To run the label properly, Grant needed a second in command. The first person he approached was Phil Carson. "I was going to do it, but Ahmet talked me out of it," he says now. "Ahmet said, 'Don't tie yourself to this thing when you could be running Atlantic,' so I turned Zeppelin down at the last minute."

Grant took it as a personal snub. "It caused a big rift," admits Carson. "I got married that summer, and Zeppelin was meant to come to the wedding. They made a band decision not to—all except Jonesy. It calmed down eventually, but it was tough for a while. After I turned the job down, they got in a slew of people who were clueless."

Grant offered the position to Mark London, who also refused ("I said I didn't think it was going to work out"). After which, Danny Goldberg was approached. Grant flew him to London and had him chauffeured to Horselunges, where he sat downstairs for several hours waiting. Grant finally emerged from the great chamber, clad in a dressing gown, and the meeting lasted ten minutes.

"Peter sold it to me that I was going to be his ambassador in New York," says Goldberg. "I said, 'What does that mean?' He said, 'Do the press for our artists, liaise with Atlantic, the bookers, and promoters.' I said, 'Can I be called vice president? It sounds better than head of publicity.'

"I had a sense of entitlement and arrogance, disproportionate to my real value," he adds. "Peter wasn't remotely threatened by anybody else, so he was happy to let me look important."

Goldberg swapped Solters, Sabinson & Roskin for Swan Song's New York office. Unlike 484 Kings Road, 444 Madison Avenue had a corporate air. "It was in the *Newsweek* building. We had a suite on one floor and shared it with Steve Weiss and his assistant, Shelley Kaye."

It made sense having Grant's attorney nearby. "Steve was considered to be a tough guy who knew other tough guys," says Goldberg. "He had a swagger about him consistent with the way Peter wanted to present himself to the world. When Peter said, 'Jump!' Steve jumped. I heard those phone conversations in the office—'Peter wants what? Oh my God, Peter said, *What*?'"

Goldberg's first project as Swan Song's VP was Maggie Bell's solo album, *Queen of the Night*. Because Page and Grant were still considering names for the label, it was released on Atlantic. "I was employed by a holding company called Culderstead Ltd, until Jimmy came up with the name, which took ages. But we were told to get behind Maggie's record. Peter treated her with tremendous deference and respect."

Queen of the Night was pitched as Maggie Bell's debut album, but she'd already recorded two solo records, one of which was produced by ex-Cream collaborator Felix Pappalardi. Both records had been shelved. "I was told they weren't right by Peter and Mark," she says. "I still have no idea what happened to the tapes. Then Jerry Wexler said he'd produce *Queen of the Night*, which we thought was a fantastic idea."

Wexler had had a pristine track record with Aretha Franklin and Ray Charles. For Maggie's album, he handpicked Atlantic's greatest session players and songs by seasoned writers JJ Cale and John Prine. *Queen of the Night* received glowing reviews and American radio airplay, but it didn't sell as well as expected.

Everybody blamed Wexler's production. "The album lacks balls," Grant later told *Melody Maker*. "It lacks Maggie Bell." "Jerry Wexler made Maggie into an ordinary singer," adds Mark London. "We should have done a rock album."

"Peter and Mark never really knew what to do with me," says Maggie now. "I just wanted to sing and earn a living doing what I loved. Fame never interested me. I didn't want all that madness."

Maggie was at her best when she was performing live, and she toured solidly, opening for Peter Frampton and the Who that year. Grant and London joined her on the road, where it often seemed Peter was at his happiest.

"Mark and Peter were hilarious together. Neither liked flying, so they'd take a couple of Valium to knock themselves out. It would be a nightmare waking them at the other end. Mark had grown up in New York and had that Jewish humor. He and Peter would smoke a couple of spliffs and do these Mel Brooks/Don Rickles comedy routines. We had a lot of fun together."

Grant was careful never to let Maggie see him taking cocaine, though. "My band laughed at me because all I ever did was drink beer. Peter never showed me that side. The Peter I knew liked afternoon tea and buns and scones with jam," she adds, laughing. "I'd go to Horselunges, and we'd sit by the fire, drinking glasses of mead and wondering if the house was haunted. I was the only girl in that world, and I often think he wanted to protect me."

Maggie had seen Peter's sensitive side before, but Danny Goldberg hadn't, until now. Director Brian De Palma's horror-comedy, *Phantom of the Paradise*, was about to be released and included a rock star named Swan and a company called Swan Song.

"The filmmakers contacted Steve Weiss to ask permission to use the company name," says Goldberg. "Peter asked me to come to a private screening and count how many times 'Swan Song' was mentioned to see if they'd violated the trademark."

Of greater importance to Grant was a scene when Swan was electrocuted on stage. "Peter was devastated," says Goldberg. "He was in tears. It reminded him of Les Harvey, and he still felt this residual responsibility. He told us to tell the filmmakers to take the scene out, which they wouldn't, of course, as it wasn't breaking any rules."

As Goldberg spent more time with Grant, he saw more of this other side. "He was a tough guy who could be unpleasant and difficult to people, sometimes because he didn't like the way they looked. But he also had this notion of himself as the protector of artists. Every decision was always about what was best for them. And nothing could shake that."

*I*n June 1974, *Melody Maker*'s Michael Watts interviewed Grant at Horselunges. It was a PR exercise of sorts. Led Zeppelin had just turned down a festival on the grounds of a English stately home, Knebworth House.

Letters poured in to the music press accusing them of neglecting their home country.

In the interview, Peter offered his customary mix of bravado and sensitivity. "If somebody is gonna do something snide to one of my artists, then I'll fucking tread on them without thinking," he declared. Later, though, he discussed being a tour manager during the Don Arden era and seeing "good, good artists" treated poorly. "I said to myself, if I ever become a manager, I would never be like that."

Michael Watts sounded as bemused by Grant as the *Daily Mirror*'s writer Don Short had three years earlier. Here was this big brute of a man (looking "like a bodyguard in a Turkish harem," he suggested) proudly showing off his tapestries and the antique liqueur decanter Jimmy Page had bought him for Christmas.

However, Knebworth wasn't discussed, and Grant mentioned Swan Song's new signing, Bad Company, only in passing. Bad Company's debut album would be the label's first US release.

It was former Zeppelin roadie Clive Coulson who bought the group to Grant's attention. Coulson had quit Zeppelin's crew in 1972 and gone on to tour manage Jeff Beck before former Free singer Paul Rodgers approached him about his new band.

Free's soulful hard rock peaked with the hit single "All Right Now" in 1970. However, their guitarist Paul Kossoff's drug problems soon skewered the music and the band's morale. In the summer of 1973, Rodgers formed Bad Company with ex-Mott the Hoople guitarist Mick Ralphs and former Free drummer Simon Kirke. King Crimson's ex-bass player Boz Burrell joined a few months later.

Rodgers had grown up in the industrial north of England. Being blessed with a rich blues voice was his ticket out of a life in the coal mine or the factory. By his own admission he wasn't a businessman, though. "I remember our manager in Free saying, 'You need to sign a publishing contract.' I said, 'What's a publishing contract?' It hadn't occurred to me I was a songwriter. . . . That's why we needed someone like Peter Grant."

Grant was invited to hear the new band rehearse at Albury village hall in Surrey. "About an hour past his planned arrival time, G walked in," says Simon Kirke. "He apologized profusely, and we asked him if he would like to hear the set, but he said, 'No need.'"

Grant had been sitting outside in his Porsche with Clive Coulson, listening through the open window. "I heard them playing something called 'Can't Get Enough' and knew they had what it took," he said later.

Clive Coulson would handle the band's day-to-day management, and Grant would use his reputation and expertise to negotiate on their behalf and be recognized as their official manager. Coulson then hired Zeppelin's former roadie Phil Carlo to head up Bad Company's road crew.

"Clive put the whole thing together and took a percentage of Peter's management fee," says Carlo. "Peter's attitude was, 'As far as anyone is concerned I am the manager, and people will tremble and do whatever we ask.' And it worked."

Among Grant's first tasks was releasing Mick Ralphs and Paul Rodgers from their previous label, Island Records. Free's manager John Glover says Rodgers asked him to go to war with Island boss Chris Blackwell, but he refused.

"I said, 'I don't mind talking to Chris for you.' Paul said, 'No, I want you to go in and tell him to fuck right off,'" recalls Glover. "I replied, 'I am not the person to do that at this point in time. I have too much respect for Chris. But I know someone who will—Peter Grant.'"

Grant struck a deal with Blackwell, but for the time being Swan Song would have Bad Company in America only. They would be signed to Island in the UK. Nevertheless, Grant took the same approach to the new group as he had with Zeppelin, setting them up with its own publishing company and structuring a business around them.

"Peter said to us, 'You guys make the music, and I'll take care of everything else,'" says Rodgers. It was a familiar mantra. Bad Company started recording its debut album at Headley Grange at the end of 1973. "Peter gave us the opportunity to work as we could only have dreamed about. Complete freedom to play to our heart's content and make as much noise as we liked in this big old haunted mansion in the country."

It was a testimony to the money being generated by Led Zeppelin that Swan Song could celebrate its launch with three lavish parties: in New York, Los Angeles, and later at the UK's Chislehurst Caves.

In May, Swan Song's $10,000 gathering at New York's Four Seasons Hotel was marred only by the organizers being unable to find any swans. Instead, they'd hired a flock of geese and hoped nobody would notice. Everybody noticed, particularly Grant, Plant, and Bonham who lived on farms. Bonzo and Richard Cole later chased two of the hapless birds out of the venue and into the Manhattan traffic with inevitable consequences.

With money and success, though, came jealousy and resentment. A week later, Maggie Bell joined Grant on a flight from New York to Los Angeles for the second gathering at the Hotel Bel-Air. The label's entourage took up most of the first-class cabin. Before take off, Grant popped two Valium and washed them down with champagne.

He woke later to find Maggie being harassed by a very loud, drunk businessman. He wanted to know who these English reprobates were and why they'd been allowed to fly first class.

"This guy was being very obnoxious," she says. "Peter called a stewardess and asked if she could tell him to go back to his seat. Which is when the guy pulls out a gun and starts waving it around."

A pilot and some of the crew overpowered him and confiscated the weapon. The plane was met at LAX by FBI agents, who questioned Peter. He turned up "the Englishness," explaining he was on a business trip with a world-famous singer and this impertinent man had become a nuisance. As Maggie and the others waited to collect their luggage, their would-be assailant was led past them in handcuffs, shouting, "Have a nice day!"

It was a strange start to the trip, and it would get only stranger. At the Hotel Bel-Air party, Grant and Bell were introduced to the now eighty-three-year-old comedian Groucho Marx, who immediately barked at Maggie to "Show us yer tits!" But few celebrity guests, even Marx, could possibly compete with Elvis.

On May 11, Grant and Led Zeppelin attended Presley's concert at the LA Forum. When his band fumbled the intro to "Funny How Time Slips Away," Elvis called a halt. "Wait a minute, wait a minute, hold it," he drawled. "If we could start together fellas, cos we got Led Zeppelin out there." For Grant, there could be no greater endorsement. "Dad loved Elvis and loved that he'd stopped the show for Led Zeppelin," remembers Helen.

Promoter Jerry Weintraub had arranged for Grant and Zeppelin to meet the star. After the show, they were ushered into Elvis's hotel suite. Presley had long been cosseted from the outside world by a group of gofers and minders, nicknamed the "Memphis Mafia." He didn't know Led Zeppelin's music but was intrigued by these longhaired Brits who sold more records and concert tickets than he did.

"It was Bonzo who broke the ice," Jimmy Page told me. "He asked, 'What was that hot rod you drove in *Loving You*?' After that, we were off." At one point, Bonham surprised Presley by pushing him hard on the shoulder to demonstrate the kickback on one of his sports cars. His minders looked concerned, but he waved them away.

"We stood in a circle for two hours, talking," remembered Robert Plant, "and people kept coming by from his entourage thinking he'd had enough, and he kept saying it was OK."

Grant was talking to Elvis's drummer, Ronnie Tutt, when he sat down without looking behind him. Peter later explained he had a compacted lower disc in his back and needed to take the weight off. The story changed slightly with each retelling, but the outcome remained the same. "All of a sudden I heard this voice behind me saying, 'Jesus Christ!'" Grant recalled. "It was Elvis's dad, Vernon. I'd sat on him."

Grant told the story again at a music business conference in 1994. "I said to Vernon, 'Mr. Presley, if anyone in this room was going to sit on you, it might as well have been me.' Later when we left, I said to Elvis, 'I'm sorry for sitting on your father.'" Grant paused for comic effect, like an English Don Rickles, "And Elvis replied, 'Stick around kid, you might get a permanent job.'"

The Memphis Mafia's Jerry Schilling claimed it never happened, but the tale of Grant squashing Elvis's dad never died. A year later came another enduring legend, after Grant encountered Bob Dylan at a party in LA.

"Bob Dylan was chatting with Paul McCartney," reported *Rolling Stone* magazine at the time, "when a well-oiled guest butted in: 'Hi, I'm Peter Grant and I manage Led Zeppelin,' he told Dylan with an outstretched hand. 'I don't bother you with my problems,' Dylan replied."

Behind the humor, Dylan's response was typical of how Zeppelin was viewed within the industry. Launching Bad Company presented Grant with a challenge. They were an unknown group, and he needed Frank Barsalona, the promoter he'd fired, to give them a support slot in America. Hoping for a piece of the "next" Led Zeppelin, Barsalona's Premier Talent Agency hired Bad Company to open for blues-rocker Edgar Winter.

It was a tour of contrasts. "We were opening for Edgar in arenas, but we had a private plane, and limos to meet us on the tarmac," says Paul Rodgers. Phil Carlo remembers Grant once persuading Winter's manager, Teddy Slatus, to let Bad Company play for longer. Slatus agreed but was worried there wouldn't be enough time to clear the stage afterward.

"Bad Company overran by two or three minutes," says Carlo. "Next thing, G walks on stage, picks up one of the Marshall cabinets—'OK, where do you want this?' Teddy couldn't believe Peter Grant was loading the band's gear. G said, 'You wanted a quick changeover. I used to do this for a living.'"

The opposing sides of Peter Grant were rarely more apparent. One minute, he was working as a humble roadie; the next, he was snorting cocaine on Bad Company's private jet and warning a visiting journalist to "make sure you write something nice about the show." The problem was no one could be sure which "Peter Grant" would make an appearance at any given time.

Within days, Bad Company was upstaging the Edgar Winter Group, just as Led Zeppelin had done with Vanilla Fudge. Unlike Zeppelin, there was nothing deep or mysterious about Bad Company's music. It was macho blues-rock and big ballads that sounded magnificent in America's cattle-shed arenas.

During the Edgar Winter dates, "Can't Get Enough" swaggered up the Billboard singles charts. Soon after, came the band's debut LP, unfussily titled *Bad Company*. It reached the top five in Britain and number one in America.

Having watched Swan Song's first US release conquer the charts, Grant could be forgiven for thinking it would always be this easy. Jimmy Page told *Rolling Stone* he wanted Swan Song to "promote acts that have had raw deals in the past." Both he and Plant wanted to sign their friend, folk singer Roy Harper. However, his manager wouldn't budge, and Harper remained on EMI.

Page and Plant had better luck with another of their favorite artists. In the early 1960s, the Pretty Things had briefly challenged the Rolling Stones in the battle of the dirty English R&B bands, but they'd fallen on harder times since then. Lead singer Phil May agreed to their signing with Swan Song on the proviso Peter Grant became their manager. "Peter said, 'Fuck off, I've heard you're unmanageable,'" May recalled in 2011. "But it went well."

The Pretty Things remained on the label for two years. May's strongest memory of Peter Grant was witnessing the power he wielded over Atlantic Records. Phil would sit cross-legged on the floor of the Kings Road office, puffing on a joint, listening to Peter on the phone, saying no to everything Ahmet Ertegun asked him to do.

Grant dispatched the Pretty Things to Headley Grange to record their next album, *Silk Torpedo*. On the first day, a brand new Bösendorfer piano fell off a delivery truck and shattered before it even made it into the haunted house. In the coming weeks, the band racked up an astronomical bill, hiring the London Philharmonic Orchestra and relieving Headley Grange of several rare antiques, including a pair of Chinese dueling pistols. "In the end Swan Song paid for everything," admitted May.

The label celebrated *Silk Torpedo*'s release with what it called "a freakish Hallowe'en party" at Chislehurst Caves—a subterranean tourist attraction on the outskirts of south London. "Do what thou wilt but know by this summons that on the night of the full moon on 31 October 1974, Led Zeppelin request your presence" read the invite.

Ex–New Vaudeville Band trumpeter Bob Kerr's band was among those providing the musical entertainment. "It was a most interesting evening," he remembers. "Things I'd never seen before." Maggie Bell and random members of Led Zeppelin and Bad Company roamed the caves, gawping at female wrestlers, strippers dressed as nuns with the back of their habits missing to reveal stockings and suspenders, and a naked woman lying in a coffin covered in jelly.

"Who would ever think of that?" says Sherry Coulson. "'Hey, let's lay a naked woman in a casket and cover her in jelly, but don't put any over her nose in case she can't breathe and dies.' Where did that idea come from? Where is that woman now?"

Presiding over the madness, and looking like a pirate captain in a nautical cap, was Peter Grant.

After the party came the comedown. *Silk Torpedo*, Swan Song's first UK release, fused sixties R&B with seventies glam-rock. Jimmy Page declared it "absolutely brilliant," but it was too offbeat for American radio or the mainstream rock crowd.

It was also a victim of Grant's scheming. When Bad Company took off, Peter dumped Frank Barsalona again and others who'd promoted them as an opening act. From now on, Concerts West would reap the benefit and promote Bad Company as arena headliners.

Grant assumed Swan Song's pulling power was enough for the spurned promoters to support the Pretty Things regardless. "Peter overplayed his hand," says Danny Goldberg, who struggled to book the group as an opening act anywhere.

Silk Torpedo sold but not as much as Swan Song had hoped for, and it failed to reach the Billboard Top 100. The follow-up, 1975's *Savage Eye*, would be their last album before Phil May quit. "The Pretty Things nearly came back, big time," says Phil Carson, "but not quite."

However much attention Grant thought he could give his other artists, he still deferred to Led Zeppelin. This meant when Jimmy Page spoke, everyone at Swan Song stopped what they were doing and listened.

"1974 didn't happen," Page told the press. He wasn't wrong. The year had started badly for the band, when John Paul Jones told Grant he wanted to leave. "He turned up at my house, told me he'd had enough, and said he was going to be the choirmaster at Winchester Cathedral."

Grant and Jones talked, and during their conversation Peter admitted he'd thought the group had wanted to fire *him* during their Australian tour. "I got very insecure and thought the band wanted to blow me out. John said he thought it was the other way around—that I was going to blow them out."

The conversation was endemic of what Ed Bicknell calls "the constant fear" that plagued all managers. Zeppelin was due to start recording a new album at Headley Grange. Grant told Bad Company that Jones had the flu and they could use the studio to make their debut album instead. They were none the wiser.

In reality, the Winchester Cathedral choirmaster story was an in-joke. Jones's problem was the impact Zeppelin was having on his family life. Having postponed the recording sessions, Grant talked him out of leaving and implemented some new rules. "We didn't tour in the school holidays as much, and there was more notice given for when we were touring," said Jones later. "I trusted Peter to put it right."

Jones hadn't been the only member of the Zeppelin family considering a life away from the band. In January 1974, Richard Cole married his actress and model girlfriend, Marilyn Woolhead. It was a brief courtship, greatly encouraged by his boss.

"I'll always remember the first time I saw Peter," says Marilyn now. "It was at the Mayfair Hotel. He walked in, saw me, and went, 'Woargh! Cop the nanny!' Nanny meant 'nanny goat,' cockney rhyming slang for 'coat,' and I was all dolled up in this lovely coat. I did a little twirl for him, but I think Peter was dumbfounded that I knew rhyming slang. I think we stayed up all night, and after that we all just hung out together. It was a mad time, and in no time Richard and I were married."

Grant paid for a reception at London's Playboy club, where *Oliver!* songwriter Lionel Bart bashed out tunes on the piano. Unlike some of the band wives, Marilyn was invited into Grant's inner circle. "Peter was adorable, and I think he was fond of me. He was what Italians call the 'capo.' He was powerful, and he knew it—and he was Richard's mentor."

Tour managing Led Zeppelin meant Marilyn's husband zoomed around America in a better private plane than Hugh Hefner, but it wasn't a well-paid job. After six years' loyal service, Cole expected better. "I thought they'd make me a shareholder in Swan Song," he admits now. "They didn't, so I thought, fuck it."

Eric Clapton had conquered his heroin addiction and was touring for the first time in four years. Clapton's handler, Robert Stigwood, who'd supposedly been dangled from a fourth-floor window by Peter Grant, offered Cole the job of tour manager. It was $16,000 for eight weeks' work—significantly more than Grant was paying. However, leaving Zeppelin's secret society came as a culture shock. "To start with, I wasn't used to other promoters," Cole admits. His Peter Grant–endorsed working methods also unsettled his new employers.

"I ran my business like a military general. The first gig at the Yale Bowl, I started shouting at Eric's musicians because they were so disorganized and all over the place. I also brought in my own security." Zeppelin's favorite ex-cop Bill Dautrich was soon arranging police escorts. "Bill Oakes [Stigwood's right-hand man] said to me, 'Fucking hell, Richard, the only thing you've missed are helicopters flying overhead.'"

The Clapton tour was a success, and after a few weeks Ahmet Ertegun joined them in New Orleans. Over drinks, he told Cole Zeppelin was going back on the road next year, and Richard was going with them. It was almost a done deal. "It was then I realized I'd been played," Cole says. "I wouldn't be surprised if Ahmet hadn't got on the phone to Peter already and said, 'Sort this out with Richard because it's all working good.'

"Peter, Jimmy, and Robert came down to mine and Marilyn's and offered me three times what I was earning and a Jag," he says. "The trouble is, me, Peter and Jimmy were all like schoolboys together. So I came back. It ruined me in a sense, but you can't blame anyone else for your own behavior."

One evening in late 1974, the White Hart's regulars arrived at Horselunges for one of Peter and Gloria's parties. Among them was Dave Northover, a local insurance broker and weekend rugby player. Northover had met Zeppelin's manager during a wild night in the pub. "At the time, my knowledge of Led Zeppelin went as far as the theme tune to *Top of the Pops*," he admits.

Northover and his then wife, Carol, arrived at the manor to see their local postman and doctor drinking side by side with rock stars and their minders. The smell of pot and amyl nitrate filled the air, and several guests were already disappearing into Peter's study, "where they were doing whatever they were doing."

At one point during the night, Carol wandered onto the grounds looking for her husband and saw him through the study's open window. In a repeat of Grant's earlier mishap with Gene Vincent, she climbed through, fell, and landed on sixties pop star Adam Faith's leg—the same one he'd nearly lost in a car accident a year before. There was no lasting damage, but driving home, Northover marveled at the world he'd just entered: "That party was my first inkling of what was to come."

One week later, Grant asked if Northover wanted to go on tour with Led Zeppelin. "My work as an insurance broker was ending; I was thirty and

The young Peter Grant and pet
dog, Chummy, in the garden of
33 Norhyrst Avenue, South
Norwood, London.

Peter's mother, Dorothy Louise.
She was very straitlaced, says
granddaughter Helen.

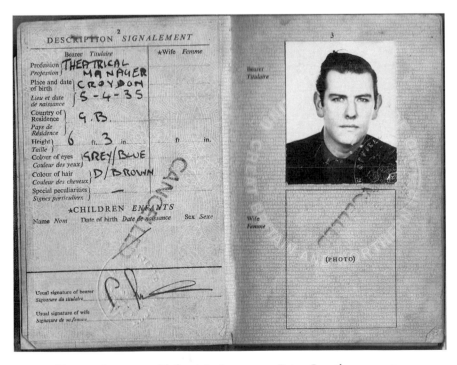

Twenty-five-year-old theatrical manager Peter Grant's passport,
summer of 1960.

Peter shortly before his wedding to singer Gloria Cutting in Hull, Yorkshire, summer of 1962. © *THE GRANT FAMILY COLLECTION*

Dressed as Santa Claus with the Yardbirds (from left: Chris Dreja, Keith Relf, Jim McCarty, Jimmy Page), Chelsea, London, Christmas, 1967. © *THE GRANT FAMILY COLLECTION*

Sunbathing with future Led Zeppelin tour manager Richard Cole, on tour with the New Vaudeville Band, Las Vegas, May 1967. © *THE RICHARD COLE COLLECTION*

Peter with Led Zeppelin, Marine Drive, Mumbai, India, 1972.
© *THE RICHARD COLE COLLECTION*

Peter Grant, the capo, and his soldiers, Derek Skilton and Richard
Cole, shot for *The Song Remains the Same* movie, outside Horselunges
Manor, Sussex, 1974. © *PETER CLIFTON*

Inside the great hall at Horselunges Manor, Sussex. © *THE RICHARD COLE COLLECTION*

Father and daughter: Peter and Helen in the great chamber at Horselunges. © *THE GRANT FAMILY COLLECTION*

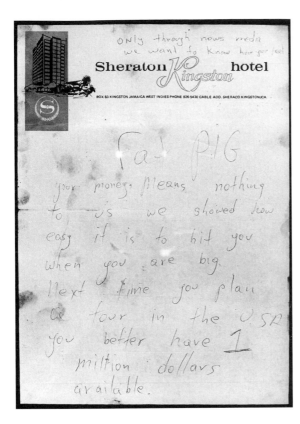

The Jamaican death threat letter, 1973. © *THE GRANT FAMILY COLLECTION*

The letter reads:

"only through news media we want to know how you feel . . . fat pig . . . your money means nothing to us . . . we showed how easy it is to hit you when you are big. Next time you plan a tour in the USA you better have 1 million dollars available. Since you can't get to us that could be a problem for you. Dont forget you are nothing without your boys. Now you wont want Robert to loose his voice or Jimmys guitar to blow up.

Dont forget you are dealling with
U . . . . D"

Peter with Atlantic Records mogul Ahmet Ertegun.
"Dad always called him 'Omelette,'" says Helen.

John Bonham, Grant, and Jimmy Page, flying high on
Led Zeppelin's private jet, *The Starship*, January 1975.

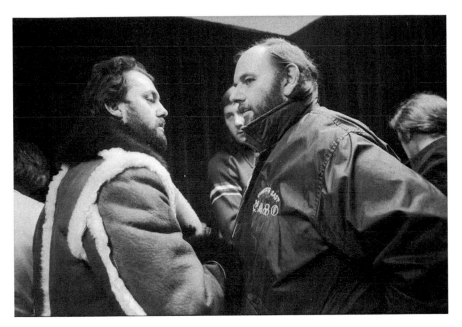

Richard Cole and Peter, with security guard Bill Dautrich (center) and Swan Song VP Danny Goldberg (from behind, right), America, 1975.

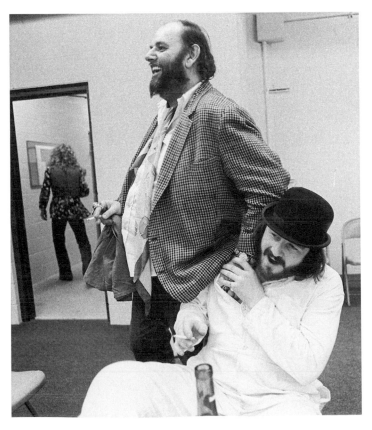

Enjoying a touching moment with John Bonham, backstage at Market Square Arena, Indianapolis, January 25, 1975: "Bonzo was the best mate I ever had," said Grant.

PHOTOS © NEAL PRESTON

Peter and Richard Cole dressed to impress at a Mississippi River-boat party, New Orleans, 1975. © THE RICHARD COLE COLLECTION

Grant leaving his mark in the parking lot, America, 1975. © NEAL PRESTON

(*Top*) Valhalla! I am coming!: waiting to board *Caesar's Chariot*, Chicago O'Hare airport, April 12, 1977. (*Bottom*) Dazed and confused: crew member Dave Northover watches Peter transport a delicate Jimmy Page to *Caesar's Chariot*, April 1977.

PHOTOS © NEAL PRESTON

Masters and servants. From left: Atlantic Records' Phil Carson, Plant, Page, crew member Dave Northover, Concerts West promoter Terry Bassett, and Zeppelin attorney and consigliere Stevens H. Weiss, America, 1977. © NEAL PRESTON

Peter, Jimmy, and Robert with security guard and royal escort John "Biffo" Bindon (far right), Tampa Stadium, Florida, June 3, 1977. "Bindon was a nice guy . . . when he wasn't being a killer," says Phil Carson. © TERRY O'NEILL

Celebration day: Peter blows out the candles on his birthday cake while Phil Carson chats to his friend, April 1977. © NEAL PRESTON

Father and son: Peter and Warren, shortly before all hell broke loose backstage at Oakland Coliseum, California, July 23, 1977.
© MICHAEL ZAGARIS

(*Right*) You're gonna need a bigger boat: enjoying a Jaws moment with Warren and the catch of the day, Miami, Florida, 1977.
© THE GRANT FAMILY COLLECTION

(*Middle*) Three amigos: Richard Cole, Cindy Russell, and Jimmy Page at Page's house, Plumpton Place, East Sussex, 1978.
© CINDY RUSSELL-FOSSEN

(*Below*) Hey, hey, mama!: Robert Plant and Jimmy Page, Ibiza, 1979, "where Robert and Jimmy asked me to manage the band," says Phil Carson.

(*Top*) Grant with Plant, Jones, and the obligatory bottle of Blue Nun, Knebworth Festival, August 1979. © *NEAL PRESTON*

(*Bottom*) Dinner and laughter with Peter, Helen (second left), and friends, Peppermint Park restaurant, St. Martin's Lane, London. © *THE GRANT FAMILY COLLECTION*

Sleeping it off:
in bed at Horselunges.
© CINDY RUSSELL-FOSSEN

Achilles last stand. From left: Plant, Carson, John Bonham's personal assistant Rex King, Bonham, and Grant, Led Zeppelin's final tour, Cologne, Germany, June 1980.
© THE DAVE LEWIS COLLECTION

Cindy Russell reading Robert Plant's rejection letter to Grant, December 1982: "Peter took a photo, then asked me to tear the letter up."
© CINDY RUSSELL-FOSSEN

The lesser-spotted G, with Jimmy Page's bass guitarist Durban Laverde and tour manager Phil Carlo, at Jason Bonham's wedding reception, Kidderminster, April 1990. © *THE PHIL CARLO COLLECTION*

Straight shooter: at a Porsche owners club rally with the Bad-1 licence plate.
© *THE GRANT FAMILY COLLECTION*

Elder statesman: with friend and tour manager Phil Carlo, In the City music conference, Manchester, 1994.
© THE PHIL CARLO COLLECTION

Bring it on home: Helen and Warren Grant, Surrey, June 27, 2018. © ROSS HALFIN

looking for something different. I asked him, 'What would I have to do?' and he replied, 'Just don't take any shit from anyone, and you'll be fine."

The next time Northover saw Grant was at the Ambassador Hotel in Chicago. "It was the beginning of the tour, and there was a meeting with Peter and Richard Cole," he says. "I noticed a few scantily clad ladies around, and one of them—I think she was one of the Plaster Casters—led me into another room, knelt down, and undid my trousers."

Unfortunately, despite his new friend's best efforts, he couldn't rise to the occasion. "She smiled and said, 'Oh, you must have taken too much speed,' zipped my trousers back up, and walked out." Northover reemerged, looking embarrassed, to see Grant and Cole grinning knowingly. "I later found out it had all been prearranged for the new boy."

Northover made his Zeppelin debut in January 1975, escorting John Paul Jones to the stage in front of seventeen thousand people at the Minneapolis Metropolitan Sports Center. From here on, his jobs included guarding the lighting tower and stage monitors and ensuring Grant's hotel suite fridge was stocked with his favorite tipple, Blue Nun white wine. "Peter always had a bottle of it in his pocket. You never knew if he was going to drink it or hit you with it."

Prior to the tour, Northover had mentioned he was a qualified physicist (he'd worked as a junior scientist at the Harwell Atomic Energy Research Establishment). When this information was relayed to the band, he'd somehow become a "pharmacist." "I think they liked the idea of having someone around who knew about chemicals."

Page, Bonham, and Richard Cole had all tried heroin for the first time on the 1973 tour. A dealer claiming he was unable to find cocaine had offered it as a substitute. Cole had been snorting the drug regularly since then, and he wasn't the only one. "That 1975 trip through America was the first tour in which heroin circulated freely among our entourage," he admitted.

For Northover, the whole tour was an extraordinary experience. Late one night in the "Riot House" he found himself balancing Keith Moon on his shoulders, as the Who's drummer attempted to climb from his seventh-floor balcony to John Bonham's on the eighth. "As I stood there lifting him up, I wondered what the headlines would read like if I let him drop."

In New York, Northover was in Robert Plant's hotel suite when David Bowie arrived unannounced. "Robert was getting changed in the bedroom, and Bowie ran straight past me," he recalls. "I heard Robert shouting 'Get him off me!'—and there he was, semi-naked, with David wrapped around him. I calmed him down and told him to wait in the lounge until Robert was dressed."

Everything had expanded for this latest tour, including the crew, the production, and the entourage. Grant wanted to control every aspect of Zeppelin's image and had hired twenty-three-year-old Neal Preston as their official tour photographer, and brought Atlantic Records' promotions manager Danny Markus with them on the road.

Both recalled the obvious hierarchy but also the constant nagging tension. "Peter was very protective of me right from the start," said Markus. "But you could see he got angry quite often."

"The first thing I realized was Peter held the keys to the kingdom," says Preston now. "No offence to Robert, but it was Jimmy and Peter's band."

Also joining mainstays Cole, Mick Hinton, and Page's tech Ray Thomas, was returning sound engineer Benji Le Fevre and Maggie Bell's ex-road manager Brian Gallivan. Showco had also provided what Grant described as "half a jumbo jet's" worth of lights, lasers, and special effects. These included a neon-lit Zeppelin logo that glowed like a baseball stadium scoreboard to remind everyone of their magnitude.

The band and their manager's personalities also seemed to have grown. Everybody had become an exaggerated version of themselves. Even John Paul Jones, who kept his own counsel and was almost invisible when he wasn't performing.

John Bonham looked menacing onstage, dressed like an ultra-violent "droog" from Stanley Kubrick's *A Clockwork Orange* in white boiler suit and black bowler hat. He was menacing offstage, too, once punching Dave Northover in the stomach without warning. "He said, 'I heard you play rugby, so I wanted to see if you could take it.'"

Visiting journalists found Robert Plant amiable and vain and keen to spread peace and goodwill. "I'm just a fun-loving guy, a bubbly character," he announced. Meanwhile, *Creem* magazine's Lisa Robinson and *Rolling Stone*'s cub reporter Cameron Crowe were treated to the full Jimmy Page experience.

Jimmy arrived for *Rolling Stone*'s cover shoot, looking ethereal and clutching two bouquets of dead roses. "I was looking for black roses," he whispered. "They exist, you know."

"The party line was that Jimmy was a genius, and a delicate, sensitive soul," recalled Lisa. "The truth was, his heroin use had escalated, but this was never acknowledged around me."

To keep this circus on the road, Grant and Cole also turned up the more excessive sides of their personalities. Richard now carried a knife or a hammer ("I felt more confident with them in certain situations"), and Peter just carried himself.

In Greensboro, North Carolina, Grant took control after hundreds of fans tried to gate-crash the venue, damaging the band's limousines. Their two remaining chauffeurs wanted to leave before the gig was over. "Peter wouldn't allow that," says Neal Preston. "He said to these drivers, 'How much are these cars? I'll fucking buy 'em'—and pulls out a wad of bills. The drivers couldn't believe it, 'They're not ours to sell.' He said, 'Then I'll fucking take 'em.' God knows what he and Richard did, but the next thing I know they've got the keys."

Zeppelin came offstage and was whisked straight into the first limo. "All four got in, and Peter squeezed behind the steering wheel. Then Richard pushed me into the second limo. As he did so, my bag tipped over, spilling lenses and rolls of films down the stage ramp and the loading deck."

To his amazement, Cole helped Preston collect them all. "Richard was uttering the vilest words I'd ever heard while picking up my stuff. He then pushed me back in the car, so I was lying face down across the laps of three of the hottest groupies on the planet. He got behind the wheel and followed Peter. I'd never seen driving like it. To this day I don't know if they drove on the left or on the right side, but they went so fast we lost our police escort."

When the cars arrived at the airport, Grant performed a victory lap around the *Starship* before bringing the limo to a tire-screaming halt. "I said, 'Amazing bit of driving, Peter.' He looked at me and replied, 'Fuck off.'"

Joe Jammer also flew with Zeppelin on a few dates. He'd presumed Grant wanted him on the crew, but it was really a precursor to asking him to join Maggie Bell's band. "I remember Peter was being mother hen and trying to keep it all together," he says. "Jimmy was getting a little deep into certain things by then."

Grant's ribald humor helped take the edge off difficult situations, and Peter had a new favorite: the English comic actors Peter Cook and Dudley Moore and their vulgar alter egos Derek and Clive.

Led Zeppelin's engineer Eddie Kramer had recorded a drunken Cook and Moore, ad-libbing in New York's Electric Lady Studios. The results were later released as an LP, even though they were originally meant for their own enjoyment.

"I think Eddie gave Peter a bootleg copy," suggests Joe. Grant and the band adored these filthy, funny sketches in which the two comics discussed "The worst job I ever had," which included "collecting Winston Churchill's bogeys" and "retrieving lobsters" from Hollywood actress "Jayne Mansfield's arsehole."

"We were on the *Starship* once, and Jonesy put on the new Neil Young album. Peter stopped it straight away—'Turn that fuckin' whining off,'" says Joe. Derek and Clive were quickly put back on the stereo. "Peter loved his comedy, also those American Jewish guys. He used all the old Jewish sayings. Bill Graham was always a 'schmuck' and making a quick getaway after a show was always 'a quick smeitz.'"

In New York, Joe joined Grant and Zeppelin for an evening at wisecrack- ing stand-up Rodney Dangerfield's club. "We tipped Rodney off, so he made an announcement, 'Hey, we got a band in the house, the Led Zeppelins, hell- uva name.' He knew what was going on when people started getting up from the table—'Hey, everybody keeps going to the bathroom and coming back sniffing, everybody got a cold?'"

After the show, the visiting party trooped downstairs to Dangerfield's dressing room. "You had to be careful what you said around Peter. Rodney sees this huge guy bending his head to get in—'Wow, you're a big boy ain't cha. You ain't hurting for food.' Peter didn't mind. He loved it."

Grant indulged in the madness of the road and knew when to step back, at least, most of the time. *The Observer*'s music correspondent Tony Palmer joined the band in New Jersey. He was shielded from the excess but reported on the humdrum aspects of touring life: how John Bonham had diarrhea and how Jimmy Page wandered listlessly around the dressing room, looking for a missing sock.

Peter Grant ("in his torn jeans, 20p Oxfam shirt, and Davey Crockett hat") made quite an impression. Palmer described Grant as "worrying exces- sively and endlessly about his two children" and beaming with delight when Gloria called to say her pupils had come first, third, and fourth in a national dancing championship.

Nevertheless, Grant wasn't immune to temptation and opportunities on the road. Richard Cole remembers an earlier tour, where Zeppelin had a day to kill in Winnipeg. "I remember suggesting a boat trip," he says, laughing. "Peter said, 'Fuck off, order sixty screwdrivers and a couple of hookers.'"

"Peter's girlfriends on the road were never called girlfriends or even mis- tresses," remembers Joe Jammer. "Peter was like a mandarin. So they were called concubines."

However, a friend from the outside world had noticed one of Grant's female companions. "We were in a 'green room' somewhere in America, and I saw this woman hovering around Peter," recalls Chris Hayes. "I said to Mickie, 'Something's going on with her and Peter.' He said, 'Are you raving mad?' I said, 'No.' I could just *tell.*" Her instincts would soon be proved right.

Three weeks into the US tour, Led Zeppelin released its sixth album. *Physical Graffiti* mixed crushingly heavy blues, folk, pop, and R&B across four sides of vinyl. Grant thought it was the best record they'd ever made and singled out "Kashmir," an epic song that suggested dinosaurs trampling through the Himalayas, for special praise. "I remember Bonzo saying, 'Oh, you've *got* to come down. We ain't half done something today. . . . Get in the Porsche and get down here.'"

Physical Graffiti was the first Led Zeppelin album on Swan Song. With $15 million worth of advance orders, it reached number one in the UK and in the United States. In an unguarded moment, Grant told the press they hadn't wanted a Zeppelin LP to be Swan Song's first release, "Because Zeppelin could be on a shit label and still sell 2 million records."

If 1973 was the year Led Zepplelin reached their artistic peak, 1975 was the year they wondered how much bigger it could get. However, in Grant's mind, Zeppelin's size also made them a bigger target. At Madison Square Garden, Bill Dautrich's men confiscated three loaded revolvers and twenty knives from the audience.

In LA, a girl arrived at the "Riot House" and claimed she'd had a vision that something terrible was going to happen to Jimmy Page at that night's concert. It was Lynette "Squeaky" Fromme, one of cult leader Charles Manson's disciples. Months later, Squeaky was arrested for pointing a loaded gun at President Gerald Ford.

"That's how we lost a little of the camaraderie," Grant admitted, "because there were now armed guards outside the hotel rooms all the time."

It was on this tour Grant told a journalist he'd been approached by the Mafia wanting to latch on to the band. Organized crime and the music industry had been bedfellows since the days of the 78 rpm record. The mob followed the money, and nobody was making more than Led Zeppelin.

Bad Company had heard rumors about Grant before they signed with him. Back in England, known associates of the Kray twins had been seen hanging around the Swan Song office.

Simon Kirke broached the subject with Grant early on. "When I got a few minutes alone, I asked Peter point-blank about his underworld dealings. He looked me in the eye with a charming smile and said, 'Simon, would I be in the position I'm in today if any of that was true?' He said it with such sincerity, I swallowed it completely."

Days later, Kirke joined Grant and the rest of Bad Company for a meeting. "The moment we walked in, Peter said in that menacing way, 'Simon, close the door behind you. I want to answer the question you put to me a few days ago in a different way.'

"On a prearranged signal, the rest of the band stepped away, and Peter pulled out a Tommy gun." Kirke froze, until the toy weapon unleashed a stream of Ping-Pong balls. He never raised the matter again.

However, working in such a huge cash business in the 1970s did present challenges. "As Peter and I became closer, he would dig deeper about stuff," says Ed Bicknell. "I don't know if he was involved in organized crime, but if you worked in certain markets in a cash business, there would often be fronts—a steak house somewhere in, say, Minnesota. In a cash situation, you encounter people—and I'm sure Peter did."

"There were attorneys and underworld figures in Vegas, New York, and Chicago who would do anything for Peter," says Danny Francis. "The first time I went to Chicago with him, we went to an Italian restaurant, and it was like a scene from *Goodfellas.* They treated Peter like a king."

In Britain, Don Murfet's Artistes Services routinely supplied minders to watch over Grant and his bands, "But Peter was increasingly drawn to anyone who seemed to be connected, whether in government circles or in the underworld," admitted Murfet.

These connections often paid off. When one of Murfet's men was refused a US visa due to a string of previous convictions, Peter made a call, and the visa miraculously appeared forty-eight hours later.

Bad Company soon enjoyed the same level of elite protection as Led Zeppelin in the States, after Steve Weiss enlisted former detective Steve Rosenberg to organize their security. "All these cops, FBI men, and CIA agents used to take holidays and come on the road with us," says Phil Carlo. "Our guys could work in different states and had the power of arrest. There was one we called Dirty Harry who had a revolver in a leg holster. We'd get him to dive on the floor, roll over, and pull the gun, like in the movies."

Carlo was amazed to see their private police force impose its own rules. When Boz Burrell ran out of dope before a show, one of Bad Company's cops walked into the arena and busted the first kid he found with a bag of grass. "He said, 'I'll let you off, but I need to destroy this.' Then he took the bag backstage and gave it to Boz.

"The power we had was incredible. At this point I discovered the only people who could jump red lights with a police escort were the president of the United States and Peter Grant."

Years later, Grant claimed to the film researcher Mark Long that much of this power came from one Herb Atkin, a man who would play an increasingly influential and divisive role in his life. Even now, despite Atkin's death, some former members of the Zeppelin organization are reluctant to discuss him, or they remain vague about who he was and what he actually did.

"I knew who Herb Atkin was," says Phil Carson now. "He helped the band with some security issues. That was it. He wasn't a bad guy."

"Herb supposedly used to work for the CIA and had all these government ties," says Richard Cole. "The first time I met him was through Steve Weiss in Chicago, and I think he was carrying a gun. I didn't know who he was or what he was involved in, but all of a sudden he's involved in Led Zeppelin. Nobody knows the full story."

The full story is so extraordinary that a Hollywood scriptwriter might reject it for being too far-fetched. On December 15, 1968, the *New York Times* published an article, "Itkin's Story: A Contradictory Web," which described how a forty-one-year-old labor lawyer, Herbert Itkin, had been working undercover as a government informer and was currently "living in fear of his life in protective custody at an undisclosed military installation base."

Itkin's evidence in a recent pension fund and New York City contracts kickback case involving the teamsters union had been led to the conviction of more than a dozen local officials, politicians and organized crime figures. Among them was Mafia boss, Antonio "Tony Ducks" Corallo, who was imprisoned on several charges including extortion.

During the trial, Itkin claimed the CIA and the FBI had employed him as an informant. Both agencies confirmed this to be true, saying Itkin had supplied vital information about Mafia activity in Central America, which he'd gathered while working undercover as a mob lawyer. It was also claimed he'd worked for the CIA in London, where he'd investigated the escape of the British agent-turned-Soviet-spy George Blake in 1966.

Itkin and his family went into a witness protection program soon after the trial, but in a farcical turn of events, he barely hid his new identity. Instead, he relocated to Southern California, changed his name to "Herbert Atkin," and with the FBI's assistance became a private detective, setting up the Continental Investigative Agency in Los Angeles.

On August 7, 1975, the *New York Times* revealed Atkin's true identity after he became embroiled in an industrial espionage case between two computer manufacturers. Atkin acted on behalf of one of the companies but was subsequently accused of falsifying evidence and committing perjury. Atkin granted the newspaper an interview, further exposing his identity and confirming his involvement in sending "Tony Ducks" Corallo to prison.

Shortly after, Atkin and his then wife, who, Grant claimed, worked undercover for the British Secret Service, showed up in London. Grant told Mark Long that Steve Weiss had introduced him to Atkin shortly after the Drake Hotel robbery and that Atkin had advised him during the subsequent police investigation.

However, the *New York Times* also noted Atkin's tendency to talk publicly and indiscriminately about his agency connections. "Striving in his singular way for status, he bragged of his undercover work despite the obvious risks," they wrote.

"You never knew what was true and what wasn't with Herb," confirms Richard Cole. "I remember him boasting once about how he'd been one of the last people to see Jimmy Hoffa alive." The teamsters union boss had disappeared in a Detroit restaurant parking lot in 1975 and was missing or presumed dead.

The overriding impression was that Atkin was an opportunist with serious connections and power, but also vulnerable and dangerous. Neither Helen nor Warren Grant knew the nature of Atkin's business with their father. "I did wonder why Dad had him on board," says Helen. "Herb used to come down in a helicopter with his wife, and it was like JFK and Jackie Kennedy rocking up."

While Grant's new agency-affiliated contact helped smooth Led Zeppelin's and Bad Company's way through America, not everyone Peter hired proved quite so effective. In 1974, Grant was also introduced to John Bindon, a part-time actor and bodyguard with connections to various London crime figures, including the Krays.

Bindon's onstage and offstage roles blurred. Away from the screen, he was involved in protection racketeering. On screen, he played a gangster alongside Mick Jagger in the 1970 movie *Performance* and appeared in numerous hard-man TV roles.

Nicknamed "Biffo," after a bear in the British comic *Beano*, Bindon could be as witty and charming as he was aggressive and intimidating. "He was a funny guy," recalls Phil Carson, "except when he was being a killer."

Bindon was also an enthusiastic womanizer and notorious for the unusual size of his penis. He would routinely whip out his appendage in the pub and hang several pint glasses off it to amuse his fellow patrons.

By the midseventies, Bindon had also become a minor newspaper celebrity, thanks to his stormy relationship with baronet's daughter and model

Vicki Hodge. The couple were regulars in the gossip columns and regularly sold stories to the tabloids.

One tidbit kept out of the press involved whispers of a relationship between Bindon and the Queen's sister, Princess Margaret. The couple had been photographed together on the island of Mustique—with Bindon wearing an "Enjoy Cocaine" T-shirt—and, so the gossip claimed, had begun a clandestine affair back in Britain.

According to one eyewitness, Bindon joined Led Zeppelin's organization after a fracas at the Speakeasy, which involved Richard Cole and Roy Harper. A champagne bottle was thrown by one of the party and accidentally hit the would-be "twisting wrestler"-turned-DJ Jeff Dexter, a close friend of the club's co-manager Tony Howard.

"Bindon was mates with Tony," says Dexter now. "Cole, Harper, and the others were all banned after that, and there was a bit of aggravation. Eventually they apologized, and Richard brought Biffo into the firm." Bindon would start work as one of Grant's security guards soon after.

*G*rant and Zeppelin returned to Britain at the end of March 1975. Back in Hailsham, Dave Northover opened his luggage to find a souvenir from his first rock 'n' roll tour: a big bag of dope.

"I have no idea how it got there," he insists. "I had passed out halfway through packing my suitcase." Northover's days of selling insurance were officially over.

Grant always believed Led Zeppelin shows should be treated as events, and "An Evening with Led Zeppelin" was due to run for three nights at London's Earls Court Exhibition Centre in May. The title could have come straight from the Croydon Empire in 1950. "I know it sounds corny," he said. "I guess that was a by-product of my days as a fourteen-year-old stagehand, but I was proved right. It was an event."

When fifty-one thousand tickets sold out in two hours, an extra two dates were added. "We could have done ten shows that month," Grant said. As Zeppelin was playing only London, Grant and the show's promoter Mel Bush arranged for British Rail to supply extra intercity trains, nicknamed "The Zeppelin Express," to transport fans into the capital. "That was Peter's idea, and I thought it was genius," said Jimmy Page.

In keeping with the old-fashioned "An Evening With" theme, Grant invited several radio DJs to act as modern-day masters of ceremony and introduce the group on stage on different nights. These included the BBC DJs Alan Freeman and Bob Harris and Capital Radio's Nicky Horne.

With its smoke machines, lasers, and overhead video screen relaying the action to even the cheapest seats, it was the biggest production ever staged at Earls Court. And the music was just as thrilling. "It was a great honor to introduce them," remembers Nicky Horne, "and the power coming off that stage was incredible."

Four days after the concert, Horne was in his new flat in North London when there was a knock on the door. A black Daimler was outside, and a liveried chauffeur stood on the doorstep. "He said, 'I'd like to give you something from Led Zeppelin and Mr. Peter Grant.'"

The driver handed over a box. Inside was a solid silver goblet from luxury jewelers Asprey. It was engraved with Nicky's name, the Swan Song logo, Led Zeppelin, and the date of the show. "I was shocked," he says, "but what a wonderful gift."

Watching the Daimler glide off into the distance, Horne suddenly started to feel uneasy. "I had just moved into the flat and hadn't told anyone my new address," he says. "Nobody else knew, but somehow Peter Grant had found out where I lived."

What Grant didn't know, though, was that Earls Court would be one of the last times the four members of Led Zeppelin played in Great Britain.

8

Have You Been a
Naughty Boy?

*"It was a big schoolboys' outing,
and we had the money to do anything we liked."*

—PETER GRANT

*I*n spring 1975, Paul Rodgers was walking up the stairs at 484 Kings Road, as the rock group Queen was coming down. "We nodded at each other," Rodgers says. "I certainly knew who they were." Queen was difficult to ignore. They'd just had a hit with "Killer Queen," and their showboating lead singer, Freddie Mercury, was tipped to become a superstar.

However, Queen was unhappy and seeking new management. Peter Grant had known their managers—brothers Norman and Barry Sheffield—since the 2i's days. The Sheffields invested heavily in Queen but were paying them poorly. Grant listened to the band's tale of woe: how they'd just sold out everywhere on tour but could barely afford the rent on their flats.

Meanwhile, Queen listened as Grant told them Led Zeppelin had just "gone in for a quick garden" in New York. Peter had to explain this meant playing several nights at Madison Square Garden. "It amused us greatly because at that time doing such a thing was somewhere in our wildest dreams," said Queen's guitarist Brian May.

Grant later claimed he'd "made a few calls to help get Queen their money" and squeezed £125,000 out of the Sheffields. Harvey Lisberg insists he and Grant had several meetings about co-managing Queen: "Peter wanted to sign them to Swan Song, and they didn't want to."

Either way, Grant passed on managing what would become one biggest rock groups of the seventies and eighties. "I said to them, 'Fellas, I would love to do it, but I haven't got that many hours in the day.'"

Events during the rest of the year and into 1976 suggested he made the right decision. No sooner had Led Zeppelin finished touring when Bad Company and Maggie Bell went on the road together. Grant considered it his managerial duty to join them.

Bell's new album, *Suicide Sal*, and Bad Company's second, *Straight Shooter*, both arrived in April. *Suicide Sal* cut across rock, blues, and soul and featured Jimmy Page playing on two tracks. But there would be only one winner. *Straight Shooter* raced into the Billboard Top 10, buoyed by the hits, "Good Lovin' Gone Bad" and "Feel Like Making Love." Within the space of two records, Bad Company had jumped from nowhere to filling arenas.

However, money and success couldn't negate problems within the band. Grant later described Paul Rodgers as "the most difficult person I ever had to work with." Rodgers was a keen boxer and would later become a seventh dan in karate. On more than one occasion, there were fights, which required Grant or Steve Weiss to pay people off to make the problem go away. "I was only ever arrested twice," revealed Grant in a previously unpublished interview. "In New York after the Drake Hotel robbery and in New Orleans with Bad Company."

Po experienced Paul Rodgers's wrath first hand. Hipgnosis designed Bad Company's album sleeves, and Po was taking photographs on their European tour. "We were in Ludwigshafen. Everyone was drinking, and Simon and Boz were playing the organ in the hotel bar. I was sat with Paul Rodgers, tapping my fingers on the table. He asked me to stop, and I didn't."

Without warning, Rodgers lashed out. "He decked me," says Po. "I was drunk and furious, staggered back to my hotel room, and smashed the TV set, and then I smashed up the room. I passed out on a vibrating waterbed and woke up later with the worst hangover ever, wondering what I'd done. To avoid Clive Coulson, I made my own way back to London. And then I waited."

Peter Grant's phone call didn't come straight away, which only prolonged Po's agony. "Finally, he rang: 'Hello Po,' he said in that quiet nasally voice. 'Have you been a naughty boy? I've got a hotel bill here for £2,000 in damages. What have you been up to?'"

Po explained what had happened and then apologized profusely. "Once I'd thrown myself at his mercy, Peter started laughing, 'So tell me one thing—did you enjoy smashing up that room?' I was shocked. I said, 'Yes, I did. I loved it.' And he replied, 'Good. Then we'll pay the bill, just this once. . . . but don't ever fucking do it again.'"

Bad Company's crew boss Phil Carlo found Grant much easier to deal with than Paul Rodgers. Peter's approach to the road combined his fastidious attention to detail with his love of hard cash.

When Bad Company played in Boston, Jimmy Page and his new companion Bebe Buell (the future mother of Hollywood actress Liv Tyler) showed up at the backstage door unannounced. "It was pouring rain, and Jimmy and Bebe stood there in sunglasses, looking a bit wobbly and soaked to the skin," remembers Carlo. "We had a guy from the college football team on the door, and he would not let them in, as Jimmy's name wasn't on the guest list.

"Peter found out and let them in later. Then he told me to go and get this football player. The poor guy was terrified. As soon as he arrived, Peter thanked him: 'Well done, you were given a job, and his name *wasn't* on the list. You did the right thing.'"

Weeks later, Carlo saw Grant rubbing his hands with glee as the tour's T-shirt money was brought into the dressing room in a large bag. "He couldn't wait to divvy it up. Everyone, Peter, Clive, the band would all get a fat envelope full of cash.

"It didn't matter how much they were getting paid for the shows—how many noughts were on the end of the bank account—they still wanted to make a few quid on the side. 'It's readies,' G used to say, 'Let's keep *shtum* about this. Not a word to anyone, especially Joan Hudson.'"

*H*it records, sold-out shows, and hard cash made it easier to excuse the bust-ups and the violence. Until next time. On the last night of the tour, Grant ushered Bad Company into their dressing room. Like a magician performing a trick, he pulled back a white tablecloth to reveal four gold discs underneath.

"Peter had tears in his eyes; we all had tears in our eyes," said Simon Kirke. "He gave a lovely little speech and then said, 'Now get the fuck out of here and knock 'em dead.'"

Touring America back-to-back with two groups was exhausting, but Grant had another reason for staying out of the country. At Earls Court, Robert Plant had dedicated Led Zeppelin's "In My Time of Dying" to Dennis Healey, the UK government's chancellor of the exchequer. Healey had vowed to raise taxes high enough to cause "howls of anguish from those rich enough to suffer." And he'd kept his promise.

Grant, Led Zeppelin, and Bad Company would all become nonresident for a year to avoid paying 83 percent tax on their earnings and 98 percent tax on unearned income. "It kicked off in January '75," said Peter. "That was the start of [Zeppelin's] nonresidency, which we were only told about three weeks up front. Joan Hudson told us of the problems we'd have if we didn't go."

Grant and the band retained their houses in the UK, but to avoid paying the full rate now they had to spend nine months outside the UK. Like traveling gypsies, they individually set up temporary homes in France, Switzerland, and Jersey, with the bands later heading to Malibu.

"I have a vivid memory of log cabins in the Swiss Alps and messing around with John Paul Jones's kids—like *The Sound of Music*," laughs Warren. "At the time it just seemed like fun."

Becoming tax exiles brought home to Peter's children the reality of his profession. Helen Grant already had mixed feelings about the job. In England, Helen, a talented ballet dancer, attended the Bush Davies School of Theatre Arts. "But I never told anyone what Dad did for a living," she admits.

It wasn't easy keeping the secret. "I boarded at the school during the week. On Fridays, kids would get picked up by their parents, usually in a regular hatchback." Meanwhile, Peter would come tearing up the road, wearing flying goggles and sitting behind the wheel of a Bentley. "You'd hear the car backfiring before it reached the drive. I'd say, 'For God's sake, Dad, bring the Volvo next time.'"

However, Tony Palmer's *Observer* story in May 1975 cost Helen her anonymity. "When I went back to school on Sunday, my friend's dad had seen this massive article, and everyone knew about it," she says. "For a while after, I was terribly bullied. I didn't tell Dad. If I had, it would have been like opening up a box of fireworks. I felt I had to get through it myself."

Grant took the same approach, regardless of the effect it had on him and his family. Peter was in the south of France in August when Robert and Maureen Plant's car crashed on the Greek island of Rhodes. Both were seriously injured.

Plant had fractured his right leg and ankle and was encased in plaster from hip to toe. "Colesy had to get a forklift truck to wheel Robert onto the plane," remembered Grant. For tax reasons, Plant recuperated in Jersey while his wife recovered in England. "It was a nightmare," Grant said. "There was a lot of tension, all holed up in houses we didn't really want to be in."

Grant later remembered being on a plane with Page and Plant when they realized they couldn't afford to enter British airspace until after midnight. Their chartered jet circled Ireland three times before resuming its flight to Gatwick Airport.

To ease the pressure, Peter suggested Zeppelin find somewhere overseas and glamorous in which to write and rehearse their next album. They decided on the Malibu Colony in California, a private stretch of beachside villas overlooking the Pacific. Peter rented a bungalow himself and attempted to turn it into Zeppelin/Swan Song headquarters. "A crazy idea," he admitted later.

John Bonham's wife, Pat, had just given birth, and he was loath to leave his family or his farm. Robert Plant arrived in Malibu in a wheelchair, while Jimmy Page kept such nocturnal hours, his villa was soon nicknamed "Henry Hall" ("henry" being English slang for heroin). It said much about the state of the group that John Paul Jones booked himself into "The Riot House" instead. "Robert and I seemed to keep a different time sequence to Jimmy," Jones later told writer Dave Lewis. "We just couldn't find him."

Among Page's fellow libertines was Michael Des Barres, whose group Detective had just signed to Swan Song. Des Barres was the public school–educated son of an English marquis, and was now married to "Miss Pamela." He met his new label boss in Hollywood that summer.

"Peter looked so incongruous in the Californian sunshine," he remembers. "He was a huge man, but there was a gentleness about him. I remember him eating a gigantic plate of eggs benedict, and I was shocked because he was so precise in the way he held his knife and fork," he adds, laughing. "And he was very charming to women. The girls loved him because he was the ultimate daddy. I was in the fug of narcotics myself, but Led Zeppelin used me to pass messages between them, as they weren't talking to each other."

Becoming embroiled in their soap opera, Des Barres realized how demanding Grant's job was. "We were just rock stars—dildos in velvet trousers. Peter Grant had to look after us *and* everything else, which meant dealing with all these crooks. To be truthful, I saw him lose it only once, and it was just verbal. Richard Cole was worse. Cole was fucking murderous."

Danny Goldberg was still employed by Swan Song in New York, when Grant hired former Atlantic Records executive Abe Hoch to run the European operation from London. "I had no idea what I was letting myself in for," says Hoch now.

After Hoch accepted the job, Grant booked him into New York's Plaza Hotel, where he remained for three months, waiting to be told what to do. "Friends would say, 'What are you doing here?' I'd say, 'I'm waiting to go to London.' Everything was paid for. Finally, Peter turns up from the Colony or hovering over England because he'd have to pay tax if he landed and says it's time to go."

In November, Hoch joined Grant in Munich, where Led Zeppelin was meant to be recording a new album, *Presence*. Grant later described the process as "an uphill struggle." Plant was limping around Musicland Studios on crutches, while everything ran on what one insider calls, "Jimmy Page time."

"Musicland was underneath the Arabella Hotel, where we were staying," recalls Hoch. "Days were going by, and we were waiting for Page, and the Rolling Stones were due in after us. Finally, Jimmy wakes up, wanders into the studio, and starts playing. Everybody says the same thing, 'Oh my God, Jimmy's playing.' Bonzo's kit was in the hotel dining room, and he started banging away, while people were still eating dinner. That cleared the room. It was the most incredible noise I've ever heard."

Page worked fifteen- to twenty-hour days with engineer Keith Harwood, the two men nodding off over the studio desk, until one woke the other and they carried on. Recording one day, Plant lost his balance, fell and almost broke his leg again.

Both Grant and Abe Hoch recalled the singer struggling to write lyrics for the album. "Robert once said to me, 'What rhymes with Achilles' Last Stand?'" laughs Hoch.

Grant remembered sharing a cab with Plant and John Paul Jones in Munich. "It was freezing outside," he told Malcolm McLaren. "Robert was behind with his lyrics and apologized to Jonesy, who said, 'Personally Robert, I've never bothered to listen to the lyrics on any of our albums.' I think it became colder in the cab than it was outside."

Presence was completed in a three-week, chemically assisted blur. When it was over, Grant ordered Abe Hoch to accompany the master tapes back to London. "There were two flight cases filled with fifteen spools—overdubs, outtakes, everything," Hoch says. "Peter insisted we cover the cases with the Rolling Stones 'tongue' stickers, just to piss off the Stones when they came to the studio."

En route, Hoch's plane developed a fault and landed in Bonn, Germany, where he was told the luggage would be moved to another aircraft. "I grabbed a steward and said, 'I need to see you move my luggage.' He said, 'Why?' I said, 'It's worth millions of pounds.' 'What have you got that is worth millions of pounds?' "It's the new Led Zeppelin album.' He said, 'I *love* Led Zeppelin.'"

The steward allowed Hoch off the plane and onto the runway. Within seconds soldiers surrounded him. "I heard rifles clicking, and I put my hands in the air. Then the steward shouts, 'It's OK, he has the new Led Zeppelin album.' Immediately, the guns go down, and the soldiers surround me, wanting to see this precious thing. After that, they let me watch the flight cases being put on the plane. What else could I do? Peter Grant told me I had to stay with those tapes."

Swan Song planned to release *Presence* at the exact same time worldwide, and Grant wanted to trailer its release with a PR campaign based around Hipgnosis's cover art. The sleeve showed a black object spliced into a photo from a 1950s *National Geographic* magazine. Was it solid matter or a black hole into another dimension? Its creator, Po, doesn't know. "It was obtuse and bizarre, and it suited Led Zeppelin," he says now.

A model of the object was to be photographed outside landmarks including 10 Downing Street and the White House. "Then three weeks before the album was due, *Melody Maker* got hold of the cover," explains Po. "Peter went ballistic and assumed it had come from me. It hadn't, but he was on the phone screaming."

Later, Po was asleep when he heard his doorbell ringing. "It was three in the morning, my wife and child were in the house, and Richard Cole and John Bindon came stomping up the stairs, shouting, 'You fucking cunt! You gave them the picture!' I was terribly frightened and phoned Peter who, of course, was still awake. Peter then discovers a boy in Atlantic's PR department had given *Melody Maker* the image."

Presence arrived worldwide at the end of March 1976. It was Zeppelin's darkest, gnarliest album yet, almost devoid of choruses, and remains one of Jimmy Page's personal favorites. "It's a bit of a muso's album, isn't it," Page told me. "So many times, I speak to people, and they say *Presence* is their favorite, and I'm always surprised."

The Zeppelin name alone would sell it, and *Presence* went straight to number one in America and in the UK. In contrast to their labelmates' tortured new record, Bad Company's latest, *Run With the Pack*, was another collection of painless blues-rock songs.

"Unlike Led Zeppelin, there was never any menace around Bad Company," points out Sherry Coulson, who understood where Zeppelin's aura came from. "It was partly Jimmy, but also G. I adored Peter, but there was always a drama. I saw a thousand Zeppelin shows but usually from behind a speaker. I used to sit there and embroider. Only once were we allowed in the audience, and G said it was too dangerous, so we had to have the FBI or Johnny Bindon with us."

However, the drama followed Bad Company when they started doing a tax year out. Sherry remembers renting a house in the Hamptons, while the band was touring America.

"I came down one morning, went to get a broom from the kitchen closet, and Bindon was inside. He was hiding from Vicki Hodge. He'd taken some Mandrax, climbed in, and fallen asleep while his missus went screaming around the neighborhood. I took out the broom, shut the door, and left him there."

When Bad Company decamped to the Malibu Colony, Bill Dautrich spotted intruders inside Robert Plant's empty villa. He found two young women trying on Plant's clothes and claiming he'd contacted them through the spirit world. As with Jimmy Page's stalker, Lynette "Squeaky" Fromme, the intruders were part of the Manson Family.

Soon after, Phil Carlo spotted another uninvited guest outside his beachside bungalow. "I whacked him over the head with a log," he says. "Within five minutes, there were cops with guns and a helicopter with a searchlight overhead. It turns out Boz Burrell, the friendly old hippie, had told this guy in a bar where we were staying, but after the Manson girls we weren't taking chances."

Carlo was especially worried, as his pregnant wife, Julie, was in the villa ("G had paid for her to come out and stay with us"). The following morning, Grant summoned Carlo to his bungalow, where he found last night's intruder tied to a chair. "Bill Dautrich was there, and it turned out this guy was wanted in three different states. G asked me what I wanted to do, but I didn't know. So he said, 'Bill, get the boys to take him up the mountains and drop him off.'

"The guy freaked out. 'Please Mr. Grant, no!' He thought this ogre was going to have him dropped off a mountain. Of course, it was the English interpretation of 'drop him off,' meaning 'give him a lift somewhere and kick his arse out the car.'"

In Malibu, Bad Company realized how big a bubble their manager had built around them. When Carlo, Burrell, and Simon Kirke requested a Chevrolet Camaro each, they arrived a couple of days later. When Phil was stopped for driving his without shoes, a shirt, or any identification, Bill Dautrich smoothed it over with the police chief. When everyone ran out of dope, a fixer, known as "Harold with the wooden leg," made a trip to Mexico and returned with the goods stashed inside his hollow limb.

Meanwhile, the Colony's other quieter residents counted down the days until Bad Company went home. When music had been booming out of one of their villas for hours, *Waterloo* movie star Rod Steiger suddenly appeared from behind a sand dune.

"Rod was in a housecoat, dark glasses, and smoking a cigar but still looked like he did when he'd played Napoleon," remembers party guest Maggie Bell. "He looked down at us and shouted at the top of his voice—'Shut the fuck up!'"

Since working on Led Zeppelin's film, director Peter Clifton had spoken to Peter Grant almost every day. Midway through the project, Clifton took a rare day off to watch the cricket. He'd not long arrived at Lord's cricket ground to see England play Australia, when he heard his name over the loudspeaker.

Clifton was chatting to fellow cricket fans Mick Jagger and Charlie Watts at the time. "They were terribly impressed that I was so important," he said. "So was my father, watching the game live on TV in Australia. Of course, it was Peter Grant needing to speak to me urgently. About what? I have no idea."

On one level, Clifton had been welcomed into Zeppelin's world as an equal. He attended Earls Court as a VIP guest, enjoyed a private audience with Jimmy Page at his Holland Park mansion, and indulged in the same habits as the band ("I wasn't a big drug taker, but I did a lot of coke with Peter"). However, he could never become complacent. Clifton had to chase Joan Hudson for his money, and Grant and Steve Weiss refused his repeated requests for a signed contract. "Peter argued that he'd never had a contract with Zeppelin, so why should I?"

During a private screening of *The Song Remains the Same* in New York, Ahmet Ertegun fell asleep. It was a bad omen. "Great film," he muttered later, "but who was the guy on the horse?" Ertegun had failed to recognize Robert Plant making his swashbuckling movie debut.

Grant was deeply upset by Ertegun's reaction. He needed Ahmet's approval for Atlantic's parent company, Warner Bros, to distribute the film. Zeppelin was too big for them ever to have refused, but in business Peter was becoming more suspicious and mistrustful than ever.

Clifton soon experienced Grant's paranoia first hand. While working on the movie in Los Angeles, Swan Song gave him twenty-four-hour use of a chauffeur-driven limousine. Foolishly, he'd sent his chauffeur to collect some film for *The London Rock and Roll Show*, a movie he was directing about Chuck Berry's UK comeback concert. The chauffeur told Grant, who became convinced Clifton was bootlegging Zeppelin's film. Richard Cole and Zeppelin's burly Welsh roadie Brian Gallivan ransacked his hotel suite, looking for evidence, and confiscated the other film.

Back in Britain, Grant and Robert Plant talked up the movie on the BBC TV music show *The Old Grey Whistle Test*. Standing on the deck of a boat as it puttered up the River Thames, Grant, wearing a T-shirt bearing his motto "In for a Quick Garden," let Plant do the talking. Neither was entirely engaged. "They took us out to lunch beforehand and plied us with the best claret," revealed Peter.

The Song Remains the Same finally had its premiere in New York and London in October 1976. It had taken almost three years from inception to reach the big screen. "I think we all went in with a bottle of brandy or whatever our tipple was," Page admitted. "We were so nervous of this thing we'd created."

The concert footage was a welcome memento of Led Zeppelin on stage, but the fantasy sequences were unconvincing. "You can look at those as either an attempt to break new barriers . . . or just Spinal Tap," said Page. Nevertheless, he recognized the message in Grant's sequence straight away. "That was Peter completely living up to it," he told me. "He was putting two fingers up at the music business. He was having some fun with the image."

In Grant's backstage scene, though, Clifton had been obliged to mute the offending "fucks" and "cunts." "Otherwise it would have been a bit like Derek and Clive," said Page.

"What did we know about making films?" said Grant later. "What we wanted to avoid was making just another rock 'n' roll movie. We jokingly felt that, even if it flopped, we'd at least get a video cassette copy each, making it the most expensive home movie in history."

For Peter Clifton, directing *The Song Remains the Same* was a bittersweet experience. Before its release, he was appalled to discover his name missing from the posters, and Zeppelin's accountants refused to pay his final £12,000 bill. The film was a box-office hit and made an estimated $10 million within a year of release. Despite Grant's assurances, Clifton never saw a penny.

At the London premiere, Clifton's son, Kieran, presented each of the band with a gift-wrapped reel of outtakes, showing them with their families. "There was footage of Helen and Warren, and Gloria with her ballet dancers in the studio. These were scenes that weren't included in the film."

However, Grant believed Clifton was hiding footage of Zeppelin and arranged a court order to have his house searched. Clifton was away, but his son's nanny answered the door to Joan Hudson and a roadie. Between them, they took everything with Led Zeppelin's name written on it. "I was horrified," said Clifton. "It was Peter Grant's absolute drug paranoia."

In the years ahead, Clifton would describe Led Zeppelin as "the rudest, most arrogant, and inhuman people I ever encountered." By the early 1990s, his attitude toward their manager had softened enough for them to meet for lunch in London. "Life goes on, and I made a good film," he said. "Peter had changed too. We shared a bottle of wine and made our peace."

However, during the final negotiations with Warner Bros, Grant had missed some meetings. Hipgnosis had created the movie's Art Deco–style posters and Po was delighted to present the artwork to Warners' senior management, but surprised by Grant's absence. "At the time I heard Peter had a heart problem," he says. Clifton was also shocked to attend a meeting only to find a drunken Richard Cole and Benji LeFevre in Grant's place.

Peter blamed his nonappearance on urgent family business. In fact, his marriage had broken up, and Gloria had run off with his farm manager.

By 1975, the touring, the drugs, the nannying of Jimmy Page, and the tax exile had left its mark on the Grants' relationship. "Peter would always call home when we were on tour," says Richard Cole. "And then he stopped calling home. Gloria had been in the entertainment business; she knew what went on. Then the cocaine took over, and when you've got a big bag of coke, you think you can do anything."

"Peter had a very good marriage," insists Chris Hayes, "and then he got involved in drugs and that circus in America." Her earlier hunch was also correct. "Gloria told me when the tour ended, Peter said he was exhausted and wanted to crash out in a hotel before coming home. Glo used to do his mail while he was away, and a letter arrived from this woman. She was heartbroken."

Peter's infidelity was an issue, but when Gloria began an affair with their new farm manager, Jim Thompsett, the marriage broke down completely. "Peter told Mickie he came back off a tour and realized there was something going on," remembers Chris. Grant, with his customary droll humor, told Mickie Most he'd guessed after he and Thompsett sat down together for breakfast, "And I got the burnt sausage."

The comment came from his time staying in boarding houses on the road. It was always assumed the guest who didn't receive the burnt sausage at breakfast had spent the night with the landlady.

Gloria moved out to consider her future, but then decided to leave for good. Richard Cole remembers an urgent phone call from Grant, asking him to come down to the manor. Gloria had returned with Thompsett to collect her belongings. Cole could sympathize with the boss: his own marriage to Marilyn was falling apart at the time.

"I put a shotgun in the boot of my car and drove to Horselunges," he says. "When I got there, I could see the three of them talking outside but didn't want to get involved. You could only get into the manor over the drawbridge, but I decided to go around the back, climb up a tree, and try and climb over the wall."

Cole hadn't noticed the branch was rotten and fell into the moat, into which the manor's malfunctioning septic tank had been leaking. Filthy and dripping wet, Cole then decided to remove the distributor from Gloria's car engine to stop her driving away, "But Peter made me put it back again. He didn't want to upset her."

There would be no reconciliation. "I remember getting called to the study, and Dad told me Mum was leaving," says Warren, who was ten years old at the time. "I asked why, and he said she'd found another man. Then I realized who it was.

"One of reasons I was so cut up about it was because I knew I'd been used. With Dad away, Jim had befriended me, and he used to take me out on the farm. I now realize he'd started an affair with my mum. After he'd gone, he had a Transit van parked down the road, and I poured a bag of sugar into the petrol tank."

Thompsett had lived in a gamekeeper's cottage on the grounds, which, some years later, Warren partly demolished with a farm tractor. "I was traumatized by it all," he admits now.

With Gloria gone, Grant wasted little time seeking custody of his children. Before flying to LA for a premiere of *The Song Remains the Same*, he applied for a temporary high court injunction, prohibiting Gloria from having the children in Thompsett's company while he was away. To Grant's surprise, the judge went even further and granted him a permanent injunction.

"In the midseventies, women automatically got custody," points out Mark Long. "That Gloria *didn't* says more about Peter Grant's power than anything."

"Gloria always said, 'He had better lawyers than I did,'" adds Chris Hayes.

Helen Grant maintains her parents never fully got over the end of their marriage. "Dad asked Mum to come back, but she wouldn't. Then a year later, she wrote him a letter saying, 'May I come back?' And he said 'No.' I think it was his pride that stopped him. I don't think Mum ever loved anyone the way she did my dad."

Nevertheless, the couple divorced; Gloria married Thompsett in 1977 and they had a son together one year later. Reflecting on her parents' breakup now, Helen lays the blame squarely on the music industry. "Led Zeppelin was the best and worst thing that ever happened to my dad. My mum always said, 'We were happiest when we had no money. If he hadn't made all that money, we would have still been together.'"

With Gloria gone, life at Horselunges changed dramatically. Ray Washbourne, a no-nonsense Londoner who'd previously worked for Don Murfet's Artistes Services, became Peter's right-hand man. "When Dad was away, he'd look after us and make sure I went to school," says Warren.

"He was like a male nanny," adds Helen. "But you didn't fuck about with Ray."

Crew members and security staff were also hired to help out. "I got the call after Gloria left," says Dave Northover. "I think I did Tuesday to Friday. There were all these bad vibes—people talking about how Peter was going to get this bloke, Jim."

When Northover took the children to visit their mother, he noticed they weren't alone. "I'd spot Peter's people keeping an eye on things. What could he do? I think in the end he accepted it was over."

"Dad wanted us to stay with him, but not out of spite to my mum," insists Warren. "He gave us the choice. It was the same when I was moving to a new school." Warren was offered the choice of boarding, like his sister, or being schooled locally. "All my friends were going to the local Hailsham School, which we all called 'Battle Road,' so I said I'd go there.

"Unfortunately, I was a bad kid. From a young age I thought, 'What do I have to go to school for?' I live in a massive house with a moat around it; my dad manages this band known all around the world. So why do I need to learn geography? So I went only because I knew I had to.

"Then I'd get comments from teachers like, 'Just because of who your dad is, don't think you don't have to do any work.' That immediately made me think, OK, they think I'm not working because of my dad."

"When Mum left Horselunges, it became a very macho household," says Helen. "I noticed it whenever I came home from school. There was always an atmosphere there. At night, you'd hear unexplained noises and doors banging. I'm sure the house was haunted."

Grant's latest bodyguard, John Bindon, contributed to the macho atmosphere, trailing an air of menace and dark comedy. "Biffo came with us to Monaco one year," recalls Warren. "I was walking to the pool, and he was sitting on his balcony smoking the most enormous joint—'Morning Warren!' To us he was just one of the guys."

Later, Bindon enlivened Guy Fawkes Night at the manor by accessorizing the Guy with a gigantic exploding penis fashioned from a loaf of French bread and a firework. "He then took a scaffolding pole, filled it with rockets, and started firing them at the Martlet," recalls Warren.

The Golden Martlet Pub earned well out of Horselunges, but catering to Grant and his merry men had its drawbacks. "Biffo could be terribly funny," says Dave Northover, "but also very dangerous. He really didn't care."

Northover joined Bindon in the Martlet one evening. He was chatting to the landlord, when he spotted something out of the corner of his eye. "Biffo had his back to the bar, bold as you like, while the woman he was with was on her knees giving him a blow job. It was early, so there weren't many in the pub to see his giant tool. I remember thinking, Jesus Christ, John."

It wasn't always such fun, though. Late one night, Grant woke Northover and ordered him to make Warren a cup of tea. "It was two in the morning, and Warren was still up and about. I said he should make it himself. Peter told me to come up to his bedroom straight away. He was in there with Bindon. He said, 'Make him a cup of tea!' I refused, and next thing, Peter hit me on the shoulder with a hammer.

"I don't know why he had a hammer in his bedroom. I went downstairs and probably made the fucking tea, but I left the next morning. A couple of days later, Ray calls, and I got talked into coming back. Later on, the 'hammer story' would come up as a funny thing in conversation, but I was distraught at the time."

John Bindon wasn't the only one nominated to sit up all night with the boss. "Now Peter's wife had gone, he borrowed everyone else's," says Sherry Coulson. "He was good fun. G always had the best gossip—'Ere, you'll never guess what Keith Richards has done.' So we hung out with him, as he always dished the dirt and could be quite feminine and bitchy."

"He'd phone at ten o'clock—'Wotcha doing, Marilyn? . . . I got plenty of champagne,'" remembers Marilyn Cole. "Then he'd send his chauffeur, Norman, up to London in the Rolls to take me to down to Hellingly."

For a time, Peter insisted on having a chauffeur on call twenty-four hours a day. Norman was Grant's regular and most trusted driver. "Norman was the first person to introduce me to cockney rhyming slang," recalls Dave Northover, "I didn't have a clue what it meant when he described someone as 'a right shirt front.' Then I realized, oh, 'cunt.'"

"Norman would pick me up and take me back to Horselunges," says Marilyn, "and Peter and I would watch movies, drinking and doing coke, while Warren—bless him—was being looked after by the boys."

Both Grant and Jimmy Page were fascinated by *The Night Porter*, the 1974 film in which Dirk Bogarde's SS officer resumes a sado-masochistic affair with Charlotte Rampling's concentration camp survivor.

"Peter was always interested in what was not said," Marilyn explains. "And that film is all about what was not said. There was all this passion and troubling contradictions and tense emotions that were never discussed. I think Peter was unbelievably hurt and lonely after Gloria."

"I think there was a wounded side to him that caused all his bad behaviors," suggests Sherry. "It always interested me how G couldn't get over any slights. If someone spelt his name wrong or forget to mention him in an article. And you don't get much more personal than your wife leaving you for your farm manager."

"After Gloria, Peter would make excuses for you to go and see him," remembers Po. "I owed him so much. So when he said we needed to talk, I went, even when we didn't."

Po was summoned one night, only to find Grant and Richard Cole in an especially paranoid state. "There was copious amount of alcohol and Peruvian marching powder on the go. It felt very weird at Horselunges that night. It was November, and there was mist everywhere, like something out of the *Hammer House of Horrors*."

"We were sitting in Peter's bedroom, and suddenly his big old black dog started barking. Peter was convinced there was somebody in the garden—'It's that bloke, Jim.' So we all ran downstairs, and there was a silver pistol on the table. I remember Peter saying to Ricardo, 'Get the gun,' then to me, 'Po, get the poker from the fireplace, and hit him on the head if he comes in.'

"They ran into the garden, and I could hear them shouting by the swimming pool. Then 'Bang!' A gunshot. 'Have you got him?' 'I think I got him!' I'm standing by the door with a poker and this old dog at my feet, wondering what the fuck I'm doing.

"Of course, it was all the realms of fantasy. There was nobody there. After forty-five minutes they come back inside, full of bravado, and went upstairs to carry on. At 6 a.m., I got in my car and drove home, thinking, 'This is completely out of control.'"

*I*n December, Britain's *Ideal Home* magazine ran a story on Grant's London apartment, 41 Gloucester Place Mews. The article showed how designers

Paul Reeves and Jon Wealleans had transformed the property into a visual riot of sandblasted glass skylights and geometric wall designs.

"I sent Peter a breakdown of costs," says Reeves. "He sent back a blank check with a note that read, 'Leave it to you, love Peter.' Which was very clever. Because he was a friend, he got it cheaper than he would have done otherwise."

The Mews was meant as a gift to Gloria, but Paul Reeves thinks she never even saw it. The flat's centerpiece was a dining table with cylindrical glass legs. "I doubt anyone ever ate a meal off it," he admits. "It was probably just used for chopping up noxious substances."

Abe Hoch moved in for a time after arriving in London. "Peter said 'You can stay in my mews flat.' I said, 'What's a mews flat?'" Hoch's appointment as vice president of UK and European operations coincided with the end of Danny Goldberg's tenure in New York. Goldberg had put all his energy into managing a spiritually minded singer-songwriter named Mirabai. He'd signed her to Atlantic but couldn't get a hit.

"That was a Goldberg investment I persuaded Ahmet to bankroll," explained Grant. He eventually made Goldberg choose: the singer or the label? He chose Mirabai.

It was an amicable split, but in Grant's eyes, Goldberg had left the family. Danny was surprised to see Peter in tears, again. He'd also given him a warning as a parting shot. "Peter told me, 'All these friends of yours wouldn't talk to you if you didn't work for Led Zeppelin.'" It was partly true, but Goldberg also wondered if Peter wasn't subconsciously talking about himself.

Besides Abe Hoch, the Kings Road office also included new recruits, secretary Cynthia Sach and publicist Unity MacLean. "We had the scruffiest offices you've ever seen," said Cynthia in 2011. "For all their millions, Zeppelin didn't spend a penny doing the place up."

"Peter looked like a bit of an ogre," remembers Unity, "and to be honest, I was rather nervous of him."

Unity witnessed Grant's ogre-like tendencies at the launch for *The Song Remains the Same* in Covent Garden. "There was a Japanese photographer trying to get into the party, and I remember Peter pushing him down the stairs. I thought he was going to fall, and I found it rather scary. When I went up there, the only people at the party were Paul and Linda McCartney. I realized later everything had to be so exclusive with Peter, we sometimes ended up with nobody.

"Peter was nice to me to begin with," she says. "He always called me 'U,' never Unity. But I do think he had ulterior motives. He once asked me to go to Horselunges with him. I didn't want to upset him, but I was married and didn't think it would be appropriate."

The following morning, Unity arrived at work to find a dead chicken draped over her desk. "I thought it was a warning, like the horse's head in *The Godfather*," she laughs. "I went to see Cynthia—'Cyn, there's a dead chicken on my desk.' She pretended she didn't know, and then admitted Peter had asked her to get it. Apparently, he thought I was a chicken for not going on a date with him.

"Gloria had left him, and he was alone. And Peter cared desperately for Helen and Warren. I gave Warren a wide berth. He needed his dad, not bossy old me. And if you put a foot wrong with him, Peter would be all over you. But he did ask me and Cyn to look after Helen," she adds. "I think he was concerned because her mother wasn't around. Cynthia took her to the ballet, and I took her to lunch. We talked about things at school and what she wanted to do. Helen was a charming girl."

While Grant's drug use amplified existing problems and scrambled his judgment, he still hadn't the time to run a record company. However, nothing was allowed to happen without his approval.

"Swan Song was more like an illusion than a reality," says Abe Hoch. "There was a billboard for Durex condoms across from the office. I used to look at it and think, 'This is a good indication of where my life's going.'"

It had already become too much for fellow tenant, Mark London. He gave up co-managing Maggie Bell and left Number 484, leaving behind some beautiful antique furniture. "I never saw or spoke to Peter again after that," he says. "It had all got too heavy for Mark," admits Maggie.

"There was a lot of politics, a lot of games being played," says Hoch. "Phil Carson was a good guy, but I never understood his hold over Zeppelin. They'd offered him the Swan Song job, but he wasn't stupid, so he didn't take it. Then there was our attorney, Stevens Weiss. He was more like Ray Donovan [the fixer in the US TV drama] than a lawyer."

Tapes from new artists arrived daily, and it was impossible to get Grant to listen to them. "Hundreds of hopefuls sent in cassettes and tapes," says Simon Kirke. "They all stayed in a huge bowl in the center of the conference table."

One day Hoch opened a package from Atlantic. It was a tape of a group from Seattle and a note that read, "This girl sings like Robert Plant but with more balls." "Robert was in the office and, like an idiot, I showed him the note. That went right in the wastebasket. A girl singing with more balls than him wasn't going to float. The group turned out to be Heart."

Hoch and the others quickly learned Led Zeppelin took priority over everything else. The office's telex machine was their vital link to America. If the band needed to use it, the staff had to wait. "We were trying to work something for the Pretty Things," recalls Hoch, "and Robert had lost a bathrobe in a spin dryer in a hotel in Nice, so he needed to send a telex to track it down."

"I walked in one morning and saw the office girl, Jenny, sitting in a corner sewing," remembers Unity. "She said, 'Oh, Jimmy came in with his jeans and asked if I could turn up the hems.' I thought, oh, great, now we're running a sewing circle."

At Robert Plant's recommendation, Swan Song signed Welsh guitarist Dave Edmunds. Nobody knew what to do next, though, as Led Zeppelin had to sign off on all decisions. "Which was impossible," says Richard Cole, "because you could never get them all together in the same room."

Unity succeeded in bringing all of Zeppelin, except for Jimmy Page, to the boardroom table for a meeting. "I wanted to run that label properly," she insists. "I wanted to do good things for Dave Edmunds and Maggie."

"We sat and talked and after a while John Bonham took me aside. He said, 'Unity, I admire your loyalty and everything you're trying to do, but if you want to know about tractors, farm equipment, or which bull to mate with your cow, then I'm your man. But I'm not a record company person. None of us are.' I said, 'Bonzo, what am I supposed to do?' He said, 'You need to speak to Peter.'"

Speaking to Peter wasn't easy, either. Days went by when he didn't appear in the office. When he did, Grant was reluctant to make any decisions. "I honestly think he'd had enough of the business," says Unity. "He had no interest other than joking around with the boys and talking about the old days.

"He'd sit there, chatting for hours and shoving a key into a huge bag of cocaine and sniffing up these giant rocks. I'll say this for Peter, he was generous. He'd always give you some, holding out his key—'Come on U, sniff it up before it falls off.'"

"Peter's office was below ours, and he and Richard used to lock themselves in there, doing substances," remembers Hoch. "Roy Harper was often around—or Harpic, as they called him, after a brand of toilet cleaner, I later discovered."

Locked in his office and revved up on cocaine, Grant would start making phone calls. They could come at any time of the day or night. The *NME*'s Nick Kent received a call after *The Song Remains the Same* received a drubbing in one of the music papers.

"He sounded like he was in the throes of a full-blown, drug-accelerated breakdown," Kent recalled. "He sounded like a cross between a wounded bear and Darth Vader with a slight East London lisp. 'I just want to know if you're still our ally,' he kept asking me. It made my blood run cold."

Dave Northover realized how much cocaine was passing through the office when he was sent on an errand. "Norman the chauffeur took me to this block of flats near Gloucester Place Mews," he recalls. "There was a man there who said, 'I've got something for you' and took out a big canister and poured out a kilogram of coke onto a sheet of plastic on the floor. It was a mountain of pharmaceutical cocaine, which we had to take back to Peter."

If Grant and his accomplices weren't in the office, they were usually in one of the local pubs: the World's End, opposite the office, the Man in the Moon, the Roebuck, or the Water Rat, where John Bindon and his cronies drank.

Helen remembers walking along Kings Road with her father and seeing people staring. "I think that's when I realized he was a bit different. So I'd stick two fingers up at them." Later, Peter took her to the World's End pub, "Where I met some guy who was supposed to have robbed the Bank of England."

The pubs were full of scoundrels, and many found their way back to Swan Song. "We had all kinds in and out of the office," admits Phil Carlo. "Bindon's villain mates, the cobbler Terry de Havilland who made shoes for the band, attractive ladies in very little clothing, dodgy looking people nodding off in the corner, and then the colonel in his blazer sorting out the poppy tins."

"There were all these terrible characters, like Bindon and guys with nicknames like Paddy the Plank," says Abe Hoch. "As an American I found this East End villainy really intimidating. Peter and Richard gave off that aura. They also looked wild, with their hair and their beards and those teeth. They were like something out of a film.

"Neither of them raised a hand to me, but it was how they said things. They'd come right up to you and go, 'Did you tell so and so this?' in that London accent they had, staring at you with glazed eyes. You'd be scared, even if you didn't know what they were asking."

One night, a friend invited Abe on a double date with David Bowie's estranged wife, Angie, and Vicki Hodge. "I didn't know who Vicki was," he insists. "We're hot to trot, and she suddenly says, 'I'm so glad you're a man, because most men find out who my boyfriend is and back off.'

"With all the Brooklyn bravado I could muster I said, 'Fuck your boyfriend. . . . Who is he anyway?' She says, 'John Bindon.' Truthfully, I started to cry. I'd heard a story Bindon had ripped a man's bollock off with his bare hands. Thank God, he never found out."

Besides the threat of violence, there was also the politics. Deep down, Hoch knew it was time to leave Swan Song not long after he'd arrived. "Jimmy came over to my house on Old Brompton Road and wanted to talk," he says. "He said, 'I need your advice. G is out of it all the time. We don't know to deal with it. How would *you* deal with it?'

"I remember thinking, 'This guy is full of shit. There is no upside for me in this conversation. If I suggest I could run their operation, it's the door or death.'"

The two men sat in silence, Page waiting patiently for Hoch's reply. "In the end, I said, 'You can't replace him, he's the fifth member of Led Zeppelin. If he is having problems, we should all get together and try and help him.' It was all a game. Everything at Swan Song was a game."

9

Doctor Larry's Bag

"In 1975 Peter Grant had to turn around
and say, 'There's nothing else I can do for you.
Now you really can go to Saturn.'"

—ROBERT PLANT

"**B**ad Company was a force of nature," declares Detective's ex-lead singer Michael Des Barres. "They were a great top-down, shades-and-leather-jacket rock 'n' roll band. By comparison, the rest of us were a bunch of wankers."

Four years after the band formed, Bad Company had achieved three US top-five, platinum-selling albums, and Clive Coulson had more than earned his cut of Peter Grant's management fee. Yet, despite Des Barres's glowing endorsement, the wheels were starting to come off.

In the summer of 1976, Bad Company finished another grueling American tour. With barely time to unpack, they went straight to the Château d'Hérouville studio in France to record the next album. There was just one problem. "When we arrived, Mick Ralphs turned around and said, 'We haven't got any songs, we haven't got *anything*,'" recalls Phil Carlo, who phoned Grant to break the bad news.

At the time, Iggy Pop and David Bowie were at the "Honky Château," as it was nicknamed, working on Pop's *The Idiot* album. "Peter asked to speak to Bowie," says Carlo. "I could hear him talking and Bowie chortling." Grant had known David Bowie when he was still Davie Jones, a wannabe pop star in the early 1960s.

After thirty minutes reminiscing about the old days, Grant asked him to put Carlo back on the line. "He said, 'Tell Mick to stop panicking; tell the boys to take as long as they want. I've told Bowie he can stay in the studio and take his time.'"

Two weeks later, Bad Company had cobbled together the bones of a new album. However, *Burning Sky*, released the following spring, would be the first not to make the top five in Britain or America.

Rock music was undergoing another periodic shift, and it was happening outside Swan Song's front door. Kings Road boutique owner Malcolm McLaren had recreated himself as a music manager and maneuvred his group, the Sex Pistols, into the tabloids and the charts. What nobody knew was that McLaren identified completely with Peter Grant and his generation of hustlers and star-makers.

The Pistols with their sloganeering song titles and confrontational image upset the British establishment more than any pop act since Elvis. The phrase "punk rock" now appeared in newspapers as well as the music press. What unified punk groups such as the Pistols, the Damned, and the Clash was a return to raw, uncomplicated songs.

Punk's year zero policy meant Iggy Pop and David Bowie were excused. However, Bad Company, with their beards and cowboy hats, and Led Zeppelin, with their double-neck guitars and expensive home movies, were considered terminally unhip.

The adulation and sales didn't disappear overnight. Far from it. However, the arrival of these young upstarts unsettled the old guard. "All of a sudden I felt terribly out of touch," admits Simon Kirke.

Page and Plant went to see the Damned play the Roxy in London and thought it reminded them of the primal rock 'n' roll of the fifties. "I understand why punk happened," Plant told me. "When you have an audience all over the world, like Zeppelin did, you become more and more remote, and you're a generation removed from the average kid on the street."

However, America hadn't fallen for punk's charms, and Led Zeppelin was booked to play its biggest US tour yet, starting in February 1977. After final rehearsals, the group's equipment was flown ahead to the States. Then it was announced Plant had contracted laryngitis, and the tour postponed for four weeks. Thousands of tickets had already been sold for every date. "The loyalty of the fans astounded me," said Grant. "There was no hype, no MTV. It was down to pure demand."

Zeppelin's 1977 North American Tour finally began in Dallas in April. The numbers were huge: forty-nine scheduled concerts playing to an estimated 1.3 million people. "By then, I'd started to think, how much bigger could it get?" admitted Plant.

The *Starship* was grounded with engine failure and replaced with a repurposed Boeing 720 from Las Vegas's Caesars Palace. *Caesar's Chariot* had similar fixtures and fittings, as well as a rudder painted with the Swan Song emblem of a winged messenger falling from the sky—an unlikely image, perhaps, for an airplane.

Grant joined the party a day later than the others, turning up by Learjet and strolling into the Dallas Memorial Auditorium with Steve Weiss on one side and John Bindon on the other. Both men were emblematic of Grant's power but in different ways. Nobody else, though, had known Biffo was joining the tour.

According to some, Special Branch officers had advised Bindon to cool his relationship with Princess Margaret or risk the consequences. He was also struggling financially. "I never saw John in gainful employment," said his old friend and Kings Road shoemaker, Terry de Havilland. "He was a good actor but didn't get that much work." Grant's job offer couldn't have come at a better time.

Peter had his reasons for wanting Bindon around. "During one US tour the band received a lot of death threats," he said later. "It was an extremely stressful time, but I dealt with it in the way that was necessary."

"Every band had death threats," insists Phil Carson. "You didn't take them seriously, but the paranoia was amplified because of the cocaine. Those of us around Peter knew it was bullshit; he had to be indulged, and there was money changing hands for such indulgence, hence Bindon coming along."

Of the band, only John Bonham seemed comfortable around the new bodyguard. "My memory is Robert, especially, hated Bindon being on that tour," says Dave Northover. Even Grant's lieutenant, Richard Cole, was confused. "We were never told why Bindon was there."

In footage from New York, Bindon can be seen shepherding Page and Plant to their limousines. Wherever Led Zeppelin and their manager went, Biffo wasn't far behind: muscles bunched, flinty eyes scanning the area for wrongdoers, ready to let fly with a volley of expletives or worse.

But it didn't matter how much manpower Grant assembled, he couldn't dispel a lingering air of suspicion and paranoia. Where once it was Zeppelin, Grant, Cole, and their road crew against the world, the entourage now included various personal assistants, gofers, and random drug buddies. "The tour had become all about camps," says Cole. "There were no camps before. Now it was all becoming fragmented."

Among the latest recruits were Plant's new assistant Dennis Sheehan (who would later go on to tour manage U2 until his death in 2015) and Rex King, a carpet fitter from London who was hired to keep John Bonham company. "We took Rex out to be his whipping boy," said Grant.

There was also a physician on the payroll. "Doctor Larry" had already brought his pharmaceutical expertise to the Rolling Stones and appeared in their infamous tour movie *Cocksucker Blues*. Larry's bag of pills and potions made him one of the most popular members of Zeppelin's retinue. From the vantage point onstage, Led Zeppelin often noticed how the doctor and his good-looking female guests always occupied the best seats in the house.

In Britain, the Sex Pistols' "God Save the Queen" would soon become the unofficial anthem for Queen Elizabeth II's Silver Jubilee. Nobody in America was listening, and the States rolled over for Led Zeppelin, just like it always did. During the first leg of the tour, hundreds of fans without tickets tried to force their way into a show in St. Paul, Minnesota. One week later, fans, unable to get into two sold-out dates in Cincinnati, threw bottles through the Riverfront Coliseum's plate-glass doors and tried to smash their way inside.

Any outsiders allowed into Zeppelin's inner circle had to adhere to Peter Grant's rules. Swan Song's US press officer, Janine Safer, handed journalists a list of instructions, which included never asking about anything other than the music. Some wondered if the second rule on the list wasn't for the journalists' own safety: "Do not talk to Peter Grant or Richard Cole—for any reason."

The *Los Angeles Times* ran an interview with Grant under the headline, "The Pilot Who Keeps Led Zeppelin on Course." Writer Robert Hilburn met "the huge Buddha-shaped manager" in New Orleans and regaled his readers with war stories: "Like the time Grant poured a bucket of water over a video machine being used to illegally film a Zeppelin concert." Grant, meanwhile, preferred to talk about how many tickets the band had sold.

Onstage, Robert Plant roared bansheelike through "Achilles Last Stand." Shirt open to the waist, he shook his hips as usual but was dosed up on painkillers to help make it through the show. Jimmy Page matched his singer pose for pose but was so thin, his white stage suit, embroidered with Chinese dragons and poppy heads, seemed to dwarf his body. Page looked positively consumptive. The tour gossip was that he was surviving on a diet of alcohol, chemicals, scraps of solid food, and very little sleep.

On April 6, the tour reached Chicago for a run of sold-out nights at the twenty-thousand-capacity stadium. On the first date, Page materialized on-stage, wearing leather jackboots, aviator shades, and a German SS officer's cap. There were shades of his and Grant's beloved *Night Porter*.

The third Chicago date was cut short after an hour. From the start, Page seemed listless and disorientated. "We're going to take a necessary five-minute break," Plant told the audience. The show was abandoned with the excuse given that Jimmy had gastroenteritis.

"I told Jimmy, you can't go back on," said Grant, still sounding like a concerned parent in 1994. "I sent someone out to tell the audience the show would be rescheduled, but I decided they needed to hear an English voice." Zeppelin's stage designer, Ian "Iggy" Knight, was given the job. Grant insisted his accent worked: "There was not one boo, and only two people asked for their money back."

Creem magazine reporter Jaan Uhelszki was granted an audience with Page during the Chicago run, and found him in a tetchy mood after a luke-warm review of a recent show.

After a few minutes of stilted conversation, Page passed a new rule. "Jimmy informed me the only way I could converse with him for the interview would be by directing my questions to his PR," said Uhelszki. She completed the interview, asking her questions to Janine Safer, who was seated four feet away. Safer then repeated them to Jimmy, and she relayed his answers back to Uhelszki.

Day after day, Grant marshalled Led Zeppelin and its foot soldiers from his throne on *Caesar's Chariot* or whichever presidential suite he was sequestered in. Grant was still coping with the collapse of his marriage. "It was hard for me because I had to leave the kids, and my divorce was starting," he admitted later.

"The whole thing with Gloria had hit him hard," concurs Cole. "Peter was the boss, and if the boss doesn't look as though he's right on it every minute of the day, the rest of the people, me included, weren't."

Cole had demons of his own. He had been using heroin before the tour. Other crew members, and journalists especially, were wary around him. When Cole's "Ricardo" or "Dirty Dick" alter ego took over, few were safe.

"Ricardo was not a man to be messed with on that tour," remembers Po. "Even with something simple like getting into a limo, the door would fly open, and you'd hear his voice from inside—'Get in, you *cunt!*'"

Tour photographer Neal Preston remembers Cole nearly bringing the plane down during one flight: "Something happened, and Richard was really angry. We were coming in to land but still a thousand feet up, when he tried to kick out one of the plane's windows.

"I was sitting next to Peter, and he was as white as a ghost," he adds. "Every time I've asked Richard about this since, he maintains he knew the windows were double paned and he'd only cracked the first one. That may be, but I still remember that overwhelming feeling of, What the fuck!"

As the tour progressed, there were times when the shows seemed to happen as much by luck than judgment. "All the timekeeping went out the window," admits Phil Carson. "One night we didn't even leave the hotel in New Orleans until nine o'clock, and we were supposed to be onstage at eight. There were real problems, but because there was so much money coming in, it was papering over the cracks."

There were reasons for the band's tardiness. One evening, Dave Northover was sent to rouse Jimmy Page from his hotel suite. After several minutes searching, he discovered Page's hiding place: "Jimmy was so skinny, he was passed out inside the bolster at the end of the bed."

This was Northover's second Zeppelin tour. No matter how many times he told everyone he was a physicist and not a pharmacist, they ignored it. One night, Page was writing a letter and mistakenly emptied his fountain pen into a $1,000 stash of cocaine. His inkpot and stash had been next to each other on his desk.

"The best I could do was empty the mess onto a plastic lid and leave it to dry on a hotel radiator," says Northover. For the next few days, it was easy to tell which girls and gofers had been in Jimmy's suite, by a telltale trickle of blue mucus around their nostrils.

There were late-running shows, and there were poor shows, but there were plenty of times when the energy coming from the stage was almost tangible. Led Zeppelin still thrilled the audience, and their manager still knew how to play the charming host.

Grant's connections led to an invitation to the Russian Embassy in Washington. Peter returned the compliment and invited his hosts to the show in neighboring Landover, Maryland. They watched from the side of the stage and declared Led Zeppelin was better than the Rolling Stones. Business cards and numbers were exchanged, and Grant envisaged Zeppelin laying waste to the USSR. Events later on the tour derailed those plans, and as Grant observed, "Elton John went there first."

The tour's first run ended at Detroit's Pontiac Silverdome in front of a record-breaking seventy-six-thousand-strong crowd. The day before the show, Neal Preston fell foul of Grant. It was an experience he's unlikely to forget. "We kidnapped Robert Plant," he explains—the "we" being Neal, Janine Safer, and Atlantic's marketing manager, Danny Markus. "We had some time off before the Silverdome gig, and I told Robert that Little Feat was having a press party in Detroit. Robert loved Little Feat, and we were going to the city anyway, so we went a day earlier."

Preston had forgotten to tell Grant, though. "When the band turned up in Detroit the next day, I received an urgent call from Richard. He said, 'G needs to see you. I don't care if you're taking a shit, pull your fucking pants up and get here now.'"

After a severe dressing down, Grant told Preston he had to deliver a set of prints of John Bonham from the night's show under his door by twelve noon the next day. Grant knew it would take all Preston's ingenuity to complete his mission on time.

"It was horrible," Preston says. "I tried to get anyone I knew in Detroit to make the prints for me, but they'd been up all night doing blow. I called the local newspaper, and they couldn't help. I had to get cabs everywhere, so it was at great personal expense. I managed to get the prints under the door with two minutes to spare." Neither Grant nor Bonham ever mentioned the pictures again.

After playing the Silverdome, the touring party returned home—to wives, girlfriends, families, and some semblance of normality. Although the definition of "normality" differed depending which band member it was.

There was no respite for Grant. That Zeppelin was briefly off the road didn't excuse him from taking care of the band's every need. On May 19, he put on his best velvet jacket and joined them at the Ivor Novello Awards in London, where Zeppelin was honored for its "Outstanding Contribution to British Music."

"It wasn't like all those disc awards," he said later. "That really meant something." Visitors to his Eastbourne home in the 1990s saw only one piece of memorabilia on display: the Ivor on top of the television set.

Peter and the band were off the road for a little less than a month before the second leg resumed in Birmingham, Alabama. The melodrama and spectacle continued, onstage and off. DJ Nicky Horne had introduced Zeppelin at

Earls Court and was now making a documentary about the group for London's Capital Radio.

Horne flew to New Orleans to join the tour. A limousine was waiting to take him to the group's hotel on Bourbon Street. "It was late at night, and there was nobody to meet me," he recalls. "I knew Peter was on the floor above mine, so I decided to find him. I got out of the lift on his floor and walked toward the end of corridor. There was this huge guy sitting on a chair outside the room. I presumed he was Peter's security guard. He was, but he had no intention of letting me go anywhere."

As Horne walked toward him, the guard stood up, pulled a gun from his waistband, and pointed it straight ahead. "He was holding it in a proper two-handed stance, and shouting 'Where's ya pass?' I suddenly became very English and said in a high voice, 'I haven't got a pass!' and held my hands up. Eventually he realized I wasn't an assassin and put the gun away, but I was scared shitless."

Horne's first trip on *Caesar's Chariot* was to Baton Rouge. There it became obvious this was no ordinary flight. "Richard Cole told me there'd been a fight on the plane, and one of the portholes had cracked," he marvels. Cole neglected to mention he was the one who'd cracked it.

Soon after takeoff, stewardesses in matching hot pants appeared in the aisle carrying what looked like a wooden cocktail cabinet. "It was covered in Chinese dragons, lettering, and gold leaf," says Horne. "It was full of all sorts of different kinds of grass, pills, anything you wanted."

After the plane landed in Baton Rouge, limousines sped onto the tarmac to take everyone to the LSU Assembly Center. There had been more talk of death threats: "I remember speaking to the roadies about it. There was a palpable sense of paranoia about one of the band members being assassinated. The security was so tight."

The extra manpower recruited from the local police department looked wonderfully incongruous alongside Zeppelin's entourage. Grant, with his Dickensian cap and South London accent, could have come from another planet next to these good old Louisiana boys with their crew cuts and sports shirts. Nobody was taking any chances. The cops flanked the stage, while Grant and his aides watched from the wings, wired on adrenaline or something from Dr. Larry's bag or the pharmaceutical cocktail cabinet.

There may have been threats on Led Zeppelin's lives, but Grant's humor endured. After the show, Cole summoned Nicky Horne to Grant's hotel suite: Peter wanted to do his interview now. Horne walked into the room to find the manager naked and reclining beneath black satin sheets on a vast circular bed. It was an imposing image.

As soon as Nicky asked his first question, a woman's head appeared from beneath the covers. There was a lot of giggling followed by the appearance of a second woman's head. "Peter had two female friends in bed with him, and both were naked," remembers Horne. Cole and Grant had staged the whole thing. "It was the strangest interview I'd ever done, and weirdly intimidating. The band was in on it as well because when I went back downstairs, Jimmy came over with a big grin on his face—'How did the interview go, then?'"

If Grant still needed convincing of how far he'd come since the days of the Embassy Ballroom circuit, he was left in no doubt one day in Texas. Zeppelin and Bad Company's touring schedules overlapped, and their private jets were parked side by side on the same airstrip.

"It was a wonderful moment," says Po, who'd spent weeks on the road with Bad Company. "These were mad, hedonistic days, and we all swapped around and got into each other's planes."

There was more mischief to come, when Grant strolled onto Bad Company's jet with the tallest woman Po had ever seen, "Taller than Peter. This unbelievable-looking Amazonian black model. Peter said, 'Wait here a moment darling, and I'll come back for you in a minute.'"

He returned to *Caesar's Chariot* just as Bad Company's jet prepared for takeoff. Within minutes, it was airborne. Peter's abandoned consort was distraught. She needed to get to New York; this plane was going to Austin. "I remember Clive Coulson going, 'What the fuck? Peter's dumped us with his girlfriend.' And Clive had to buy her a ticket home."

Po also spent time on the road with Zeppelin in '77 and was reminded of how much of their mystique and power radiated from Jimmy and his manager. After one show, he was summoned to the guitarist's hotel suite.

"Page was wearing his SS outfit and had filled the room with candles. I thought, 'Hang on, has he got a Ouija board in here?' But Jimmy was very clever at creating an atmosphere of mystery—with the cigarette dangling from the lip and the hair all over his face. It was all about the mystique."

Bad Company's press officer Sam Aizer also saw Page holding court in his *Night Porter* costume when Bad Company played Texas. "The Nazi uniform. What was that about? I mean, *really*. What was going on there?" he sighs.

Both Powell and Aizer also saw how the macho atmosphere around Led Zeppelin had escalated since John Bindon's arrival. "To this day, Bindon was the scariest man I'd ever met," says Aizer. "I didn't even want to look in that guy's direction in case I caught his eye."

On a flight to Tampa, Bindon sat next to Po and, aware of his friendship with Pink Floyd, began making threats against their manager, Steve O'Rourke.

"Steve had recently accused Biffo of ripping off £3,000 from a briefcase he'd left in the back of his Jag," explains Po. "Which he did because I was in the Speakeasy with Steve when it happened. John was determined he should pay for this slander and was basically plotting his murder. I remember thinking, 'I don't feel comfortable about this man discussing killing Steve O'Rourke.'

"At the same time, you've got Dirty Dick marching through the plane yelling at everybody, and some woman doing cartwheels down the aisle of the plane with no knickers on."

As if on cue, Grant arrived to interrupt Bindon's plotting and told Powell to join him instead: "Peter was very gracious—'You don't wanna be with those monkeys, Po, come and sit with us.' He knew I wasn't comfortable with Bindon talking about the things he was talking about."

Later, in Tampa, Powell watched Grant salvage a potentially disastrous situation. Backing up Richard Cole's assessment that nobody on the tour was "right on it every minute of the day," it was on the plane to Tampa when Cole noticed the ticket for the seventy-thousand-capacity stadium date contained the clause "Rain or shine." Zeppelin always insisted on a clause that would allow them to postpone an outdoor show in the event of bad weather. Not this time, though, and Tampa was experiencing a tropical downpour.

"A big mistake," admitted Grant. "If an outdoor show was rained off, a rain date was booked, and you did it the following day. Now we missed the detail on this one. I should have sent Richard out to check, but he'd been sorting out some trip for Robert and Jonesy to visit Disneyland with their kids."

As per John Paul Jones's request, Grant had accommodated the school summer holidays into the touring schedule. Jimmy Page rarely saw daylight, but his bandmates and their children had been to see Mickey Mouse. Helen and Warren also joined their father on the road.

"That was the tour when the penny dropped," says Warren. "I was backstage with John Bonham and realized this wasn't something all my friends were doing with their dads on the school holidays." However, there was a never-to-be-crossed divide. Helen and Warren sat with their father on the plane, insulated from the madness, even if, just a few feet away, John Bindon plotted some bloody revenge and a woman cartwheeled half-naked between the seats.

Once they arrived at the Orange Bowl, Grant realized the stage was covered by a canvas roof instead the metal covering they normally insisted on. The rain had stopped briefly, but the awning was already sagging. "There was something like ten thousand tons of water resting over the drums," Grant claimed.

The black Tampa sky matched the mood inside the stadium. Most of the seventy-thousand-strong audience was bedraggled, drunk, stoned, and restless. Earlier, several hundred had stormed the stadium gates. The police had used tear gas to quell the invasion. Now riot cops surrounded the amphitheater. They were wearing white helmets like storm troopers from the new movie *Star Wars*.

Three songs into the show, Jimmy Page stoked up the riff to "Nobody's Fault but Mine," and the heavens opened. "We're gonna give it a fifteen-minute break—are you cool?" Plant told the audience. The crowd jeered, as Zeppelin trooped off. With the rain only getting worse, Grant cancelled the rest of the show. A volley of bottles soon littered the empty stage. The riot cops waded into the fray, as Zeppelin escaped in a fleet of limousines.

Po found himself in a car with Grant and a flight case stuffed with cash, as they sped through downtown Tampa, police motorcyclists on either side. In all the chaos, John Paul Jones's family had become separated from the others. By the time they made it to the airstrip, fans had arrived from the stadium and were crowding the perimeter fence. "They were hanging off it, screaming and shouting," says Po.

Caesar's Chariot was grounded until Jones arrived, and two US Air Force jets flew ahead to see if it was safe to take off. "The pilots then radio'd back that there was a break in the cloud, and off we flew," remembers Po. "It was like a military operation."

While kids scaled the chainlink fence below, the plane and its moneyed cargo disappeared into the clouds. "Peter sat there with this big grin on his face. The gig had been rained off, but Zeppelin had been paid. 'I got the fucking cash, Po,' he said, tapping the flight case. Being around Peter always made you feel like you were part a big conspiracy or a bank robbery—and we were all getting away with it."

Within hours, Grant had booked two pages in Tampa's local newspaper and published a statement laying the blame for the aborted show on Concerts West. Tampa Council was meeting on Monday, and Grant didn't want to jeopardize his chances of rescheduling the date.

As always, Peter knew somebody who'd get them out of trouble. This time, it was Elvis's manager, Colonel Tom Parker, whose relative ran an ad agency. "So we got him out of bed early on Sunday to get the ad in for first thing the next morning. So no matter what the council said, we were in the clear for all to see." But Led Zeppelin would never play Tampa again.

After Florida, the second leg drew to a close with six nights at New York's Madison Square Garden and the same at the Los Angeles Forum. The Garden shows had sold out without a dollar spent on advertising. Instead, Grant had used radio DJ Scott Muni to announce the dates on air. "The power was unbelievable. At that point, I really did wonder how much bigger this all could get."

The venues, the fees, and the limos kept getting bigger. In New York, the chauffeured vehicles inched their way from the Plaza Hotel to the Garden in one long, bumper-to-bumper convoy. There were even empty limousines as decoys to distract overzealous fans.

Mitchell Fox, one of the young staffers at Swan Song's New York office, joined the tour after the Garden dates. "Based on the fact I could get things done, Richard Cole came up to me after the shows and said, 'Pack your bags, you're coming on the road with us,'" he recalls. "That was it. I was in. There was very little guesswork as to who was the boss. I was twenty-three years old and was told, 'Keep your eyes and ears open and your mouth shut.' I learned quickly."

In Led Zeppelin's new song "For Your Life," Robert Plant described Los Angeles as "the city of the damned." Many of the groupies who'd flocked around them on their early tours were still there at the Rainbow, but they were older, colder-eyed, and burned out. There were casualties-in-waiting everywhere, including among the musicians.

In LA, Keith Moon arrived at the band's hotel a day early, looking for Grant. Keith had known Peter since the early days of the Who. During one drunken night at the Hyatt House, Moon asked Grant to become his manager. "I said, 'Keith, as much as I love you, I've got John Bonham. How could I manage you as well?' Keith had this big ring with stars on it and said, 'Peter, if anyone ever did anything to you, I'd do *this* to them.'" Moon then ran the ring's sharp edge along the curtain, shredding the material to ribbons. "It cost me $2,300," Grant complained.

Grant was still en route from San Diego, and Dave Northover had traveled ahead. He was preparing Grant's suite when he spotted Moon's car parked haphazardly on the steps of the hotel. "Moonie was looking for Peter," says Northover. "He didn't seem to care that Peter wasn't around, as long as he had someone to talk to." Keith pulled out a wrap of cocaine, started talking, and didn't stop.

Moon later appeared onstage with Led Zeppelin at the Forum. He commandeered the microphone and shouted at the audience like a circus barker before Plant steered him away. As the band careened through a grand finale of "Whole Lotta Love" and "Rock and Roll," Moon joined them on tamborine and tympani. It was his last live performance in America. He'd be dead within twelve months.

After three weeks respite, the tour's final stretch commenced in Seattle. Back in London, Richard Cole had knocked out one of his front teeth and hadn't had the time to get it fixed. When "Ricardo" rejoined the tour he looked more menacing than ever.

As ever, John Bonham was homesick and volatile. In Cleveland, he convinced himself Neal Preston's hotel room was bigger than his and demolished it with a metal billy club. At Seattle's Edgewater Inn, Bonzo threw his malfunctioning hotel refrigerator off the balcony and into the Puget Sound below.

Bonham and Dave Northover spent a night fishing off Bonzo's balcony in Seattle. In the early hours of the morning they caught an octopus. They wrestled the poor beast into Bonham's suite with the aid of a broomstick and put it in the bath where it discharged black ink. Later, after spotting Richard Cole's case in the corner of the room, they emptied its contents and stuffed the dead octopus inside. It was around 5 a.m. when they had the bag delivered back to Cole's room.

"Sure enough, a few minutes later there was screaming and yelling outside," says Northover, "and I'm pretty sure a knife came through our door. Ricardo was *not* happy."

Cole's hotel suite was next door to Grant's. "I believe they had a row; whether it was anything to do with us, I don't know. Peter wore those huge rings, and Richard appeared the next day with a huge black bruise on his face where I think Peter had smacked him."

Unfortunately, all this rage and paranoia would soon find another outlet.

*T*hree days after Seattle, Led Zeppelin flew to San Francisco to play two shows for promoter Bill Graham. Graham's Day on the Green concerts had become a fixture at the Oakland Coliseum. There had been three since May, headlined by Fleetwood Mac, the Eagles, and Peter Frampton. Zeppelin was the biggest draw yet. Both their weekend dates on July 23 and 24 had sold out in record time.

At Oakland, Grant's dual roles as band manager and family man finally clashed. He and Bill Graham fell out before Led Zeppelin even played a note. In an unpublished interview from 1994, Peter claimed Bill wanted to add a third warm-up act—the local group Journey—to the bill. Zeppelin rarely played with a support band, but Grant had already agreed to two at Oakland: the British heavy metal group Judas Priest and homegrown guitar hero Rick Derringer.

Grant had known Journey's English drummer, Aynsley Dunbar, since the late 1960s, as he'd been briefly mooted for the Zeppelin job. "And Bill really hustled me on that, but I didn't have room to put Journey on, and that soured things between us."

Graham then asked Grant if Zeppelin would play an extra date on the Friday before the weekend shows. Peter refused, believing it could be seen as a snub by the thousands who'd camped overnight and queued for hours to buy tickets for the original dates. "Bill and I had cross words about it," he admitted. "And it all snowballed from there."

Graham's official version of events eschewed these details. Instead, he re-counted how Grant's people contacted him the day before the first show, de-manding a $25,000 cash advance on Zeppelin's fee. Graham was furious but afraid Zeppelin would cancel the gig with some fabricated excuse if they didn't get the money. He managed to raise the cash, stuffed it into three empty shoeboxes, and took it himself to Peter's suite at the San Francisco Hyatt.

As soon as Graham walked into the room, he spotted the city's biggest drug dealer and realized what the money was for. "What I should have done was walked right out of there with the money and not gone back," he wrote in his autobiography, *Bill Graham Presents*. "But I didn't."

The show would go on, no matter how much the promoter disapproved. The following afternoon, Led Zeppelin swaggered onstage in blazing sun-shine. Robert Plant, in a torso-hugging T-shirt that read, "Nurses do it better" looked like he belonged in daylight hours—a vampiric Jimmy Page less so.

"I'd heard stories about the drugs Jimmy was doing," says Michael Zagaris, who photographed both Oakland shows. "Supposedly, they had to pick him up in his room, carry him to the freight elevator and then into the limo." After a few uncertain minutes, Page seemed to come alive midway during "The Song Remains the Same."

Led Zeppelin's performance that afternoon would take second billing to the drama offstage. The show had already become a battle of wills between the great rock promoter and the great rock manager. It was Graham's chosen support acts on the bill, and Graham's design on the stage. Led Zeppelin's airship floated overhead, but the stage was surrounded by Bill's clunky-looking replica of Britain's prehistoric Stonehenge monument. Seven years later, a similar stage set would appear in the spoof rock movie *This Is Spinal Tap.*

Punches were thrown before the show began. When stagehand Jim Downey saw Grant walking up the ramp toward the stage, he made an off-hand remark about how steep the walkway was. Grant overheard and took it as a jibe about his weight. Seconds later, John Bindon had punched Downey unconscious. Other stagehands witnessed the assault but couldn't intervene. The show had to go on.

What happened next has since passed into Peter Grant mythology. Toward the end of the show, one of Graham's security team, Jim Matzorkis, claimed to have seen Warren Grant remove a sign from one of the backstage trailer doors. He intervened. "It wasn't a violent act," said Matzorkis later. "I just took the signs from him."

"I was backstage, and this guy came along with these signs," says Warren now. "One of them had 'Led Zeppelin' written on it. It was a piece of timber with the name routed out, and I thought it looked cool. I asked if I could have it, and he said, 'No.' I was eleven years old, a little twat, and I tried to grab it. And he pushed me over."

The late Dennis Sheehan witnessed the incident. "I don't think the guy meant it," he said in a 2012 interview. "He put his arm out to one side and Warren was off balance and fell."

"So, I did what any kid would have done and told my dad," continues Warren. "The next thing I know, him and Richard Cole were chasing this bloke. The last thing I saw was him trying to get over a barrier."

In Matzorkis's version of events, he took the signs to a trailer for safekeeping, where he was challenged by Grant. "He kept saying, 'You don't talk to my kid that way. Nobody talks to my kid that way!'" John Bonham had come offstage and had also seen the altercation with Warren. Bonzo strode up the trailer steps and kicked Matzorkis in the groin.

Zeppelin's security guards pulled Bonham away, and Matzorkis limped to another trailer nearby. Bill Graham told his side of the story in his autobiography: "I went into this long, long speech. I said, 'Peter, remember, you're a very big man. You have a lot of security with you, and they're big. I don't want anyone to get hurt.'" Graham suggested they go together to hear Matzorkis's explanation.

Graham's book included a graphic account of what happened next. As soon as they were in the trailer, Peter threw a punch at Matzorkis and sent him reeling. When Graham tried to intervene, Grant picked him up and dumped him outside—"like a fly."

John Bindon, who'd been shadowing his boss, now joined in. Matzorkis claimed Bindon held his arms while Grant repeatedly punched him. Graham heard his cries for help and with another of his security team, Bob Barsotti, tried to get into the locked trailer. But Richard Cole stopped them. "I stood guard outside," Cole says, "but I didn't realize how bad the situation had gotten in there."

According to Barsotti, Cole stripped the aluminium pole from a backstage table umbrella and used it against anyone who tried to get into the trailer. In the meantime, Matzorkis was on the floor and convinced Bindon was trying to gouge out one of his eyes. It was only then, he said, that enough adrenaline kicked in, and he was able to break free.

Legend has moved in on what happened next. Some claim Matzorkis was carried unconscious to an ambulance. Matzorkis himself has always maintained he lost a tooth in the attack. "I saw this guy come out of the trailer, and his face was covered with blood," remembers Michael Zagaris. "I thought he'd had some kind of accident."

"He had a bloody nose, but he was walking," says Dave Northover. "The way it all kicked off that day was just ridiculous. I'm sure it wouldn't have gone down like that if Bindon hadn't been there."

Graham's security staff wanted revenge, but Grant was free to lead the band and his army out of the stadium unchallenged. Hard commerce put paid to any retaliation. Led Zeppelin had another show to play, and Bill Graham wouldn't jeopardize that for anyone.

Instead, Graham struck a deal with his team: allow Zeppelin to play the second Oakland show, and then let him try and have the guilty men arrested. Graham told his security detail that if he failed, they had his blessing to take the law into their own hands. "You can do it here, or I'll fly twenty-five guys of your choice to the next stop on their tour, and you can do them there."

Warren and Helen left with bodyguards in a limousine, oblivious to the scale of the violence. "I don't know why it got as bad as it did," insists Warren. "The wives and children were told the security guard was sacked. Later I found out what happened, and you think, Oh, was this was my fault? Am I to blame?"

Apart from Bonham, the rest of the band was unaware of the altercation. For Jimmy Page, though, the conflict backstage mirrored the turmoil out front. "All I could see were people getting pulled over the barriers and beaten up," he said. "There was a very nasty, heavy energy about the whole day."

That night, Steve Weiss telephoned Bill Graham. He refused to discuss what had happened and flatly told the promoter, "The band would find it difficult to play tomorrow unless you sign a waiver indemnifying them against all lawsuits."

Graham called his attorney and said he wanted everybody involved in the assault arrested—"starting with Peter Grant"—but not until after the second concert. The lawyer advised him to sign the document but claim he'd done so under "economic duress"—a get-out clause that would render his signature legally worthless and allow him to pursue criminal damages.

Graham waited until 3 a.m. before telling Weiss he'd sign, but he wasn't the only one willing to stall. Led Zeppelin was due onstage at 1 p.m. the following day. At 12:30, and with sixty thousand people already inside the stadium, Grant and the band were still at the Hyatt.

Weiss eventually appeared backstage with the indemnity letter, and Graham signed the document. "If I hadn't, Zeppelin wouldn't have played, and we'd have had a riot."

Zeppelin arrived at the stadium ninety minutes later than scheduled to find the mood backstage caustic. The band was essentially playing behind enemy lines.

"I was told I couldn't go on stage with a Zeppelin laminate; I had to have a Bill Graham pass," says Michael Zagaris. "I told Peter, who told me 'Fuck 'em! If anyone touches you, our security will blow them away.'" Graham had hired extra muscle in the shape of several hulking semi-pro football players, but Grant had brought in two moonlighting Los Angeles Police Department SWAT cops.

There was one moment of light relief during the show when a dancer talked her way onstage and wafted around Robert Plant during "No Quarter." When one of the band asked who she was, Bonham apparently shouted over the mic that it was "Bill Graham's missus." "Bill went ape shit," claimed Grant.

When Plant came offstage before the encore and tried to speak to Graham about the fight —"I told him the whole thing was absolutely, totally ludicrous"—the promoter refused to even look at him.

Long before the show ended, the band's getaway cars were lined up by the stage ramp. Zeppelin's entourage flanked either side of the walkway to chaperone them straight into the vehicles. Graham spotted an imperious-looking Peter Grant through the window of his limo, just as it pulled away. To salt the wound further, two police motorcyclists flanked the car.

Graham's team also included a retired police sergeant, who advised him Grant and Bindon could be charged with inciting assault, and Cole with assault with a deadly weapon. However, the Oakland PD didn't consider the incident serious enough to class as a felony and couldn't serve a misdemeanor warrant on a Sunday. They'd have to wait until Monday morning.

Graham's people had already spoken to the band's chauffeurs who'd agreed to tip them off if anyone tried to leave. These were local drivers without any allegiance to Grant, and many had witnessed some heavy-handed behavior over the previous days.

But nobody was going anywhere. On Monday morning, detectives and a SWAT team from the Oakland and San Francisco police departments descended on the hotel. Within seconds, the lobby was swarming with baton- and gun-carrying officers. Grant's security detail had been expecting them. There had been tip-offs from both sides. Many of Grant's hired security were policemen who knew the arriving officers. They, in turn, allowed their colleagues to give Grant and his men the chance to turn themselves in. There was another reason for letting them come quietly. Grant had booked so many empty rooms at the hotel as a decoy, the arriving police would have to search them all otherwise.

Later, Grant claimed he was watching television with Warren and Helen, when one of Zeppelin's private cops, Greg Belper, told him it was time to hand himself in. He later told Malcolm McLaren he went into the bathroom, changed his shirt, snorted two lines of cocaine, and called John Bindon.

In Grant's account, Bindon initially refused to hand himself in, as he was certain the police would discover his criminal record in the UK. Grant told him that when they arrived at the station he should fill in his date of birth "the English way," with the day first, followed by the month and year, instead of the American way. "It will confuse the computer."

Grant then chopped out a further line of cocaine, wrapped it in a dollar bill, and stuck it in his pocket, before going down to meet the police. Grant knew he wouldn't be searched until after he was interviewed and about to be transferred to a cell, at which point he'd ask to use the bathroom. This show of bravado convinced Bindon to go with him.

Grant, Bonham, Bindon, and Cole arrived together in the hotel lobby. With their matching beards and wild eyes, they looked like a pirate crew, with Peter, in his rings and scarves, resembling a modern-day version of their captain.

Graham's people had tipped off the local TV station, which filmed the men being led away. Nobody was handcuffed. At the station, Grant and Bonham were booked on single battery counts; Bindon and Cole on two counts of battery. Shortly before being taken to the cell, Grant asked to "use the can." Once inside the stall, he snorted the cocaine and flushed the dollar bill down the toilet. The police were none the wiser.

Nobody was going to stay locked up for long. Steve Weiss posted bail of $250 for each count. As usual, he knew someone or did something to make the problem go away. Led Zeppelin's next date wasn't until a week later in New Orleans. "Once we got let out of jail, we had our pilots on standby and got the fuck out of there," says Cole.

Despite the police presence, John Paul Jones had demonstrated his uncanny knack of becoming the invisible man and had already left. Nobody noticed. Jones had planned a weeklong road trip with his family in their motor caravan. By the time Grant and the rest were released, the Joneses were en route to Oregon.

They were joined by a now-armed Brian Gallivan. "Gally was worried about Jonesy's safety and had somehow got hold of a shotgun," reveals Dave Northover. "The SWAT team had found out, which is another reason they'd turned up at the hotel the way they did."

The exact details of the Oakland Incident are obscured by misinformation and hearsay to this day. In 1978, the *Sunday Express* reported how John Bonham and his accomplices had been "convicted of battering security guards with guitars." Until recently, one of Grant's former employees presumed Graham's security guard had died as a result of his beating. Nobody ever told him otherwise.

Joe "Jammer" Wright was in the Kings Road office when a telex arrived from Steve Weiss. "It read, 'Is it true manslaughter charges are being drawn up against Led Zeppelin in San Francisco?' I said, 'What!' But Carole Brown said, 'You did not see that, Joe.'"

Unity MacLean remembers Grant trying to keep the details secret from his staff. "He didn't want anything tainting the group."

Meanwhile, Bill Graham's official statement published in the *San Francisco Chronicle* detailed everything: "There were ten years of an ongoing respectful relationship between members of the Led Zeppelin organization and myself," he wrote. "However, the incident in question . . . encroached on moral boundaries. . . . Now that I've seen the horror of seeing two men whose total weight exceeds five hundred pounds wreak physical havoc on one man weighing around two hundred pounds, I cannot help but wonder how much of this did in fact go on in the past with these people."

However, when news broke that Bill Graham had had John Bonham arrested, the Bay Area radio station KSAN's switchboard lit up with calls from angry fans. Graham went on air to read a pre-prepared statement but dumped the script and instead raged about their heroes' abuse of power.

Graham filed a $2 million lawsuit. Zeppelin's lawyers offered significantly less, knowing they could afford to wait whereas Bill's people couldn't. It would be a year and a half before the case was resolved.

In 1978, Grant, Bonham, Bindon, and Cole pleaded "nolo contender," whereby a defendant in a criminal prosecution accepts conviction but does not admit guilt. Bindon was given a sixty-day suspended jail sentence and a $300 fine, while the others received $200 fines each. According to Jim Matzorkis, Graham's lawyers eventually squeezed just $50,000 damages out of Led Zeppelin in an out-of-court settlement, one-third of which was swallowed in legal fees.

"I didn't like those people," wrote Graham in his autobiography. "I didn't like their influence on society or their power. They surrounded themselves with physical might. The element around them was oppressive. They were ready to kill at the slightest provocation."

Grant and his men had behaved badly, but Grant's power as Led Zeppelin's manager had always made Bill Graham uneasy. At the Fillmore in the 1960s, Graham had been the undisputed boss. Ten years on, there was Grant, screwing promoters for the privilege of promoting the biggest group in the world. The game had changed, and not in Bill Graham's favor.

"Bill had this attitude that he owned San Francisco, and you did what Bill said," offers Ed Bicknell. "As a promoter, Bill was the best, but he could still be a complete pig about things. There was tension, because Bill and Peter were very similar. Both of them were 'my way or the highway.'"

"Oakland was one empire-builder moving into an area where there was already an empire with some kind of Tartar head," said Robert Plant. While Grant's strong-arm tactics insulated Plant and his bandmates, the singer loathed the violence and intimidation. "Finally, all the heavies were released," said Plant, when asked about Bindon's role in the incident. "It was like, 'Ah. At last, I'm going to earn my money.'"

Loyal to the end, Grant would never publicly denounce Bindon. "He had a lot of good points," he insisted. "He took care of my situation."

Privately, it was a different matter. "He told me hiring Bindon was a huge, huge mistake," says Ed Bicknell.

Similarly, Grant would discuss Oakland only in the broadest terms and would always blame others. "It was a flashpoint situation that got out of hand," he said in 1993. He was even more dismissive in a Canadian radio interview the following year: "There were a few people running around, knocking into people. John Bonham flew at a fella. . . . Very unfortunate."

The fight in Oakland was about more than what did and didn't happen in that backstage trailer. It would become a turning point, and one forever bound up in the terrible event that followed.

While the Jones family headed for the Midwest, *Caesar's Chariot* flew the rest of the touring party to New Orleans. After arriving at the Maison Dupuy Hotel early in the morning, Robert Plant took a call from his wife. Their five-year-old son, Karac, was seriously ill with a viral infection, and Plant wanted to check on his progress. Less than one hour later, Maureen called back to tell him Karac had died.

That Plant had to hear the news while embroiled in the madness of a Led Zeppelin tour only heightened the pain. For once, all his manager's threats and money couldn't fix the problem.

Jerry Greenberg says he was with Peter and Warren when the news broke. "I had a boat, and we'd all gone deep sea fishing," he says. "They tracked down Peter to tell him Robert's son had died."

Grant focused on getting the singer back to his family as fast as possible. *Caesar's Chariot*'s pilots were forbidden by law from flying again for several hours, so it was late afternoon when they finally left New Orleans. Plant then made the overnight trip from New York to London. John Bonham was by his side.

Grant cancelled the remaining shows, including in New Orleans, where the band had been due to receive the keys to the city. One radio station then played Zeppelin songs for twenty-four hours straight.

Bill Graham also received a phone call. His secretary answered, and a whispering voice at the other end announced it was Peter Grant. Bill picked up the receiver. "I hope you're happy," Grant said, quietly. "Thanks to you, Robert Plant's kid died today." Then the line went dead.

This anecdote was the sign-off to Bill Graham's account of the Oakland incident. His autobiography, *Bill Graham Presents*, was published in 1992, one year after Graham's death in a helicopter crash. By then, Grant was sober, and Oakland was a distant bad memory.

After reading Graham's book, Peter telephoned Ed Bicknell. "He rang me at the office," Ed said, "and he was sobbing. I honestly thought somebody had died. He sounded really deeply hurt, very disturbed. But he managed to tell me what had happened—'This book has come out.'"

Bicknell asked Grant to fax him the relevant pages. "So I read them, and I asked him outright, 'Is this true, Peter?' And he said, 'Yes.' But he kept saying, 'I don't want to be thought of as a bad person.' Toward the end of his life, that was a constant mantra. He knew he'd lost the plot back then, but also that he'd changed since."

Neither Grant, Page, nor Jones attended Karac Plant's funeral. Their absence would be interpreted by some as evidence of a rift between Plant and the organization. Others suggest Robert never forgave himself for being on the road when his son passed away, and their presence would have been an uncomfortable reminder.

After what had happened, the violence and the drugs seemed more sordid than ever. "The illusion had run its course," said Plant, years later. "My mojo for life, for music, for everything just vanished." Led Zeppelin and Peter Grant would never tour America again.

10

A Big Hell of a Man

"We've given up. There's nothing left to do now,
except blow up the stage."

—PETER GRANT, 1980

*E*lvis Presley died suddenly on August 16, 1977, at his home in Memphis, Tennessee. Months earlier, Peter Grant had flown to the States to see his manager, Colonel Tom Parker. Presley and Led Zeppelin were both represented by Concerts West; the Colonel was floating the idea of Elvis's first European tour, and Grant wanted to promote the shows.

Don Arden had tried to bring Presley to Britain in the early sixties, but Parker turned him down. The popular theory was that the colonel, a Dutchman by birth, was an illegal immigrant and couldn't risk leaving America, which was why Elvis never performed abroad.

But "Colonel" Tom Parker was the American Dream writ large—a once penniless fairground carny who'd built a $4 billion music empire. Parker had befriended US presidents. He had the money and contacts to acquire a proper US passport. The real problem was Elvis's addiction to a cocktail of prescription painkillers, which made passing through customs and maintaining his habit impossible.

Grant never discussed his meeting with Parker publicly, but he talked to Ed Bicknell about it in the early nineties. "Peter was going to promote an Elvis Presley tour of Europe," he says. "And Parker spoke to him about bringing Elvis to Britain without him getting busted. Elvis had a horrendous issue with painkillers, as did some of his minders."

Ahmet Ertegun once said Grant reminded him of an English version of the Colonel. By 1978, Grant and Parker must have seen a lot of themselves in each other.

Like Peter, the Colonel rarely discussed his childhood or his upbringing. As young men, both had hustled a living—with Parker working the fairgrounds and carnivals. There was also the effect they had on their employees. Concert agent Byron Raphael described Parker to his biographer, Alanna Nash, but he could just as easily have been talking about Peter Grant.

"The Colonel had an astonishing power over the people around him," Raphael said. "They would have done anything he asked them to do. There was no way to keep a secret from him, and his personality was so overpowering, when he walked into a room, he took it over, no matter who was there."

Had the Elvis tour happened, it might have given Grant the challenge he needed. After 1975, there was nothing left for Led Zeppelin to conquer, and nobody else on Swan Song was going to take their place. Detective's first album was released in spring 1977 and symbolized the label's indulgence and lack of direction.

"We were raring to go and had this vision of what we should do," says Michael Des Barres. "Then suddenly we had to make this record, but we couldn't get hold of anybody."

Jimmy Page was supposed to produce the album. An official press photograph of Detective showed him in the background, passed out on a couch; something he blamed on too much Valium. "Jimmy was compromised, let's just leave it at that," says Des Barres. Instead, Detective burned through a $1 million recording budget and produced most of the album themselves.

"I didn't have conversations with anyone at Swan Song about it," explains Des Barres. "I had conversations with drug dealers. I couldn't speak to Peter. Nobody could speak to Peter."

Detective's manager, Elliott Roberts, became so frustrated by Grant's inaccessibility, he offered Swan Song's Sam Aizer a bet. "He said to me, 'I'll bet you ten thousand dollars you can't get hold of Peter right now. Even if you said, 'Put Peter on the phone or Aizer's going to be killed.'" Sam already knew Grant wouldn't take the call. Detective's debut sank without trace.

Meanwhile, in London, Dave Edmunds had bucked the trend with a hit single, "I Knew the Bride." Edmunds had been making records since the sixties, but was now managed by Jake Riviera, co-founder of the punk-friendly Stiff Records. Edmunds's brisk, unpretentious pop suited the new era.

"Jake Riviera didn't like Peter," remembers Unity MacLean. When Edmunds wanted to form a new band, Rockpile, with songwriter Nick Lowe, Riviera needed Grant to release him from his contract.

Fellow Stiff Records act Elvis Costello composed a song, "Hand in Hand," inspired by the Riviera/Grant standoff. "It was a satire about a paranoid rock 'n' roll star with a thuggish entourage," he wrote in his autobiography *Unfaithful Music*. Costello was fascinated to hear how Riviera wasn't allowed to drive his own car to Horselunges because Grant would lower the drawbridge only if he recognized the vehicle.

Nevertheless, Grant agreed to Riviera's request. "I just didn't have the time to oversee Dave Edmunds," he admitted. "Dave had Jake Riviera anyway, which brought its own set of problems." Riviera was combative and ambitious. He was Peter Grant ten years ago.

By summer 1977, Abe Hoch had grown tired of staring at the Durex sign outside his window and attempted to leave Swan Song. "Peter was in Paris, but he said we'd talk when he came back. A week later, Unity says, 'Peter needs to see you now.' So, I went to the office, and he closed the door behind me and locked it."

Grant then opened his briefcase and took out a bag of cocaine and a knife. He slit the bag open, scooped out a mound of powder and offered it to Hoch on the side of the blade. "This was Tuesday; I think it was Thursday when we left the room. I couldn't even remember what day it was, I was so disorientated, but it meant I didn't quit."

Weeks later, Hoch realized he hadn't received his paycheck. "I phoned Peter. He said, 'We decided to accept your resignation.' It was typical G weirdness. I felt devalued, but Swan Song devalued everybody."

Hoch's replacement was Alan Callan, an old friend of Jimmy Page's, who would become a close confidante of Grant's. Callan (who died in 2014) found his job description as nonexistent as Hoch had. Early on, Ahmet Ertegun told him to sign whomever Led Zeppelin wanted him to sign. Quality control took a back seat to keeping Grant and the band happy.

Instead, Callan aimed high and tried to woo John Lennon, who was holed up in New York and hadn't made an album for two years. Neither Peter nor the band would commit; he had nothing to offer. Lennon signed with the newly formed Geffen Records instead.

"I think if we'd had Alan Callan in from the start, Swan Song might have been OK," claimed Grant. "He knew what we wanted to do."

"I don't know what Alan was doing," says Unity MacLean. "It was a grace-and-favor position. He was a buddy of Peter's." Unity remembers walking into one of the offices to see the walls newly painted dark red. Callan jokingly told her it was "so it won't show the blood."

Grant's fearsome approach filtered down and influenced his courtiers, regardless of their individual power. The first to leave was Carole Brown, the woman Helen Grant remembered as "being like Mission Control." "Carole had enough of Peter and walked away," says Unity. "It was a very male-dominated office. I remember once giving Clive Coulson some paperwork for Bad Company. He snatched it out of my hand, saying, 'This is nothing to do with you. Women are not included in my band.'"

"Anybody who worked for Peter had the power to do anything they wanted," admits Hoch. "That was the problem. And I'm afraid that power affected us all."

For all the darkness, there were moments when Swan Song's reputation became more comical than fearsome. The cleaning lady, Dolly, had known Grant for years. Week after week she arrived at Number 484, ignoring the stoned musicians and Kings Road villains to tidy up the offices.

"Little Dolly must have been eighty-four years old, stood four-foot-nine, had no teeth and the bandiest legs you've ever seen," remembers Phil Carlo. "She called Peter 'son' or 'the boy' and used to tell him off—'You'll catch your death, son, coming up here without a jacket.' G would even apologize, 'Yeah, sorry Dolly.'"

Phil, his wife Julie, Grant, and John Bindon were in the office when Dolly finished her shift one day. "As she was leaving, she said to G, 'I hope those yobbos ain't hanging around my flats.' Straight away, Peter wanted to know, 'What's this all about, Dolly?' 'Oh, just some lads lurking about and causing trouble.' G said to Bindon, 'Biffo, go with Dolly. Make sure she gets home safely.'"

At that point, Dolly reached into a carrier bag. "She said, 'Don't worry about me, son. If I get any grief, they can have some of *this*.' And she pulled out the handle for an old wooden mangle."

Julie Carlo, watching from across the room, put her head in her hands. "Oh my God," she said, "even Dolly's tooled up.'"

*F*ormer Playboy bunny and model Cindy Russell met Peter Grant soon after Zeppelin's doomed US tour. Within a year she was living at Horselunges. Cindy was from Chicago, and by the late 1970s was traveling to Europe for modeling jobs and appearing in a marketing campaign for Smirnoff vodka. In one advert, plastered across the London Underground, she could be seen skydiving in a bikini.

Cindy was introduced to Grant through Richard Cole. It was summer 1977, and she was in a London restaurant when Cole breezed in. "Richard was fresh off a tour and missing a tooth," she says now. "He said to my agent, 'Who's this bird?' and then to me, 'Do you wanna go out?' I just got up from the table and left with him. I had no idea who he was."

Before long, she was staying at Cole's Chelsea flat. "They were fun times but strange times. I once let myself into Richard's apartment, and Jimmy Page was lying on the couch, surrounded by flickering candles. I was told not to worry, that's just what Jimmy does."

The couple came back one day to hear a noise upstairs. "I think Peter owned the flat above Richard's," she recalls. "I could hear all this thumping around upstairs. Suddenly this great big hell of a man appeared."

The pair met again when Cole took Cindy to Horselunges. Peter flirted with Cindy. "We were only joking around. However, for the next few months, Richard and I would be on and off and on."

With Robert Plant in mourning, Led Zeppelin was on hiatus. Nobody knew for how long. Without a tour or recording session to occupy their handlers, there were long days to be filled, waiting for something, anything, to happen. As Richard Cole admits, "I had too much time to fill, and I filled it with drugs." Before long, Cole called his heroin dealer.

When Cindy arrived in London after another assignment, she realized the extent of Cole's problem. "I went to the Water Rat, and Richard came to see me. He was in a bit of a state, not in a good place. I called Peter and said, 'You better get hold of your boy because he's in trouble here.'"

Cindy was ready to catch the next plane home. Then Norman the chauffeur arrived. "Peter had sent him to get me. I planned to stay at Horselunges for a few weeks, and a few weeks turned into 1985."

"Can you imagine what it was like for Peter's kids?" she admits. "Me walking in there and staying? Peter was very protective, and the children came first. I didn't want them to think I was trying to take their mother's place, but it wasn't easy. Helen was a beautiful girl but only a few years younger than me, so there were times when she and I went at it."

"Cindy and I had a volatile relationship," agrees Helen. "Now, looking back, I realize I was being selfish. I did spoil it sometimes. After Mum, I should have been more understanding when someone else came along for my dad."

On the one hand, there was the daily routine of ordinary family life, and on the other, the excess. "I loved the English countryside," Cindy says. "I knew how to dirt-bike. So Warren and I used to go out three-wheeling. I even went with Helen to her ballet course in Covent Garden."

And there were the drug binges, when the nights turned into days and back into nights again. Cindy once woke in Grant's four-poster to the sound of whispering voices. "I think I'd crashed out for a day or two. The curtains were drawn around the bed, but I could hear Peter and Jimmy Page talking. Jimmy asked, 'How long's she been asleep? You gonna wake her up?' And Peter replied, 'Nah, let her sleep.'

"I stuck my head through the curtains, and there's Peter trying to grind up a rock of cocaine, but the top of the grinder had come unscrewed, and the whole thing's rolling across the rug. Next to him is Jimmy Page, peering down the barrel of a shotgun."

Cindy clambered out of bed and gently confiscated the weapon. "It wasn't loaded, and Jimmy was just looking at it, but I wasn't taking any chances."

Everybody, including Grant, needed to get back to work. For all their artistic merit, Led Zeppelin was a multimillion-pound business, generating an enormous amount of revenue for an even larger corporation. But they don't break working, and important people were becoming impatient.

"A huge part of Atlantic's money came from Peter Grant and Led Zeppelin," says Phil Carson. "I'll admit it, nobody wanted to kill the golden goose."

Abe Hoch's memory of being taken aside by Jimmy Page and asked, "What shall we do about G?" wasn't an isolated incident. According to Grant, in an interview with Mark Long, by mid-1978 the wheels were in motion to remove him as Led Zeppelin's manager. The men behind this attempted coup were Stevens Weiss and Herb Atkin.

None of the surviving band members have ever publicly discussed this alleged plot, and former members of the Zeppelin organization disagree on whether it even happened.

"It's true," says Richard Cole. "Completely true."

"It was Peter's drug paranoia," insists Phil Carson now. "I don't think it happened. I *did* hear this story much later on, but you must remember Peter had serious issues at that time. Stevens was very loyal to Peter, even at times when it was difficult to be loyal to Peter."

Grant revealed his version of events to Mark Long in their final interview. "How true it was or not, I have no idea," says Long. "Was it coke paranoia? They were all paranoid, all into security and protection, they all seemed to hate each other and think everybody was after their money—and to an extent they were correct.

"Everywhere you turned in this story, there was Steve Weiss, but in the version Peter gave me, Atkin was the chief manipulator, even above Weiss."

Grant explained to Long how Herb Atkin had supplied Steve Weiss with insider-trading information that led to Weiss investing $6 million in an oil well, which turned out to be dry. "This meant Weiss was broke, and Atkin had him in his pocket."

Carson's claim that Grant had "serious issues by this time" was certainly true. Peter's drug use had accelerated and made him vulnerable. Around this time, Weiss oversaw the deal in which Zeppelin sold its song publishing rights to Atlantic Records and Warner/Chappell for what one insider called a "paltry sum by today's standards."

Grant and Zeppelin happily took the money, unaware that if they'd retained the rights they'd have made much more in the decades ahead. The compact disc was coming and with it came huge profits from repackaging old music in a new format. In the late seventies, though, few outside Silicon Valley foresaw the CD revolution.

The sting in the tail was that Steve Weiss retained his share of their publishing at the same time as negotiating the sale. This sleight of hand and vested interest went undetected at the time. It meant that, unlike his clients, Weiss would retain a piece of Led Zeppelin in the lucrative age of CDs and box sets.

"In the meantime, by 1978, you had the richest band in the world, and nothing was happening," says Mark Long. "Peter was losing control, he'd become isolated, Swan Song was falling apart, Jimmy and Robert weren't talking."

Weiss and Atkin's first move was to get to Grant's lieutenant, Richard Cole. Cole's heroin addiction made him susceptible. "I was not on my game," he admits now, but he clearly remembers a meeting at London's Montcalm Hotel in which the two men quizzed him about Grant. They discussed how poorly they thought Cole had been treated by the management and questioned why he hadn't shared more in Zeppelin's financial success.

"They got me pissed," Cole says. "They were giving me whiskey. I didn't even like whiskey, and I remember Herb was watering it down from the ice bucket." Cole also didn't realize their conversation was being secretly recorded. After some prompting from Atkin, he explained that Grant's weakness, his Achilles' heel, was his children. "That was quite obvious to everyone who knew him," says Cole. This innocent remark would come back to haunt him.

Grant then told Long he was invited to a meeting with Weiss and Atkin. They told him he'd made many enemies in the business after Zeppelin's 90/10 split—and the money it had cost several mob-connected promoters. This, again, was true. But Atkin fueled Grant's paranoia by telling him he wasn't sure how long he and Weiss could continue to protect him or, crucially, his family: "They said, 'The wolves are closing in. Who can you trust?'"

At which point, they played Grant a doctored recording of what now sounded like Richard Cole making vague threats against Peter's children.

"Weissy and Atkin didn't know what to do with me," explains Cole. "I was the one with the memory. I'd been collecting the money on the road, and I knew things. And the next thing I know I'm in fucking exile."

Grant paid for Cole to go to Montreal for three months. "To do fuck all, but get drunk," he admits. Weiss and Grant sent him money and made sure he was looked after, but the trip was intended, he says, "to get me out of the picture."

While in Montreal, Cole met a girl in Thursday's, a club on Crescent Street, who turned out to be the niece of a New York mob family boss. "She told me she had a bodyguard watching her, as she'd been kidnapped on Rhode Island," he explains. "What I didn't know was he thought I'd been involved in the kidnapping."

The following day two men came to Cole's hotel room, claiming to be acting on the mob uncle's behalf. They threatened his life. Cole persuaded them to let him make a phone call. "I rang Herb Atkin, who spoke to them, and he apparently had the contract taken off me."

Whether there *was* a contract or not, the incident was a further reminder of Atkin's power and influence. Some time later, Grant realized the recording of Cole talking about Helen and Warren had been deliberately edited to mislead him. In the meantime, though, Atkin claimed they'd unearthed a plot to kidnap Warren, and his fear escalated again.

Grant had already received death threats against Led Zeppelin and had recently hired a South London private detective to investigate a stalker who'd tried to break into Jimmy Page's house. Now there was a threat being made against one of his own children.

All this drama ensured Atkin had Grant's attention whenever he needed it. It didn't go unnoticed at Horselunges. "When Herb walked into a room,

my stomach flipped, and the hair stood up on the back of my neck," remembers Cindy Russell. "As soon as I met him I heard about these threats against
Warren. I never knew if he was full of shit, but he *knew* people. I remember a
story about Herb hanging a guy out of a helicopter in Central America. I'm
sure he was scoping out my family. Every time I went home to Chicago, I was
followed."

Something had to give and, soon enough, it did. Grant collapsed with a
heart attack and was rushed to the Wellington, a private hospital in St. Johns
Wood. "My heart had ballooned up like a small football," he said.

Grant remained at the Wellington for ten days and then flew to the south
of France for two weeks' recuperation. His doctors recommended a
700-calories-a-day diet. "The doc said I was to make healthy meals," says
Dave Northover. "Peter stuck to the diet for a time, but how many calories
were there in vodka and orange made with loads of vodka and heaps of
oranges?"

In the aftermath of his hospital stay, Grant purchased a white Mercedes
ambulance. In a blackly comic twist, the vehicle came with several pieces of
emergency medical equipment, including an oxygen mask. Despite the double dealing and machinations going on, Peter's sense of humor hadn't deserted him.

Grant reasoned that owning an ambulance meant he'd be fully prepared
in the event of another heart scare. But the vehicle also proved a blessing
when confronted by heavy traffic on the A12 to Eastbourne. Peter would simply order Ray Washbourne "to stick on the siren and the blue light" and start
overtaking everything in sight.

*T*he loss of Robert Plant's son, Karac, had been a greater turning point
than anyone realized. "As far as I was concerned, I was finished with
the band and was going to retrain as a teacher," said Plant, who even applied for a place at a teacher-training college in Sussex. "I thought there was
something far more honest and wholesome about putting the ego away in
the closet."

It was John Bonham who persuaded Plant to reconsider. In doing so, it
meant Led Zeppelin went back to work and strengthened Grant's now fragile
role as band manager. It was also a stay of execution for Richard Cole. But
there were several false starts before the singer was ready to return.

"Robert kept saying he'd do it and then back down," said Grant. "Bonzo
was a tower of strength. We had a meeting at the Royal Garden Hotel, and
they started talking about Bad Company and Maggie Bell and all that with

their Swan Song hats on, and I said, 'What the fuck are you talking about? You should worry about your own careers.'"

Grant suggested the group meet at Clearwell Castle, a gothic retreat in the Forest of Dean that had been used recently by Bad Company. There was no pressure to do anything more than jam. Plant finally joined them in May.

At Clearwell, Jones introduced his new toy: a Yamaha GX-1 keyboard. "Stevie Wonder had one," said Page. "We called it 'The Dream Machine.' Immediately John Paul started writing full numbers on it." Then, Plant and Jones were writing together. It was a subtle shift of power that would have been incomprehensible the last time Zeppelin made a record.

"I'd done a serious amount of writing all the way through and all the writing on *Presence*," Page told me. "Robert and John Paul are writing numbers together? Let them do it."

In November, Led Zeppelin flew to Stockholm to start work at Abba's Polar Studios. Later, John Paul Jones revealed the group had split straight down the middle. "There were two distinct camps, and Robert and I were in the relatively clean one," he said. "We'd turn up first, Bonzo would turn up later, and Page might turn up a couple of days later."

Page and Bonham had found something else to distract them. Cole had made contact with a heroin dealer near the studio: "When he turned the light on in his living room, that was my signal he had some stuff for me." While Jones and Plant tinkered in the studio, others were watching and waiting for the light.

The album titled *In Through the Out Door* was completed in just under a month, with Page producing. "When I needed to be focused, I was really focused," he insisted. It would be the only Led Zeppelin release on which he didn't at least co-write every original song. For the first time, he seemed to have weakened his vice-like grip on the band.

While Zeppelin was making the new album in Stockholm, back in London, Abe Hoch's worst fears about John Bindon were confirmed. On November 21, Biffo was accused of murder and fled the country.

Bindon had been drinking that afternoon in the Ranelagh Yacht Club, a private members' establishment in Fulham. A scuffle broke out involving John Darke, who was an armed robber from South London, and one of Bindon's friends, another convicted criminal named Roy Dennis. Both Roy and his brother, Gerry, had been visitors to Swan Song.

The scuffle escalated into a knife fight that involved Bindon, Darke, and several associates. Darke was stabbed nine times and died before he could reach a hospital. Bindon was repeatedly knifed in the back and chest but survived. Bleeding heavily, he was driven to a friend's house where a private doctor attended to his injuries. One chest wound was so deep, the blade had nicked his heart.

While Biffo was being sewn up, arrangements were made for him to catch a flight to Dublin. From here, he'd be taken to a hospital, where he'd be treated under his mother's maiden name while he considered his next move.

Bindon was driven to Heathrow by another Kings Road associate and one of Grant's occasional minders, Johnny Gillette. The Aer Lingus clerk was told Bindon had been injured playing rugby. He was wrapped in a red blanket to disguise the blood and allowed to board the plane.

Interviewed in 2011, the late Cynthia Sach said an injured Bindon had arrived at the office looking for Grant after the attack. He wasn't there, and Cynthia refused to call him. Richard Cole is certain he and Peter were in Stockholm when Bindon was stabbed.

Cole was married to his second wife, Tracy, at the time. "She called me up and said some of Biffo's mates had been round and semi-threatened her. They wanted the phone number of Peter's heart surgeon, and they thought I'd have it. I found out later that Bindon had been stabbed in the heart."

Dave Northover remembers Grant being involved in Bindon's escape: "It was a busy time upstairs in the bedroom. There were calls backward and forward to Ireland. I also think Peter organized Biffo's solicitor."

"Vicki Hodge asked Peter to help," reveals Phil Carlo. "G knew someone in Ireland who looked after Bindon until he could come home. In return, Biffo did a couple of favors and collected some money for the Irish."

With Bindon missing, the police soon arrived at the manor. "The old bill turned up and raided Horselunges," remembers Warren. "All these flying squad officers and plainclothes detectives with a warrant looking for John. Dad said, 'He's not here, but crack on.'"

Bindon remained in Ireland and eventually negotiated his return with Scotland Yard. A year later, he stood trial for the murder of John Darke at the Old Bailey. The actor Bob Hoskins, the future star of one of Grant's favorite films, *The Long Good Friday*, was called by the defence as a character witness. It was a masterstroke. Incredibly, Bindon was acquitted of murder, manslaughter, and affray and walked out of court a free man.

Neither Bindon's part in the Oakland incident or his murder trial helped Grant or Swan Song's damaged reputation. But Grant had stood by Bindon, just as he stood by all his friends. "Everything was black and white with

Peter," said Alan Callan in 1996. "If you were friends, he would go to the end of the earth for you. He was the most straightforward man I've ever met."

Nothing else about Grant was quite as straightforward. "I think Peter became overwhelmed," says Ed Bicknell. "He was trying to protect his musicians, trying to keep a band together that's been afflicted by chemicals and booze, and he's got this ramshackle road crew with lunatics like John Bindon bashing people. Then he had his own drug demons on top of all that."

*T*wo months before John Bindon's trial, Led Zeppelin released their new album, *In Through the Out Door* and played their first British shows in four years. Po created an image for the LP cover that showed an elaborate re-creation of a New Orleans bar, photographed from six different angles. He visited Horselunges to show Grant and Page the artwork. Clive Coulson was also there, and Peter suggested the four of them toast the great city of New Orleans with a bottle of his vintage absinthe.

Po was aware of the spirit's potentially hallucinogenic qualities. "I was more cautious because I didn't want to get out of control in a business situation," he says. "So, I left my drink on the table while they all knocked back theirs.

"Suddenly, all three of them nodded off mid conversation. Their heads went down, one by one. I sat there, wide awake, thinking, 'What should I do? Do I dare wake up Peter Grant?' After twenty minutes, they all came around and carried on talking, as if nothing happened."

Grant had once joked how Led Zeppelin's albums would sell, even if they were packaged in a paper bag. For *In Through the Out Door*, he decided to put his theory to the test. The LP's expensive cover art was then concealed inside a brown paper bag.

Grant's theory was proved right. The album sold 1.7 million copies within weeks of release and reached number one in the UK and the United States. Songs such as "In the Evening" had a familiar swagger and bombast, while others, including the bouncy samba "Fool in the Rain" seemed like a reaction to all that. Jimmy Page later described the album as "too polished" and "not really us."

Freddy Bannister had organized the 1970 Bath Festival and now promoted a regular festival at the grounds of peer David Lytton-Cobold's stately home at Knebworth Park. He'd tried to book Led Zeppelin to play Knebworth twice before.

Grant knew Plant didn't want to tour. The Knebworth festival would ease him back into performing but would be enough of an event to launch Led

Zeppelin's comeback. "We didn't want to start all over again," Grant explained. "I said, 'We're the biggest band in the world, so we better get out
there and show them we still are.'"

Bannister realized how much Grant had changed since their last meeting
when he arrived at Horselunges. The security cameras over the drawbridge
hadn't been there before. "The control panel in Dad's bedroom was like
something off the Starship Enterprise," admits Warren.

Inside the manor, Grant informed Bannister of Led Zeppelin's fee (rumored to be £1 million), and that Showco would be bringing a stage set from
America, costing £315,000. Bannister suggested they meet again with Showco
to discuss those figures.

He later described the all-night meeting with Grant and Showco boss Jack
Calmes. "Peter kept himself going with long lines of cocaine," wrote Bannister in his 2003 memoir, *There Must Be a Better Way*. "God knows how much
he got through. The cost, if set against the freight charges, would have reduced them quite significantly." Eventually, Showco's costs were whittled
down to £100,000, making the dates financially viable.

Tickets for the first show on Saturday, August 4, went on sale in June.
Grant had decided not to announce the second date on the 11th until later.
After four weeks, Zeppelin had sold just 115,000 of the expected 150,000 tickets. Bannister allocated 100,000 tickets to the first show but sent 15,000 postal
applicants tickets for the second date instead.

It was an unorthodox way to drum up business, but Bannister promised
to refund these tickets if the applicants couldn't attend. As it was the vacation
season, he was inundated with requests for refunds.

Reluctantly, Bannister suggested to Grant they cancel the second Knebworth show and try and sell out the first. Peter told him to wait. "I said to
Bannister, 'This is the biggest fucking band in the world, and we can do two
dates.' I was absolutely confident."

According to Freddy, Grant also suggested he'd renegotiate Zeppelin's fee
in light of the slow sales. Without a written contract, though, Bannister could
only hope he kept his word, whatever his word turned out to be.

In the meantime, Grant tried to bolster the bill with some high-profile
support acts. Swan Song's artists were noticeably absent. The second biggest
act on the label, Bad Company, was promoting a new album, *Desolation Angels* and about to tour America.

Grant and Bannister looked elsewhere. Ian Dury and the Blockheads, the
Boomtown Rats, and Dire Straits were all approached to play and refused.

These were current groups who'd distilled punk's back-to-basics approach; opening for Led Zeppelin was not part of their career plan.

"I said no, because Dire Straits wasn't ready," explains Ed Bicknell. "Mo Austin, the chairman of Warner Brothers, phoned me up and said, 'I hear you were offered shows with Led Zeppelin, and you turned them down? You do know their manager is Peter Grant?'"

The final bill zigzagged between the impenetrable progressive-rock of Todd Rundgren's Utopia and former Outlaw Chas Hodges's pub-pop duo, Chas and Dave. When Grant suggested adding seasoned British folkies Fairport Convention, Bannister presumed they'd split up years ago.

For the second date, Grant secured Keith Richards and Ronnie Wood's side-project-meets-drinking-club, the New Barbarians. The Rolling Stones connection gave them kudos and curiosity value, but the Barbarians had never made a record.

"I talked to Peter about this years later," says Bicknell. "He asked why Dire Straits didn't do it. I said the band wasn't ready, and I didn't fancy playing on your stage with your sound and lights or rather *without* your sound and lights, on a bill where the audience has only come to see Led Zeppelin. He said, 'Hmmm, very wise, Ed.'

"The trouble is, Peter was in a goldfish bowl operating out of the Kings Road office, and he'd overestimated how many Led Zeppelin could draw. They also hadn't recognized how tastes had changed. Which is how you ended up with the New Barbarians."

Regardless of weak ticket sales and support bands, both shows went ahead. Knebworth was sold as Led Zeppelin's great comeback, and it almost lived up to its billing.

The Grants took a helicopter from Horselunges to the site. "As we arrived, we heard Jason on the drums during the sound check," remembers Warren. Bonham's son had been seen behind the kit in *The Song Remains the Same.* Now aged thirteen, he was a formidable player. "John was at the mixing desk, and Jason was playing. We could hear the drums from the PA in the helicopter as we flew over."

Despite punk's antipathy toward Led Zeppelin, members of the Sex Pistols and the Clash were among those seen loping around backstage. "I'd suggested to Dad we have a liggers enclosure," says Helen. It was a designated holding pen, away from the VIP area where "anybody who looked a bit suspect" could be contained.

The band had played two warm-up dates in Copenhagen, but it had been two years since Oakland. Onstage Led Zeppelin, especially Plant, seemed visibly nervous. "Robert didn't want to do it," admitted John Paul Jones. "I could understand why. But we thought he'd really enjoy it if we could just get him back out there."

Plant looked as if he wasn't sure if he should be wiggling his hips the way he did in 1972. In contrast, Jimmy Page, grinning beatifically, was soon soaked in sweat and lost in the moment. When Zeppelin gelled on "Nobody's Fault but Mine" or "Kashmir," it sounded magnificent. And there was still another show to go.

Then the problems began. Three days later, Led Zeppelin's accountant Joan Hudson contacted Freddy Bannister, requesting Zeppelin's fee for the following weekend. Bannister explained they didn't have the money, as they hadn't sold enough tickets for the first date. He'd also presumed Grant would reduce their fee for the second show. Bannister insisted the official attendance figure for Saturday had been 104,000. Hudson told him Grant had it on good authority there were 250,000 people there, and the band expected their money.

The following day, an American wearing a suit and dark glasses and claiming to represent Peter Grant arrived at Bannister's office. He introduced himself as Herb Atkin. "Everything about his appearance was intended to suggest he was CIA or the Mafia," wrote Bannister in his memoir. An Englishman claiming to be a retired police superintendent accompanied Atkin.

The two men told Bannister that Grant had aerial shots of the audience, which had been analyzed by a contact at NASA. They'd proved there were 250,000 onsite. Swan Song's Mitchell Fox had sent Neal Preston up in a helicopter to photograph the crowd. Soon after, Preston remembers receiving a call from the New York office: "I was told to put the negatives of the photo in an envelope, someone would come to my house tomorrow to pick it up, and I was not to ask any questions. The next day, this guy in a jacket and tie arrives. 'I'm here for the envelope. Thank you, goodbye.' And that was the last I heard of it for a long time."

Bannister was never shown the aerial photograph or any data from NASA. Instead, two days before the second date, he was told Grant's people were taking over the festival, including the box office. There'd been a complete breakdown of trust. Bannister had no choice but to withdraw.

Later, Grant claimed he'd been told by Herb Atkin that "a firm from the East End," knowing how much cash there'd be backstage, was planning a robbery during the second Knebworth date. "Herb was very well connected, and a few people got their collars felt and were kept away from us for twenty-four hours," he said.

In the meantime, Grant put his cashiers in the office and his security guards at the gates. Despite the addition of the New Barbarians, the attendance was lower than the previous week; Bannister even claimed as little as forty to fifty thousand people turned up; a figure disputed by others.

The DJ Nicky Horne had been hired to introduce Zeppelin onstage. "When I came in for the second weekend, I didn't know what was happening," he says. "Freddy paid me for the first weekend. Then on the second, Richard Cole turns up and gives me an envelope stuffed with cash."

There were bags of cash everywhere, being moved between trailers and limousines. These included the bands' fees, merchandising money and, according to some, the cash for the car park tickets, all of which had become Grant's responsibility.

When the New Barbarians remembered they didn't have a manager, Ronnie Wood asked Peter to collect their money for them. "I remember sitting in their trailer counting it out for Ronnie," says Richard Cole.

The Barbarians were reluctant to go onstage that afternoon. "Keith Richards wouldn't come out of his trailer," remembers Maggie Bell. "Peter was outside going, 'Come on, time to go!' And Keith was inside saying, 'I'm not doing it.' So G started shaking the caravan—'Yeah, you fucking are.'"

The day didn't get any better for Keith and Ron. Two of Don Murfet's security men, John "JB" Bettie and his brother, Paul, were at the side of the stage when Zeppelin played. They'd been given orders not to let anyone up without a pass, and Grant was impressed when they stopped Richards and Wood.

"Peter came over, and he was laughing," says Paul Bettie. "He said, 'What are you two boys up to?'" before offering the brothers a job at Horselunges.

"At Knebworth I remember being given two bags," continues Bettie. "G said, 'There's two hundred grand in one and a sawn-off shotgun in the other.' I said, 'I hope I open the right bag first, Peter, otherwise I'm fucked.'"

"I was told to collect, I think, a million pounds from Freddy Bannister," recalls Cole. "Peter and Zeppelin had two hundred grand each, in bags, thrown into the back of their cars." When Grant's chauffeur, Norman, took him back to Horselunges, Peter walked into the house, leaving the bag behind. He wouldn't remember the missing money was there until the following day.

A month after Knebworth, Herb Atkin contacted Bannister again and requested a meeting at London's Dorchester Hotel. Rumors about the conflict between the promoter and Grant had found their way into the music press.

"It seemed Grant wanted me to absolve him and the band of any bad publicity and wanted me to sign a letter to that effect," wrote Bannister.

Atkin had previously intimated that he knew "people in Miami" who would create problems for Bannister if he didn't cooperate with Grant at Knebworth. Atkin repeated these threats at the Dorchester. "I was scared for the safety of my family," wrote Bannister. "I wanted to put everything behind me and get on with my life. So, I agreed to sign the statement."

Grant then paid for a full-page advertisement in *Melody Maker* and published the letter on September 20. Bannister stated, "Led Zeppelin had voluntarily reduced their guarantee. . . . Led Zeppelin, the manager, and his staff have been completely cooperative. . . . The group's performance at Knebworth was really tremendous . . . " and "Finally, it would be a privilege and pleasure for me to promote another Led Zeppelin concert."

It read like a letter written at gunpoint. Bannister's company, Tedoar Ltd, went into liquidation soon after, and he retired from the music business.

Grant cautiously addressed the problems in a 1993 interview with Dave Lewis, the editor of Led Zeppelin fanzine, *Tight But Loose*. "We did have a bit of a row over the attendance," he conceded. "But I had it photographed from a helicopter that first week and sent to NASA to be analyzed. There was 210,000 in there, give or take 2 percent, they told us. So we got paid in full. There was some battle over VAT. And I think it was 180,000 the second week."

Some years later, Neal Preston was told his aerial photograph of Knebworth had been sent to a NASA laboratory by Grant's fixer. He was told they had software to separate the picture into four quadrants, "And they could estimate plus or minus a hundred people how many were in each quadrant and work out the size of the crowd."

The story of Grant, the Knebworth photograph, and the NASA laboratory quickly passed into Led Zeppelin folklore. Not everyone is convinced. "I'm afraid I think it's bollocks," says Ed Bicknell. "Peter told people it was true, and human beings have this natural will to believe." The power of fear and suggestion had worked again.

According to Grant, Weiss and Atkin hadn't abandoned their plan to depose him. Atkin was still whispering in his ear and others close to Led Zeppelin. As long as Grant believed his family and his band were in danger, "from an East End firm" or persons unknown, there was money to be made. "Cindy told me that whenever Herb left Horselunges, he was carrying a stack of hundred-dollar bills inside a rolled-up magazine," says Richard Cole.

In 1980, Cindy joined the Grants and Phil Carson's family on the Warners' private jet for a trip to Miami. They stayed at the exclusive Fontainebleau hotel on Miami Beach, met with Ahmet Ertegun, and went deep-sea fishing. Grant was delighted to see one of his favorite comedians, Don Rickles, lounging in a gazebo by the pool.

Early one morning from the window of their suite, Cindy watched an unmanned boat wash up on the beach. Within seconds it was surrounded by men driving four-wheelers who quickly unloaded its cargo and disappeared into the dark. Before flying home, Cindy remembers Peter washing their money, "Because he said most of the cash in Florida had coke on it, and he didn't want to take any chances."

However, drug squad detectives were waiting to meet them when their plane landed at Gatwick Airport. The police headed straight for Cindy and took her into a room for interrogation. "They said, 'We hear you're bringing in a kilo of coke.' They were serious, and they were pissed when they couldn't find anything."

Then one of the officers discovered the tiny remnant of a joint in Cindy's purse. She was questioned again, and strip-searched. "Then they went through the Carsons' luggage. Phil and his wife had a baby daughter and were carrying a huge plastic bag of baby formula. The cops were going, 'Great! We've got it. Here's the coke!' I said, 'Honey, believe me, that's nowhere near a kilo.'"

There was nothing for the police to find, and the story of the baby formula "drug bust" amused them all for years. But the experience left Cindy unsettled. "Herb told me my name was known to Interpol," she says. "And he said he could get it taken off. He scared the crap out of me."

John "JB" Bettie began working at Horselunges not long after the Knebworth festival. His brother, Paul, joined him later. It was easier work than their regular jobs—throwing drunks out of nightclubs in London's West End—but it had its drawbacks.

"At times, it was like working in an ivory tower," says Paul. "It was a beautiful house, but there wasn't always much to do." Nevertheless, one of the first things Grant told him was if Herb Atkin called, "I had to come and get him, no matter what he was doing, even if he was taking a shit."

Bad Company's security guard, Danny Francis, had just returned from the band's last tour when his son, Daniel, was taken ill. Grant was as supportive as a second father. "He sent Norman the chauffeur round with the Daimler and a check and told me to take him to Harley Street, no waiting." Francis later named his second son Grant in his honor.

"There were good days and bad days," says Francis now. "On the good days, Horselunges was fantastic. But on the bad days it was dark, like the house was haunted."

By April 1980, it had been more than a year since Grant had toured with any of his bands. But he brought the uncompromising rules of the road into civilian life. When he threw a fourteenth birthday party for Warren, it became the scene for what Grant's old friends now refer to as "the helicopter incident."

Warren had taken up motocross, and Peter had acquired a new Suzuki bike straight off the production line as a birthday gift. He'd arranged for the bike to be flown by helicopter to Horselunges and for Po to photograph its arrival.

Unaware of what was about to happen, Warren was told to stand in front of a window at the manor and look into the distance. "I heard a whirring sound, and then I saw the helicopter," he says now. "And then I saw something fall off the bottom of it."

The chopper had taken off from their local hotel, the Boship Farm Inn, with Warren's motorcycle secured by a length of chain. Shortly after, the chain snapped, and the bike fell into a field. By the time the helicopter landed at Horselunges, Grant was incandescent with rage. "Dad went mad," says Warren. "He charged across the lawn and started ranting at this poor guy."

"Peter was furious," remembers Po. "He told Richard Cole to bring the pilot into the house. I think Bindon was there, too, because I remember Peter telling him to take the distributor cap out of the helicopter's engine, as if it was a car."

Grant and Cole marched the pilot into the house. Po went with them, as he'd caught everything on camera, and Peter wanted the photos as evidence. "There was a lot of finger prodding, and Peter told the pilot in no uncertain terms, 'I want £5,000 for a replacement bike, and you're not leaving until I get it.'"

The pilot asked to call his boss at the helicopter company, Bristow, and was told to use the phone in the next room. A few minutes later, he returned. "He said, 'It's all sorted, Mr. Grant; we'll pay you the money, so I'll take the helicopter back now.' And I'll never forget what happened next."

Po watched aghast, as Grant approached the pilot until his face was a few inches from his. "He leaned right in and said, 'What's it like to be called a fucking liar?' The guy visibly shrank back. Peter had become so paranoid, he was taping his phone calls. He said, 'Listen to this, cunt,' and played the tape recording back.

"You could hear the pilot's boss's voice, 'Tell him whatever he wants to hear and get out of there.' This guy was terrified. 'I am so sorry, Mr. Grant.' But Peter wasn't having it—'Get back on the phone and tell him I want £5,000 or this fucking helicopter's not leaving my property.

"Somebody eventually arrived with some cash because the helicopter was allowed to leave just before it became dark. Peter got his way, but we were amazed he didn't kill the guy."

"When Dad had those moments, he didn't like himself very much," says Helen. "It used to make him anxious and upset. I think there were times when he went to bed and thought, 'I was wrong and shouldn't have done that.' I think he felt guilty; he knew he'd been out of order. But he would never show it."

By now, Grant's bands and his business colleagues had also learned to work around his absences. With Alan Callan on board, Grant spent less time in the Swan Song office.

"I'd get a lot of tapes from groups, and any which stood out I'd send to Horselunges," explains Unity MacLean. "Then I'd call the house and speak to Ray or Dave. 'Did Peter get the tapes?' 'Oh yeah, he got them, he's very pleased.' 'Can I talk to him?' 'Oh, he's not up yet, Oh, he's on the other line . . . ' Always an excuse."

When she did speak to Grant, it was usually so he could fire her. "He was always firing me," she says. "It was usually something to do with Jimmy Page: 'Jimmy says you said this. . . . ' The first time it happened was twelve o'clock at night, and I was devastated.

"I called Richard, who said, 'Ignore him. He'll have forgotten about it by the morning.' And he did. Except for once, when I took him at his word and didn't turn up the next day. Then he phoned to tell me to get my arse down to the office right away."

Nobody was spared. "By this time, Peter needed delicate handling," Carson explains. "I bought a house halfway between London and Horselunges, partly so I could be available. But by this time, it wasn't easy.

"If I needed to see Peter I had to pick my times carefully. I'd arrange to meet him on, say, Wednesday at two o'clock. And if I was lucky, I'd get to see him, maybe, Thursday night, but more likely Friday. So I would go down there, with all my work papers and a change of clothes and sit in Peter's study until I was summoned."

In New York, Mitchell Fox had discovered a band called Itchy Brother and wanted to sign them to Swan Song. The group later changed their name to the Kentucky Headhunters, and Fox still manages them today.

Mitchell arrived in Hellingly to see Grant and checked into the Boship. "I spent five days waiting for Peter to call," he says. "I watched a lot of cricket on TV and even learned the rules. Finally, the call came, and a Rolls Royce Silver Shadow turned up to give me a ride to the house."

Still, Grant wouldn't come out of the bedroom. "I arrived one morning, and this guy called Mitch was there," remembers Paul Bettie. "He'd been sitting in the living room since yesterday. I made him some food, and we sat together all day. At one point, Peter phoned and asked, 'Is Mitch still there?' But he still didn't come down.

"Mitch saw the phone and asked what button you pressed to speak to Peter upstairs. I didn't think it was a good idea, but I told him, and he pressed it. Peter said he'd be down in a minute. Then he rang again. He said, 'Tell Mitch, there's a cab coming for him. Tell him to go back to New York, and I'll speak to him there.'"

"I slept in the living room for three days," admits Fox, "then went back to the hotel for another five, and I still didn't get to speak to Peter."

Horselunges ran to its own rules, and Warren was used to seeing their father's business associates marooned in the living room for days on end. "Dad used to say, 'Light a fire, Ray, they'll be all right.'"

Whatever intrigue was going on behind the scenes, Grant's inaccessibility had affected his relationship with Led Zeppelin. In Peter's version of events to Mark Long, Phil Carson was poised and waiting to take over the band's management. Though he acknowledges Weiss and Atkin's attempted coup, Richard Cole never heard Carson was involved, adding, "*Every* fucker in the world wanted to manage Led Zeppelin."

Carson, meanwhile, insists Page and Plant approached him directly and asked if he would consider taking over. "This was in Ibiza in 1979, I think," he says. "We were all together on the beach. And I said, 'No, let's give Peter another chance, I'll talk to him.' That I do regret. Because I *could* have managed Led Zeppelin. I gave it my all to try and help him."

After Knebworth, Robert Plant had cautiously agreed to another tour, and promoter Harvey Goldsmith had lined up provisional dates in Europe, but nobody could make a move until Peter said so.

"There were six weeks to go, no signed contracts, and Harvey's going nuts," says Carson. "Peter's in his bedroom, he hasn't showered for days, he's in this old fucking tracksuit. And he says to me, 'Ere, Phyllis—he always called me Phyllis—I hear you can do a good impersonation of me?' It's true I used to impersonate Peter.

"So he told me to call Harvey and pretend to be him. So I phoned Harvey Goldsmith, impersonating Peter Grant while the real Peter Grant is sitting next to me. Harvey believed it was him, and the deal was done. I didn't tell him the truth until years later."

News of Led Zeppelin's "Tour over Europe 1980" was announced soon after. There were to be thirteen dates, crisscrossing Germany, Belgium, Austria, the Netherlands, and Switzerland, but not the UK. The shows were meant as a precursor to a possible American tour, but Grant didn't want to spook Robert Plant.

"Robert kept insisting he wouldn't go back to America," he said. "But we had to go if we were to carry on. That was where a sizeable amount of the market was, and I purposely played it down with Robert. Bonzo would tell me he'd say to him, "How come G hasn't said anything to me about America yet?" I never said a thing."

But for the first time since 1968, Richard Cole wouldn't be going with them. Grant had decided Cole's drug problems were too serious. "I'd paid for the doctor's visits, and it just wasn't getting better," he said. "So I thought the only way to shake him up was to blow him out."

"There was also a certain mistrust of Richard by Peter, which, to this day, I find unjust," says Phil Carson. "Richard Cole lived and died for Led Zeppelin and for Peter. But you never know what somebody is whispering in someone's ear.

"I always felt Richard should have been given more responsibility within the organization, but Peter never gave it to him. Then he couldn't give it to him because he got so messed up."

A few months later, Cole decided to go to Italy to get off heroin. "The idea was Peter would pay for it, and I'd clean up," he says. "But it was obvious Herb also wanted me out of the way because I was telling Peter things."

Cole flew to Rome with a girlfriend. "Before leaving, Herb told me to meet someone who wanted to talk to me about some business with Zeppelin. We were meant to meet at the Excelsior Hotel, but his name wasn't on the register. If I'd had my wits about me, I'd have realized it was a setup and wouldn't have gone in there."

Astonishingly, Cole was arrested by armed police the following morning in his hotel suite. He was taken to a maximum-security jail, where he was told he was also being held on suspicion of terrorism.

"They thought I'd blown up the Bologna train station, which had been attacked by terrorists the day I arrived in Italy. The strange thing is, nobody knew I'd been arrested. Then two days later, I got a letter from Steve Weiss's office. They'd got me a lawyer already."

Mysteriously, a bag containing 32 grams of cocaine was also found in Cole's suite. Even when it was obvious Cole wasn't involved in the bombing, Italian justice moved slowly. Eventually, he was sentenced to six months for possession and transferred to a more comfortable facility, Rebibbia, on the outskirts of Rome.

Grant paid for both of Cole's lawyers, Julio Gradaloni and New York attorney Jeff Hoffman, whose previous clients included John Gotti, the head of the Gambino crime family. Inevitably, Herb Atkin was among Cole's prison visitors. "Hoffman didn't like him at all—didn't trust him," says Cole.

Cole's spell in prison had the desired effect of weaning him off heroin but also kept him out of Britain and away from Grant and Led Zeppelin. He would never work for the band again.

Instead, Phil Carlo had replaced him for Zeppelin's European tour. "When I first got the call, I thought, 'Shit! What have I done?'" Carlo admits. "I was told to get the train to Polegate. Peter picked me up in his black Porsche with the Bad 1 number plate, the one Bad Company had given him.

"Eventually, after an hour of small talk, G said, 'Zeppelin is going out again, but it has to be different this time.' He said, 'Your job is to make the tour smooth, keep it low key, and keep it happy.'"

After a month-long postponement, the tour finally began in Dortmund, Germany, on June 17. It was low key on every level. "I was keen to stop the self-importance and the guitar solos that lasted an hour," said Robert Plant. "We cut everything down, and we didn't play any song for more than four and a half minutes."

This was very much a Led Zeppelin for 1980: jeans and T-shirts; a light show half the size of the one they'd used before; and a set that began with bluesman Tiny Bradshaw's "Train Kept A-Rollin,'" as played by the Yardbirds. "Punk kinda woke us up again," admitted John Paul Jones.

Away from the pomp and spectacle of Knebworth, the group had time to reacquaint themselves with the music and each other. Grant also seemed pleased to be back on the road and was visibly relaxed.

Zeppelin uber-fan Dave Lewis followed them to Cologne and then on to five more shows. "Their security guard said, 'Here's your passes, stand where you like,'" says Lewis. "So I stood on the side of the stage. If Peter trusted you, you were OK."

Helen and Warren joined their father when the tour reached Zurich in June. "By then it was becoming quite normal for us to jump on these Learjets and fly out," says Warren.

As low key as the dates were, though, some old habits still had to be accommodated. Arrangements were made for a drug dealer to fly out from London. "She turned up at the airport wearing dark glasses, a big floppy hat, and a veil," remembers Phil. Carlo and Grant quickly nicknamed her "The Beekeeper."

Bonham was still drinking heavily, and Phil remembers Peter intervening during a car ride in Germany: "Bonzo was swigging from a bottle of scotch and kept putting his hands over the driver's eyes. Not a good idea when you're doing a hundred miles an hour down the autobahn. In the end, G took the bottle, pretended to have a swig and then pretended to pass out on him. He stayed that way, slumped against Bonzo, trapping his arms by his side for the whole journey."

Carlo noticed Grant sometimes seemed happier around the crew and the drivers than anybody else. In Frankfurt, Ahmet Ertegun arrived with Steve Weiss, but Grant was nowhere to be seen.

"Weissy sent me to find Peter, and I found him looking underneath somebody's truck," says Carlo. "He'd been out in the car park, introducing himself and shaking hands with all the drivers. I said, 'G, there's a load of important people in here.' He said, 'Go and tell them I'm already with important people.'

"He said to me later, 'Those truck drivers, they go all night, all weathers, and if there's a ruck they'll always pile in, Phil.'" Grant sounded almost wistful for his own days behind the wheel.

The European tour ended in Berlin on July 7. Grant cornered Carlo just after the plane landed. "As we were coming down the steps at Heathrow, G turned around and said, 'I've just had a word with Jim and Robert. You're in. We're going to America.'"

Grant and the band met later at London's Blakes Hotel to finalize their plans. A nineteen-date US tour billed as "Led Zeppelin, The 1980s: Part One" was arranged for October and November that year.

Despite his demons, Grant hadn't lost his nose for business. If the dates went well and Plant was happy, there was time for "The 1980s: Part Two" later. "We were fully operational again," Grant said.

Paul Bettie remembers a box of T-shirts for the upcoming American tour being delivered to Horselunges. Six months later they were still there, where he'd left them. The tour wasn't to be. On September 24, Rex King picked John Bonham up from his farm and drove him to Berkshire's Bray Studios for the first day of tour rehearsals. It would be the last rehearsal Bonzo ever played.

11

Crocodiles in the Moat

"There were times I wanted to wring Peter's neck, but I wish him well."

—ROBERT PLANT, 1988

*I*t was Led Zeppelin's sound man Benji Le Fevre who discovered John Bonham's body. It was September 25, and Benji and John Paul Jones stopped by Jimmy Page's house, the Old Mill in Windsor, on their way to rehearsals. Rex King and Page's man Friday, Rick Hobbs, were up and about while a rumpled-looking Jimmy was gently easing himself into the day. Everybody presumed Bonham was still asleep upstairs.

Jones suggested they wake him and followed Le Fevre into the bedroom where the two men were confronted by the awful scene. In a daze, Jones walked back downstairs to break the news to his bandmates. He later remembered hearing Plant and Page laughing and joking, blissfully unaware of what he was about to tell them.

Plant wanted to see his friend's body, but Le Fevre persuaded him otherwise. The emergency services were called, and a doctor and an ambulance arrived, but it was too late. Later, Robert and Benji would break every speed limit driving to Worcestershire to tell Pat Bonham and the family before they heard it from anyone else.

Before that, though, Le Fevre called Horselunges. Knowing how difficult it was to reach Grant, even under normal circumstances, he told Ray Washbourne what had happened. Ray's subsequent exchange with Peter said much about his careful handling of the boss.

Grant recalled the conversation in a 1993 interview. "Ray came up to me and said, 'Come downstairs.' He sat me down, handed me some Valium, and said, 'Take these.' I said, 'Why do I want to take them?' And he said, '*Take* them.' I said, 'Tell me what it is.' He said, 'There's somebody on the phone for you.' I said, 'What *is* it?' He said, 'John Bonham's died.'"

Cindy Russell found Grant a few minutes later. He was visibly upset and shaking. "I couldn't believe it," she says now. "I asked him, 'How can John be dead? The band is with him. They're all together.'" Grant told her how Bonham had been downing huge shots of vodka from yesterday morning until midnight. Then came the anger and recrimination.

"My God, it was like trying to nail down an elephant. Peter was blaming himself—'I should have been looking out for him, I should have been there'— but blaming others as well. John had been drinking Smirnoff vodka, and of course I was the Smirnoff billboard girl."

Calls were made to Phil Carson and Don Murfet. "I was at Horselunges for thirty-six hours after Bonzo died," remembers Carson, "sitting with Peter and working out what we were going to say to the press."

Meanwhile, Murfet and his team went straight to the Old Mill to dispose of anything incriminating before the police arrived. Paul Bettie remembers Grant telephoning and asking numerous questions. "Peter was saying, 'You have to tell me this, this, this . . . ' All these personal questions about how Bonzo died. He wanted to know everything."

In the event, there was nothing for the police to find, and nothing suspicious about Bonham's death. It was a terrible accident and a wasteful loss of life. After a day's steady boozing, the rehearsal at Bray Studios was abandoned, and Bonzo and Rex King went back to Page's house for the evening.

Bonzo fell asleep on the sofa around midnight. Rick Hobbs and Rex King put him to bed, later telling the coroner they'd placed him on his side bolstered by pillows. It was not the first time either had put a drunk musician to bed.

Hobbs checked on Bonham later and noticed he hadn't moved. But at some stage in the night, he'd rolled over. It was later revealed Bonham had consumed the equivalent of forty single shots of vodka. When his unconscious body started rejecting that much alcohol, he suffocated in his own vomit. The coroner's eventual verdict was "death by accidental suicide."

Warren Grant was in a lesson at Battle Road when he was summoned to the office. "Ray was there and said, 'I have to take you home right now.' Straight away, alarm bells started ringing. I thought something had happened to my dad, to Mum, to Helen. . . . "

Washbourne had been told not to say anything until they were back at the manor. "Ray kept saying, 'Wait 'til we get home,' but I said, 'No, I want to know now.' He did tell me in the end. When I got home, Dad was in his study. He said, 'Bonzo's died.' He wanted me out of school because it was going to be on the radio, and he didn't want someone telling me before he did."

By early evening, John Bonham's death was on the TV and radio news across Britain. Even in the snail's paced, predigital age, it didn't take long for the story to reach America, where fans were about to buy tickets for Zeppelin's upcoming tour.

"I was in the office doling out tickets for the New York show when Scott Muni announced it on WNEW-FM," says Mitchell Fox. "I went into Steve Weiss's office. I'm not sure if Steve knew already. It was the days of multiple lines on a switchboard, and they were all flashing, with people wanting a statement from us. We just stood there, looking at these flashing lights in a state of shock."

Confusion reigned at Swan Song in London. "Peter just said, 'Everybody out, lock the doors and don't come back until I tell you,'" remembers Unity MacLean. Although she was used to Grant's erratic working methods, Unity suspected something was wrong. "I didn't know what. So, I went home and then went with my husband to a bar around the corner."

At home later in the evening, she found a message on her answering machine: "It was the journalist David Wigg—'Do you have any comment on the death of John Bonham?' So I had to hear it from the *Daily Express*. Peter didn't have the courtesy to tell us. It chokes me up to think about it, even now."

Bonzo's funeral took place on October 10 at St. Michael's Church in the Worcestershire village of Rushock, near to the family's farm. Bonham's shell-shocked family sat up front. Behind them were row after row of stony faces belonging to his bandmates, Swan Song contemporaries, and Midlands peers, among them ELO's Jeff Lynne and Bev Bevan.

After the service, Bonham's coffin was taken to Worcestershire Crematorium. The wake was held in his favorite pub, the Chequers, in Cutnall Green. "Everybody was drunk," remembers Cindy. "I don't drink, but I got drunk that day, and Peter got so pissed at me, I had to travel back with the Carsons.

He was just upset. The whole thing with John took the breath away from everybody."

Don Murfet noticed how subdued Grant had been when they'd met soon after Bonham's death. "Peter hadn't been in his normal, control-freak manager mode." Grant had lost a close friend. Like Peter, John Bonham had come from the simplest of backgrounds and achieved success beyond anything his family could have imagined. His and Grant's lives were interwoven outside the recording studio and the concert arena.

Like Grant, Bonham sometimes hid his insecurities behind a bluff exterior. Robert Plant remembered him complaining bitterly during a car journey before their final rehearsal. "Bonzo said, 'I've had it with playing drums. Everybody plays better than me,'" said Plant, after which the drummer tore off the car's sun visor and threw it out the window.

"On every tour before rehearsals, John would be worried about not playing as good as last time," said Grant.

Bonham's death had been widely reported in the press. The *Daily Mail* had even run the story on its front page; their prurient interest piqued by the story of a rock star expiring after "a night of heavy drinking." Bonham wasn't a household name, like a Beatle or a Rolling Stone. More than one newspaper ran the story of his death, but with a photograph of Rex King instead.

What stoked Grant's anger more than anything was the press speculating on what they called "the jinx of Led Zeppelin." *NME* posed the question, "Why do people associated with Led Zeppelin seem to die?" While the *Evening News* quoted an unnamed source, claiming Robert Plant feared Jimmy Page's fascination with the dark arts had been the reason for their drummer's demise.

A decade later, the scriptwriter Barrie Keeffe raised the topic with Grant. "I got the impression Peter wished Jimmy hadn't gone into all that stuff with Crowley and black magic," he says now. "Peter did wonder if the band was cursed, but he wasn't serious. It was just because he loved Bonham, and it ended so tragically."

"Peter once said to me, 'All that black magic stuff was a pile of shit,'" offers Ed Bicknell. "Pagey had a few books, and bought a couple of houses that looked spooky. That was it, really. But he understood how it added to the aura. Peter said he'd sometimes take Jimmy with him to Atlantic, and people would run into their offices because they thought he'd cast a spell on them. All bollocks."

However, others also viewed Bonham's death as an opportunity. "G was very disappointed," remembers Phil Carlo. "People were dangling checks in front of him to make Led Zeppelin carry on, and people he respected were phoning up, even before the funeral."

Several drummers, including Simon Kirke, ELP's Carl Palmer and Carmine Appice, were mentioned as possible replacements by the press. "I was flattered when I saw my name in the papers," admits Appice, "but I didn't want to piss off Rod and told him there was nothing in the rumors. Rod thought it was funny, told me to encourage it, as it was good for selling tickets." Twelve months later, Stewart fired Appice. "He said he was tired of hearing rumors I was about to join Led Zeppelin."

Meanwhile, hundreds of letters for the Bonham family and Led Zeppelin poured into Swan Song's London office and ended up with the Grant family. Many were from America and remained unopened for years.

In an age when emotions can be conveyed online in an instant, there's something arcane about these handwritten messages: "Bonzzo [sic] was amazing. . . . I am sorry for your loss." Though, inevitably, some asked for an audition. "If you need a drummer, I play in a group in Medina, OH," wrote one hopeful. "But I will save the money and come to England."

Unity MacLean fielded calls from fans and drummers alike. Grant was furious, though, when she contacted Richard Cole to tell him about Bonham. Another inmate at Rebibbia had heard one of Zeppelin had died, but not which one. "My lawyer told me it was Bonzo, and I thought, 'That's it then. That's the end,'" says Cole.

"I wrote to Richard because he was getting garbled information," says Unity. Then came the warning: "Ray Washbourne told me, 'Peter says you're not to contact Richard again.' I said, 'Peter can't tell me what to do.' Ray said, 'You wanna know what Peter can do?' Like he was making a threat. I said, 'Peter can do what he likes. Peter can't get off his backside to run a record label. I can speak to whoever I like and tell Peter from me . . . '"

Bonham's death marked the beginning of the end of Unity's tenure with Swan Song. "I was close to Bonzo," she says. "He was the only one who was sympathetic and ever told me I was doing a good job."

Unity was now pregnant with her son. Bonham's death convinced her it was time for a change, and she left a few months later. "I thought, 'I'm out of here.' I didn't want to be bringing a child into a world where people are dropping like flies around me." A year earlier, she'd had to deal with the fallout when a young photographer had died of a suspected overdose at Page's house, Plumpton Place.

With Carole and Unity gone, it was left to Cynthia Sach and a new secretary, Sian Meredith, to run the office. In early November, Plant joined Page and Jones for a meeting on the island of Jersey to discuss their future, but the singer had already made up his mind. "The band didn't exist the minute Bonzo had gone," he said. "There was no Led anything."

"They came back, and I booked a suite for afternoon tea at the Savoy," recalled Grant. "And they asked what I thought. I said it just couldn't go on because it was the four of them, and they were relieved because they had decided the same. For Led Zeppelin to make that music, it needed the four of them to do it. And now one was gone."

Zeppelin released an official statement on December 4: "We wish it to be known that the loss of our dear friend and the deep respect we have for his family together with the sense of undivided harmony felt by ourselves and our manager, have led us to decide that we could not continue as we were."

In hindsight, the mention of "our manager" was pivotal. Phil Carson helped prepare the final statement. "It was never really on for there to be another drummer coming in," he said. "But I think, had there been any other manager, it could have carried on. They could have let time pass a bit and then bring in someone new. Another manager who was not going through what Peter was going through would probably have tried to encourage them to go on."

"After John died, Dad did his manager's job," says Warren. "It was when Led Zeppelin decided not to continue that the reality sank in. There was a lot of backstabbing, jostling for position, and people thinking they could get a piece of it and taking advantage."

Grant told Mark Long that after Bonham's death, Steve Weiss was among those pushing for the band to re-form with another drummer. Some in the organization recall Weiss being devastated by Bonzo's death. "Because he realized his cash cow had gone," suggests one. When it became obvious Zeppelin wouldn't continue, the vultures eventually stopped circling.

In one of his last letters to Grant, Herb Atkin never mentioned Led Zeppelin but instead told him his health was suffering and pleaded with Peter to give up smoking before it was too late. It read like the words of a concerned older relative rather than a man trying to steal his business.

Atkin's letter arrived in an envelope stamped with the words "Continental Investigative Agency," suggesting he was the world's most indiscreet private detective. He died after suffering a heart attack in February 1989.

After Zeppelin, Herb's so-called accomplice, Stevens H. Weiss, married his longstanding girlfriend, Marie, and moved to Florida. He passed away in Fort Lauderdale in June 2008. The obituary in the *Sun-Sentinel* paid tribute to his "integrity, wit, and devotion to his many high-profile clients."

*I*n the meantime, 1980 turned out to be a terrible year. "Bonzo passed, Zep broke up, Peter went into seclusion, and Bad Company stumbled on toward our own breakup," says Simon Kirke. "Everybody was doing an incredible amount of drugs, myself included. And on top of that, John Lennon was shot at the end of the year."

A generation of musicians and fans were suddenly confronted by their own mortality. Bonham was just thirty-two when he died. His bandmates and the members of Bad Company were all still in their thirties, with Grant the grand old man at forty-five.

In 1980, record companies and audiences were still coming to terms with the concept of the aging rock star. For Dylan, Neil Young, and the surviving members of the Beatles, the Stones, the Who, and Led Zeppelin, the 1980s would be a confused and confusing time. They would all try on the new clothes, hair, and technology with variable results. "I'd never felt so out of place and vulnerable as I did at that time," admitted Robert Plant.

Page was the first Zeppelin member to start playing with new musicians. Page and Yes's ex-bass guitarist Chris Squire agreed to a studio jam after meeting at Phil Carson's Christmas party. Yes was one of Carson's Atlantic acts and had just broken up. Squire and Yes's drummer Alan White were now looking for a new opportunity.

"Jimmy just wanted to start playing again," Squire told me in 2015. "I remember he was on a health kick, really behaving himself. . . . Would you believe, only smoking cigarettes through a holder?"

The studio jam led to the beginning of a new project. By spring 1981, Page, Squire, and White had demoed a handful of songs. Chris Squire's father had suggested a band name, XYZ, in acknowledgement of their previous groups. Grant listened to the demos and summoned Squire to Horselunges, where they had a long, chemically assisted discussion.

"It was the funniest conversation," Squire told me. "I said, 'XYZ. It's a great name, isn't it?' And Peter replied, 'Hmmm, but the Y comes before the Z. That means Yes comes before Zeppelin.' I said, 'But you can't have XZY Peter. It has to be XYZ, or it won't make sense.' 'Hmmm, but that means Yes comes before Zeppelin.'"

Yes's ex-members were also still tied to their old manager, Brian Lane. According to Squire, a meeting between the two managers "did not go well." Sam Aizer also believes Yes had once approached Grant for management. "They went to Peter for the same reason Queen and Bad Company did, because he was a powerhouse."

XYZ's biggest stumbling block, though, was the absence of a lead singer. "Jimmy said he'd get Robert Plant," said Squire. "He kept saying Robert was interested, that he was coming to the studio. But he never did. I think it was too soon after Bonzo. Eventually the whole thing just fizzled out."

Squire and White soon assembled a new version of Yes, and Page was asked to write a film score. In 1974, director Michael Winner's movie *Death Wish*, starring granite-faced Charles Bronson dispensing vigilante justice on the streets of Chicago, had been a box office hit. It was time for a sequel.

Winner's producers had soul singer Isaac Hayes lined up to record a soundtrack. But Winner wanted Jimmy Page. The director had lived next door to Page in Holland Park for years, but had never met him. Winner's knowledge of rock music was sketchy, but he knew Led Zeppelin had been huge.

Winner called Peter Grant, who told him Page was unreachable for the next ten days. The director needed an answer before then. Grant made the call, "And Jimmy said, 'Yeah, let's do it.'" After which, Michael Winner pulled off the most extraordinary coup in the history of Peter Grant and Led Zeppelin.

"I said, 'Isaac Hayes is doing the music for free and [the film company] Cannon Films is getting a share of the album and a share of the publishing,'" wrote the late Winner in his 2004 autobiography. Hayes's record label wanted to revive his career and had agreed to their client delivering the score for free. "Peter Grant then said the most amazing thing: 'Well, how do I beat free?' I said, joking, 'Jimmy Page has to pay to do our music.' To my amazement Peter Grant said, 'How much?'"

"Peter did the most absurd deal," reveals Phil Carson. "Winner told him, 'All you have to do is beat nothing.' So Peter said, 'I'll give you $100,000.'" Winner claimed the actual figure Grant paid was $175,000, plus a greater percentage for Cannon Films than Hayes's label were offering.

Whatever the numbers, it was an astonishing turnaround from the man who'd once cowed promoters with his brutal 90/10 split. "So, Peter paid for Jimmy to do the soundtrack," says Carson, "which really stuck in Jimmy's throat for a long time."

However, when Winner dispatched a driver to Horselunges with a contract, Grant refused to sign it. "Winner sent some heavy down to my house," Grant complained. "He was wasting his fucking time. I just left him outside."

Paul Bettie remembers the forty-eight-hour standoff: "The driver was there so long, he'd knock on the door and ask to use the toilet. We'd have to say, 'Sorry mate. Go down to the Martlet.' Peter knew he'd been told to wait until he got a signature, so it was a case of 'Right, I'll show him.'"

Winner repeatedly phoned Grant to find out why he was stalling, but he couldn't reach him. At first, he was told Peter "was in the bath" or "had gone for a walk."

"I answered so many times, in the end I said, 'Look, you won't believe this, but Peter's gone paragliding,'" says Dave Northover. 'What? Good God, man!' 'Yeah, he's gone paragliding . . . on the Isle of Wight, but he'll be back in a couple of hours' time. He does this quite often.' Then I put the phone down."

After two days, Winner threatened to cancel the deal unless the contract was signed that night. Peter relented, but he'd made his point. Soon after, Winner finally met his elusive nextdoor neighbor. "One evening my doorbell rang. A thin and slightly wobbly Jimmy Page had come to see the *Death Wish II* movie in my private cinema," he said. Page watched the film and decided where the music should go. "And then Jimmy said to me, 'I'm going to my studio. I don't want you anywhere near me, I'm going to do it all on my own.'"

Winner was used to eccentric actors and agreed to Page's terms. His trust paid off. Jimmy created the soundtrack—a mix of spooked-sounding instrumentals and the occasional splash of blues—in an eight-week burst of activity at his new home studio.

Death Wish II was panned by the critics but made a comfortable $45 million at the box office. Jimmy Page's soundtrack was released in February 1982 but didn't trouble the top thirty anywhere. It was Grant's first experience of a new decade without the guaranteed certainties of the previous one.

"Winner said to me, 'I thought I was getting a soundtrack I could just about use, but it would be a hit record,'" says Phil Carson. "'Instead I got an unbelievable soundtrack that was not a hit record.'" And it had cost Grant at least $100,000.

Robert Plant hadn't been idle since Led Zeppelin's demise. He grieved deeply for John Bonham but at thirty-three years old wasn't ready to give up music. He'd turned one of the barns at his home, Jennings Farm, into a four-track studio, and by the end of 1981 was playing small gigs around the Midlands with a group of local musicians using the name the Honeydrippers.

Plant's new ensemble played soul and rockabilly songs in college halls and the back rooms of pubs. Audiences gawped at Led Zeppelin's lead singer shaking his tail feathers in venues normally reserved for wedding functions and retirement parties.

While these gigs were far from Zeppelin's sixty-thousand-seaters, not everything had changed. Plant still stuck to Peter Grant's Golden Rule and demanded 90 percent of the door. "I was happy," Plant told me. "I was finding my feet again after Bonzo, and I didn't want or need all the trappings, all the stuff that had come with Led Zeppelin toward the end."

Grant watched Plant's return with curiosity and bemusement. Before long, the singer had assembled another group of musicians and was planning to make a record. He told his new bandmates he was offering an equal collaboration.

This was a group effort, not a solo project. However, Plant's new friends were a far cry from Page's mooted supergroup. Guitarist Robbie Blunt had been in Michael Des Barres's seventies glam-rockers Silverhead, while keyboard player Jezz Woodroffe worked by day in his family's music shop in Birmingham. They were fine players but comparatively unknown.

Plant and his band eventually checked in at Rockfield Studios to make their album. The location was perfect. Rockfield was a remote residential facility in Monmouthshire, hundreds of miles physically and spiritually from London and Atlantic Records. Genesis's Phil Collins played drums on most of the finished record with ex-Rainbow drummer, Cozy Powell, performing on two songs. Only when the album was finished did Plant allow any outsiders, including his manager, to hear it.

Peter Grant and Phil Carson were both invited to Rockfield for the playback. Jezz Woodroffe recalled Grant's reaction in a 2013 interview with Plant's biographer Paul Rees: "He said to Robert, 'I think you better just pay these guys off, because you've got a career here.'" Grant thought it beneath Plant to be working with unknowns.

Plant refused to back down, and Ahmet Ertegun was asked to mediate. At a later meeting, Plant told Grant, Carson, and Ertegun that either they support the record or any deal between them was off. Reluctantly, they agreed. Plant also compromised. There was no more talk of a new band. Robert Plant's debut solo album, *Pictures at Eleven*, was released on Swan Song in June 1982.

The front cover showed the singer, freshly shorn and wearing this season's pop-star fashions. But hearing that voice without Jimmy Page's guitar or John Bonham's seismic drumming required a mental adjustment. Nevertheless, *Pictures at Eleven* still sounded enough like Led Zeppelin to push it into the top ten in Britain and America.

The emergence of Robert Plant as a solo artist would be a learning curve for all, including the singer and his manager. "When we got the slick of the

Pictures at Eleven sleeve, there was a problem with the lettering," said Grant. "I phoned Robert and told him we've got to put it right, but he made me laugh because he said, 'I didn't know you got so involved in all the cover designs and stuff,' which says something for all the battles we had with sleeves in the Zep days. It was me and Jimmy who did the sweating then."

Plant had long been frustrated by his junior-partner status in Led Zeppelin. Inevitably, Grant still regarded him that way. Grant and Phil Carson negotiated Plant's five-album solo deal, but it would be the last negotiation Grant ever did for the singer, and Plant neglected to pay him for the deal. "Dad was furious," remembers Helen.

Plant chose not to tour *Pictures at Eleven*, but he played the Prince's Gala Trust charity concert in July. Grant was invited to the show at London's Dominion Theatre. He made the trip into town with Dave Northover but refused to leave his hotel suite.

"Peter couldn't fit into the clothes he wanted to wear," says Northover. "So I went to the show on my own. I sat near Maureen Plant and met Prince Charles. Very nice. But it should have been Peter doing this, not me. It was very sad."

Soon after, Northover left Horselunges and bought a pub. "There was nothing going on anymore," he says, "and I needed to be doing more things financially."

Family life continued at the manor in its own unique fashion. Warren was now increasingly absent from Battle Road. Cindy Russell tried to maintain order, but it wasn't easy.

"Peter was a fantastic dad, but I don't think he knew how to discipline them," she says. "It might sound crazy now, but I was a conformist. I used to say to Peter, 'You have to keep an eye on things. You cannot allow Warren and these other kids to come into the house and get fucked up. What if something happens?' I knew they were smoking dope."

"Me and my mate used to bunk off school," Warren explains. "We'd spend the day riding our bikes around the farmer's field and eating magic mushrooms." On one occasion, Warren was under the influence when the school inspector arrived for crisis talks. "I was tripping out of my head, but I went inside and sat with him and my dad. The inspector had these big rubbery lips, and while he was talking, they seemed to get bigger and bigger. In the end, I ran out the room, laughing. Dad knew what was going on."

Not long after, Warren was summoned to the headmistress's office. She began complaining about his attendance, his behavior, and the parties he'd been holding in the old dance studio at Horselunges. "She said parents were upset about their kids going around to a rock star's house, and that it had to stop. I said, 'What's it got to do with you? It's not in school hours.'"

Harsh words were exchanged, and Warren was expelled. He was fifteen, the same age as Peter when he left school. Instead, Grant hired a private tutor for his son. "I sat in my dad's study—the one you see in *The Song Remains the Same*—and learned more in a few months than I had in all the years before."

Newcomers and old friends alike were surprised when they came to Horselunges. One night, Helen Grant introduced Tom Porter, a local night-club doorman and barber, to her father. "Dad usually didn't like anyone I brought home," she says, "but he told Tom to put the kettle on."

"I was a lad from Hailsham, meeting the manager of the biggest band in the world," says Porter now. "It was a bizarre way of life at Horselunges. The house was a bit of a mess, there were all these gofers looking at me as if to say, 'What's he doing here?' And I'll never forget there was a dog called Shithead. He was called that, because when a bit of meat went off in the fridge, one of the so-called minders threw it out the kitchen window and it landed on this dog's head."

Long after he'd stopped seeing Helen, Porter continued to visit Peter and cut his hair. "I enjoyed his company, but he could be frightening. You never knew what mood he'd be in. On a good night, he'd sit and tell stories about the old days, about sitting on Elvis Presley's dad and how he'd turned down managing Queen. I got the impression he'd been happier then.

"But on a bad day, he wouldn't speak to me. I called round once, and he opened the door and told me to fuck off. A week later he'd be fine again. I learned never to take it personally."

"I still used to see Peter, but he wasn't in the best of health," remembers Maggie Bell. In 1977, Maggie had sung the theme song to the hit TV detective show, *Hazell*. Later, Grant arranged for her to do the same for *Taggart*, a long-running show about a hard-bitten Scottish detective. "I said, 'Peter, what is it with these shows about coppers?' He said, 'Don't worry, Mags, just take the money.'"

Maggie had just had a hit single, "Hold Me," with fellow Scottish singer, B. A. Robertson. "We went to see him, and Peter said, 'Yeah, that's great' and told us we should do another song together, but I don't think he was interested anymore."

Robert Plant wasn't the only Swan Song vocalist going solo. In August 1982, Bad Company released *Rough Diamonds*, their final album with Paul Rodgers. By then, all the swagger and promise of the band in the seventies had dissipated. Rodgers was now teetotal; the others were not. And now they'd come to blows.

"There'd been a fracas between Paul and Boz at Ridge Farm," says Phil Carlo. "Simon stood in the middle of it and said to Rodgers, 'If you want to hit anyone, hit me'—and he did. And that was it."

Rodgers walked away and signed a solo deal with Atlantic. Grant could only stand back and watch, as Swan Song's second biggest group fell apart. "I said, 'OK, fellas, if that's really what you want to do.'"

In the meantime, though, Grant had to deal with the business of a new Led Zeppelin album. Ahmet Ertegun had met with Grant in Frankfurt on the 1980 tour, where he'd verbally agreed to renew Zeppelin's contract within the next year. John Bonham's death changed everything, but only for a time. Atlantic still expected a "new" Led Zeppelin album of some description.

The group agreed to assemble an album's worth of previously unheard material from the vaults. "Ahmet paid an advance, knowing that if it was substandard and we couldn't find enough material for a decent set, then the advance would be refunded," said Grant.

Unbeknown to the others, Page had a recording of an instrumental (later titled "Bonzo's Montreux"), which he and Bonham had recorded when the drummer was domiciled in Switzerland. "'Bonzo's Montreux' gave us some credibility," Page told me. "It was a very difficult album to make. Really, it was a contractual thing."

The finished album, *Coda*, included seven unreleased songs from 1970 to '78. It was unlikely to become anybody's favorite Led Zeppelin album. But one track, the furious "Wearing and Tearing" offered a clue to where they might have gone next.

Coda was held back so as not to quash *Pictures at Eleven* and eventually appeared in November 1982. It reached the top five in Britain and the top ten in America but was eclipsed, like so much that year, by Michael Jackson's *Thriller*. The game had changed, yet again.

Hipgnosis had designed *Coda*'s Spartan artwork. However, like two of its biggest clients, the agency was coming to an end, with Po and Storm Thorgerson about to go their separate ways. "That whole period was an unbelievable mess," says Po. "The last thing I did with Peter was *Coda*, and it was a real mishmash." Po wouldn't see Peter again for more than ten years.

On December 4, a month after *Coda*'s release, Grant received a handwritten letter from Robert Plant. It explained why he no longer wanted Peter to be his manager. "Representation at this stage of the game requires availability and on a day-to-day basis," Plant wrote. "It's impossible and maybe unfair . . .

to expect a return to the routine of all those years ago." Plant also addressed what he called "the distance between us" and added, "I always had the utmost respect for you."

"Peter helped me at the beginning of my solo career, but he wasn't really in the right place by that time," says Plant now. "I wish he could have been, but he wasn't."

"Peter found Robert's letter devastating," remembers Cindy. "He handed it to me to read and then took a photograph of me reading it." After taking the picture, Grant tore the letter in half. One half was lost; the other discarded under piles of Swan Song ephemera at the bottom of a box for the next thirty-five years.

Grant never mentioned Plant's letter publicly. "Robert and I did have a bit of a falling out, and I said the best thing would be for him to manage himself," was his only comment.

"The thing with Robert was a kick," adds Warren. "I know there was a lot of tension and disappointment there."

Several months after sending the letter, Plant arrived unannounced in Ed Bicknell's office. "Robert strode in like a big beaming Viking and plonked himself down," says Bicknell. "I realized he wasn't there to pass the time of day. I said to him, 'Does Peter Grant know you're here, because I've no wish to be dangled out of a window?' He replied, 'Well, I've written to him.' 'When?' 'About a year ago.' 'What was the answer?' 'I haven't had one.'"

Instead, Plant hired Phil Carson to be his new manager. A second solo album, *The Principle of Moments*, arrived in summer 1983 and gave Plant a hit single with "Big Log."

That summer, Grant went to see Jimmy Page play the ARMS charity concert in London. Page joined Jeff Beck and Eric Clapton at the gig for ex-Faces bassist Ronnie Lane, who'd been diagnosed with multiple sclerosis.

Page was still dabbling in various substances and looked almost cadaverous. "In 1982 my doctor said I was living on borrowed time," he told me. Up on stage, he pursed his lips and threw shapes just like he'd done in the not-so old days, and played an instrumental version of "Stairway to Heaven." "Let's face it, people want to hear Led Zeppelin songs," Grant said.

*G*rant pinpointed the release of *Coda* as the moment after which he sank into "a real period of blackness." "I'd just had enough of most things in life," he explained. "I just shut up shop."

The popular image of the reclusive giant in his moated castle started to take shape. Years later, Ed Bicknell was amused when local cab drivers told him they wouldn't go to Horselunges "because they thought there were crocodiles in the moat." However, the popular image wasn't the whole picture. Grant was still accessible to his children and a few close friends, but as 1983 turned into 1984, he withdrew further from the music business.

"A lot of things have been written about him becoming a hermit," explains Warren. "I was there, and he wasn't like that all the time. He became depressed. If you're a musician and your band breaks up or they lose someone, you can still channel that energy into the music. If you're a manager and suddenly you've got nothing to manage, what do you do?"

When it came to urgent business, Grant's unavailability was a problem for others, just as it had been for Robert Plant. "Peter managed me for a while," said John Paul Jones, "but I couldn't contact him. Nobody could contact him. So I wrote him a letter saying, 'Oh I don't think it's working out, maybe another time.' And it ended like that."

By now, the band's former members realized it had been a terrible mistake to sell their publishing. "There's no doubt about it, the scale of the band ended up just enveloping [Grant's] business acumen. Quite badly," complained Page.

"Peter had got so much into the Peruvian marching powder, his brain wasn't working properly," explains Ed Bicknell. "On top of that, he had Steve Weiss dabbling. When you're a manager and you don't have a legal or accounting background, something like this could get past you without you noticing it. That stuff wasn't Peter's forté. So he ended up doing one of these crackpot deals of selling the rights—like Colonel Parker did with Elvis."

Before long, Robert Plant, Paul Rodgers, and Jimmy Page were all being managed by Phil Carson. Peter's loss of Jimmy hurt more than the rest. "I met Peter again in the early nineties, and he confessed a lot of things," said Peter Clifton, "one of which was that Jimmy Page had broken his heart."

While his relationship with most of Led Zeppelin crumbled, Grant's ties with the Bonham family were stronger. Jason was a talented drummer, and for a brief time he and Paul Inder, the thirteen-year-old son of Motörhead frontman Lemmy, jammed together at the Bonham family farm and Horselunges.

"Paul was an amazing guitarist," remembers Warren. "I think the idea was, if it worked out, Dad would look after them." The collaboration was cut short when Inder's mother accused Warren and Jason of leading Paul astray. "She thought we were getting him to smoke dope. Of course, we weren't."

Soon after, Jason joined Phil Carson's latest signings, a nouveau hard rock band called Airrace. "Peter came to the Marquee to watch us," remembers

Airrace's guitarist Laurie Mansworth. "We already had a drummer, but Peter was looking for a place for Jason, so of course we said yes.

"I'd have fascinating talks with Peter about the Zeppelin days, about musicians, and how the business was always changing." However, by the time Airrace released its debut album in 1984, neither Grant nor Phil Carson were still involved. "There was never any big falling out. We all just seemed to go our separate ways."

Ex–Thin Lizzy guitarist, Gary Moore, and pop-punk singer Adam Ant were among those who also had meetings with Grant around this time, but they never led to anything. Peter would show an interest in a new project, and it would just as quickly fade away.

After Bad Company's split, Simon Kirke joined a new group, Wildlife. Grant signed them to Swan Song and became their manager, leaving Clive Coulson to do the day-to-day work. The process took numerous phone calls and urgent telegrams from Kirke, who ended up wasting days in the Boship until Grant would see him. "I think signing Wildlife was Peter's way of keeping me happy until Bad Company came back," he suggests.

Wildlife's bass guitarist Phil Soussan, who would later play with Jimmy Page and Ozzy Osbourne, experienced what he calls "a Wizard of Oz moment" when he first visited Swan Song's office.

"It really was like peering behind the curtain," Soussan says. "I thought I'd be entering some Tolkienesque dungeon with Icarus flying around. What I found was a house with hardly any furniture in it and a roadie, Brian Gallivan, shouting out the window for fish and chips and a pint from the World's End pub across the road.

"My first impression of Peter was of that wonderful villain in the old Charlie Chaplin movies," he continues, referring to silent movie actor Eric Campbell. "He had these incredible piercing eyes and a look that said you couldn't bullshit him. Peter and Clive Coulson told us the rules—'The band never argues in public, and if you have a problem with anybody, you come to us, and we sort it out.' It was all very Marlon Brando in *The Godfather*."

However, Soussan also saw how physically fragile his new manager was. When Wildlife played a support slot at the Hammersmith Odeon, Grant arrived backstage to congratulate them. "Ray and J. B. Bettie were with him, and they cleared the stairwell before he arrived. It took Peter ages to get up the stairs, and he was completely out of breath when he reached the top."

Cocooned for days on end and continuing a ruinous love affair with cocaine, Grant's health was suffering. One day, Cindy Russell was so concerned by Peter's grey pallor she called his heart specialist. "Peter was about to do a line of coke, then saw the doctor's car pull up on the CCTV monitor. He was not impressed. 'You bitch!' I thought, yeah, OK, I'll pack my bags and go, but at least I knew I did the right thing."

After the doctor checked Grant over, he turned his attention to Cindy. "I'd done a lot of coke and lost a lot of weight, so he bawled the pair of us out."

Like the boss, Swan Song Records was grinding to a halt. The label hadn't had a top-ten album after *Coda*. Wildlife's debut came and went in April 1983, and Simon Kirke left the group soon after.

Led Zeppelin fanzine editor Dave Lewis continued visiting the office but never once saw Grant. After *Coda*, there was very little to write about, and the music took a back seat to the human drama. Once, Lewis was with Unity MacLean, when they heard Richard Cole barreling up the stairs. "There was a load of commotion, and Richard was shouting, 'I'm gonna fucking kill him!' I think he'd had a row with one of the Kings Road drug barons." A wild-eyed Cole stormed into the office, "Which was when I noticed he had an axe stuffed down his trousers."

It wasn't just Led Zeppelin and Bad Company; everybody else had gone too. The Pretty Things had temporarily split, and Detective had long since broken up, with lead singer and resident drug fiend Michael Des Barres on the road to sobriety.

When Alan Callan told Grant he was leaving the company, Peter barely acknowledged the information. Weeks later, when he realized Callan had actually quit, he sent Ray Washbourne to collect his company car. Atlantic withdrew its backing, and Swan Song went into liquidation at the end of 1983.

One cupboard at the Kings Road office was later found to contain piles of tapes from hopeful new artists, including 1980s pop star Paul Young's band Q-Tips and heavy metal giants Iron Maiden—some still in unopened envelopes. It was as if everything had frozen in time, Miss Havisham–style, around the late 1970s.

Maggie Bell was the last musician in the office. "I turned up one day to have lunch with Sian Meredith. There was nobody there, but the front door was open to the street," she says. "I went upstairs and there were papers everywhere, most of the phone and the fax lines had been ripped out. Suddenly I heard voices I didn't recognize downstairs and whoever it was was coming back.

"I locked myself in the toilet and sat on the seat. Whoever these people were, they came back upstairs. They tried to open the toilet door, but I had my

foot on it and they gave up. Then they took everything else that was left—
Mark London's paintings, the Chesterfield sofa, the stereos, everything. . . .

"I stayed hiding until they'd gone. There was one phone still working, and
it kept ringing, but when I answered there was nobody at the other end. It was
scary. I called Peter, and Ray answered, so I left a message. After that, I
thought, that's it, I'm out of here. This place is finished."

Meanwhile, Jimmy Page was assembling a new group with Phil Soussan
briefly playing bass. One day, Grant turned up unannounced at their rehearsal studio. "Peter was so upset and pissed off," Soussan recalls. "He'd
gone to the office, and it had been shut down, closed. It was his label, and he
didn't even know."

"I regret not getting someone in to run Swan Song properly," Grant said.
"We kept getting it wrong—or I did."

"G just walked away. He'd stopped going there," says Phil Carlo. "I was
the last employee. When it ended, I got a week's money for every year I'd
been there and not a shilling from Led Zeppelin or Bad Company."

The New York office remained operational for a little longer, but after
Bonham, many of its employees had already walked away. "I finished in 1980
and went to work on Wall Street," says Sam Aizer. "Paul Rodgers wanted to
fire me every day, and you could never get Peter Grant on the phone. I'd had
enough. What summed it up was that in New York if something needed doing, you could reach Steve Weiss in a minute. In London, you'd make an appointment to see Peter next Wednesday, and he'd turn up three weeks later,
which is probably why Weiss made all that money."

Prior to Swan Song's launch, Grant and Zeppelin had purchased Hammerwood Park, an eighteenth-century manor house near East Grinstead,
which was briefly glimpsed in *The Song Remains the Same*. "The idea was
they'd convert it into a studio and flats, and it would become Led Zeppelin
and Swan Song's headquarters," says Perry Press, who brokered the sale.

"We bought it derelict and didn't improve it because of what they wanted
to do with the property. We hired architects, and we had plans, but nothing
was ever done, as they were so busy, and everything stopped after John died."
Much like Swan Song itself, Hammerwood Park was neglected and effectively
left to rot. It was finally sold in 1982.

After Swan Song's collapse, Phil Carlo was soon working shifts at
Horselunges. Though they happened less frequently, there were still times
when Grant left the manor to take care of business. Phil was reminded of his
high-level connections when the Sussex police pulled over the Mercedes they
were driving. The pair was on their way to visit Joan Hudson.

"We must have looked a sight," Phil admits. "Peter had on his dark glasses, his red Swan Song jacket, the rings, the big beard, and a cigarette in his mouth, and we're in a car that cost thousands."

The policemen wanted to know who owned the Mercedes, but Grant couldn't remember which company it was registered to. When they asked to see his ID, Peter's wallet opened, concertina-like, to reveal business cards from around the world.

"There were cards from the Russian embassy, US senators, congressmen, the FBI in Florida. . . . The policeman looked at Peter and said, 'Who *are* you?' He said, 'I'm Peter Grant.' Right then, another car pulls up, and the coppers all stand to attention. It was the chief constable of Sussex. He said, 'This man is a personal friend of mine,' and we were allowed on our way."

Most of the time, though, Phil's job was simply to keep Grant company. "I usually did weekends. So I'd leave home on a Friday afternoon and come back Monday, and if I'd had a couple of hours sleep I was lucky. That was a big part of my job—sit up in the bedroom with Peter, telling stories."

"Sometimes Peter would phone Clive and ask him to come down," remembers Sherry Coulson. "G would ring us, and in those days the old phones would ring a hundred times before cutting off, and Peter was the only person who'd let it ring that long.

"Afterward, I'd hear Clive on the phone to Phil Carlo: 'You go, it's your turn, I'll pay you.' If my husband went, I wouldn't see him for four days. Never three and never five. Always four, and he'd come home green, sweating and hallucinating."

At the manor, Phil Carlo's daily duties ranged from the mundane to the bizarre. One day, he found himself on his hands and knees, rummaging in the fireplace. Peter had removed his broken dentures the night before and wrapped them in a wad of tissue, which the cleaner had mistakenly thrown into the fire. "Warren asked what I was doing. I said, 'Don't tell your dad, but I'm trying to find his teeth.'"

Inevitably, the shotguns came out, with a bored Grant once challenging Carlo to see how many times out of ten they could hit the bell on the drawbridge. Later, when Peter told Phil they were going fishing, he threw him a .410 shotgun instead of a fishing rod.

Like some rock 'n' roll version of *Moby Dick*'s Captain Ahab, Peter had become obsessed with hunting down the pike that was eating the baby ducks in his moat. It also became a family outing. "Dad loved those ducks," says Warren. "So the pair of us would get our shotguns—Dad had a sawn-off—put a couple of stepladders against the wall around the moat and try and shoot the pike."

Both the Bettie brothers were now working at Horselunges. Among their regular tasks was a trip to the nearest Marks & Spencer's store, eleven miles away in Eastbourne, to stock up on Grant's favorite foods.

"We were there so often for sandwiches and buying so much, the manager used to help us carry it to the car," says Paul. "My brother put out the story we worked at a children's home. We didn't want to admit it was for one man and most of the sandwiches would be thrown away.

"Peter always insisted there had to be four fillet steaks in the fridge at any time," he recalls. "But they were never touched and were thrown to the dogs. Then one day he came down and there wasn't any steak. Peter went fucking crazy."

Eventually, J. B. quit, and Paul carried on alone. "There was a lot of sitting around without much to do. Helen and Warren were growing up. Warren was out, usually causing havoc down at the Martlet or in one of the other pubs in Hailsham. Jason Bonham's driver would bring Jason over, and the two of them would go off together, which could be a nightmare."

"Warren and Jason ran up a huge tab at the Martlet," remembers Helen, "but the landlord was too scared to come to the house and ask Dad to pay it."

Like Carlo and the others, Bettie also saw the debilitating effects of his boss's drug habit. Late one night he was disturbed by the sound of gunfire. "I jumped up, thinking, 'Who's shooting?' And it was Peter. The gardener had cut the lawn and put a tarpaulin over it, and Peter thought he could see people crawling out from underneath.

"We were in the garden once when a Harrier buzzed overhead. Next thing, G's got his shotgun—'Fucking bastards! Shaking my roof!'" Bettie persuaded him to put the weapon down. "I said, 'Peter, can you imagine tomorrow's *News of the World*? "Led Zeppelin Manager Shoots Down Harrier Jet!"'"

On his good days, Grant still gravitated toward his friends' wives for company. "There'd be a group of them," remembers Phil Carlo. "My wife, Julie, and Sherry Coulson, who were both blonde, and Ronnie Wood's ex, Krissy, and Simon's wife, Desiree Kirke, who were both dark. G used to watch them tottering up the driveway—'Fucking hell, here they come, Charlie's Angels. Some dark, some blonde and some . . . well, I'll leave the rest to your imagination.'"

"I used to say to Peter, 'You're like Howard Hughes, you are,'" recalls Julie. "If I rang, he wouldn't answer the phone until I told him it was me. There were very few people he trusted. One day I was upset about something, and Peter found out. Next thing, there's a car outside waiting to take me to Horselunges."

Once Julie arrived, she and Cindy Russell fell into a deep conversation. "We started chatting and didn't stop for hours. Peter said later, 'Jesus Christ, I have never heard so much shit in all my life.' I said, 'How did you know what we were talking about?' He said, 'Cos I taped your conversation.'" Peter then told them he'd like to release it on an album. "And he wanted to call it the Drivel Sisters."

The Carlos still witnessed the darker side of Grant's behavior. One day, Julie overheard him having a furious argument on the phone: "We all ran for cover. After it was done, he walked into the room, picked up a Tiffany vase, probably worth thousands, and smashed it into pieces. I said, 'Peter! No! That was one of a pair.'"

Grant replied, "Not anymore," picked up the other, and smashed it as well. "Later, he calmed down and was very apologetic—'I'm sorry if I upset you.' If he was angry, he could be frightening."

"Horselunges might have been built in whatever century, but it wasn't a show home; it was a family home," insists Phil. "Our kids would come over and swim in the pool. Warren would crank up the temperature, until there was steam coming off it like a Turkish bath."

Children and dogs trampled dirt over the antique rugs, lit cigarettes would be left on the corner of an oak table instead of in an ashtray, and when an expensive oil painting fell off the wall, it was left, abandoned, behind the refrigerator for months, "Where it ended up covered with ice cream and Coke. But Peter didn't mind."

"It wasn't that Peter didn't care about lovely things," explains Julie. "I once said to him, 'What would you take if you had to leave this house quickly?' He said, 'Nothing, just the kids.'"

"There were a lot of liggers and ponces around Dad, people who wanted something from him," remembers Helen. "Phil and Julie never did, they were happy just being his friends.

"I used to come back from school, though, and find people I didn't know in the house and find things had gone missing from my bedroom. I became the old cow, shouting, 'Fuck off!' and throwing people out the house. Then I'd get shouted at for shouting at them."

Items including large amounts of cash had been disappearing from the manor for some time. Warren Grant knew there was a problem when he was in Uckfield one day and saw one of their employees' sons wearing a Led Zeppelin at Knebworth T-shirt, and there was still a week to go before the gig.

However, with Swan Song in receivership, Grant now had less reason than ever to leave the manor. "I'd try and get him to do things," says Cindy Russell. "Hey, let's take the Porsche out, let's go down to Brighton, let's go buy Taco shells because I'm craving Mexican food, but it wasn't easy."

"He'd be sociable sometimes, and there'd be other times when he just wanted to be left alone," remembers Warren. "We might want to see a band, and he'd say he wanted to go, but sometimes getting him out of the house was impossible."

Many close to Grant hoped that if the right project came along, he'd reengage with the music business. In 1984, Richard Cole met up again with his old boss. Since his release from jail, Cole had been living in Los Angeles and had become a father. However, he was struggling to conquer his addictions and find work in the music industry.

Cole was living with his mother in London and was working as a scaffolder again. "My mum still had a tin bath," he says, drily. "A bit of a comedown from the days of hotel suites with marble bathrooms."

Then he received a telegram from Caesar Danova, an entrepreneur and old friend from the Zeppelin era. Danova had negotiated with the Japanese government to stage Rock for Hiroshima, a charity concert to be held the following year on the fortieth anniversary of the atomic bomb. Danova needed experienced people. He offered to put £2,000 in Cole's bank account and pay for a round-the-world airline ticket. "I didn't know how confident I felt about it all," Cole admits, "but I knew it was better than scaffolding."

Richard brought in Peter Grant as his co-partner and, later, Don Murfet to handle security. They set up headquarters in Mayfair and hired a young Matthew Freud, the future PR guru, as their publicist. Soon the world's newest rock stars Bryan Adams and Prince were rumored to be playing. "Caesar showed us a video of 'Purple Rain' and said, 'We have to got to get this guy,'" remembers Warren.

"We didn't actually have anyone booked to play the festival," Cole admits. "I don't think any of us knew how it was going to work, or even who the investors were. All we knew was people wanted to give us some readies and a trip to Japan."

Everybody took their money and plane tickets. It was Warren's eighteenth birthday, and he joined his father on the flight to Tokyo. During a four-hour stopover in Bangkok, Grant tried to get some sleep in the business class lounge, "But the chairs were airline seats bolted to the floor. Dad ripped the armrest out of one them, so he could lie down. He had a kip, and I got drunk."

Once they arrived, Grant and the others realized the site earmarked for the festival was completely unsuitable. The festival was doomed to failure. Cole was the first to walk away. The others soon followed. The dream team that had once taken Led Zeppelin around the biggest arenas in the world wasn't destined to make a comeback, and Rock for Hiroshima was quietly abandoned.

*I*n 2007, when it was announced Led Zeppelin was reuniting for a one-off charity show, more than a million people registered online for just twenty thousand tickets. It was different in the mid-eighties. After John Bonham's death, Grant received regular letters from the Led Zeppelin Revival Society, a group of fans that petitioned the group to re-form. By 1984, even their letters had stopped. The eighties were all about the here and now, today and tomorrow. The commonly held view was that Led Zeppelin belonged in the past.

Phil Carson was now handling Plant and Page in their solo and new band ventures. He had his work cut out. The previous summer, Plant revived the Honeydrippers and released an EP of fifties R&B songs, co-produced by Ahmet Ertegun.

To his surprise, they scored a big US hit with a revival of the romantic ballad "Sea of Love." Suddenly, Led Zeppelin's old singer was recast as a middle-of-the-road crooner. It was not what he'd expected.

Having had a hit album, Plant responded by firing Phil Carson and hiring the Who's handler Bill Curbishley instead. As if to confound his new audience, his next solo album, 1985's *Shaken 'n' Stirred*, sounded like the anti-Honeydrippers. It was a collection of modish electro-pop songs with barely a chorus between them. It sold slowly and an accompanying US arena tour saw Plant performing, for the first time since Zeppelin days, to empty seats.

Meanwhile, Jimmy Page's new group, the Firm, was a collaboration with Paul Rodgers. On paper, it made sense: two Swan Song veterans joining forces in the new decade. It didn't work as well in practice. The Firm's 1984 debut was sinewy blues-rock with a few vogueish flourishes, but sales were modest.

Then the impossible happened. In summer 1985, Page, Plant, and Jones reunited to perform at the biggest charity concert in history. Live Aid was the brainchild of the Boomtown Rats' lead singer, Bob Geldof. Geldof, an outspoken Irishman, had persuaded, pestered, and emotionally blackmailed some of the world's biggest pop stars into appearing at the event in aid of drought-stricken Ethiopia. The concerts were to be held at London's Wembley

Stadium and Philadelphia's JFK Stadium in July and televised around the world.

The Live Aid lineup now reads like a Who's Who of eighties pop with a few seventies survivors for good measure. U2, Dire Straits, Queen, Elton John, and Paul McCartney were booked for London, while the Philadelphia lineup included Zeppelin, Madonna, Tom Petty, Neil Young, Black Sabbath, and Bob Dylan.

There were several links between Live Aid and Grant's old life. Zeppelin was supposed to play JFK Stadium on its aborted 1977 tour, and Live Aid's co-promoters were Harvey Goldsmith and Peter's old nemesis, Bill Graham.

Grant had also had a difference of opinion with Bob Geldof. Years earlier, Peter had taken Warren to see the Boomtown Rats. After the show, he'd asked for an autograph, only for Geldof to seize his pen and scrawl across Warren's face: "Dad went nuts, and there was a lot of finger prodding."

This latest Led Zeppelin reunion happened by accident. Robert Plant had been asked to perform, solo or with the Honeydrippers. He then invited Page, and John Paul Jones invited himself. "It was the old trap," Plant said in 1988. "It was like George Harrison was saying that he had to be careful in case Paul and Ringo were invited to do the same show, and it would be, 'Oh, as the three of you are here, why don't you give us 'Love Me Do'?' And that's exactly what happened to us."

Plant had asked Phil Collins to play drums, but when it became a Zeppelin reunion, they added a second drummer, Tony Thompson from the funk band Chic. The message was clear: John Bonham could not be replaced by one man. Phil Carlo was working as the Firm's tour manager and saw trouble brewing long before the show.

At rehearsals, Plant announced he wouldn't sing "Stairway to Heaven." He'd back down later, but Page was incensed by the singer trying to hold them all to ransom. Later, while watching Queen's showboating performance from Wembley on TV, Plant turned to Carlo and said, "Fucking hell, we've got to follow *that*.'" He had grounds for concern.

In an unwitting display of hubris, Phil Collins had performed at Wembley Stadium and then flown to the States on the Concorde to play in Philadelphia. When he arrived at JFK, the atmosphere in Zeppelin's dressing room was poisonous. Plant had invited Collins when it was still a solo gig, but now it was Led Zeppelin and with all the baggage that entailed. "Robert on his own—a lovely bloke," said Collins. "Robert and anything to do with Zeppelin—a strange chemistry happens. Everything becomes very dark."

That said, Collins had missed two days of rehearsals. He was woefully unprepared and had underestimated how difficult the music was to play. "Jimmy came up to me after the second song, pointed at Phil and said, 'Get him turned off,'" reveals Carlo. As they lurched through "Rock and Roll," "Whole Lotta Love," and "Stairway to Heaven," Collins wasn't the only one struggling. "I was hoarse and couldn't sing," admitted Plant, "and Page was out of tune and couldn't hear his guitar. . . . We sounded so awful."

Grant hadn't been invited and watched Live Aid on TV, like everybody else. "He was really pissed off by the whole thing," remembers Warren. Having suspended all contact with his old clients, there was nothing Grant could do about it.

During Zeppelin's performance, the JFK stage was crowded with stewards, security guards, rubberneckers, and hangers-on, some standing three or four deep. It was hard to have imagined Grant tolerating this in the seventies. And while he'd seen plenty of bad Zeppelin shows, there hadn't been TV cameras recording them for posterity. So much had changed since he'd been away.

That night, though, the audience ignored the bum notes and fumbled solos. Instead, they were carried away by the history, the occasion, and a tantalizing glimpse of what Led Zeppelin had once been.

It was a turning point in the band's fortunes. The world outside the diehards and obsessives slowly started to rediscover the music. Led Zeppelin's rehabilitation had begun. The rehabilitation of Peter Grant would take a little longer.

12

Looking Good and Dangerous

"Peter Grant loved the game,
and he turned it upside down."

—ROBERT PLANT

aul Bettie knew it was time to leave Horselunges when he'd worked ten days straight and not seen the boss once. "I'd heard Peter walking around, but it was a life lived upstairs," he says. "One day I realized I was sitting there, pulling my hair out, literally. I'd had seven great years with Peter and the family, and I left in '86."

Bettie wasn't the first to go. A year earlier, Cindy Russell flew home to Chicago. She had been staying on and off at the manor since 1978 and decided it was time to go for good. "My father was ill, and I thought I was losing him. I loved Peter to pieces, but I was also young and wanted to have children. Peter was so much older, and he'd done all that."

"Cindy upped and left," remembers Helen. "Just went in the middle of the night, which I thought was bad."

"Peter would call up and say, 'When are you coming back to get your stuff?'" says Cindy. "It was over, and it was the end of an era, but I always felt love for Peter and those kids."

With Cindy's departure, there wouldn't be a significant other in Grant's life. However, Warren remembers women visiting and occasionally staying for days. Sometimes, one might arrive by helicopter as Norman the chauffeur was ferrying another over the drawbridge in the Rolls.

"There was a *Penthouse* model called Janet, who was around for a while," he remembers. Warren also returned one night to discover an actress he'd seen in a soft porn movie sitting with his father. "She was wearing a fishnet veil, like the one she'd worn in this video. She stayed for a few days and told us she was an acupuncturist."

"Dad never got over not being with my mum," believes Helen. "Not really. But he was also a huge flirt. Despite being a very big man, women loved Dad. He had an amazing charisma and sense of humor."

Grant was also a manager without anybody to manage, and he hadn't forgotten the lessons learned on the road. Once, Peter and Helen were coming home by helicopter after Christmas shopping in London when they flew into dense cloud. "We couldn't see anything. I was screaming at Dad, but he stayed cool. We had to land in a field full of bulls," she recalls.

Unfortunately, Helen was wearing a bright red Swan Song jacket at the time. "I just ran, with Dad following behind clutching a Fortnum and Mason ham. A farmer's wife eventually shuttled us back to Hellingly in her station wagon."

Before their comical getaway, Helen noticed her father's unwavering calm. Grant had survived everything the touring life could throw at him: guns, tear gas, a drunk John Bonham. What was there to worry about?

Old habits with money also remained, and cash was still kept in supermarket carrier bags. "Ray once told me he'd gone to the Dorchester with Dad for a meeting," says Helen. "Dad went to the toilet, wearing his gold Rolex and with twenty-five grand in a Somerfield bag. When he came out, Ray asked him where everything was. He'd left the watch and the bag in the toilet. When they went back, the Rolex had disappeared, but they'd left the tatty old carrier."

"They were strange times for Peter," says Perry Press. "I'd still get the odd phone call. There was no 'Hello, how are you?' just straight in with, 'Have you seen Charlie Watts lately? He looks like Bela Lugosi.' Which Charlie did at the time. The calls were apropos of nothing, but it was nice to hear from him."

By the time he was eighteen, Warren would also sit up with his father. "We had lots of nights like that. He talked about the war, the films he was in, and how he used to do the curtain call at the Croydon Empire. He didn't talk about his problems. He wouldn't allow anybody to worry about him."

"I was very protective over Dad, and him over me," says Helen, "but we did have a very feisty father and daughter relationship."

In summer 1986, Grant discovered he was going to become a grandfather. His daughter had fallen for a rock star. Helen was now living at Krissy Wood's house, where she'd met former Moody Blues and Wings guitarist Denny Laine. "Dad said, 'Of all the people, why the fuck have you chosen him?'"

Later, the couple went to Horselunges to tell Peter about the pregnancy. "Dad chinned Denny, who nearly fell in the moat," claims Warren.

"Then Denny got up and hit Dad back," says Helen. "The two of us went and lived on a houseboat near Windsor, and I didn't have much contact with Dad for the next few months."

Helen's daughter, Lucianne, was born the following February. "After that, we moved into a cottage in the middle of nowhere, with an oil tank and no phone. One thing Denny taught me was how to survive with nothing. Dad hated that I was living like this, but it was the making of me. I think there was also a part of him thinking, 'Go on then, Helen.'

"Dad came to see us when Lucianne was six weeks old," she recalls. "He'd asked if we needed anything. Later, he pulled up in the Range Rover, and it was filled with nappies of every kind, a pram, a cot, and all sorts of baby paraphernalia."

Grant now had the perfect reason to get healthy. After suffering another heart scare, doctors advised him to lose 150 pounds. At his heaviest, his weight had ballooned to over 300. His seventies contemporaries still remember Peter's huge appetite for Blue Nun, chocolate milkshakes, and "big plates of food followed by big lines of the Peruvian rocket fuel," says Michael Des Barres. "I'd think, Wow! How does he do all that?"

But he couldn't carry on. By the time Paul Bettie left Horselunges, Grant's drug use was tailing off. "Where it was once seven days a week, now it was two or three. I did wonder if his money was running out."

"He used to have these bumper wraps of cocaine," says Warren. "There'd be half an ounce in them. Then one day he said to me, 'It's gone, I've flushed it down the toilet.' Later on, he got rid of all his booze and really started trying to lose weight."

"I threw the stuff away," Grant said. "My minders said, 'We could have got you a refund on that.' Then I stayed in the bedroom for three days and drank fresh orange juice. I got myself off it without having to go to a clinic."

Grant had begun the long road to recovery. So too had Richard Cole. "I got sober in '86," Cole says. "I was living in America and later started working for Sharon Osbourne. Peter and I would meet up for tea on the Kings Road whenever I was in London."

However, Grant and Cole's past lives were never forgotten. Music critic Stephen Davis's 1985 book, *Hammer of the Gods: Led Zeppelin Unauthorized*, had become a *New York Times* best seller. Before his sobriety, Cole had supplied the author with plenty of scurrilous insider anecdotes.

It was all there somewhere: the drugs, the groupies, the brawl at Oakland, even the shark. "I've read parts of the book, and it disgusted me," said Grant. "It's horrendously inaccurate." The band was similarly appalled, but none of them sued.

"I had this conversation with Robert Plant a while ago," says Abe Hoch. "We all misbehaved. We thought we were bigger than God. Bad things happened when we were all together, and Peter Grant condoned it. Sure, it was fun, but we didn't always behave as appropriate human beings. We did things we wouldn't do now as adults."

It wasn't the 1970s anymore. The world Peter Grant helped create had moved on in his absence. His pioneering 90/10 split was almost industry standard, and the biggest bands were reaping huge profits from tickets and merchandise, thanks in part to Grant's foresight.

In 1981, just after Led Zeppelin split, the Rolling Stones, whom Grant helped secure their first radio session, had cleaned up with a $50 million grossing US tour. Four years after Peter turned down Queen for management, they were listed in the *Guinness Book of Records* as Britain's highest-paid company executives.

The music television channel MTV had also changed the game. The idea of selling Zeppelin's music with glossy videos would have been an alien concept to Grant, but his old clients couldn't be so precious now.

With the Firm, Page stuck to his old moves: putting his hair over his eyes and jamming a cigarette in his mouth. Robert Plant, meanwhile, sold his shiny new techno-rock album *Now and Zen* with a film showing him looking moody and windswept in the desert.

They weren't alone. Most of Zeppelin's contemporaries sucked in their cheeks and fluffed up their hair. How else could they compete with this new wave of twentysomething, MTV-endorsed rock bands?

Among them was the American group Bon Jovi, whose guitarist Richie Sambora had been signed to Swan Song as a teenager. Led by vocalist and pinup Jon Bon Jovi, they'd repurposed the most obvious parts of Led Zeppelin and Bad Company and given it a glitzy makeover. Their 1986 album, *Slippery When Wet*, would sell 12 million copies in America alone.

Bad Company's former security guard Danny Francis now worked for Bon Jovi. "And Jon and his manager, Doc McGhee, all wanted to talk about Led Zeppelin and Peter Grant," he remembers. "Even today, no matter what country I go to, someone says, 'Tell us a story about Peter Grant.'"

These Zeppelin-inspired new groups reignited interest in the band and its former manager. In 1980, Don Murfet had offered Grant a cut of Adam and the Ants' management but Grant passed. Six years later, Murfet came to Grant with a young Irish band, Blue Russia. The group had been doggedly playing the London pub circuit and were still waiting to become the next U2.

"Don had picked up Blue Russia and thrown a few quid at us for wages, haircuts, and rehearsals," explains their former bass guitarist, Tony St. Ledger. "We were in the studio when Don told us he was bringing Peter Grant down. He said Peter didn't come out of his house for anybody, but he thought we'd spark his interest. We were shocked—'Are you sure?' Of course, I'd read *Hammer of the Gods*, and I'd seen *The Song Remains the Same*."

The group was similarly shocked when Grant arrived one week later. "We'd expected a big man, but he looked like a broken man. He came shuffling in wearing old tracksuit bottoms. I thought, Fuck, is this what rock 'n' roll looks like when it spits you out? I found it a bit emotional. But Peter was so nice to us, said he liked what we did. He had these amazing eyes, and I remember thinking, 'OK, he's a gentleman.'"

Grant put Blue Russia in a rehearsal studio on the south coast and watched them play the Half Moon pub in Putney ("We couldn't believe Led Zeppelin's manager was at *our* gig"). But it didn't last. "Don told us what we wanted to hear. Really, nothing was happening." Murfet paid for Blue Russia to go home for Christmas. They never came back.

"Truthfully, when record companies heard Peter and Don were involved, they became wary," says St. Ledger. "Suddenly they said the numbers didn't add up. By then, I don't think those two had the greatest reputation."

Record company executives had also read *Hammer of the Gods* and seen *The Song Remains the Same*. However, while Grant's reputation made some cautious about signing his artists, others saw pound and dollar signs.

A fter the Sex Pistols split in 1978, Malcolm McLaren shapeshifted again. The punk Svengali turned himself into a pop star, with his hip hop/dance hit "Buffalo Gals." By the mid-1980s, he wanted to make films.

McLaren was fascinated by Peter Grant. "Peter was an extraordinary underling," he enthused. "A gigantic character out of a Dickensian novel."

However, his interest had as much to do with late-fifties Soho and the British class system as it did Led Zeppelin.

McLaren identified with a bygone world where nightclub doormen became music managers. He also believed Grant craved respect more than money: "He wanted to usurp his class." In 1986, McLaren approached Peter to make a film about his life.

Glinwood Films signed up to make the movie. McLaren would co-produce with John Goldstone, whose credits included Monty Python's *Life of Brian*. When the Python team struggled to fund their biblical comedy, Led Zeppelin helped raised £75,000 for the project. Completing the team was *Chariots of Fire* director Hugh Hudson, and Barrie Keeffe, who'd written the 1980 gangster movie *The Long Good Friday*.

Grant agreed to the project after seeing McLaren in the Sex Pistols' spoof documentary *The Great Rock 'N' Roll Swindle*. "There was a part where Malcolm talked about how to play the record companies," says Barrie Keeffe, "and Peter said he'd got it absolutely right."

Keeffe vividly remembers his first meeting with Grant at Horselunges. He was ushered into the manor and told to wait. After a few minutes came an ominous noise from the minstrel's gallery overhead. "'Clunk,' 'clunk,' 'clunk.' It was Peter coming down the stairs with a walking stick."

On his drive in, Barrie noticed a shire horse in one of the fields. He nervously asked if Peter had had a horse-riding accident. Grant peered at him in disbelief. "No," he said. "I was walking downstairs, and some cunt had left a bottle out, and I slipped." He paused and settled himself in an armchair. "And the worst thing is, I was the cunt who left it there." That rather broke the ice.

In *The Long Good Friday*, John Bindon's former character witness, Bob Hoskins, played Harold Shand, an East London crime lord whose empire is threatened by crooked politicians, the Mafia, and the IRA. McLaren envisaged Led Zeppelin's manager as the Harold Shand of rock 'n' roll.

"Peter said he liked Hoskins in the film because his character rarely raised his voice," remembers Keeffe. "He said, 'That's real danger, Barrie.'"

After a couple of hours, Grant gave Keeffe his blessing and agreed to meet again. "I asked his son, Warren, what his dad drank, as I wanted to send him a bottle as a thank you," says Keeffe. "I'll never forget, Warren said, 'That'd be great, because everybody takes from my dad, nobody gives.'"

Over the next three weeks, Keeffe and Grant met in restaurants and at a health spa in Sussex. "We chatted and chatted, and it ceased to be an interview and just became spending time together. Peter was wonderful company.

He was on a diet, but food was still very important—'None of that nouvelle cuisine shit, Barrie,' he'd say. I only saw him with a glass of wine once, but he was still getting through three packets of cigarettes a day. He was also what my mother would call 'a real gentleman.' All the women we met seemed to be in love with him."

Grant talked for hours, about Gene Vincent, Don Arden, and Robert Stigwood's "disgusting skinny ankles." He discussed the merits of a "big bag of readies" versus a check ("If in doubt leave a zero off, Barrie"), and the time he'd accidentally attacked a noise pollution officer. But there were places he wouldn't go. One day I just came out and said, 'Did you cry, when your wife left you for another man?' And he looked at me, and said, very quietly, 'My God, that man is lucky to be alive.'"

Barrie learned that Grant had been "the" Peter Grant for so long, he wasn't comfortable showing a sensitive side. "He wanted us to stick with the legend."

Keeffe saw this version of Grant in action once at a restaurant near Heathrow Airport. "There was a man at the next table, obviously in the music business, and trying to impress a couple of air stewardesses. He said something disparaging about somebody Peter knew.

"Very quietly, Peter said, 'Barrie, I think you better go to the bar.' I asked why. He said, 'No, Barrie, just go to the bar.' I saw Peter get up, and a few seconds later, this guy ran out the restaurant."

Slowly, though, Grant's mask slipped. Keeffe's wife had died, and he was raising her two young sons on his own.

"I became their stepfather, and Peter was very taken by that. It was all about family for Peter," he says. "He came to my house in Greenwich to meet the boys. I said, 'It's a bit second class after your gaff.' He replied, 'No, Barrie, this is a real home.' He ended up staying for tea.

"He wouldn't talk about his own childhood," remembers Keeffe. "The only time I sensed anything about it was when I had an important meeting coming up. I was apprehensive, and Peter picked up on it—'You look nervous, what's going on?' So I told him, and he said, 'No, Barrie, no!'—very emphatic—'Bullies smell fear. They *always* smell fear.' Peter told me never to be intimidated.

"Looking back, though, I think there was a loneliness about him. He never got over the drummer dying, and he insisted he wasn't the fifth Zep—'Jimmy would never have stood for that.' He reminded me of a scene in the film of the Beatles at Shea Stadium. The whole place is going mad, and the manager Brian Epstein's at the side of the stage looking like the loneliest man in the world. There was a touch of that with Peter."

Keeffe spent a year working on the screenplay, while Malcolm McLaren talked up the movie. He claimed Bob Hoskins and Ray Winstone (star of the British prison drama *Scum*) were being considered for the lead role. Grant was six-foot-three; neither of them were more than five-foot-eight. Malcolm didn't foresee a problem, telling another interviewer Grant would be played by Daniel Day Lewis: "We'll fatten him up like Robert De Niro in *Raging Bull*."

After a working title "The Godfather of Rock 'N' Roll," McLaren unwisely changed the proposed film's name to *Hammer of the Gods*. A synopsis circulated around the industry, quoting a budget of $18 million and promising A-list stars, but Grant was unimpressed.

"Peter O'Toole said it best," offers Keeffe. "He said, 'There's three types of madness: madness, divine madness, and film madness.' One minute you're getting phone calls in the middle of the night, the next everything goes horribly quiet. We were told Peter's daughter didn't like the script."

"It was a bit sensationalist," says Helen.

Grant complained the screenplay was McLaren's perception of how his life had been, not how it really was. "Malcolm's idea came from Peter and Richard Cole as gangsters in *The Song Remains the Same*," points out Keeffe. "We wanted to portray Peter making his way through the jungle of the music business and doing right by his artists. But the stories were his. Normally with a screenplay, you're looking for the good bits to embellish. We didn't have to fictionalize anything."

Keeffe and Hugh Hudson would later disappear from the project. "There wasn't a falling out," Barrie insists. "That's just the business. I miss Peter, and he always made me laugh." After they'd gone their separate ways, Grant sent Keeffe a Christmas card. "It said, 'Dear Barrie, long time, no see. Hear you're still looking good and dangerous.' It made me smile."

McLaren's next move was to bring in Internal Affairs director Mike Figgis and Jeremy Thomas, the co-producer of *The Great Rock 'N' Roll Swindle*. "Malcom said he wanted to make a film about the godfather of rock 'n' roll—his words—and would I take the project on," says Figgis now. "So I did—initially. I read *Hammer of the Gods* and brought in a friend of mine, Mark Long, whom I'd worked with in experimental theater."

To help them in their research, McLaren, Figgis, and Long hired a hotel suite and spent several hours interviewing Grant about his life and career.

Peter was amusing, candid, guarded, vague, clever, contradictory, and prone to exaggeration. He was, simply, "Peter Grant."

The filmmakers' plan was to use Led Zeppelin's music in the soundtrack. "Malcolm McLaren's idea is to use twelve songs that meant something to me," explained Grant at the time. However, Figgis soon realized that securing the rights to the music would be harder than they'd imagined.

Figgis and Long then developed a script based around Grant's interviews, only for McLaren and Thomas to reject it. "Let me be diplomatic," says Figgis. "It was too . . . truthful. They basically crapped themselves and said, if we go ahead with this, we will never get the rights to Zeppelin's music.

"I was disgusted by a lot of what we unearthed—all that stuff with Johnny Bindon," he adds. "So I started to distance myself from it, and I was busy with other projects anyway. Then I discovered they were having meetings without me. In the end, I suggested to Mark Long that he have a crack at the script on his own."

"I enjoyed Peter's company," says Long. "He was from a completely different planet than me, but we got there in the end. We met for a couple of hours, and it felt a bit like an audition. Then, typical of how people are in the music business, I got the call—'Peter wants you to go to Toronto with him. Next week.'"

In the meantime, news of a Peter Grant film had stirred up interest among journalists and publishers. Everybody was suddenly interested in his story.

In 1989, Grant was interviewed at Horselunges for an item about music managers for the Tyne Tees TV show, *Wired*. Later, he joined fellow ex-Yardbirds manager Simon Napier-Bell on a program for Sky TV. "I spent four hours with Peter, and he was amusing and insightful and totally toned down," says Napier-Bell.

In May, the music magazine *Raw* ran Grant's first interview in almost a decade. His conversation with writer Malcolm Dome ranged across many topics, including Led Zeppelin's recent reunion.

A year earlier, Page, Plant, Jones, and Jason Bonham had headlined Atlantic Records' fortieth anniversary concert in New York. It wasn't the first time they'd reconvened since Live Aid. In January 1986, the three originals and drummer Tony Thompson booked a rehearsal space in Bath but gave up after a few days. Since then, Page had made guest appearances at Plant's solo shows, suggesting a collaboration was pending.

The Atlantic concert also featured Yes, Wilson Pickett, and Foreigner and was filmed by HBO. Zeppelin arrived onstage, jet-lagged, at 1:30 a.m. "Atlantic invited me to attend, but I declined," Grant said. Though he later admitted he hadn't been invited at all, claiming, "Phil Carson felt I wasn't healthy enough."

Zeppelin played five songs, including "Stairway to Heaven." They were hampered by sound problems, and Page and Plant looked tense and uneasy. "I know for a fact that up until five minutes before the band was due to go onstage, Robert was refusing to sing 'Stairway to Heaven,'" Grant told Malcolm Dome. "And he was totally out of order on that."

An old stagehand like Peter couldn't fathom why the talent wouldn't want to play their biggest hit. But Zeppelin's power struggles were not his problem anymore. With the film in progress, Grant was now considering offers for an autobiography. He met with several potential ghostwriters, including Dome, ex–*Melody Maker* editor-in-chief Ray Coleman and *Rolling Stone*'s David Dalton.

Dalton spent a strange couple of days with Grant in Miami. "Peter seemed depressed," he says. "And it was raining, and Miami in the rain is horrible, but he was so cagey about everything. He said, 'I don't want to talk about the shark.' I phoned my publisher, and he told me to get the next plane home."

It was also time to leave Horselunges. Helen, Warren, and the minders had all moved on. Warren had met his future wife, had trained as a greenskeeper, and would eventually become the head greenskeeper at the East Sussex National Golf Course. "I'd had years of going between jobs, and it was the best thing I ever did," he says now.

The rather dilapidated manor and its 86 acres was too much for a retired music manager on his own. "And the taxman needed paying," admits Warren. Peter later told Simon Kirke he'd had to sell Horselunges as "the VAT men stitched me up."

Grant eventually sold the property to a local couple, Barry and Anna George. The Georges allowed him to remain there until he'd found somewhere new, so he moved into a self-contained flat above the garage.

"The whole situation was weird," says Helen. "I couldn't understand how Dad could live in a big manor house and then move into the garage and see other people in what used to be his home. But he seemed quite happy. Perhaps he thought, 'That was then, and this is my situation now.'"

Grant was again tempted to go back into management. Two new acts came onto his radar. Thomas McLaughlin, known by the stage name "Thomas

McRocklin," was a nine-year-old whiz kid guitarist in the style of a young Eddie Van Halen.

Grant watched him play a showcase in a London studio. "It was basically fifteen, twenty minutes of me playing these shredding solos," says McLaughlin now. "Peter was sat on a low couch at the back of the studio."

When it was over, record executives and roadies alike queued up to shake the famous manager's hand. After the fifth or sixth time, young Thomas overheard Peter whisper to his latest well-wisher, "Give me a hand off this fucking couch. I'm stuck."

Grant said he was interested in managing McLaughlin, but it wasn't to be. "My dad was managing me, and he was totally into rock," he explains. "Peter thought I should go down the pop route. In hindsight, it wouldn't have been such a bad idea."

Grant was then introduced to the Scottish pop-rock group Goodbye Mr Mackenzie. Their keyboard player, Shirley Manson, would later form the hit nineties band Garbage. In 1989, Goodbye Mr Mackenzie enjoyed a UK top-forty hit, "The Rattler" and were determined to win over America.

"We already had two managers," explains ex-lead vocalist Martin Metcalfe. "They thought bringing in Peter Grant would help us break the States. The thing is, these two guys had watched *The Song Remains the Same* so many times, they knew the lines off by heart. They even walked around impersonating Peter, speaking through their noses. I think they thought it would be fun to meet him. So they wrote him a letter."

Grant liked "The Rattler" and asked to meet the group at Horselunges. "We drove down to this big house and had to wait in the car until they'd rounded up the dogs, in case they attacked us," recalls Metcalfe. "Then we realized Peter wasn't living in the actual mansion but above the garage."

Grant's young visitors anticipated a wild night like the ones they'd read about in *Hammer of the Gods*: "I think I had a carry-out with three cans of beer in it." Instead, they found Led Zeppelin's former manager sitting quietly in an armchair, sipping a cup of tea and missing his top set of dentures.

"We thought he'd be racking out lines of cocaine, but it was like visiting an elderly relative, your Uncle Peter," admits Metcalfe. "We sat there while he told stories. He talked about Bad Company and how Zeppelin made "Kashmir." I couldn't believe he'd been Robert Morley's body double. Morley was so posh and Peter was so working class."

Metcalfe glimpsed some of Grant's familiar ire after he mentioned Phil Lynott. Before his death in 1986, Thin Lizzy's hard-living frontman had fallen out publicly with his father-in-law, the TV gameshow host Leslie Crowther.

"I don't know what happened, but Peter was very much in the Phil Lynott camp, saying 'Fucking Leslie Crowther!'—in that nasally voice we'd heard in *The Song Remains the Same*—'Let me tell you about Leslie Crowther, I had his number.' I doubt Phil Lynott was the ideal son-in-law, but Peter had certainly picked his side."

Then again, in the early '60s, Grant had played an Arab on the children's TV show *Crackerjack*. Its host was Leslie Crowther. Who knows what happened? But Peter never forgot a slight.

Nothing more came of the meeting. Grant claimed Goodbye Mr Mackenzie wanted him to manage them in America, but he couldn't commit. Martin Metcalfe remembers a different conversation: "Our managers told EMI we were talking to Peter Grant, and they shat themselves. They said, 'If you get that guy in here we're going to drop the band.' They were so afraid of his gangster reputation."

The character Grant created had been a blessing in the seventies but was something of a curse in peacetime. He was still trapped in an image, even if it was changing slowly.

In summer 1990 Grant was interviewed in the heavy metal magazine *Kerrang!* He told writer Paul Henderson how Jimmy Page was "stubborn" and said John Bonham "was probably the best mate I ever had in my life." Peter also revealed the results of his recent diet. "I used to be twenty-eight-and-a-half stone, and I've lost ten stone," he divulged. "I'm fitter and healthier now than I have been since the early seventies."

Music photographer Ross Halfin captured this new, streamlined Peter Grant at London's Conrad Hotel. "He was charming and friendly and easy to deal with," he remembers. Grant also shared Zeppelin anecdotes, illustrating the needling tension within the band.

"Apparently Robert once walked to the side of the stage during *Dazed and Confused* and said to Peter, 'The problem with this band is it's one long guitar solo,'" Halfin recalls. "Grant poked him in the chest and said, 'Yeah, and remember whose fucking band it is, and it's *not* yours.'"

Unlike in the early 1980s, Grant was now often seen in public. He arrived by helicopter for Bon Jovi's big outdoor date at the Milton Keynes Bowl and showed up at the Marquee Club for gigs by Goodbye Mr Mackenzie and Jason Bonham's new group, Bonham.

At Jason's wedding reception in Kidderminster, Grant watched the groom, Jimmy Page, Robert Plant, and John Paul Jones blast through a handful of Zeppelin numbers, including "Rock and Roll" and "Bring It On Home."

In May 1990, Grant turned up unannounced before a Notting Hillbillies show at the Congress Theatre in Eastbourne. This visit would have a great consequence on the rest of his life.

The Notting Hillbillies was Dire Straits guitarist Mark Knopfler's side project, and their drummer was Dire Straits' manager, Ed Bicknell. Since first meeting Grant as a student at the RAK office, Bicknell had worked for the NEMS agency with several of Peter's Don Arden–era contemporaries. He'd since steered Dire Straits from playing South London pubs to headlining the world's biggest arenas.

The Notting Hillbillies were preparing to sound check when the fire doors at the back of the theater opened. "In waddled Peter Grant and a bloke in a sheepskin coat who looked like a second-hand car dealer and turned out to be one," remembers Bicknell. "Peter said, 'I came down to thank you for those nice things you said about me on television.'"

Ed Bicknell had also been interviewed on the TV show *Wired*. "I was surprised when I heard they'd interviewed Peter, as I thought he was a recluse. So I spoke to them about how important Peter had been, and I talked about the ninety-ten split."

Ed invited Grant and his friend into the dressing room and made them both tea. The show's promoter, Paul Crockford, wandered past, spotted Grant perched on a flight case, and did a double take.

"As a joke I said, 'Oh Paul, this is Peter Grant, my manager,'" says Bicknell. "Paul, who is quite a nervous individual, looked concerned. Peter picked up on the joke straightaway and said, 'I've come to count the dead wood,' which is an old-fashioned word for ticket stubs.

"Crockford panicked and said, 'But it's a council venue, it's all on computer.' Peter said in that low voice of his, 'Oh, dear me, we haven't got off to a very good start.' I said, 'Never mind that, can you get a couple of tickets for Peter and his mate?' Poor Paul was quaking in his boots. 'But the show's completely sold out.' Peter did that look and said, very quietly, 'Oh, dear me, we're *not* getting on very well, are we.'"

After the show, Grant joined Bicknell and a couple of roadies backstage, where they talked until the early hours of the morning. "We talked about Chuck Berry and Gene Vincent, not Led Zeppelin," says Bicknell. "I remember thinking, I'm talking to Peter Grant, but he's nothing how I thought he'd be."

Bicknell had recently moved to nearby Polegate in Sussex. He and Grant swapped numbers and arranged to meet again. "That started what became a very close friendship. I would visit my kids nearby, and most Saturday evenings Peter and I would go to a local gastro pub, Moonrakers in Alfriston, and just sit and chat. We ranged over every imaginable subject."

Bicknell was from the next generation of music managers after Grant. The two dynasties had worked a couple of floors apart at 155 Oxford Street in the sixties.

"Terry Ellis and Chris Wright at the Chrysalis agency were the ones just before me," he explains. "We were social secretaries who'd booked bands at our colleges and come into the industry with university degrees. Peter said the only qualification you needed in his day was being able to drive a van. But Peter and those guys laid the rough-and-ready foundations for the business.

"In Peter's day, there were no computers, and you didn't study music management. It was bags of cash, and people really would run off with your money in the middle of the night. Peter and Don needed their reputations to stop people running off. The difference between Peter and Don was Peter saw himself working for the artist. He was actually very enlightened."

Bicknell had occasionally spotted Grant around Soho during the early seventies. "At the Ship or the Speakeasy, usually surrounded by these grubby acolytes and forlorn roadies geeing him up," he admits.

"Peter came from an era where if somebody upset you, you didn't get a lawyer, you paid a visit. I'd hear gossip about people being slapped around, but I didn't judge. I'm not being an apologist for him, but that wasn't the Peter Grant I came to know."

Eventually, these over-dinner conversations touched on Led Zeppelin. Ed discovered how much the business had consumed him and how distraught he felt about Bonham's death. "He'd say, if I only I had been there, I could have saved John.' And I used to say, 'You might have been able to save him in that moment, but what about the next time?'

"Peter always saw Zeppelin as Jimmy Page's project. He used to say to me, 'Fucking Robert Plant, he always wanted to be the leader of the band.' But that's what happens. When you've attained everything you've ever aspired to, success turns around and bites you on the arse. When acts get to the top, they fall to bits, and all sorts of inner turmoil is exposed. Zeppelin was no different.

"What people don't realize, though, is the manager is sometimes as likely to go off the rails as the act," he says. "It all gets too much. Everybody wants something. In Zeppelin's case, either a share in the financial success or a share in the glory. Then Peter tried to build an empire and launched Swan Song, and I think that almost did him in."

Grant's family encouraged their father's new friendship. "Hooking up with Ed really shaped Dad up," believes Helen. "He loved his company, and it was a real meeting of minds."

Bicknell didn't drive and used the services of a local cab company. "The drivers believed all these stories about Horselunges and said they wouldn't go there. Once I told them who Peter was, they used to say, 'Oh, I saw your mate in Waitrose on Tuesday.' Because Peter was driving around in a black Range Rover with an LZ1 license plate and they'd spotted it in the car park.

"Weeks later, I'd say to Peter, 'Did you have a good time in Waitrose that Tuesday?' And he could never understand how I knew, even though he had the most recognizable car in the area."

The two phoned each other regularly to swap stories and gossip. When Grant was asked to judge a Battle of the Bands talent contest on Eastbourne pier, he persuaded Bicknell to join him. "And these bands were just appalling," remembers Ed. "So we chose a winner at random. Nobody would believe you had Led Zeppelin and Dire Straits managers judging a local talent contest."

In return, Ed asked Peter to attend a lecture he was giving to a class of students on a boat on the River Thames. "Eighty people had paid for this course. And they got to hear the two of us pontificating about the music business and telling anecdotes. They were completely bemused."

Before long, Grant had moved out of the garage at Horselunges and into a rented flat in the Sussex seaside town of Eastbourne. "He found a nice apartment with an underground car park where he could keep his Porsche," remembers Warren. "He'd go down there, fire it up, fill the place with smoke, and upset the neighbors."

Grant continued his health regime. He took daily walks on the seafront and used homeopathic remedies from an alternative therapist. "He also got into super-juices," says Warren. "In the old days he'd have had a doctor's bag of coke and Valium; now it was full of Vitamin C."

For Helen, this was the period when the real Peter Grant reemerged. The turquoise jewelry and garish scarves were long gone. Grant now cut an increasingly traditional-looking figure on his seafront strolls.

"One of my fondest memories of my dad is seeing him in his suit and his sensible lace-up shoes," she says. "Deep down, he was very old-fashioned. I still think that person was in there when he was on tour with Led Zeppelin and wearing all that regalia. Inside there was still this very ordinary guy."

"He wasn't living the rock 'n' roll lifestyle. He'd sit at home watching TV," adds Warren. His favorite shows were *Lovejoy*, a gentle Sunday-night drama about a roguish antique dealer, and the BBC soap opera *EastEnders*, "which he watched religiously."

Ed Bicknell soon realized the importance of family and friendship to his new friend. "Peter showed up one day at my place. He had this big cardboard box under his arm. Inside was a piece of Tiffany glass.

"There used to be a store on Tottenham Court Road with an Art Deco frieze. When they knocked the building down, Peter bought some of this frieze. He gave it to me and said, 'This is for you. You've helped me live again.' I was incredibly touched.

"After my dad died in '92, I had two older male figures come into my life at different stages," says Bicknell. "And they almost became like second fathers. George Martin was one, and Peter Grant was the other. Peter and I had an uncomplicated affinity. I didn't want anything from him, and he didn't want anything from me."

Warren's daughters, Amy and Tiffany, were born in 1990 and 1992, giving Peter another opportunity to play the doting grandparent. "With me he had this tenuous connection with what he used to do, and we would laugh about it," explains Bicknell. "What Peter enjoyed most were his grandchildren."

But he hadn't changed his opinion of Denny Laine. Ed raised the subject one Christmas after some of the Grant family joined him for a Boxing Day lunch. "Peter and I were sitting in the living room together, watching the embers in the fire, and I just said, 'What's it like having Denny Laine as your kind of son-in-law?'

"There was a silence. Then Peter replied, 'Waste of food.' We both laughed. He turned to me later that afternoon and said, ''Ere, what do you think Denny Laine's doing on New Year's Eve?' I said, 'I haven't the faintest idea.' He said, 'Playing a gig in Latvia . . . with Rick Wakeman.' Peter thought this was hilarious."

Despite considering the idea of managing new acts, Grant abandoned the idea for good after watching Bicknell at work. "Peter once asked if he could spend the day with me in the office," says Ed. "He came in, sat in the corner with his cup of tea, and then told me how boring it was. And he was right. The game had become corporate and administrative. It wasn't creative like it was in his day.

"When the second Led Zeppelin box set [*Boxed Set 2*] was being put together, Peter was acting for Pat Bonham and called up to ask about a packaging deduction on the discs. I said it was 25 percent, and you won't get any company to shift on this. He said, 'That's outrageous.' He called Ahmet and, something was worked out. CDs and boxed sets were a whole new thing for him.

"I don't say this critically, but there are many myths about Led Zeppelin's deals. What was considered an absolute fuck-off royalty rate in 1969 would not be considered one in the age of streaming. You have to consider all this in the context of the times. The business was still developing. Peter didn't get a bad deal."

Bicknell also realized there'd been others in the organization interfering in Zeppelin's affairs. "Sitting in those gastro pubs with Peter, he'd start opening up. He did not like Steve Weiss. When Zeppelin sold their publishing, Weiss, of course, kept a piece, but it was more than that. There's a saying that if your accountant shows up backstage at Wembley, wearing a blue satin tour jacket with a tiger on the back, you've got a problem. People who are qualified as bean counters suddenly want to be rock stars and hang out on the bus—and Weiss was one of those."

By now, Grant's business legacy was right there, in the new groups filling concert halls and topping the charts. By early 1992, Nirvana and Guns N' Roses were two of the biggest rock bands in the world.

Nirvana, led by troubled frontman Kurt Cobain, merged punk's scuzzy energy with radio-friendly choruses. Guns N' Roses mixed silver coke-spoon rock with punk's bad attitude, courtesy of volatile lead singer, Axl Rose. Both wouldn't have sounded the way they did, though, without Led Zeppelin.

Nirvana was managed by Danny Goldberg, the young PR Grant hired to help run Swan Song in 1973. "Nirvana was from the punk generation, but they respected Zeppelin," he explains. "I'd say to Kurt Cobain, 'This is how Peter Grant and Zeppelin would have done it,' and he'd listen. Back then, Peter was always in my head because he was the ultimate manager."

When Axl Rose's unpredictable behavior threatened Guns N' Roses' future, their manager at the time sought Grant's advice. "He rang up and said, 'How do I cope with him?'" remembers Helen. "Dad told me Axl was out of control."

Managing rock stars' fragile egos was now somebody else's responsibility. Grant preferred watching golf at Gleneagles or attending Porsche Owners' Club events. Together with his friend, ex-racing driver "Lord" John Gould, Grant had begun hiring out his vintage motorcars for wedding functions. He even played chauffeur to some of the happy couples. "Peter used to say, ''Ere, I got a wedding on Saturday. Can you imagine what the punters would think?'" says Bicknell.

One evening, Ed realized how much his friend's life had changed. He and Grant were dining at Elvis Hau, a Chinese restaurant in Eastbourne, where the proprietor leapt out from the kitchen, wearing a jumpsuit and a wig to perform Presley's greatest hits.

"After 'Elvis' had sung 'All Shook Up' in the middle of the pork ball course, Peter started chatting with two guys on the next table," Ed remembers. "When we left, I asked who they were. Peter said, 'The Lord Mayor and his mate. They asked me if I wanted to become a magistrate.' I told him he'd be good at that.'

"Grant looked bemused, 'Yeah, but it wouldn't look good on the CV.'"

*F*amily and friends now sensed Grant was increasingly at ease with himself and his past. But the publication of Bill Graham's autobiography in 1992 was an uneasy reminder of the violent times. "Peter knew he'd behaved badly," says Bicknell, who'd heard his friend in tears after he'd read the book. "But he didn't want to be thought of that way anymore."

A year later, in October 1993, Grant took a call from a newspaper reporter, asking for a comment on John Bindon's death. Biffo had been Peter's accomplice at Oakland, but the two men hadn't seen each other for years. Both Bindon's acting career and his appearances in tabloid gossip columns had waned since his murder trial. Bindon had been living in reduced circumstances when he died, purportedly of cancer. "I didn't know anything until the *Evening Standard* rang me for some quotes," Grant said.

Oakland was a long time ago. But Grant's reputation still followed him on his occasional forays into the music business. That summer Peter joined Ed Bicknell at In the City, an industry conference in Manchester organized by Simply Red's co-manager Elliot Rashman.

"Peter said, 'I've been invited to a conference,'" says Bicknell. "'What's a conference? I'll go if you come with me.'

"We arrived the night before. The hotel was packed with people, and nobody knew who he was," says Bicknell. "I asked Elliot Rashman and his co-manager Andy Dodds if they'd join us for dinner, and they both said, 'Are you sure?' They'd heard the rumors about Peter, like we all had. But they came, and Peter started telling stories, and they were amazed because he was nothing like they thought he'd be.

"At about 12:30 Peter benignly said to Elliot and Andy, 'Now, now, young men, big day tomorrow, time to go to bed.' Like something your dad would say when you were a kid. And they went. They toddled off to bed because

Peter Grant told them to. They said later, they couldn't equate that other Peter Grant with this Peter Grant—couldn't put the two together."

The following day, the former music journalist Paul Morley interviewed
Grant onstage. "It was fucking awful," says Bicknell. Morley arrived flanked
by comedy bodyguards, and the conversation was stilted and awkward. "Is it
true you would hang people from a hotel window fifteen floors up?" Morley
asked.

Grant grinned, "No, but it could be a first time today."

If he'd wanted to, Grant could have found work as an after-dinner
speaker. He returned to In the City the following year and later shared a stage
with Bicknell at the Canadian National Music Week conference in Toronto.
This time, Ed interviewed Peter. "They were always a good double act," says
Helen.

Grant had fully refined his stories and comic timing. He talked about
"helping Allen Klein out of his chair by his lapels" and joked about Jimmy
Page ("There's a man who knows how to save a penny"). But he also candidly
discussed his drug problems and the aftermath of John Bonham's death.

"The Peruvian economy rocketed, believe me," he admitted. "The marching powder went on for some years. I got to point where I couldn't face the
phone calls. All these drummers phoning up, saying they'd been promised a
job."

Mark Long joined Grant and Bicknell in Toronto. "Peter and I sat in a
room with this guy," remembers Ed. "He seemed to be stunned by everything
that came out of Peter's mouth—and it was pretty tame. I honestly don't
think Peter was bothered whether the film got made or not."

Nevertheless, Grant still discussed the planned movie in interviews,
claiming that Robbie Coltrane, the burly Scottish actor (later known for playing Hagrid in the *Harry Potter* film franchise) was tipped to play him. But he
also couldn't resist a joke, telling Iron Maiden's lead singer and BBC DJ Bruce
Dickinson that Gary Oldman, fresh from performing as the vampire lead in
Bram Stoker's *Dracula*, would be ideal as Jimmy Page.

At Grant's suggestion, Mark Long also interviewed many of Peter's other
friends and co-conspirators, including his ex-wife Gloria, Mickie Most, Richard Cole, and Phil Carlo. As time passed, Grant took Long into his confidence—finally discussing his childhood in more detail, but also Steve Weiss
and Herb Atkin's alleged plot to take over his band.

"The impression I had was that the last four years of Led Zeppelin were a
nightmare, a horror story," says Long. "They were worth more money than
any other band on earth, and everybody wanted a piece. The more I talked to

people, the more stories I heard. There was so much self-protection, money, thievery, and greed—everybody seemed to be suspect."

However, despite Grant's assurances to the filmmakers, none of the members of Led Zeppelin made themselves available for interview. "They were virtually incommunicado and all hiding in castles somewhere," remembers Mike Figgis. Nor were they willing to licence their music.

"The story we got back from Zeppelin was, 'Who the fuck wants to make a film about Peter Grant? They should be making a film about us,'" says Long.

"Zeppelin wouldn't let him use their music," confirms Phil Carlo. "Peter was furious about it and very hurt."

Grant, the man visible for three seconds in Stanley Kubrick's *Lolita*, finally returned to the big screen in somebody else's film. Producer John Goldstone had revived the *Carry On . . .* comedy film franchise. *Carry On Columbus*, a spoof of the life and times of the Italian explorer included Grant in a cameo role as the cardinal, looking vaguely menacing in papal robes and a mitre.

"I think he'd been an extra in one of the original *Carry On* films," says Warren, "so they thought it would be good to have him in the final one."

It wouldn't be the last time Grant revisited his old life before Led Zeppelin. In the summer of 1994, he saw the Everly Brothers at London's Royal Albert Hall. Grant had been their road manager and driver in what now seemed like another lifetime. Afterward, Grant attended a party where Phil Everly introduced him to his fellow guests.

"This man made everything possible," Everly told the audience. "Without his efforts, musicians had no careers. He was the first to make sure the artists came first and that we got paid and paid properly."

By 1995, Grant was living at Ilex End, in Upper Carlisle Road, Eastbourne. Before being converted, the property had been a garage and chauffeur's accommodation. Perhaps Peter hadn't come so far from his days as a driver.

Helen and Denny Laine's relationship was over, and she was now living nearby. "It meant I saw more of Dad," she says. "It also meant if we had a falling out, I was just around the corner. Then we'd go out to lunch, and it would all be forgotten."

Helen saw the changes in her father up close. "Led Zeppelin made him, but it broke him as well," she admits. "He really did become quite humble in old age. I understand there were people who hated him, but there were a lot of dimensions to my dad. Whatever people say, about the violence and the drugs, he had a softness and was a very ordinary basic man."

Grant had always been an animal lover and now owned a Jack Russell named Blackjack. "He'd disappear with that dog for days on end," says Helen. "He'd take him for a walk on one of those long leashes, so the dog ran around while he sat in the Range Rover smoking a cigarette. Typical Dad."

Grant turned sixty in April. "At Christmas the year before, he said he'd be down to sixteen stone by his sixtieth birthday, and he was," recalls Bicknell.

Peter phoned Mickie Most and told him he'd lost so much weight, it was like "losing a whole person." The last time Mickie's wife, Chris, had seen Grant, they'd shared a flight from Los Angeles to London in the seventies. "Peter was being very nice to me, but he was completely out of it, and it was heartbreaking to see."

Grant told Mickie Most there were times he didn't think he'd make it to sixty. Mickie quietly agreed.

That summer, Grant was reconciled with the two musicians he'd nurtured and groomed and once acted as referee and bodyguard for. Robert Plant and Jimmy Page had reunited and were touring as Page and Plant, performing Led Zeppelin's songs with an Egyptian orchestra. Their *No Quarter: Unledded* album had been a Billboard top-five hit.

Helen Grant tried to convince her father to go with her to their show in London. "He said, 'No, I want no part of it.' He was being stubborn. I went, and it was fantastic, and, of course, his curiosity got the better of him, and he came to see me the next morning to find out what it was like. I told him he should go to the show tonight, but he still wasn't sure. In the end, I said, 'Stop being so stupid, go and see them!' And he did."

The duo greeted him from the stage. "Peter was a different person from the man I saw at the end of the seventies," said Robert Plant later. "He was clean, his vision was clear. He knew that he'd moved mountains, that he'd changed the world for artists."

"I remember seeing him with Robert and Jimmy backstage with their arms around each other," says Helen, "and they looked so happy. It was a pivotal moment for him."

On September 20, Grant attended the International Managers Forum Dinner at London's Hilton Hotel. Unbeknownst to him, he was to be given the inaugural Peter Grant Award as an acknowledgement of his contribution to music management. It would be his last major public appearance.

"I bamboozled them into putting his name on the award," admits Ed Bicknell. "Some people still weren't happy because of his reputation."

Grant and Bicknell were sharing a table with Queen's Brian May, among others. After the meal, Grant quietly told Ed he needed to get some fresh air.

"He'd turned very pale and was sweating profusely," remembers Bicknell. "We went outside for a while, and he recovered himself. The award was supposed to be a secret, but then Brian May leaned over and said something to Peter, without realizing he didn't know.

"I went up to do the presentation, and Peter found it very difficult to get up on stage. He was struggling." Grant gave a modest speech in which he thanked as many people as he could remember. As always, he saved his greatest praise for the musicians he'd looked after. "He said, 'The only reason any of us got here is the talented people we worked with.'"

Grant received a standing ovation. Some of the audience had known him in the good old, bad old days. Everybody in the room had heard the stories, but they were all surprised by this new humble version of Peter Grant.

Five days after the ceremony, Grant was back in London at the 100 Club on Oxford Street. He was filmed for his brief cameo in the video for the Pretty Things' latest single, "Rosalyn." Shot in black and white, he looked like a retired Mafia don. The old Peter Grant hadn't gone completely out of fashion.

Soon after, a couple contacted "Lord" John Gould and asked to hire Grant's 1929 Pierce-Arrow as a wedding car. Peter offered to be their chauffeur. He wore the cap and the driving gloves and was paid £30 in cash.

"John Gould said afterward, they pulled over in a country lane and G said, 'Right, let's divvy up the roadies,'" says Phil Carlo. "He was delighted. It was just like the old days with the T-shirt money. It was the first time Peter had been paid in cash for years."

Grant's life had come full circle. He'd made his peace with his musicians, won over his peers, and inspired his successors in the music industry. Best of all, he'd managed to be get paid in cash—one last time.

On November 21, 1995, Grant was looking after his granddaughters Amy and Tiffany while Warren and his then wife attended a school parents' evening.

"When we got back, he was a bit wound up," says Warren. Peter asked his son for a lift, telling him he had some business to attend to. An acquaintance had been looking after some of his possessions from Horselunges, but was refusing to return the lion skin rug Peter had inherited from the manor's previous owner.

There was an argument on the doorstep; Warren intervened and eventually persuaded his father to leave. No sooner had they started to drive away when he realized something was seriously wrong. "Dad said, 'Warren, I don't feel well'—and, that was it, he was gone. I spun the car round and drove to Helen's, as she lived nearby."

His sister called an ambulance, and Peter was taken to the hospital. But it was too late. He'd suffered a fatal heart attack. "Alan Callan called me the next day to say Peter had died," remembers Ed Bicknell. "I knew he'd not been well the last couple of times I'd seen him, but it still came as a shock."

Callan had remained close to Grant after the demise of Swan Song, and assisted Warren and Helen with the funeral arrangements and their father's estate. "Peter had been fighting with the inland revenue for years," admits Bicknell. "And there was a big battle over inheritance tax."

Grant's funeral took place on the morning of December 4 at the Church of St. Peter and St. Paul in Hellingly. "It was a gathering of odd characters," remembers Ed. "I was in a pew with Robert Plant and his new Indian girl-friend. Pagey was there, being rather morose, but I don't think Jonesy came."

Clive Coulson and Phil Carlo were ushers, as Jeff Beck, Maggie Bell, members of the Yardbirds, the Pretty Things, and Bad Company joined the family at the church. Alan Callan's eulogy paid tribute to a man he described as "a generous friend, an awesome enemy, and a staggering influence on the music industry."

Callan's testimonial also captured the essence of Peter Grant. "He was a man of many parts," he understated. "A man whose mythology was a never-ending treasure trove to the storyteller in us. He could engage you in the greatest conspiratorial friendship, and you would know that, through thick and thin, he would fight with you all the way. If you were his friend, he would give you his all. . . . Wherever Peter is going now, I hope they've got their act together."

Prior to his death, Grant had compiled a list of personal items he wanted buried with him. "Who's on it?" joked one old friend. Before the funeral, Alan Callan handed Warren an envelope of documents relating to Peter's family background. Knowing how private his father had been, he placed the un-opened envelope in the coffin.

As the mourners left the church, they were accompanied by the gentle strains of Vera Lynn's "We'll Meet Again," a wartime ballad from Peter's childhood. It was the punchline to his final joke and raised a smile among the congregation.

The wake was held at "Lord" John Gould's farm in nearby Little Horsted. After Horselunges, Grant kept his vintage car collection in one of Gould's barns. "Everybody stood around looking at these stupendous vehicles. Jeff Beck was beside himself," remembers Bicknell. "But nobody was really talking about Peter. Funerals are always gloomy, but this was a really gloomy affair."

In the coming weeks, old friends and co-conspirators were quoted in the obituaries. Chris Dreja described the man he'd once witnessed bouncing an armed promoter away with his belly as "an irreplaceable guiding light."

"I missed him long ago at the end of an era," said Robert Plant, acknowledging Grant's decision to leave the business. "He was too fine a man to dance with compromise. He walked."

"Peter said to me, 'When you've managed Led Zeppelin, where else are you going to go?'" says Ed Bicknell now. "He'd done it all."

*O*n December 10, 2007, the three surviving members of Led Zeppelin reformed with Jason Bonham to headline a charity concert in honor of Ahmet Ertegun. The record company mogul had died the year before.

Helen and Warren attended the show at London's O2 Arena. They watched the group their father helped put together performing with their childhood friend playing drums. There were ghosts everywhere they turned.

Retired roadies and tour managers, reformed drug buddies, groupies, and ex-wives sat just feet away from each other; everybody confronted by a shared, checkered past. In some cases, these were people Grant's children had last glimpsed roaming backstage in America, some thirty years earlier.

Everything had changed since the late seventies. The reunion concert had required the expert mediating skills of Robert Plant's then manager Bill Curbishley and Peter Mensch, who represented Jimmy Page. Curbishley had guided the Who since the early seventies, and Mensch had managed Metallica and AC/DC, among others.

Both men followed Peter Grant into the business, but the era when a manager would do whatever a client asked, regardless, were gone. The days of unquestioning loyalty ended with Peter Grant. "Peter kept everybody away," said John Paul Jones. It wasn't so easy to keep everybody away in the current century.

Curbishley later resigned as Plant's manager, and Jimmy Page fired Peter Mensch. Page had previously fired Curbishley as his manager after he'd negotiated the return of Led Zeppelin's lucrative song publishing, sold by Grant and Steve Weiss in the seventies.

"For all their talent, musicians are often irrational and desperately insecure and always think the grass is greener," points out Ed Bicknell. "Loyalty in this business is hard to find."

It would be difficult to imagine Peter Grant, a man who put such stock in loyalty, haggling his way through the modern music industry, with its online streaming, widespread piracy, and dwindling profit margins.

"Peter's image and bearing belonged to an analog age," says Simon Napier-Bell. "He was a totally analog personality. There was nothing virtual about Peter. He was totally real."

Even in death, Grant remains real to those he employed and who forged successful careers after he'd gone. Many still ask themselves, "What would Peter Grant do?" when faced with difficult decisions. Some still have dreams about him. "They're not bad dreams, but they're recurring dreams," admits one. "He loomed large in my life, figuratively and literally."

To his children, Peter Grant never stopped being a father, even after the business had taken its toll. "Above everything, he was the most unselfish man you could ever meet," says Warren.

Since 2010, Warren Grant has managed the UK's leading Led Zeppelin tribute band, Hats Off to Led Zeppelin. Meanwhile, the business has embraced his father's legacy in ways that would have once seemed unimaginable.

In February 2016, HBO began screening *Raging Bull* and *Goodfellas* director Martin Scorsese's seventies music-biz drama, *Vinyl*. Its distorted portrayal of Led Zeppelin and its manager was singled out for particular criticism, not least by those who'd known them in real life.

British actor Ian Hart played Grant, complete with a bushy beard, elaborate comb-over, and exaggerated cockney accent. But he sounded less like Peter and more like Bob Hoskins's East End gangster in *The Long Good Friday*.

It was as if Barrie Keeffe and Malcolm McLaren's godfather of rock 'n' roll had finally made it to the screen, buckling under the weight of terrible clichés. "If I was Peter I'd have fucking sued," says Maggie Bell's old co-manager Mark London.

The International Music Managers Forum continues to present its annual Peter Grant Award to managers of note. Among its recent recipients was Queen's handler Jim Beach, who'd been the group's lawyer when they'd had meetings with Grant about managing them in the seventies.

In 2012, the Bristol Institute of Modern Music announced the launch of an annual Peter Grant Memorial Scholarship. "My father would have been both touched and honored," said Helen, at the time. "He was a great inspiration to many in the business, not only on the management front, but in how he looked after his artists in his own, infamous way."

"Could you imagine what my dad would think?" she says now. "A man who'd barely had any formal schooling, having a college course named after him. I don't know if you could ever teach what he knew, but the business owes him a lot."

In one of his last interviews, Grant was asked if he ever missed the old life. "Sometimes, yes," he admitted. "I cannot describe that feeling at eight o'clock when the houselights went down, and you felt the rush from the audience, and the band hadn't even walked out. That rush was fantastic. And I always felt so proud."

Deep down, this was always where Peter Grant belonged: standing in the wings, on the side of a stage, watching and waiting for the lights to go down and the music to start. Waiting for the adventure, the madness, and the laughter to begin.

ACKNOWLEDGMENTS

Bring It On Home would not have been possible without the trust, support, and great patience of Peter Grant's son and daughter, Warren and Helen. Many thanks to you both.

Thanks also to the following friends and colleagues, including my agents: Matthew Hamilton (Aitken Alexander Associates) and Matthew Elblonk (DeFiore and Company), and Phil Alexander, Paul Brannigan, Dave Brolan, Pat Gilbert, Ross Halfin, Dave Lewis, Sian Llewelyn, and Paul Rees.

Thanks to all at Da Capo Press and Constable & Robinson, including Andreas Campomar and Ben Schafer, and Lori Hobkirk at the Book Factory.

Bring It On Home draws on my own interviews with Jimmy Page, Robert Plant, and John Paul Jones, conducted for various magazines, including *Mojo*, *Classic Rock*, and *Q*, between 1993 and 2018 and material from several previously unpublished interviews with Peter Grant conducted between 1989 and 1994.

There were also many interviews with and contributions from the following: Sam Aizer, Keith Altham, Carmine Appice, Maggie Bell, Paul Bettie, Derek Berman, Ed Bicknell, Phil Carlo, Julie Carlo, Phil Carson, Peter Clifton (RIP), Marilyn Cole, Richard Cole, Sherry Coulson, David Dalton, Michael Des Barres, Jeff Dexter, Geoff Docherty, Malcolm Dome, Chris Dreja, Mike Figgis, Mitchell Fox, Danny Francis, John Glover, Danny Goldberg, Helen Grant, Warren Grant, Jerry Greenberg, Ross Halfin, Christina Hayes, Paul Henderson, Abe Hoch, Nicky Horne, Barrie Keeffe, Bob Kerr, Simon Kirke, Dave Lewis, Harvey Lisberg, Mark London, Mark Long, Andrew Loog Oldham, Laurie Mansworth, Unity MacLean, Brian May, Martin Metcalfe, Jim McCarty, Thomas McLaughlin, Laurence Myers, Simon Napier-Bell, Dave Northover, Sharon Osbourne, Ray Phillips, Tom Porter, Aubrey "Po" Powell, Perry Press, Neal Preston, Paul Reeves, Andy Roberts, Paul Rodgers, Cindy Russell-Fossen, Ellen Sander, Arthur Sharp, Philip Soussan, Henry Smith, Chris Squire (RIP), Tony St Ledger, Mick Underwood, and Joe "Jammer" Wright. Thanks to everybody who took the time to talk to me.

Special thanks to Ross Halfin, Mark Long, Richard Cole, and Phil and Julie Carlo for going the extra distance, and to my wife, Claire, and son, Matthew.

Additional interviews and articles have appeared in the following publications: *Billboard, Classic Rock, Kerrang!, Melody Maker, Mojo, Observer, Planet Rock, Q, Radio & Records, Raw, Rolling Stone, She, Telegraph* magazine, *Tight But Loose, Uncut,* and *Vox.*

SELECT BIBLIOGRAPHY

Appice, Carmine, with Ian Gittins. *Stick It! My Life of Sex, Drums and Rock 'N' Roll*. Chicago: Chicago Review Press, 2016.

Arden, Don, with Mick Wall. *Mr Big: Ozzy, Sharon and My Life as the Godfather of Rock*. Sun Lakes, AZ: Robson Publishing, 2004.

Bannister, Freddy. *There Must Be a Better Way: The Story of the Bath and Knebworth Rock Festivals, 1969–1979*. Bath, UK: Bath Books, 2003.

Burdon, Eric. *I Used To Be an Animal, But I'm All Right Now*. London: Faber & Faber, 1986.

Cigarini, Johnny. *Confessions of a King's Road Cowboy*. Leicester, UK: Matador Publishing, 2015.

Clarkson, Wensley. *Bindon*. London: John Blake Publishing, 2007.

Cole, Richard. *Stairway to Heaven: Led Zeppelin Uncensored*. New York: Harper Collins, 1992.

Davis, Stephen. *Hammer of the Gods: Led Zeppelin Unauthorized*. London: Pan Books, 1985.

Fey, Barry. *Backstage Past*. Brownsville, OR: Lone Wolf Press, 2011.

Frame, Pete. *The Restless Generation*. Dublin: Rogan House, 2007.

Goldberg, Danny. *Bumping Into Geniuses: My Life Inside the Rock and Roll Business*. New York: Gotham Books, 2008.

Goodman, Fred. *The Mansion on the Hill: Dylan, Young, Geffen, Springsteen and the Head-On Collision of Rock and Commerce*. London: Jonathan Cape, 1997.

———.*Allen Klein: The Man Who Bailed Out the Beatles, Made the Stones and Transformed Rock & Roll*. New York: Eamon Dolan/Houghton Mifflin Harcourt, 2015.

Graham, Bill, with Robert Greenfield. *Bill Graham Presents: My Life Inside Rock 'N' Roll*. New York: Da Capo, 1992.

Greenfield, Robert. *The Last Sultan: The Life & Times of Ahmet Ertegun*. New York: Simon & Schuster, 2011.

Harrison, Peter. *Brixton Boy Calling*. Columbia, SC: Createspace Publishing, 2013.

Hoskyns, Barney. *Trampled Underfoot: The Power and Excess of Led Zeppelin*. London: Faber & Faber, 2012.

Hutchins, Chris. *Mr. Confidential*. Seattle, WA: Ebooks, 2005.

Keeler, Christine, with Douglas Thompson. *Secrets and Lies: The Real Story of the Political Scandal That Mesmerized the World—The Profumo Affair.* London: John Blake Publishing, 2014.

Kent, Nick. *Apathy for the Devil: A 1970s Memoir.* London: Faber & Faber, 2010.

Lewis, Dave. *Led Zeppelin: Then as It Was—at Knebworth, 1979.* Bedford, UK: Tight But Loose Publishing, 2008.

———. *Led Zeppelin: Feather in the Wind—Over Europe, 1980.* Bedford, UK: Tight But Loose Publishing, 2012.

———. *Five Glorious Nights: Led Zeppelin at Earls Court, May 1975.* Berkshire, UK: Rufus Stone Publications, 2015.

Lewis, Dave, with Simon Pallett. *Led Zeppelin: The Concert File.* London: Omnibus, 2005.

Murfet, Don. *Leave It to Me.* Manadaluyong City, the Philippines: Anvil Publications, 2004.

Napier-Bell, Simon. *You Don't Have to Say You Love Me.* London: Ebury Press, 1983.

Nash, Alanna. *The Colonel: The Extraordinary Story of Colonel Tom Parker and Elvis Presley.* London: Aurum, 2004.

Neill, Andy. *Had Me a Real Good Time: The Faces: Before, During, and After.* London: Omnibus Press, 2011.

Osbourne, Sharon. *Extreme: My Autobiography.* New York: Time Warner, 2005.

Pearson, John. *One of the Family: The Englishman and the Mafia.* London: Arrow, 2004.

Rees, Paul. *Robert Plant: A Life.* New York: Harper Collins, 2014.

Robinson, Lisa. *There Goes Gravity: A Life in Rock 'N' Roll.* New York: Riverhead, 2014.

Rye, Mark. *Over Under Sideways Down: Stories from Inside the British Music Scene.* London: RockHistory, rockhistory.co.uk, 2014.

———. *Inside Looking Out: Rock and Roll Stories from Inside the British Music Business.* London: RockHistory, rockhistory.co.uk, 2017.

Scala, Mim. *Diary of a Teddy Boy: A Memoir of the Long Sixties.* London: Headline Review Publishing, 2009.

Wall, Mick. *When Giants Walked the Earth: A Biography.* London: Orion, 2009.

Winner, Michael. *Winner Takes It All.* Sun Lakes, AZ: Robson Publishing, 2005.

Wood, Ronnie. *Ronnie.* New York: MacMillan, 2007.

Wright, Chris. *One Way or Another: My Life in Music, Sport and Entertainment,* London: Omnibus, 2014.

INDEX